Ex Líbrís

GATE OF HELL

GATE OF HELL
CAMPAIGN FOR CHARLESTON HARBOR, 1863

by Stephen R. Wise

University of South Carolina Press

Library of Congress Cataloging-in-Publication Data

Wise, Stephen R., 1952–
    Gate of hell : campaign for Charleston Harbor, 1863 / by Stephen
R. Wise.
        p.   cm.
    Includes bibliographical references and index.
    ISBN 0–87249–985–5 (acid-free)
    1. Morris Island (S.C.), Battle of, 1863. 2. Fort Wagner (S.C.)
3. United States. Army. Massachusetts Infantry Regiment, 54th
(1863–1865)   I. Title.
E475.63.W57   1994   94–2921
973.7'34—dc20

Contents

Maps

Illustrations

Acknowledgments

My introduction to history came from parents who took me on vacations that were often highlighted by visits to historical sites. Among the first places I remember visiting was Charleston, South Carolina, and Fort Sumter. The Civil War history of the fort and the city fascinated me. Over the years I returned with my parents to visit Charleston, and I continued my study of the Civil War. I soon learned about the tremendous struggle on Morris Island, the deadly assaults on Battery Wagner, and the use of African American troops. At Wittenberg University, I expanded my knowledge writing research papers for Celestine Anderson and Robert Hartje, while my advisor, Joseph O'Connor, gave much-needed assistance and encouragement to continue my study of history.

At Bowling Green State University, Robert Twyman took an interest in my education and guided me through my first major work on Morris Island. I am extremely grateful to Professor Twyman for not only his patience but also his direction and support. He, along with David Skaggs and Richard Wright, initiated me into the world of primary research and writing. Special thanks go to a number of individuals at Bowling Green, including the library staff—especially those in the inter-library loan department who cheerfully filled my numerous requests. Other indespensible persons included Mary Lee Kuhtz McLaughlen, Zulma Ramos Von Ewegen, Louise Kruszewski Paradis, Kevin Himmelberger, Gary Bailey, John Surratt, and the fine masters of unique talents, Jeff Atkinson and Paul Lindstrom. Also during this time Curt Bay gave editorial advice, Martha Bergmann greatly assisted my research, Denny Walston produced excellent copy negatives of Morris Island scenes and maps, and my aunt, Anne Beehler, graciously translated a German account of the battle into English.

I first set foot on Morris Island in the company of Jeff James, Jack Von Ewegen, and Paul Walters in a canoe provided by Steve Gilbert. From this trip and others with Robbie Freeman, I came to understand what life must have been like on that little barrier island so many years ago. I also received constant aid from the rangers at Fort Sumter National Monument, including Omega East, Russ Smith, Bob Bradley, and Jim Small.

I never lost sight of my work on Morris Island and was continually given advice, assistance, and encouragement by Tom Connelly, Earle

Jackson, Larry Connin, Sarah Heron Turner, Frank Lenz, George and Cecily McMillan, Bill Still, Sharon Bennett, Doyle Clifton, Mike Adams, Bob Incas, Charlie Peery, Allen Roberson, Don Moore, Mike Taylor, Ted Banta, Bob Holcombe, Alex Moore, Jack Waldron, Bud Wass, Norma Kipp Avandano, Kevin Foster, Will Jones, and David Caffry. Allen Stokes at the South Caroliniana Library and Richard J. Sommers at the U.S. Army Military History Institute assisted in finding new research material. I also came in contact with such fine historians and researchers as Steve Smith, Robert J. Schneller, David O'Sullivan and Mona Grunden. Tom Legg was kind enough to share his research on Rear Admiral John Dahlgren, which gave me new insight into Dahlgren's personality and actions. My discussions with Antonio de la Cova, who is completing a manuscript on Colonel Ambrosio Gonzales, proved extremely valuable in helping understand Civil War era personalities. Dave Sadowski's keen knowledge of weapons kept me from making errors in discussions of arms and armaments. Mike Miller provided constant assistance and helped bring the Morris Island campaign into a broader perspective, defining the overall importance of the campaign. Tracy Power kindly assisted in researching individual Confederate soldiers, and a number of photographs printed in this work were provided by the fine work of Walter and Valentina Hobbs. Jim Legg not only assisted with research but also, after some friendly bartering, drew the wonderful maps used throughout the book.

Two people who deserve special credit include Willis J. "Skipper" Keith and Kathy Dahle. Skipper shared his tremendous knowledge of the Charleston area and provided invaluable editorial work and comments. Kathy must be singled out for generously sharing her knowledge and research. Her work opened new areas and greatly enhanced my work.

Others deserving special mention are my parents, Mary and Glenn Wise, as well as Dave Ruth and Alice Parsons. I could never have become a historian, much less finish this book, without my parents' love and support. Dave Ruth, a long time historian at Fort Sumter, has not only been a solid backer of my work but has always remained a good friend. Dave's knowledge of Civil War Charleston is astounding and he never hesitates to share it. I am much indebted to him. Throughout the final stages of this work I have been helped by Alice Parsons. She typed and edited the manuscript and assisted in its organization. Without her this book would never have been completed.

I would like to also mention the thousands of individuals who fought and labored on Morris Island. Their accomplishments inspired my study. This book is their story.

GATE OF HELL

Introduction

Morris Island, South Carolina, long since washed away by Atlantic Ocean waves, was the site of a lengthy standoff that pitted black and white, North and South, army and navy, in a struggle which resulted in blood from thousands of men seeping into the sand. In the end there was little strategic gain for either side. Yet a man-made hell on the Carolina coast tested new weapons and military doctrines which proved to be telling lessons for both sides.

In the summer of 1863, three major campaigns took place that affected the outcome of the Civil War. Two of these, Gettysburg and Vicksburg, were dramatic turning points because of their immediate effect on the war. At the same time, a third campaign directed against Charleston, South Carolina, was underway on Morris Island that proved instrumental not only for the Civil War but also future battles. Morris Island introduced a new era in the science of engineering and gunnery. It was a major testing ground for African American troops whose fine performance against Battery Wagner and in the subsequent siege convinced the Northern government to expand its recruitment of black soldiers.

The skillful, bold operations made the Morris Island campaign exceptional in the annals of military history. The British observer Viscount Wolsely, who wrote extensively about the Civil War, considered the battle on Morris Island to be the war's most important campaign. Yet the memory of Morris Island disappeared as quickly as the island eroded into the ocean; however, its story cannot be forgotten.[1]

When diplomacy failed, the Civil War began at Charleston, South Carolina. The beautiful port city became the symbolic heart of Southern secession and was forever linked with the war and its beginning. Besides its symbolic value, Charleston was also a vital seaport, munitions center, and military stronghold, one the South was determined to hold and the North determined to capture.

Located on a peninsula formed by the Ashley and Cooper rivers, Charleston stands four miles from the outer edge of a deep and spacious harbor. The mouth of the harbor is formed by two islands. On the northern side is Sullivan's Island. Morris Island forms the southern end. Directly between the two islands, built on a shoal, sits Fort Sumter.

In 1860 a vessel coming to Charleston via the main ship channel had to approach from the south, cross the bar, and sail along Morris Island until reaching the harbor's mouth, where the channel turned west and ran between Fort Sumter and Sullivan's Island. Here, in this critical spot, were Charleston's principal defenses: Fort Sumter, and on Sullivan's Island, Fort Moultrie. Together the two forts formed the linchpin defending the harbor. If warships could pass through the crossfire laid down by Sumter and Moultrie, there remained only Castle Pinckney, an old brick relic of the War of 1812, to defend Charleston. Pinckney could not stop a determined attack. If enemy warships made it past the outer forts, Charleston could not be defended.

During the first half of the nineteenth century, Charleston's defenses were planned and constructed by the U.S. Army Corps of Engineers. They paid little attention to Morris Island, even though the island paralleled the main ship channel for nearly four miles. By contemporary military thought, defensive works on Morris Island were deemed unnecessary, as pre-1860 artillery could not effectively cover the channel. Also, by the same theory, artillery mounted on the island's northern end, known as Cummings Point, could not penetrate Fort Sumter's brick walls. In fact, so confident were the engineers on the latter point, they placed Sumter's weakest wall, the gorge wall, opposite Cummings Point.

At the beginning of the nineteenth century there was no Morris Island; instead there existed three islands: Middle Bay, Morrison, and Cummings. The three islands were separated by small, marshy inlets which in time were filled to form one thin strip of land. The new island took its name from a corruption of Morrison Island and became known as Morris Island. A cheerless spot, Morris Island was typical of the many barrier islands that lined the South Carolina coast, having a sandy beach along the ocean and a large expanse of salt marsh facing inland. Measuring three and three-quarters of a mile long, the island varied in width from twenty-five to a thousand yards.

Since 1673 there has been some sort of navigational light on the island's southern tip, guiding vessels into the main ship channel. The lighthouse there in 1860 had been built during the mid-nineteenth century. Near the light was a light-keepers' house. Besides having the city's lighthouse, Morris Island also served as Charleston's lazaretto, a hospital for persons with contagious diseases, and was sometimes referred to as Coffin Island because of the numerous bodies buried among the island's sand dunes.

Until 1860 it seemed that Morris Island would be allowed to continue its quiet existence. This changed on the night of December 26, when

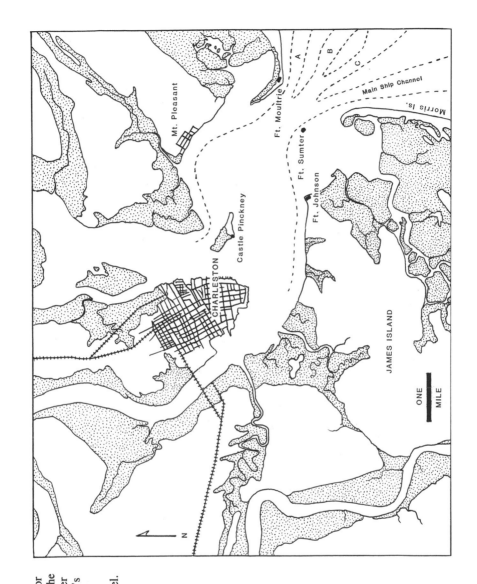

Map 1: Charleston Harbor showing the location of the Main Ship Channel. Other channels are A: Sullivan's or Maffitt's Channel, B: North Channel and C: Swash or Overall Channel.

Major Robert Anderson, fearing that troops from recently seceded South Carolina would overrun vulnerable Fort Moultrie, moved his garrison to the more secure Fort Sumter. Immediately the Carolinians began to build batteries to isolate and bombard Fort Sumter, and Morris Island soon found itself a center of military activities.

On December 31, 1860, several steamers arrived off Morris Island and landed eighty soldiers with construction equipment and horses. Fortifications were started and the harbor light was extinguished. Just north of the lazaretto, a battery was quickly constructed to cover the main ship channel. Troops were also stationed along the length of the island and, with the battery's garrison, kept the ship channel under close watch. The vigilance paid off on January 9, 1861 when the merchant vessel *Star of the West* was sighted crossing the bar and moving toward Fort Sumter. On board were 200 Federal troops with ammunition and provisions. The battery near the lazaretto opened on the vessel. Two hits were recorded, but the steamer continued on. The battery could not stop her, and it was left to Fort Moultrie to eventually turn the *Star of the West* from Fort Sumter.[2]

Since the Morris Island battery, forever known as the *Star of the West* Battery, was unable to stop a merchantman from moving down the ship channel, the Southerners redoubled their efforts. In the next few months the Carolinians were joined by men from other seceding states, and together they continued to build more fortifications. In time redoubts appeared at the island's southern end near the lighthouse. The *Star of the West* Battery was enlarged and leading to the north were a number of unconnected earthworks which led to breaching batteries at Cummings Point. Facing Fort Sumter were four separate batteries. Two were mortar batteries; another, located inside an iron casemate, mounted three 8-inch Columbiads, while the fourth had two 42-pounders and a small, rifled, Blakely cannon.

The Blakely, made in Great Britain, was a gift to South Carolina from Fraser, Trenholm and Company, the Liverpool branch of the highly influential Charleston merchantile firm of John Fraser and Company. Based on the design of its inventor and namesake, Alexander Theophillis Blakely, the cannon had a 3.5-inch bore and fired a 12-pound shot which, due to the barrel's rifling, spun as it left the gun. The spinning gave the gun incredible accuracy and penetration, more than the much larger, smoothbore, 8-inch Columbiads that fired 65-pound balls.

Though the Confederates worked hard to perfect their breaching batteries, their commander, Brigadier General Pierre G. T. Beauregard, doubted the ability of his artillery to reduce Fort Sumter, which he, agreeing with the engineers who built it, considered nearly impregnable. Beauregard knew that the Federal garrison was low on provisions and eventually would have to evacuate the fort; however, Beauregard's hand was forced when word reached him of a naval relief expedition being assembled to reinforce Fort Sumter. A demand was sent to Anderson for the immediate surrender of Fort Sumter. It was refused, and orders for attack were sent to the harbor batteries.[3]

Chapter 1

THE PRIZE AND ITS DEFENSES

The Charleston defenses are like a porcupine hide with the quills turned outside in.
Rear Admiral Samuel F. Du Pont

Early on the morning of April 12, 1861, a mortar shell from Fort Johnson on James Island traced a high arc across the sky over Charleston Harbor and exploded directly above Fort Sumter. Almost immediately, a 12-pound rifle bolt, fired from a 3.5-inch Blakely rifled cannon on Cummings Point, Morris Island, slammed into Sumter's gorge wall. In terms of rifled artillery, the little Blakely would prove to be a mere toy when compared to the later cannons fabricated during the war. However, its accurate shelling throughout the bombardment was of grave concern to the Federal garrison and aided in the fort's eventual capitulation. The Blakely also foreshadowed an even greater use of rifled artillery on Morris Island.[1]

The combination of Fort Sumter, rifled cannon, and Morris Island linked together in the war's first action. It was inevitable that they would again come together before the conflict ended. Located three-quarters of a mile from Sumter, Morris Island was not only the closest land to the stronghold, but its location also gave gunners a direct line of fire on Sumter's weakest side, the gorge wall. Here, in 1861, the Southerners established their most effective breeching batteries consisting of the Blakely rifle and the much larger 8-inch Columbiad smoothbores. These batteries punished Sumter's brickwork, with the Blakely driving its bolt twenty inches into Sumter's wall.[2]

The builders of Fort Sumter had not foreseen the development of rifled artillery. Accepted military theory of the first half of the nine-

6

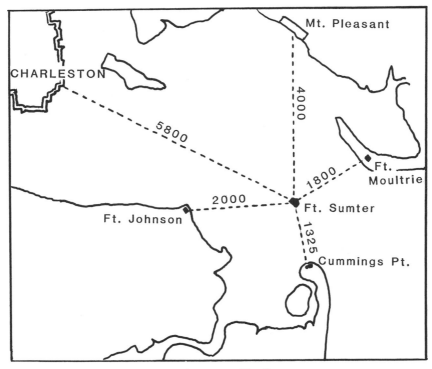

Map 2: Distances to Fort Sumter

teenth century stated that defenses on Morris Island were unnecessary because the island was covered by Sumter's barbette guns. Also, since the fort was designed to repel sea attacks and not attacks from the local populace, the engineers placed its weakest and least gunned wall, the gorge wall, opposite Morris Island. In times of trouble, it was thought Morris Island would be occupied by friendly troops, and even if the enemy did land on the little island, no one envisioned artillery capable of breeching Sumter's walls. Though the old theory was shaken in April 1861, the Confederates failed to fully grasp the significance of Morris Island and the Blakely.[3]

After Sumter's capture, the Southerners removed their cannon from Morris Island and placed them in fortifications designed to protect Charleston. The city was important to the Confederacy. Besides its symbolic value, Charleston was the South's dominant shipping point on the Atlantic coast. Not only could the port handle most sea-going vessels, it had excellent railroad connections which could distribute incoming supplies to military depots throughout the South. Charleston was also home to a number of commercial houses with connections in Great Britain. Partial to the Confederacy, and with an eye to profits, the larger firms quickly began making arrangements to ship commercial and military items from overseas to the Confederacy through Charleston. The incoming supplies were essential. Without them the Confederacy would be unable to resist the Northern armies.[4]

To protect Charleston, energetic and innovative officers were sent to improve, design, and construct the city's defenses. After Sumter's capture the harbor works were strengthened under the direction of General Beauregard and Colonel Roswell Sabine Ripley. For a brief time Charleston was commanded by Colonel Richard H. Anderson and then in August 1861, Ripley, now a brigadier general, returned.

An Ohio native, Ripley was a West Point graduate, veteran of the Mexican War, had served on coast surveys, and taught mathematics at West Point. In 1853 Ripley resigned from the army and settled in Charleston where he married into the prominent Middleton family.

Remaining active in military affairs, Ripley joined the South Carolina militia and in 1860 the thirty-eight-year-old artilleryman commanded Fort Moultrie, directing its guns against Fort Sumter. So well did Ripley perform his task that Captain Abner Doubleday, one of Sumter's defenders, later wrote that Ripley: "Like all Northern converts . . . thought it necessary to be overzealous in his new position, to do away with the suspicions excited by his birth and education." If this was Ripley's purpose, he succeeded. After the battle, the Charlestonians insisted that he be retained to defend their city.

To his friends Ripley was a kind and jovial officer, but to those who failed to please him, Ripley could lash out with a vengeance. A demanding superior and an irritating subordinate with a fondness for alcohol, Ripley alienated many of his command's aristocratic officers, but his skill as an artilleryman and engineer compensated for his abrasive personality. For Charleston's defense, he was too valuable to do without.[5]

Ripley's primary efforts went into defending the main ship channel and James Island. To guard the harbor, both forts, Moultrie and Sumter, were strengthened, given additional cannon and full garrisons. To supplement Moultrie, new earthworks were built on either side of the fort, and Moultrie's seaward brick wall was covered with sand.

Fort Sumter was repaired and prepared to repel any naval assault, but unlike Moultrie, its brick walls could not be covered with sand. However, while the fort's high walls were easy targets for enemy artillery, they also made it the harbor's main guardian. Mounted on Sumter's barbette were the Confederate's heaviest cannon, which could fire their projectiles down on enemy vessels, ripping through decks into engine rooms and magazines.

While Sumter and Moultrie watched over Charleston's water approach, other batteries and forts were constructed to keep the Federals off James Island, the most accessible land route to Charleston. Located south of Charleston across the Ashley River, James Island was bordered to the east by marsh stretching between James, Morris, and Folly islands. To the southwest was the Stono River, which was navigable by steamships for the entire length of James Island. In 1780, the British had used the Stono River to support their movements against Charleston when they bypassed the city's water defenses by moving across James Island to the mainland, crossing the Ashley River to the peninsula, and approaching Charleston from its landside. The Confederates were well aware of this history and did not want it repeated.

On the harbor side of James Island the Confederates strengthened Fort Johnson, a derelict fortification that had been turned into a quarantine station and a government storage site. As a harbor fort its purpose was secondary. Forts Sumter and Moultrie guarded the harbor entrance, and at best, Johnson's guns could only annoy vessels once they passed the outer works; however, should an enemy seize Fort Johnson, as the British had done in 1780, Charleston and the inner harbor would be exposed to direct artillery fire.

To protect Fort Johnson and James Island from overland attacks, the Confederates depended on nature, cannon, and strong earthworks. A natural barrier of salt marsh lined the island's eastern rim, separating James from Morris and Folly islands. The thick, heavy mud was virtually impassable to attackers as it would consume men nearly up to their waists, making any advance a military nightmare. Confident that even Yankees would not be foolish enough to try a major advance through the marsh, the Confederates did not build any defenses along the island's eastern rim.

Instead the Confederates concentrated on keeping the enemy out of the Stono River, therefore stopping a repeat of the 1780 British attack. To guard against this, an important set of fortifications were constructed centering on Cole's Island at the mouth of the Stono River.

The defenses on Cole's Island served a dual purpose. The well-built batteries not only denied entrance into the Stono River and protected James Island, they also guarded the water approaches to Folly and Morris islands. With Cole's Island securely held, no enemy could land on the two barrier islands without jeopardizing their communications. Because of this, for the first year of the war, the Confederates were able to leave Morris Island defenseless. For the moment, the war had passed by Morris Island. Its cannons were removed and the sand batteries deteriorated and disappeared under the constant action of the wind.[6]

The importance of Cole's Island was not lost on General Ripley, who continued to improve its defenses while his command was incorporated into a larger military department. In November 1861, Charleston became part of the newly formed Department of South Carolina, Georgia, and Florida. The department's commander was General Robert E. Lee, an appointment that initially did not set well with Charlestonians. Until then, Lee had not had a successful career. His defeats in western Virginia had resulted in his transfer south, where his engineering skills would be used in developing a department-wide defense policy.[7]

Even before Lee arrived in the region, he realized the South did not have enough men or cannon to defend every inlet along the coast. The lack of resources was made evident when, on November 7, 1861, one day before Lee arrived in Charleston, a squadron of Union vessels entered Port Royal Sound, some fifty miles south of Charleston, and easily defeated two widely separated and undergunned Confederate forts. Besides confirming Lee's belief that he could not defend his entire department, the Federal victory also gave the North a base from which strikes could be launched against Charleston, Savannah, and other important coastal sites. To counteract this and improve his position, Lee immediately began implementing strategic withdrawals, concentrating his defenses at Georgetown, Charleston, Savannah, and the Savannah-Charleston Railroad.[8]

Lee, who may have been influenced by some of his father's theories of coast defense, based his plan primarily on an army report written in 1826 by Major Joseph G. Totten, which detailed a coastal defensive policy. Totten proposed a system of harbor forts that delayed an enemy's advance until local militia could be mustered. Once ready, the militia would then move to the threatened area and defeat the enemy. Lee took Totten's concept and added the element of rail transportation. Garrisons at Savannah and Charleston were kept strong enough to meet initial attacks, and before the enemy could gain the advantage, reinforcements would arrive via the railroad. To make his plan work, Lee continued to strengthen the harbor defenses and also built a number of new fortifications along the Charleston and Savannah railroad. From this point on, Charleston's harbor works and the railroad were linked together.[9]

For five months Lee worked at implementing his plan, then in March

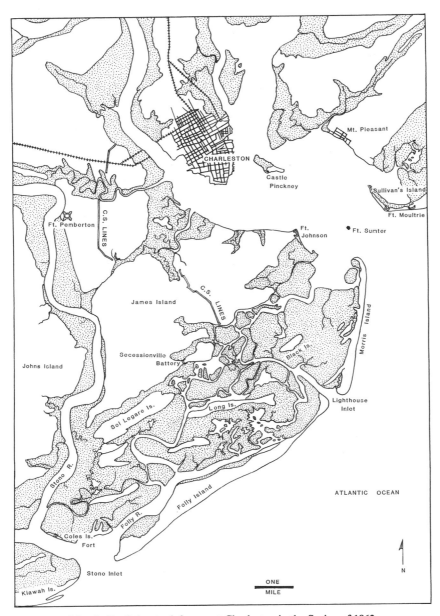

Map 3: Confederate defenses at Charleston in the Spring of 1862

1862 he returned to Richmond to serve as advisor to President Jefferson Davis. His successor was his second-in-command, Major General John C. Pemberton. A native of Pennsylvania, Pemberton, like Ripley, had married a Southerner, but unlike Ripley, Pemberton's wife was a Virginian and not a Charlestonian. He was not accepted in low country social life, and throughout his tenure the South Carolinians viewed him with suspicion. Still, he continued to carry out Lee's policies, but under a continuing personnel drain. While troops were sent to Tennessee and Virginia, Pemberton was forced to reduce his defense lines. Men were taken from guarding the railroad, and Georgetown was evacuated. Another site abandoned was Cole's Island. Though extremely important to the protection of James Island, Pemberton feared his garrison on Cole's Island would be cut off and irreplaceable men and guns lost, so over the protests of General Ripley and the island's commander, Colonel Johnson Hagood, the Confederates removed their cannon and left Cole's Island.

The evacuation of Cole's Island opened a feud between Pemberton and Ripley. Never a congenial subordinate, Ripley did not allow rank to stand in his way when arguing his position. Outraged at Pemberton's evacuation of a position he considered vital to Charleston's defenses, Ripley began a campaign to discredit his commander. At the same time, Ripley's usual irritating actions toward subordinates were causing dissent within the Charleston district. Officers who displeased Ripley were often given menial tasks away from their commands, and Ripley's habit of playing favorites also caused difficulties. To restore morale in his department and make his life easier, Pemberton, in June 1862, transferred Ripley to the Army of Northern Virginia.

Ripley's departure only solved part of Pemberton's problems. While his abandonment of Cole's Island had tightened his defense lines, it also opened new avenues for Federal attacks. The enemy now had access to the Stono River, which in turn exposed James Island and Fort Johnson. To stop the enemy from reaching the harbor side of James Island, Pemberton ordered the construction of loosely connected redoubts running across the center of the island from Secessionville in the southeast to Fort Pemberton on the Stono in the northwest.

Besides opening James Island to attack, the abandonment of Cole's Island also changed the status of Morris and Folly islands. Both were now open to Union occupation. Folly was not defended but Pemberton did return the military to Morris Island. On June 3, 1862, orders were sent to Lieutenant Colonel Thomas Wagner of the 1st South Carolina Artillery Regiment to construct a small battery at Cummings Point. Located near the old position of the Blakely gun, the new battery faced the opposite direction, with its guns aimed down the channel and away from Fort Sumter's gorge wall. Pemberton planned other works on Morris Island, but he was forced to postpone them when the Northerners took advantage of the Cole's Island evacuation and moved against Charleston.[10]

The unexpected abandonment of Cole's Island presented such great opportunities for the Federals at Port Royal that even the department's slow-moving commander, Major General David A. Hunter, was quick

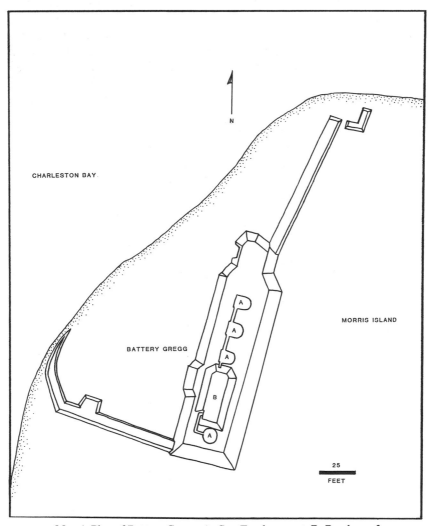

Map 4: Plan of Battery Gregg, A: Gun Emplacement, B: Bombproof

to react. By June 2, 1862, nearly seventy-five hundred Union troops were convoyed into the Stono River and landed on the southwestern end of James Island. In front of them ran five miles of unfinished redoubts and batteries held by four thousand Confederates. The Union Army was poised to turn Charleston's defenses and repeat the British triumph, but Hunter stalled. Thinking he was outnumbered, he turned his command over to Brigadier General Henry W. Benham and left James Island.

Benham was under orders not to attack, but was given permission to protect the Union camps on James Island. Since his position was under the guns of the Confederates at Secessionville, and reconnaissance had shown the work to be unfinished and undermanned, Benham sent about one-third of his force against the fort at Secessionville. The battle was sharp and confusing. Thanks to intervening salt marsh, the Federals were unable to employ their superior numbers, and after a brief hand to hand struggle, the Confederates held. When Hunter learned of the attack he had Benham relieved and withdrew his men from James Island.[11]

With the Federal threat gone from James Island, the Confederates continued their defensive work. The James Island lines were completed, and additional batteries were started on Morris Island. With Cole's Island now under the guns of Federal warships, Morris Island became an important element in Charleston's defenses. The island was now looked upon as the guardian of the harbor's southern flank.

Until the Battle of Secessionville, the only fortification on Morris Island was at Cummings Point. Designed to cover the main ship channel, the battery was vulnerable to an infantry attack, so to protect it and keep the enemy away from Cummings Point, Pemberton directed his engineers to construct an infantry outpost twelve hundred yards to the south behind the spot where Morris Island narrowed to a mere twenty-five yards.[12]

The battery was designed and its construction supervised by two of Pemberton's best engineers, Langdon Cheves and Francis D. Lee. Though neither were professional military engineers, the two South Carolinians were good examples of the local talent pool available at Charleston. Cheves, son and namesake of the director of the First Bank of the United States, had received formal military training at West Point but left the academy to become a prominent lawyer and rice planter.

Like Cheves, Lee was also a well-known figure in prewar South Carolina. A graduate of the College of Charleston, Lee became an architect and received recognition for remodeling the interior of the city's Unitarian Church and building Charleston's Farmer and Exchange Bank.

When South Carolina seceded, Cheves and Lee left their civilian careers and offered their services to their state. They received their apprenticeships in the fine art of military science during the spring of 1861 while constructing works to attack Fort Sumter. Later, they often worked as a team. Among their assignments was the design and construction of Forts Walker and Beauregard at Port Royal. Then, they were assigned to duty in the Charleston area, and in the summer of 1862, took their expertise to Morris Island.[13]

Cheves and Lee had gained knowledge from the earlier attacks against their works. They knew the Confederacy had a limited amount of war material, so they took special care in building the new Morris Island battery, combining the island's natural features with an efficient and deadly design. They placed the work about one thousand yards from Cummings Point and fifty-five hundred yards from the island's southern end. The battery looked south and had a massive land front that stretched from Vincent's Creek on the James Island side to the Atlantic Ocean. The land front joined the sea wall at a dominating bastion that gave enfilading fire against any would-be attackers. A well-traversed and fortified sea front guarded the ship channel. The rear, or northern, wall and the wall that paralleled Vincent's Creek were little more than infantry parapets, but no attacks were expected from these directions, and Lee and Cheves concentrated on perfecting the rest of the battery. They placed the land face just north of the island's narrowest point, where its guns could sweep the twenty-five yards of dry land that kept Morris Island from being split in two. When completed and properly garrisoned, the work could easily halt any enemy force trying to reach Cummings Point.[14]

Since the work had only a breastwork for its rear wall, it was technically a battery, and initially it was called the Neck Battery, an appropriate name since its mission was to choke off and stop enemy soldiers from moving down Morris Island. Five months after its completion, the Neck Battery was renamed. Following a time-honored, though somewhat grim tradition, it was named for a South Carolinian, and as was becoming commonplace, one who had died during the war. On November 4, 1862, the battery was named to honor Lieutenant Colonel Thomas M. Wagner of the 1st South Carolina Artillery.

Wagner, a Charleston native and local planter, had joined the 1st South Carolina Artillery at the start of the war as a private and soon moved up through the ranks, making Lieutenant Colonel by April 1862. A bachelor noted for his excursions into the city's seamier

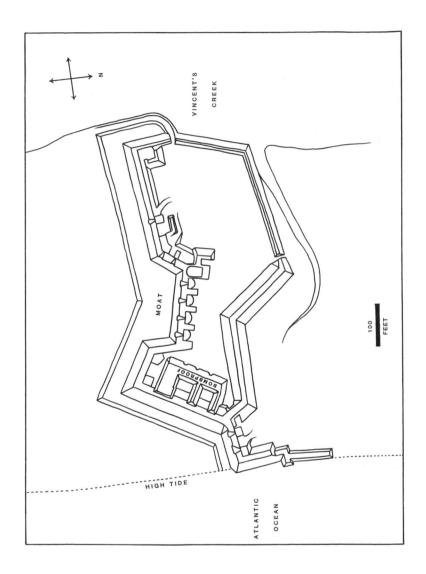

Map 5: Plan of Battery Wagner

sections, Wagner soon developed into a popular and efficient officer. He served occasionally as Fort Sumter's commander and briefly commanded at the Battle of Secessionville after his superiors had been wounded. Appointed the Department of South Carolina and Georgia's chief of ordnance in May 1862, the thirty-eight-year-old Wagner was mortally wounded on July 17, 1862, when a gun exploded during artillery practice at Fort Moultrie. His final words called for the completion of Charleston's harbor defenses. With the renaming of the Neck Battery, Wagner's name would be forever linked with the city's fortifications.[15]

To many, the term battery implies a second class fortification, a weakling in the hierarchy of military works, but depending upon its location, it can be stronger than the largest fortress. By definition, a battery lacks a complete rear wall. Some batteries have no rear defense. In Battery Wagner's case, there was a low rampart with an infantry parapet guarding the rear approaches. A formidable obstacle it was not, but it was not supposed to be. Wagner's main strength lay to its front, and here Cheves and Lee coordinated the battery's well-positioned cannon, made up of navy shell guns, howitzers, and carronades, to sweep Wagner's approaches, while the sea wall contained sheltered coastal guns that could duel with warships. Though only a battery, Wagner was a formidable obstacle, and with its strength, it often would be erroneously called a fort, a title of distinction, honor, and dread given to Wagner by its opponents.[16]

Though Wagner was exceptionally strong in its own right, Pemberton planned to aid the battery with a number of supporting works designed to keep enemy forces off Morris Island and protect Wagner's approaches. New earthworks were started on the island's southern tip near the site of the old lighthouse, while batteries were also planned for Black Island, a low, marsh island between James and Folly islands, which would cover Light-House Inlet. At the same time, what remained of the famous Floating Battery, which had been used during the bombardment of Fort Sumter, was anchored at the mouth of Vincent's Creek where it would be used as an artillery platform with its guns sweeping Wagner's land approach. Work was also started on a causeway running from James Island to Morris Island so reinforcements could be hurried out to the barrier island. If all of these defenses were finished, Morris Island would be a difficult position to assault.[17]

Pemberton did not remain at Charleston to see the completion of his defense plans. Never a favorite of Charlestonians, Pemberton regularly squabbled with influential citizens who soon began seeking his removal. He retained the confidence of both President Davis and General

Lee, but they were unable to alter the erosion that had already occurred, and bowing to political pressure, Davis transferred Pemberton to Vicksburg, Mississippi, and ordered General Beauregard returned to Charleston.[18]

The creole general who, from his childhood near New Orleans, spoke better French than English, was returning to the scene of his first triumph. Hero of Fort Sumter and Bull Run, Beauregard had planned the attack at Shiloh and executed a brilliant withdrawal from Corinth, Mississippi. His skill as an engineer and commanding general was matched by his sensitivity to real or perceived personal affronts. Beauregard also involved himself in politics and early in the war joined the anti-Davis faction in the Confederate government, thus gaining the president's animosity. After Corinth, Davis removed the troublesome Louisiana native from command, and if the president had had his way, he may well have kept Beauregard on the sidelines for the remainder of the war.

When he began looking for Pemberton's replacement, Davis first chose Major General Gustavus W. Smith, but South Carolinians continued to press for the popular Beauregard, and in mid-September 1862, the conqueror of Sumter arrived in Charleston.

Before leaving for Mississippi, Pemberton accompanied his replacement on a tour of Charleston's defenses. Beauregard discovered that Pemberton was leaving him a solid foundation from which he could continue to build. Like the previous Charleston commanders, Beauregard realized that the two most critical areas were the main ship channel and James Island. Following Pemberton's lead, Beauregard planned additional defenses, both on land and on water. Assisting him were not only the departmental engineers but also new arrivals, among them two officers detailed to Charleston at Beauregard's personal request.[19]

One was the irascible General Ripley who returned to his old command after recovering from a wound received at Antietam. Ripley's career with the Army of Northern Virginia had been less than distinguished. He had received criticism for his actions at the Seven Days and South Mountain, but had been commended for his leadership at Antietam, where he was badly wounded in the neck. After recovering from his wound, Ripley returned home and back to the more familiar duties as an engineer and artillery commander.

Though Beauregard had had the displeasure of experiencing Ripley's temper and insubordinate attitude during his earlier tenure at Charleston, the commanding general also prized his skill and competence as an artillery officer, and with combat approaching, Ripley would have to concentrate on fighting the enemy and not friends.

In addition to Ripley, Beauregard added the services of Colonel David B. Harris. Opposite in temperament to Ripley, Harris was a quiet, bookish man whose engineering skills were among the best in the Confederacy. A native of Virginia, Harris graduated from West Point in 1833, and after a brief stint in the artillery resigned to become a civil engineer. Volunteering for service when Virginia seceded, Harris soon became an important part of Beauregard's staff, serving with the general at First Bull Run. He later saw duty working on fortifications at Columbus, Kentucky, Fort Pillow and Vicksburg. Like Ripley, Harris had skills that Beauregard admired and needed at Charleston, and like Ripley, Harris would soon be linked to Morris Island and Battery Wagner.[20]

The men assembling at Charleston were skillful technicians who had to adjust to the new changes in warfare. By the end of 1862, the Civil War had brought tremendous innovations to the fields of artillery, fortifications, warships, and harbor defense.

Some of the biggest changes took place in the realm of artillery, and they had been foreshadowed on Morris Island by the little Blakely gun. At the start of the war, artillery was divided into three categories: field, siege, and seacoast. Field artillery consisted of guns, howitzers, and the hybrid Napoleon gun-howitzer. Light and maneuverable, they served alongside the infantry. The longer-ranged and smaller-bored field guns fired shot, shell, canister, grapeshot, and case shot while the large-mouthed howitzers were designed to send shell, grapeshot, canister, and case shot against attackers at close range. The Napoleon was a compromise between the field gun and howitzer. The bronze artillery piece could fire shot, shell, case shot, and canister. It had the range of a gun and the hitting power of a howitzer.

Like the field pieces, siege artillery was also divided into guns and howitzers, and also included high-trajectory firing mortars. Designed for use against an enemy's field fortification or to bolster defenses, siege artillery was light enough to transport by road, but usually too slow and cumbersome to accompany armies on the move; however, once a campaign stalled and fixed works were prepared, the siege artillery would be summoned to serve alongside the field pieces.

The war's largest class of guns and mortars was known as seacoast artillery. This large cast iron ordnance normally occupied gun chambers inside masonry forts. These guardians of the coast, firing shot and shell weighing more than 100 pounds, were rarely seen in the field.

Their massive weight, 7,000 to 15,000 pounds, prohibited most movement outside a fixed position.

At the start of the Civil War there was not a single piece of rifled artillery in the United States Army. The artillery was all smoothbore, firing either a round solid ball (termed solid shot) or a shell, an iron ball filled with powder which was exploded by the use of a timed fuse. Though very effective at close range, the smoothbores lacked certain qualities that came with a rifled barrel—a marked increase in weight of projectiles and accuracy. With a rifled cannon, enemy positions could be bombarded from a greater distance and with deadlier effect. Against masonry fortifications there was an even greater advantage. An old-style, 42-pound smoothbore firing its round shot could penetrate only about eight inches into a brickwork, but once this same gun was rifled and given an eighty-four-pound, bullet-like projectile, it could smash a hole twenty-six inches deep into the same wall.

The Confederates had taken a quick lead with their Blakely gun, but in a short time, both sides would realize the value of rifled guns, and soon the new cannon would take a major role in field, siege, and seacoast operations. The North quickly added batteries of rifled ordnance and Parrott guns to their armies. The Parrotts, which were recognized by distinctive iron bands around their breeches, were named for their inventor and manufacturer, Robert Parker Parrott. An 1824 graduate of West Point, Parrott resigned from the army in 1834 to supervise the West Point Foundry at Cold Spring, New York. His work resulted in not only rifled field pieces but eventually siege and seacoast guns.

The Confederates countered the North with imports, conversions, their own Parrott-style rifles, and a series of heavy seacoast guns known as Brooke Rifles. Invented by John Mercer Brooke, a naval officer who joined the South, the banded Brooke guns were as efficient and durable as the Parrott but could not be fabricated as quickly as the northern guns, and in many places such as Charleston, the Confederates had to use a number of the less-reliable smoothbores that had been rifled and banded in Southern foundries.

During the first campaigns of the war, both sides were able to place within their armies rifled field pieces; however, due to manufacturing time, it took longer for the appearance of siege and seacoast rifles. Initially, both sides used converted smoothbores until the new guns became available. This was particularly true for the April 1862 attack on Fort Pulaski.[21]

While the Civil War rifled guns had their beginnings on Morris Island against Fort Sumter in 1861, their first major use occurred just 100 miles to the south on Tybee Island, Georgia. Here, the chief engineer of the Department of the South, Captain Quincy Adams Gillmore, prepared siege batteries of rifled guns to attack Fort Pulaski.

Located on a marshy island in the middle of the Savannah River, Fort Pulaski guarded Savannah, Georgia. A strong casemated brickwork, the fort was considered as impregnable as the Rocky Mountains. To reduce Pulaski, Gillmore brought together mortars, smoothbore seacoast guns, recently rifled smoothbores termed James Rifles, and three newly made Parrott siege guns. At a distance of more than a mile, these guns pounded the fort, their rifled projectiles pulverizing the brick walls. Within two days rifled artillery brought down the South's "Rocky Mountains." For his success, Gillmore was promoted to brigadier general in the Volunteer Army and transferred to Kentucky, but his interests and spirit would always remain with rifled artillery and the Department of the South.[22]

Gillmore's success at Pulaski and the subsequent evolution of rifled artillery were carefully watched by the Charleston defenders. Beauregard and his staff realized that changes in their defense plans would have to take into account these new land weapons, and at the same time, they also had to prepare for new advances in naval warfare.

Closely related to the revolution in land-based artillery was the navy's improvement in shipborne artillery. By 1860, the navy was also developing and using larger and more effective guns. Though warships still carried howitzers and 24- and 32-pounders, their main ordnance was the Dahlgren gun, invented by its namesake, naval Captain John Adolph Dahlgren. At the start of the war the standard size was a 9-inch gun, but soon the North added 11- and 15-inch guns to its inventory.

The North also placed Parrott guns on their vessels, but the preferred weapon was the Dahlgren smoothbore which dominated ship armaments. The largest Dahlgren fired huge, round projectiles which by sheer weight crushed and mangled wood, iron, and masonry. Extremely effective against enemy vessels, the guns could also be used to attack land defenses, especially when mounted in ironclad vessels.[23]

Like the rifled gun, ironclad vessels had their first great test during the Civil War. At Hampton Roads, Virginia, on March 8, 1862, the Confederate citadel ironclad *Virginia* destroyed two powerful wooden vessels while sustaining only superficial damage. The next day the *Virginia* battled the Union turreted ironclad *Monitor* to a draw. In two short days wooden warships were rendered obsolete and both sides began building improved versions of the first ironclads. These new vessels were initially designed to fight one another, but they could also be used to attack fortifications.

Ironclads and rifled artillery were two new elements that Beauregard and his command would have to deal with. Besides watching James Island the Confederates had to guard against possible naval attack by ironclad warships and keep the Federal artillery from being positioned within range of vulnerable targets. To bolster their defenses, the Confederates continued to build additional fortifications and improve existing ones. Earth became their major construction material as Confederate engineers prepared for expected Federal attacks.

One work that Beauregard could not protect with earth embankments was Fort Sumter, but Sumter's vulnerability was also its strength. Its fifty-foot-high walls were easy targets for both naval and land bombardment, but heavy guns mounted on its top tier were Charleston's primary defense against naval attacks. Here the Confederates mounted Brooke Rifles and 10-inch Columbiads that could fire down on the deck of attacking warships, sending their shot and shell into vessels' hulls. No wooden warship could survive such fire, and even ironclads were possibly vulnerable to plunging shot smashing into their decks.[24]

To assist the gunners in Fort Sumter, Beauregard continued Pemberton's policy of placing obstructions in the main ship channel between Forts Moultrie and Sumter. These obstructions were woven into a log and rope boom that ran from Fort Moultrie to Fort Sumter, where an opening was left so blockade runners could enter and leave the harbor. The boom was designed to slow or stop attacking vessels under Fort Sumter's guns, thus allowing the artillerymen more time to aim and fire their cannon; however, in a short time the boom was given additional stopping power.

While Pemberton was still in Charleston, he allowed explosive canisters added to the boom. These experimental devices—termed torpedoes—were designed to explode on contact with enemy vessels. Beauregard took these torpedoes to the next stage of development and shortly after his arrival authorized the establishment of a torpedo office. Captain Francis Lee was moved from his engineering duties on Morris Island and put in charge of developing new and more powerful torpedoes. In time, Lee began mounting contact torpedoes on spars throughout the harbor and designed others that could be set off by electrical current. By the beginning of 1863, torpedoes were present in Charleston harbor, though the exact number and locations have never been accurately reported. Still, just the threat of their presence caused great psychological concern to an enemy locked inside ironclad warships.[25]

Assisting Beauregard in the defense of Charleston was a small naval contingent under the command of Commodore Duncan M. Ingraham. The squadron's main battle force was the two locally constructed ironclad rams, the *Chicora* and the *Palmetto State*. Built as smaller versions of the *Virginia*, the two vessels were casemated rams. The *Chicora* mounted six guns while her sister ship, the *Palmetto State*, carried four. Though the rams had proven their worth against wooden vessels on January 30, 1863, when they made a night raid against the Union blockaders, they were not strong enough to battle Northern monitors in a ship to ship duel. Even Ingraham's aggressive squadron commander, Commander John Randolph Tucker, realized that his crude, underpowered ironclads could only serve as auxiliaries to the land batteries in any attack against the city. To this end, Tucker kept his warships near Fort Sumter where their guns could help defend the obstructions and fight any enemy vessel that managed to pass through the barrier.[26]

Even without a formidable naval force, Beauregard developed around Charleston a well-prepared defense system. The harbor's seaward approaches were blocked by obstructions and torpedoes and heavy guns placed in well-protected fortifications. The lines on James Island were reinforced and readied to blunt any Northern attack. Beauregard suspected that any new attack might be directed against Morris Island where breaching batteries could be established against Fort Sumter, but he felt that such an assault could be repulsed. What the general feared most was a dual sea and land attack that would force him to spread thin his men and artillery.[27]

As Beauregard suspected, plans were being made to attack Charleston. Since the fall of Fort Sumter, Northern public opinion, spurred on by the newspapers, kept up a constant clamor for Charleston's capture. The city was considered by many to be symbolically more important than Richmond. It was the birthplace of secession and the heart of the rebellion. The Union military leaders needed no urging to assail Charleston. Both the army and the navy, embarassed by their inability to relieve Fort Sumter in 1861, were now eager to redeem themselves.

Besides restoring honor, the capture of Charleston would bring some tangible military results. The city was home to a government arsenal and numerous industrial plants that provided finished goods to the South's military. Once taken, the city could serve as a site to launch an invasion into the South's heartland, especially against such important production centers as Columbia and Augusta.

Charleston was also a thriving commercial seaport and was the Confederacy's main blockade running port. Throughout 1862 and into

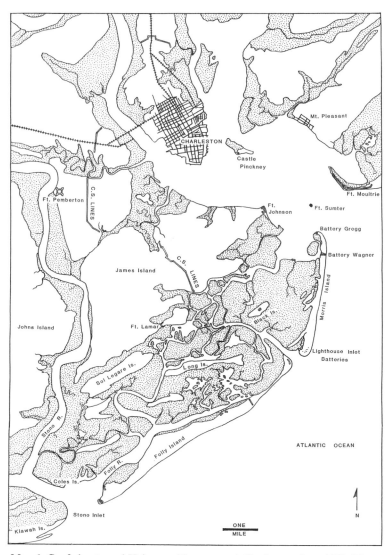

Map 6: Confederate and Union positions around Charleston, June 1863. The Confederate works on Black Island and in the marsh on Vincent's Creek were unfinished at the time of the Federal attack.

1863, the city's docks were crowded with sleek, steam-powered block-ade runners, which brought to the Confederacy thousands of arms and tons of munitions. Since the beginning of the war, the South's all-important lifeline to Europe flowed through Charleston.

To Assistant Secretary of the Navy Gustavus V. Fox, the capture of
the city had became a passion. Both he and Secretary of the Navy
Gideon Welles wanted this site of Southern defiance destroyed. Their
views were shared by their officers. As Commander John Rodgers
wrote: "I think the Nation as well as the Department has set its heart
upon the fall of that city. I think justice demands it at the hands of
fate."

As early as May 1862, Assistant Secretary Fox began urging the use
of ironclad warships against Charleston. Fox soon gained support from
not only his direct superior, Secretary Welles, but also President
Abraham Lincoln. Both saw tremendous benefits from the proposed
operations. A naval victory would bring great laurels to Welles's
Department and justify his expansive ironclad program, while Lincoln
viewed the capture of the rebellion's birthplace as a needed moral,
politcial, and symbolic victory for his party and cause.

For the attack, Fox allocated the majority of the North's ironclads.
These included the original *Monitor*, the ironclad frigate *New Ironsides,* and most of the new, improved monitor-style vessels known as
the *Passaic* class. Command would go to Rear Admiral Samuel Francis
Du Pont, the current flag officer of the South Atlantic Blockading
Squadron operating out of Port Royal Sound. Du Pont, whose squadron
had defeated the Confederate forts at Port Royal in November 1861,
was one of the navy's premier officers. Polished, urbane, and brilliant,
Du Pont combined the qualities of an Old World aristocrat with that of
a seaman who had worked his way from midshipman to commander of
the nation's most powerful squadron. Descended from French nobility
who had found wealth and prestige in the New World, Du Pont ran his
command much like a feudal state. To loyal compatriots he was genial
and complimentary and rewarded them with important positions, those
he disliked were banished. His skill as a commander of warships was
unquestioned, but Du Pont was a man of the old navy, of sails and
wooden sides. He appreciated steam engines because of the mobility
they gave to warships, but ironclads were a different matter. As he
watched the defenses grow about Charleston Harbor he became convinced that no vessels, especially the two-gunned monitors could
capture Charleston.[28]

When first contacted by Fox about the attack on Charleston, Du
Pont politely deferred from making any commitment, but in October
1862, Du Pont was brought to Washington to confer with Fox and
Welles and inspect the new monitors and their ordnance. It took all Du
Pont's social skills to survive the meetings without directly revealing
his true feelings. He was impressed by the destructive power of the 15-

inch Dahlgren guns that were to be mounted in the *Passaic* class monitors and did elicit a promise from Fox that as many of the new monitors and other ironclads as possible would be sent south, but Du Pont remained troubled. His pride in his well-earned reputation would not let him come out officially against the attack, yet his doubts remained. For a leader, Du Pont was caught in a dilemma of command that often leads to disaster. He did not believe in his vessels or his mission, but he would not remove himself from command.[29]

While Du Pont waited for his ironclads, the Northern army made preparations to facilitate the naval assault. The army, like the navy, longed to capture Charleston, and when it became apparent that General David Hunter lacked the aggressive spirit needed to assault Charleston, he was replaced by the fiery Major General Ormsby MacKnight Mitchel in Septmeber 1862. Upon arriving at Hilton Head, South Carolina, Mitchel immediately launched a probing attack against the Charleston and Savannah Railroad at Pocotaligo, but before he could organize an overland strike on Charleston, he contracted yellow fever and died, forty days after taking command.[30]

With Mitchel dead, General Hunter returned to command, and at the same time, to add a little more edge to Hunter's sword, Brigadier General Truman Seymour was also sent south. Seymour, a member of Fort Sumter's garrison in 1861, was an officer of the regular army who had earned a reputation for aggressiveness in the Peninsula and Antietam campaigns. As a Fort Sumter veteran, the outspoken officer burned with an inner desire to replace "Old Glory" over the fort's walls.

Seymour arrived in the Department of the South ahead of Hunter and quickly made contact with Du Pont and the department's acting commander, Brigadier General John M. Brannan. Before a week had passed, Seymour gathered information about Charleston's defenses and concluded that the ironclads could not capture the city without help from the army. To assist the navy, Seymour proposed an assault on Morris Island, the capture of Battery Wagner, and the establishment of a breaching battery of rifled guns on Cummings Point. With this additional fire power aimed at Fort Sumter, Seymour believed that the ironclads could then enter the harbor and capture Charleston. Though not without merit, Seymour's plan was quickly shelved once Hunter arrived and took control. The new commander effectively sheathed Seymour, by making Seymour his chief of staff and chief of artillery, positions that placed the impetuous officer firmly under Hunter's control.[31]

With Seymour sidetracked, the War Department again tried to push

Hunter to more aggressively support Du Pont by transferring some 10,000 men from North Carolina under Major General John G. Foster to Hunter's command. Like Seymour, Foster had also been a member of Fort Sumter's 1861 garrison, and he too desired nothing more than to recapture the fort. Arriving with his command in early February 1861, Foster immediately carried out a personal reconnaissance of Charleston Harbor to formulate a combined assault with both ironclads and rifled artillery. Basing his plan on a memorandum drawn up in February 1862 by the Corps of Engineers, Foster proposed an enlarged version of Seymour's plan, where simultaneous landings would occur on Morris and Sullivan's islands and the construction of breaching batteries against Sumter on both islands. Then, after the batteries had reduced Sumter, the ironclads could move in and capture Charleston.

Again, the North was given a plan that combined their two military arms into an effective strike force, and once more Hunter sabotaged the plan. As senior commander, Hunter railed against Foster's activity, which he considered insubordinate. A controversy flared and Foster left the department, so by the time Du Pont's squadron was ready, the army command was in such disarray it was unable to provide effective assistance.[32]

The lack of army support did not worry Welles or Fox, who wanted the attack to be a naval affair, but Du Pont welcomed any assistance. As his squadron began to fill out, Du Pont viewed his assembling warships with a critical eye. He liked the looks of the *New Ironsides*, an imposing ironclad frigate whose lines were similar to a wooden warship. The tower ironclad *Keokuk* was an odd piece of naval construction, which no one, including her commander, trusted. As to the monitors, Du Pont retained grave reservations.

Since capturing Charleston was such a passion of Welles and Fox, they neglected other commands in order to provide Du Pont with all available monitors. Sent south were the majority of the *Passaic* class monitors. These ironclads presented vast improvements over the original *Monitor*, which was lost in a violent gale off Cape Hatteras while heading south to join Du Pont's squadron. The new monitors were more seaworthy and carried heavier guns. The pilothouse, which on the original *Monitor* was positioned on the bow and blocked any forward firing, was now placed on top of the turret thus increasing vision and the ship's field of fire. The new ships were nearly 200 feet long, but like the original, the only portion exposed to enemy fire was the heavily armored turret.

It was the turret that made the monitors such innovative and unusual warships. Sitting on a central spindle and controlled by a system of gears, the turret was rotated by steam power. Inside were mounted one 15-inch Dahlgren and either an 11-inch Dahlgren or an 8-inch Parrott. Shot and shell, some weighing more than 400 pounds, were brought into the turret and, with block and tackle attached to a system of rails, taken to the gun's muzzles and loaded. When approaching a target, the gun ports were kept away from the enemy until the guns were loaded. Then, slowly, the turret would turn, the steam operated iron shutters opened, the cannon fired, and the shutters closed. After each firing, blowers were turned on to clear smoke from the turret. The diversion of steam to the blowers caused the ships to lose power to the main shaft, which in turn caused a decrease in forward motion and gave the illusion of disability. The process was long and laborious, but at one firing the two guns could deliver a crushing 600 pounds of metal against an enemy.

It was this ability to deliver such a potent blow from the protection of a rotating turret that made the monitors so impressive, especially in ship-to-ship combat and against masonry fortifications; however, Du Pont questioned their effectiveness against earthern works and their ability to take hits. After testing them against the earthern Fort McAllister outside Savannah, he commented to a fellow officer that they were formidable vessels—better than he expected—"but something always breaks."[33]

For months Du Pont held off attacking Charleston. Not only owing to his mistrust of monitors, but reports concerning the city's improving defenses were unnerving the rear admiral and his captains. Du Pont described Charleston Harbor as a "porcupine hide with quills turned outside in and sewed up at one end." Others among his command considered Charleston to be the best defended seaport in the world. Adding to their concerns were rumors about the Confederate explosive devices termed torpedoes.[34]

The monitors had been built to withstand concentrated artillery fire; however, due to their heavy armor and low freeboard, they could become death traps if a torpedo ruptured their hull. An explosion below the waterline could cause immediate flooding, forcing the monitor captain to run his ship aground or risk sinking. If the damage was severe, the top-heavy monitors could easily flip over, trapping and drowning its crew. Such thoughts wore on the minds of the sailors who operated the vessels. Though brave men, they were accustomed to fighting on wooden vessels, not while sealed inside an unstable iron container that could quickly become a giant coffin.

The longer Du Pont waited the more fear grew, but the dread of ruining his reputation should he not attack outweighed his hesitancy to face Charleston's defenses; and on Good Friday, April 3, 1863, nearly a year after the plan had been conceived, Du Pont ordered his squadron out of Port Royal Sound. His flag was on the ironclad frigate *New Ironsides*. Accompanying the flagship was the tower ironclad *Keokuk* and seven monitors, the *Weehawken, Passaic, Montauk, Patapsco, Nantucket, Catskill,* and *Nahant*. That night the flotilla anchored in North Edisto Sound where Du Pont and his captains made their final plans.

Though the Navy Department expected Du Pont to capture Charleston, the orders issued by the flag officer made no mention of the city. Instead, the ironclads were to move down the main ship channel to a position 600 to 800 yards off Fort Sumter's northwest face. From there they were to bombard the fort into submission. Once this was done the ironclads were to turn their attention to Morris Island. Even though the lead monitor, the *Weehawken,* was fitted with a device attached to her bow to clear obstructions, the orders contained nothing about the obstructions between Fort Sumter and Sullivan's Island, yet to reach Sumter's northwest wall, the ironclads would have to pass through the tangled mass of ropes, logs, and foreboding floating kegs. Also ominous by its omission was the lack of any mention about the dreaded torpedoes.[35]

Why Du Pont had adopted a plan of such limited scope is unclear, but considering his fears of being trapped within the harbor, he probably was looking for assistance from the army before making the final move against Charleston. By holding his immediate objectives to Fort Sumter and Morris Island, he could link up with the army and move on Charleston in short, controlled advances instead of risking it all on one reckless attack; however, reliance on the army was always a risky venture, especially with Major General David Hunter in command.

Hunter had joined the navy at North Edisto Inlet with army transports carry 10,000 soldiers and numerous siege guns. The general did not expect to take any major role in the coming action but wanted to be in a position to occupy Charleston should the attack prove successful. While Hunter viewed his role as merely supportive, some of his subordinates, most notably his chief of staff, Brigadier General Truman Seymour, and chief engineer, Captain James C. Duane, wanted the army to join the assault. The two made plans to land on Folly Island when the attack began, and Seymour hoped that once ashore he could continue on and seize Morris Island.[36]

While the troops waited on their transports, the ironclads moved toward Charleston. On April 6 the warships crossed the bar and steamed along the main ship channel just off Morris Island. Tents and earthworks were seen on the southern end of Morris Island, but no hostile fire came from those works. The day was too foggy to risk an advance, so Du Pont held his vessels off Morris Island until the next morning.[37]

In the early afternoon of April 7, the ironclad squadron again moved toward Charleston. In the lead was the monitor *Weehawken,* with its torpedo-clearing raft. Passing Cummings Point the line of ironclads moved up the channel. The battle was opened by Fort Moultrie, and soon the other works opened fire. Continuing on under a hail of shot and shell the *Weehawken* neared the obstructions when suddenly the vessel's bow was jarred by an explosion. Her commander, thinking he had struck a torpedo and not wishing to encounter any more, veered the *Weehawken* away from the obstructions. For a moment the entire line was thrown into confusion. Adding to Du Pont's problems was the inability of the *New Ironsides'* pilot to properly control the flagship. Forced to drop anchor, Du Pont signalled from the flagship for the following ironclads to move on and continue the fight against Sumter's northeastern face. The *New Ironsides* tried to join in but could not negotiate the channel, and again dropped anchor, this time directly over a submerged Confederate torpedo which contained nearly 2,000 pounds of powder. For a moment the flagship's fate lay in the hands of Captain Langdon Cheves, who was serving as the assistant engineer on Morris Island. Cheves quickly activated the ignition system to detonate the torpedo, but nothing happened. He tried again and again with the same result. Later it was learned the vessel had been spared because a wagon had run over the wires that ran between the switch and the torpedo, cutting them in two.

Unaware of his fortunate escape, Du Pont and his largest vessel remained out of the battle while the monitors and the *Keokuk* carried on the fight. It was a very uneven affair. The Confederates had three times as many artillery pieces, and they had a much faster rate of fire. The ironclads managed to fire only 154 shots, or about 16,000 pounds of metal, while the Confederates got off 2,209 shots or about 162,000 pounds of metal. In addition to this, by making use of prepositioned range markers, twenty percent of the Confederates shots scored a hit; at a time when a ten percent hit rate was considered outstanding shooting.[38]

For two-and-a-half hours the ironclads dueled with the Confederate forts before Du Pont stopped the attack, and even though three of his vessels, the *Keokuk, Nahant,* and *Nantucket,* had been forced to drop out of the fight, Du Pont still planned to renew the assault the following day. Then his ship captains began to make their reports. The *Keokuk* was sinking and five of his monitors were damaged. Turrets had been jammed, bolts shaken loose, and holes cut into decks. Appalled and unnerved by the perceived condition of his squadron, Du Pont refused to risk another attack. The next day the ironclads remained in the ship channel off Morris Island as the *Keokuk* sank off the island's southern end.[39]

While Du Pont was engaging the harbor works, Hunter allowed Seymour to land a brigade on Folly Island. Pushing a battery of two guns and the 100th New York Regiment to the island's northern end, Seymour carried out a careful reconnaissance of the Confederate works on Morris Island at Light-House Inlet. Realizing that they were unfinished, Seymour requested permission to attack, but Hunter refused. The commanding general, fascinated by the naval engagement and under no direct orders to assist the navy, remained immobile. Frustrated, Seymour established a picket line and a masked, two-gun battery overlooking Light-House Inlet, then took the remaining New Yorkers and rejoined the rest of his command on Folly's southern end.

While the battle with the ironclads was raging, the Confederates ignored the Union presence on Folly Island; however, once the warships had been driven off, a raiding party was sent across Light-House Inlet. Caught off guard, the Federal pickets were driven back, but somehow the Confederates missed the hidden battery. The artillerymen were under orders not to fire under any circumstances, so, as Confederates swarmed around them, chasing off the infantry guard, the cannoneers remained undetected at their guns. Having driven in the Federal vedettes, the Southerners returned to Morris Island, leaving behind some apprehensive artillerymen.

The affair at Light-House Inlet caused the Federals to pull back and consolidate near Stono Inlet. That night Seymour and Duane met with Du Pont to ask him to join their planned assault on Morris Island, but Du Pont, fearing any more exposure to enemy fire would cost him some of his monitors, rebuffed them. With no support from the leaders of the expedition, Seymour and Duane contented themselves with establishing a base on Folly Island for future operations against Morris Island. Here, on Folly's southern end was stationed a brigade under Brigadier General Israel Vogdes. The 100th New York garrisoned Cole's Island while Brigadier General Thomas G. Stevenson's brigade with a company of artillery and some engineers were left on Seabrook Island. Hunter then took the rest of his men and sailed to Port Royal.[40]

Du Pont also pulled his monitors back from Charleston. On April 8, he dispatched the monitor *Patapsco* to watch Confederate ironclads at

Savannah. Four days later he returned to Port Royal with the remaining monitors. Left behind to assist the blockaders was the *New Ironsides*.

At Port Royal the monitors were closely examined, and though they carried battle scars, none were seriously injured. Less than a week after they had pulled away from Charleston Harbor, five returned to duty at North Edisto Inlet. The resilience of the monitors was remarkable. After some quick repairs, they were returned to fighting trim. Du Pont was impressed by their ability to take a beating, but he firmly believed that the monitors would eventually be destroyed if they ever again attacked Charleston.[41]

However, Du Pont's views of the monitors did not match those of the administration. Though monitor fever ended, Welles and Fox would not stop, and they called for a joint expedition to capture Charleston. Orders were quickly sent to the flag officer to hold the ironclads off Charleston while the army prepared its forces. At the same time, reports criticizing Du Pont's handling of the assault began to appear. Never one to ignore an affront, Du Pont replied by condemning the monitors. He called on friends with political influence to support him, and soon the matter became a personal vendetta against the administration and anyone else who backed the turreted ironclads. Du Pont spared no one from his attacks. They included everyone from President Lincoln on down, and it soon became apparent that he could not be retained. As Gideon Welles wrote after reading one of Du Pont's dispatches: "I fear he can no longer be useful in his present command, and am mortified and vexed that I did not earlier detect his vanity and weakness."[42]

Another officer who was no longer useful was General Hunter. The army commander, long on boast and short on action, had finally convinced his superiors that he was incapable of carrying out a resolute and determined attack. Hunter would be removed, but his chief of staff, General Seymour, would be retained as would Seymour's attack plan for Morris Island.[43]

Chapter 2

THE PLAN FOR MORRIS ISLAND

I pity the poor soldiers if they land there.
Rear Admiral Samuel F. Du Pont

For the assault on Charleston, the Federal high command turned to Brigadier General Quincy A. Gillmore, the North's most proficient artillery and engineering technician. The top cadet in West Point's class of 1849, Gillmore served with the elite corps of engineers. He built seacoast fortifications, taught engineering at West Point and in 1856 was given the coveted position of heading the army's engineer office responsible for the city of New York's defenses. At the start of the war, Gillmore was assigned as chief engineer to the army-navy expedition that in November 1861 seized Port Royal Sound. After building defenses on Hilton Head Island, Gillmore ushered in the age of rifled artillery by planning and directing the attack on Fort Pulaski. This engagement, which proved the ability of rifled guns to destroy masonry fortifications, established Gillmore's reputation as being the foremost artillery and engineer officer in the army. He was rewarded with a brigadier general's commission in the volunteer army and was transferred to the Department of the Ohio where he led an infantry division in Kentucky. He always retained interest, however, in the Department of the South.

In May 1863, while on a leave of absence from his command, Gillmore learned that his name was being mentioned concerning a new attack against Charleston. Quickly, he dashed off a letter to his friend and fellow engineer, Brigadier General George W. Cullum, who just happened to be serving as chief of staff to Major General Henry W.

Halleck, the North's commanding general. Gillmore told Cullum that he was anxious to return to the Department of the South and lead the strike against Charleston. He wrote: "I have also said that I am willing to risk my own reputation upon the attempt, as I did at Pulaski, provided that I could be allowed the untrammeled execution of my plans (as at Pulaski), except so far as they involve co-operation from the navy. You are at liberty to show this letter to the General-in-Chief or anyone else."[1]

Though General Gillmore probably did not need any help from Cullum to secure the appointment, his solicitation did not hurt. He was soon summoned to Washington from New York by Halleck, where he joined a growing and impressive group of officers to plan a new Charleston expedition.

Brigadier General Truman Seymour preceded Gillmore to Washington. Sick of both Hunter and Du Pont, Seymour had taken medical leave in late April. After arriving in Washington, he immediately launched an assault on the nation's high command, calling for a renewed attack against Charleston with fresh leaders. His overtures were well received, and when Gillmore arrived in Washington for his conference with Halleck, he found in Seymour a willing ally and aide.

In meetings with Halleck, Gillmore outlined a familiar line of attack. To Gillmore's precise, engineering mind, the matter at Charleston came down to superior firepower. The Confederates had stopped the ironclads thanks to Fort Sumter's guns. They not only battered the attacking vessels but also kept the navy from removing the obstructions. To remedy the situation, Gillmore proposed adding to the fight land-based artillery located on Morris Island. These guns would reduce Sumter and allow the navy to enter the harbor and capture Charleston. Halleck was impressed. He liked what he heard, as well as Gillmore's display of confidence and efficiency. On June 3, Halleck relieved General Hunter and placed Gillmore in command of the Department of the South. With Gillmore's selection, the army was sending against Charleston its best technician. Now the navy needed to select an equally competent commander.[2]

Du Pont was not this commander. His denunciation of the monitors to save his own reputation had reached such heights that he soon convinced himself not only that Charleston was impregnable, but also that the monitors could not stand up to heavy ordnance. When Du Pont learned about the plans for an assault on Morris Island, he commented to his wife: "The plan is evidently to get Morris Island and we are to accomplish that and then the soldiers taking possession. Seymour, who is a humbug and has disgusted everybody, not excepting some of his own army, is the loudest for Morris Island. I pity the poor soldiers if they ever land there. . . ."[3]

Du Pont's opinions about the weaknesses of the monitors and the strength of Charleston's fortifications had become well known to his superiors. Secretary of the Navy Welles realized that the rear admiral's negative attitude would affect any new operation and a replacement had to be found, but the choice of a successor would have to be carefully weighed. Possibilities were Rear Admirals David G. Farragut, Andrew H. Foote, Francis H. Gregory and John A. Dahlgren and acting Rear Admiral David D. Porter. Porter was quickly dismissed because he was too young; many of the officers at Charleston were his senior in service. On the other hand, Gregory was too old for active sea duty. Welles thought that Farragut was best suited for the command, but he could not be spared from operations in the Gulf. Dahlgren, chief of the navy's ordnance bureau, was the President's choice, and had been actively lobbying for the position. Welles, however, thought he had too little sea service and his appointment would cause jealousies among officers who he had been promoted over.

All along, Welles kept coming back to Foote's name. A proven fighter, Foote was the man to send where there was immediate action. Before the war he had gained the reputation of a puritanically religious officer who led his sailors in Bible school every Sunday. He was antislavery and antidrink, and he was a fighter. In 1856 he gained national attention when he responded to a Chinese attack against American vessels off Canton and successfully led a few hundred sailors and marines against thousands of Chinese. As the first commander of the Mississippi River Squadron, Foote was paired with General Ulysses S. Grant for combined operations against Forts Henry and Donelson, the guardians of Nashville, Tennessee. During the campaign, Foote led his makeshift ironclads against Confederate batteries. With his vessels, Foote captured Fort Henry on the Tennessee River before Grant arrived but was turned back on the Cumberland River against Fort Donelson. During the battle, Foote received a leg wound from wood splinters knocked loose by Confederate shot striking his flagship. Foote repaired his vessels and himself, and while on crutches, directed his flotilla in a more tempered manner. At Island No. 10, he again supported the army in capturing enemy positions. After this victory, Foote was forced to relinquish his command to care for his wounds. Ordered to Washington, the fifty-six-year-old, forty-year veteran was placed in charge of the Bureau of Equipment and Recruiting. The desk job was not to Foote's liking, and he made it clear he wanted to return to active duty.

In Foote, Welles had the officer he wanted. Not only was Foote experienced in working with the army, but he was a close friend. His reputation would add prestige to the navy's contingent and give Welles a commander who would be sure to give the navy an equal voice in directing the campaign. Also, Foote was one of the few officers who could replace Du Pont without creating too much animosity. Welles knew full well that not all the fighting off Charleston would be with the enemy. Du Pont's influence among the officers of the South Atlantic Blockading Squadron was extremely strong, possibly affecting their willingness to fully cooperate with a new commander. Foote, Welles believed, had the character and stature to overcome all problems.[4]

In late May, Welles met with Foote at the Navy Department, and after a long interview, felt satisfied that the Mississippi River veteran would be able to meet the dual challenge of replacing Du Pont and attacking Charleston. Welles then sent for General Gillmore. After introductions, charts were produced and the men began laying their plans. Foote suggested that Dahlgren be appointed his second-in-command. Welles, who had already fended off Dahlgren's strong lobbying effort, became visibly upset by the proposal. Foote assured the secretary that he could convince Dahlgren to accompany him to Charleston in a secondary role. Welles acquiesced, and within a few days Foote gained Dahlgren's consent to be the commander of the ironclad squadron.[5]

Why Foote asked for Dahlgren is unknown. Rumors abounded that Foote had lost his aggressiveness after being wounded at Fort Donelson and was leery of serving again inside an ironclad. On the other hand, Foote knew that Dahlgren had no objections to duty on the ironclads, and Foote had even tried to persuade Du Pont to give Dahlgren command of the ironclads for the first assault against Charleston. If Foote was trying to avoid duty inside the monitors, Dahlgren was a logical second-in-command.

With his friend Dahlgren directing the ironclads, Foote could coordinate operations with Gillmore and leave the in-close work to Dahlgren. Also, by having the navy's top ordnance officer on the campaign, Foote would have an assistant who could match Gillmore's knowledge of ordnance and help coordinate joint bombardments.

With the command arrangements complete, Welles, on June 3, 1863, dismissed Du Pont. Trying to be as tactful as possible, Welles pointed out that the department could not give up its attempt to take Charleston, and since Du Pont did not concur with this plan, Welles was forced to replace him with Rear Admiral Foote. Du Pont had long expected to be relieved. He and his officers agreed that Foote would attempt to force an entrance into Charleston even if he lost all his ships trying. Foote was viewed by Du Pont as "a splendid navy officer, sort of Northern Stonewall Jackson, without his intellect and judgement."[6]

Though impatient to start, Foote, Dahlgren, and Gillmore continued to detail their plans. Using their own versions of the designs proposed by Generals Foster and Seymour, the two commanders agreed to attack Morris Island, which they believed could be quickly overrun, then easily defended against counterattacks. From Morris Island, breaching batteries would reduce Fort Sumter, and once Sumter was neutralized, the navy could remove the channel obstructions, enter the harbor, and capture Charleston.[7]

Foote often remained quiet during the discussions, leaving the navy's input to Dahlgren, who disagreed with Gillmore's proposals. Dahlgren argued that Gillmore was underestimating the Confederate defenses on Morris Island. If the island was easy for Union soldiers to hold once taken, then why would it not be as easy for the Confederates to defend, especially since they had had two years to build defenses? Instead of risking lives on a dangerous land attack, Dahlgren declared the whole affair could be handled by the navy, and if he were given six more ironclads, he could force his way into the harbor. Welles, never one to share glory with the army, undoubtedly would have backed Dahlgren's plan had the ironclads been available, but production of new monitors was slow and none would be available for months, a fact well known to Dahlgren. The attack could not be put off and Gillmore's plan was adopted.[8]

Though no detailed instructions were ever written down, the three officers did reach a verbal understanding. Gillmore left for the Department of the South confident that success would soon follow. Foote and Dahlgren remained in Washington completing final details. Foote flung himself into battle preparations with his characteristic energy, but his wound from Fort Donelson became infected and for a while Foote languished in bed. He recovered enough to leave for New York, intending to sail to Port Royal, but he suffered a severe relapse. Not wishing to hold up the campaign, Welles, on June 21, reluctantly informed Dahlgren that he would have to assume full command.

This would mean another delay as Dahlgren formed a staff and familiarized himself with the duties of a squadron commander. Welles also warned Dahlgren that there would be discontent over seniority among Du Pont's friends. Welles met frequently with Dahlgren and tried to impress the new flag officer with the importance of his command. At the completion of these conferences, Welles was satisfied that Dahlgren could handle the job; however, the secretary of navy prayed for Foote's recovery. On June 26, 1863, Foote died.[9]

While Dahlgren organized his staff, Gillmore arrived at Hilton Head on June 11, well ahead of his naval counterpart. The following day he relieved General Hunter and immediately went to work. Meetings were called with Major James Duane, the department's chief engineer, and other navy officers to discuss the situation at Charleston. Gillmore found them agreeable to his proposals, and while Hunter was being given a farewell luncheon by Du Pont, Gillmore went up the coast to inspect Folly Island.[10]

Folly Island was a key position in Gillmore's plan, as it was to serve as his springboard against Morris Island. Since Du Pont's April attack, the island had been occupied by a Union brigade under Brigadier General Israel Vogdes. Covered by sand dunes, laced with dense pine and palmetto growths, the island was described by a soldier of the 7th New Hampshire as "one of the most dreary and worthless collections of sand-hills to be found on the coast." Another wrote that "Folly Island is the name of the spot we inhabit—so called probably because as someone expressed it, some fool landed here a long time ago. He didn't stay long though." Nor did the exotic appearance of the palmetto trees appeal to the Yankees, who described them as "the worthless growth of this almost worthless state." The garrison spent its time building defenses along the southern half of the island. Other than this and some picket duty, the men had very little to do, causing a soldier to remark that the "inactivity would drive a hermit to suicidal halter, with sheer despair."[11]

Vogdes, the island's commander, was a regular army veteran who had spent most of his career teaching mathematics at West Point. Sent to Fort Pickens, Florida, with a company of artillery before hostilities broke out, Vogdes helped defend this citadel until he was captured during a Confederate attack. He was exchanged the following year and assigned to the Department of the South. Considered a skilled artillerist, Vogdes was noted for establishing well-prepared defensive positions. This he accomplished on Folly's southwestern tip, where he constructed an efficient set of works.

His personal appearance was not as attractive as his redoubts. Heavy-set and plagued with a high-pitched voice, he wore a mixed uniform of a major of artillery and a volunteer brigadier general, refusing to discard his old uniform until it wore out. Called "Old Regulations," Vogdes was a demanding officer. During his constant inspections, men were arrested for the most "trifling offenses" such as a deficiency of polish on boots or soil on white gloves, yet, though considered "peculiar" by his troops, he was a brave and kind-hearted man.[12]

Vogdes' discipline was only part of the ordeal suffered by the garrison. The sheer boredom of constant guard and fatigue duty caused many officers to resign, while others turned to drinking. Colonel George B. Dandy of the 100th New York became well known for his drunken escapades. His men would ignore him, but after sobering up, Dandy often arrested his own pickets for not firing on him when he stumbled about the picket lines.

The soldiers managed to survive Vogdes' constant inspections and the antics of their drunken officers by finding their own recreation. Surf bathing and fishing were popular. A lively exchange of goods and messages was carried on between the men of Folly and Morris islands. They traded tobacco, coffee, and newspapers. Sometimes shouting matches would break out between the Yanks and the Rebs, but once these "hostilities" ended, the men would settle down to some bartering and talking. The Union soldiers found that their officers rarely risked crossing the mud flats that separated Folly Island from its northeastern-most tip, known as Little Folly. So when on picket duty on Little Folly the men, when not fraternizing with Confederates, would relax and fish. The pickets soon found themselves spending more time watching for their own officers than the enemy. For months no one was hurt on either side, but when General Gillmore arrived the calm routine ended.[13]

The Union soldiers had mixed emotions when they viewed their new commander. Gillmore, heavily built with a full beard, was a powerful-looking man, and his appearance caused one officer to remark that "he is a live general." The men also realized that Gillmore's arrival signaled an end to the tiresome garrison duty and the beginning of fighting, which would bring to the soldiers injury and death.[14]

On Folly Island proper, General Gillmore was impressed by the works thrown up by Vogdes. The island had an excellent system of roads, and there were strong batteries sweeping Stono Inlet. Gillmore did have one complaint about Vogdes' arrangement, though. To the new commanding general, Vogdes had fortified the wrong end of the island and much to Vogdes' discomfort, Gillmore asked if he intended to "swing the island on a pivot when it became necessary to attack Morris Island?" Gillmore did give his commander a way to redeem himself. Since Folly Island was the designated jumping off point for the attack on Morris Island, Vogdes was given the all-important duty of building offensive batteries on the island's northeastern end. These works would cover Gillmore's initial assault. Surprise was essential so Vogdes had to keep their presence a secret from the Confederates.[15]

This was a difficult order for Vogdes to implement. The position of the new works would be on Little Folly, which at high tide was separated from the rest of the island. The movement of material would have to be timed to low tides and carried out under the very noses of the Confederates, who were completing their own works across Light-House Inlet. If the Northerners were discovered, not only would the men and guns be endangered, but Gillmore's entire campaign would be placed in jeopardy.

When construction began, the needed supplies and equipment were placed in the center of Folly Island so they could be transferred to the work site. All fraternization with the Confederates was stopped. Silence was necessary as the Union soldiers would be working within five hundred yards of the enemy. The work force was composed of three hundred to one thousand men under the immediate direction of Lieutenants Patrick McGuire of the New York Volunteer Engineers and James E. Wilson of the Fifth U.S. Artillery.

Taking advantage of the heavy brush and working only at night, the Union soldiers started their project. Every evening, beginning on June 15, the men marched to Little Folly and worked on the masked batteries. When trees were cut down they were lowered with ropes. All wheels were muffled and only officers could speak, whispering their orders to the men. One officer involved in the work reported that "not a rattle of a chain, nor the creak of a wheel told the enemy of our designs." Only once did the Confederates interfere. When a small blockade runner, the *Ruby,* ran aground in Light-House Inlet the Confederates lobbed a few shells onto Folly to make sure the Federals did not interrupt while they removed some of the *Ruby's* cargo. The shelling killed and wounded some Union soldiers, but no reply was given for fear of forewarning the enemy.

The work on the batteries was exhausting; even at night Folly Island was extremely hot. In the morning, the men would return to their camps and try to rest. Besides the heat, the soldiers were constantly pestered by swarms of mosquitoes and countless sand fleas. What little time was allotted for sleep was short, because five hours of each day were set aside for hard and intensive drills to prepare the men for the coming offensive.[16]

Still, some of the Northern soldiers found time to slip away from the careful watch of their officers and search for treasures on board the wreck of the blockade runner *Ruby*. On one such expedition, men from the 39th Illinois recovered a cache of pineapples, cigars, and

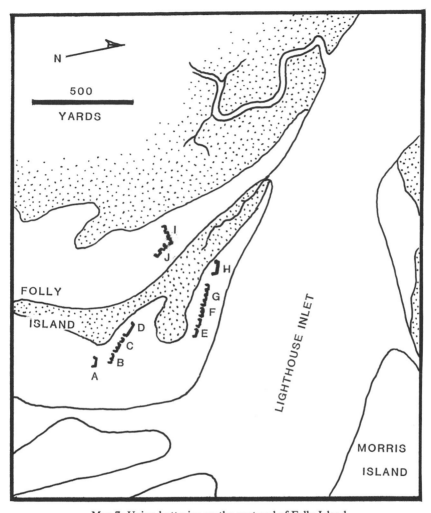

Map 7: Union batteries on the east end of Folly Island

A: two 3-inch Ordnance Rifles   F: six 3-inch Parrotts
B: four 3.67-inch Parrotts   G: eight 4.2-inch Parrotts
C: four 4.2-inch Parrotts   H: four 10-inch Mortars
D: six 10-inch Mortars   I: six 3-inch Wiard Rifles
E: two 3-inch Ordnance Rifles   J: five 8-inch Mortars

scotch whiskey. The trip had proven so successful that they returned a few nights later. This time Dr. William Woodward, an assistant surgeon in the regiment, accompanied them. Again a number of prized items were gathered up, but the men had become so preoccupied with their looting that no one noticed their small boat had drifted off. With no alternative, the soldiers swam back to Folly Island, but Dr. Woodward, weighed down by a heavy glass plate, several pineapples, and a calfskin hat box, was unable to make it, and a human chain had to be formed to pull the sputtering doctor to shore.

However, Woodward's cries of help alerted the pickets, and an enraged Vogdes arrested Woodward and ordered him to stay in a bombproof at the extreme end of the island where the new batteries were being built. For six weeks the doctor served in the bombproof with his hat box and the now broken glass plate. Though the doctor's friends appealed to Vogdes to end the banishment, the general refused. When Woodward was eventually freed, the doctor had an ambrotype taken of himself with his prizes to commemorate his ordeal.

Doctor Woodward's arrest did not stop the evening expeditions to the *Ruby,* but the men quickly learned that by sharing their goods with General Vogdes they avoided confinement. As one wrote: "I hear the men at the head of the island are going out to the blockade runner and get lots of fruit, cigars and liquor. It's a little strange that more of it has found its way to headquarters."[17]

While Gillmore approvingly watched the progress on Folly Island, he began turning his attention to organizing his forces for the attack. He brought to command positions the most capable men in his department. Brigadier General Alfred Terry was given command of one of the newly formed divisions. Although a Yale-educated lawyer, Terry was an extremely competent officer who kept his own council, rarely complained, and followed orders—qualities always appreciated by commanding officers. Terry had served as a regimental commander at Bull Run and later raised the Seventh Connecticut for the Port Royal expedition. An aggressive and demanding leader, Terry had made a name for himself through his actions at Secessionville and Pocotaligo Bridge.

Gillmore's other division leader was Truman Seymour. The veteran of Fort Sumter and the Department of the South was now finally seeing his long-cherished project become reality. An ardent rebel hater, Seymour wanted nothing more than to capture Morris Island and raise the Union flag over Fort Sumter.

To command the assault's spearhead, Gillmore brought to the department the young and energetic Brigadier General George C. Strong. Standing fifth in his West Point class of 1857, Strong was an experienced ordnance officer, having served in armories before the war and on General George B. McClellan's and Benjamin Butler's staffs before joining the Department of the South. Arriving on June 17, Strong made an immediate impression on his command. One officer commented that Strong "took control in earnest and began drilling the men." The soldiers were worked constantly, both under the hot sun and in rainstorms, marching on the loose island sand. Strong was determined his brigade be prepared. The new generals worked hard because they realized the task before them was difficult.[18]

When Gillmore took command of the Department of the South, he had an aggregate of 21,323 men. For the proposed attack on Charleston, Gillmore was bringing together some 11,000 infantry, 350 artillerymen, and 400 engineers.

Gillmore's artillerymen were a mixture of regulars and volunteers who were veterans of numerous campaigns along the southeastern coast. His regulars were composed of batteries from the 1st and 3rd United States Artillery regiments, while his largest contingent of volunteers hailed from Rhode Island. These men from the 3rd Rhode Island Artillery were among the most versatile soldiers to serve in the war. Adept at using light artillery, siege and seacoast guns, the troops were at home serving heavy ordnance behind the masonry walls of Fort Pulaski or with field artillery on exposed battlefields. They also served double duty as naval artillerymen by manning batteries onboard Quartermaster vessels. Wherever they were needed, the Rhode Islanders could play the role. Rounding out this artillery force were the solid veterans of Battery B, 3rd New York Artillery, and Captain Alfred P. Rockwell's Connecticut Battery who had been prominent in the fight at Secessionville. If needed, Gillmore could also call on soldiers from the 7th Connecticut Infantry who had received artillery instructions while serving in the forts guarding Fernandina, Florida, as well as the 48th New York Infantry whose men had garrisoned Fort Pulaski.

Gillmore had also assembled a sizeable artillery train. Available for the Charleston attack were a number of Parrott Rifles, consisting of five 200-pounders, nine 100-pounders, twelve 30-pounders, four 20-pounders, as well as twelve 13-inch seacoast mortars, ten 10-inch mortars, five 8-inch mortars, and three coehorn mortars. Besides this impressive array of artillery, Gillmore had Seymour canvass the Northern harbors for additional Parrott guns.[19]

Gillmore was planning to attack Fort Sumter with better ordnance than he had used against Fort Pulaski. No longer were his rifles converted smoothbores. They were heavy, efficient Parrott guns. The Parrott was a cast iron gun with a reinforced wrought iron hoop over the chamber. The gun was cast hollow on the Rodman plan, a manufacturing technique that gave the American cannons a longer life than their European counterparts.

The Parrott gun was inexpensive and easy to make. It was termed by European observers a typical American product because, though it was not the best rifled cannon made, it was quite practical and had a much longer service life than the European guns. While the expensive and hard-to-make European guns were of higher quality, they usually wore out at about a hundred rounds, while many Parrotts had service lives extending into the thousands of firings.

The 100-pound and 200-pound Parrotts were to be used for the bombardment of Sumter, but until that time, Gillmore's main weapons would be the smaller Parrotts and mortars that could be used both on offense and defense. If the campaign came down to siege warfare, the more mobile 20-pound and 30-pound Parrotts would prove very useful, as would the mortars. Gillmore hoped his attack would not fall into siege warfare, but if it did he was confident of success.[20]

Working with the artillery were the department's engineers, and though there were a few, young, West Point–trained officers, the majority of Gillmore's engineers were members of the 1st New York Engineer Regiment. Trained as civilian engineers, the officers and men formed a vital component of Gillmore's army. They would be responsible for preparing fortifications, mounting cannon, and if necessary, constructing siege work.

Though he was most comfortable when working with artillerymen and engineers, Gillmore had confidence in his infantrymen. Most of his men were veterans of the November 1861 expedition that seized Port Royal Sound. Since then they had taken part in joint operations, supporting the navy in the seizure of islands and coastal towns. Their only major actions, however, had been the unsuccessful assault at Secessionville in June 1862 and General Mitchel's raid on the railroad near Pocotaligo in October 1862. Besides these men, Gillmore had a number of regiments that had come to the Department of the South in January 1863. Veterans of heavy fighting during the Seven Days Campaign, these men gave Gillmore a corps of seasoned soldiers who could be counted on in combat.

Though a small army, the soldiers who made up Gillmore's command were similar to men in any eastern Federal force. All were volunteers except for a few batteries of regular artillery and some regular engineer and staff officers. Some regiments came from the midwest, but most of the units originated in the eastern states with a heavy leaning toward New England. The men were well trained, had good officers, were acclimated and eager for a fight. Gillmore's army also had something that set it apart from other Federal forces: African American soldiers.[21]

At the start of the campaign, the Department of the South contained four African-American regiments: the 1st, 2nd and 3rd South Carolina Volunteer Infantry and the 54th Massachusetts Volunteer Infantry. The South Carolina units were organized from freed slaves within the Department of the South. The oldest formation was the 1st South Carolina, which included the first black soldiers enlisted for the Civil War.

Initially raised in May 1862 by General David Hunter, the regiment was part of an overall program designed to free slaves and enlist them into military formations. In April 1862, a few weeks after his arrival as commander of the Department of the South, Hunter, a friend of President Lincoln and an active abolitionist, began organizing an African-American infantry regiment. Hunter had hoped that the former slaves would enlist and join the fight against their former masters, but he was disappointed. Still suspicious of the white man, few slaves volunteered. Undeterred, Hunter decided to give the slaves something to fight for. On May 9, he issued a proclamation declaring free all slaves within his command and the states of South Carolina, Georgia, and Florida. Hunter then ordered his white soldiers to sweep the plantations for likely conscripts, which were carried to Hilton Head and formed into a 500-man regiment. Hunter had hoped that the government would recognize his deeds and his regiment, but President Lincoln was not ready for emancipation and the formation of black fighting units. On May 20, in a kind message, Lincoln, who feared repercussions in the loyal border states, revoked his friend's proclamation, informing Hunter that only the president was authorized to deal with slavery.

Hunter only partially accepted the gentle reprimand. He rescinded his proclamation, but, with no direct order to disband the unit, he tried to keep his regiment. Outfitted in red pants, blue coats, and broad-brimmed hats, the men were kept together and drilled until August, while their fate was debated in Congress, and though Congress passed the Second Confiscation Act and the Militia Act of 1862, which opened the way for Lincoln to enlist African-American soldiers, Hunter's regiment was never recognized. Eventually, on August 10, 1862, Hunter, unable to secure authorization and pay for the regiment, disbanded all but one company, which he sent to St. Simon's Island, Georgia, to protect a community of escaped slaves. This lone company, under the command of Captain Charles T. Trowbridge, formerly of the 1st New York Volunteer Engineers, remained on St. Simon's Island for two months protecting the escaped slaves and awaiting orders.

On that isolated island, Trowbridge and his men felt forgotten, but

they were not. Even as Hunter disbanded his regiment and Trowbridge's men were deployed on St. Simon's Island, the government
was leaning toward sanctioning the use of African-American troops.
The acts passed by Congress were having an effect. Besides empow-
ering Lincoln to raise black troops, they also authorized the president
to free slaves whose masters were rebelling against the government
and to use these freed slaves in military service. At the same time,
President Lincoln began discussing with his cabinet issuing an emancipation proclamation that would free slaves within the rebelling states.

While the government was hardening its position on black soldiers,
Hunter's subordinate and officer in charge of the abandoned plantations and slaves in the Department of the South, Brigadier General
Rufus Saxton, both wrote and sent emissaries to Secretary of War
Stanton requesting permission to raise African-American troops. Stanton, aware of the administration's mood, agreed, and on August 25,
1862, he authorized Saxton to "arm, equip, and receive into service of
the United States such volunteers of African descent as you deem
expedient, not exceeding five thousand." In October, Trowbridge and
his men were recalled from St. Simon's Island and officially became
Company A of the 1st South Carolina Volunteer Infantry.[22]

Saxton offered command of the regiment to the well-known abolitionist, Thomas Wentworth Higginson. A graduate of Harvard, where
he also received a postgraduate divinity studies degree, Higginson was
a prominent supporter of John Brown and had backed Brown's attack
on Harper's Ferry. When he received Saxton's letter, Higginson was a
captain with the 51st Massachusetts, which was still in training camp
at Worcester. Within the month Higginson had resigned from his
regiment and arrived at Beaufort, South Carolina, to take over African-
American soldiers. Higginson viewed his work as both military and
philanthropic in nature. He felt that the outcome of the war and the
destiny of the Negro race might well rest on the performance of black
troops. Immediately, Higginson went to work drilling his men and
readying them for combat. In time he had his men discard what he
called the "intolerable" red trousers.

The 1st South Carolina was taken into Federal service at an impressive ceremony outside Beaufort on January 1, 1863, the day Lincoln's
Emancipation Proclamation took effect. This new regiment was only
the beginning. By February a second African-American regiment, the
2nd South Carolina, was formed.[23]

The 2nd was also recruited from former slaves, many liberated by
raids into Florida and Georgia by Higginson's regiment. Command of
this regiment went to James Montgomery, who like Higginson had

been a prewar abolitionist and backer of John Brown. Unlike Higginson though, Montgomery had actually served with the "old man" on the Kansas frontier and brought some of Brown's zeal and ferocity to his command.

Like John Brown, Montgomery was a simple man with a simple plan. He was a tall, thin man with grey eyes and a nose like a bird's beak. Bushy whiskers covered a deeply lined face. His shoulders sloped and he stooped. One officer called his movements unsoldier-like, but added that "he believes that a soldier's use is to fight and is terribly earnest." Another wrote that Montgomery was the most earnest colonel in the army and was singularly dedicated to ending the rebellion. Montgomery believed slaveholders had caused the war, so they must suffer. He also believed that once the war was over blacks and whites would be unable to live together until the memories of the conflict had faded. To this end he planned to destroy all evidence of slavocracy, thus creating an area where the former slaves could live in peace. His main weapon in this campaign was his regiment, which raided along the coast, carrying off slaves and burning plantation homes, outbuildings, and farm machinery. It was said of the 2nd South Carolina: "No white regiment for months in service has done as much to injure the Rebel cause as this handful of hated negroes, nor has any white regiment had the incentive that this fractional regiment had to distinguish themselves. They rescued their mothers, fathers, brothers and sisters from the galling servitude of the plantation."[24]

Both Higginson's and Montgomery's regiments met with opposition and racism from the white troops in the Department of the South. Most Northern soldiers thought the former slaves inferior and resented their use in the army, considering it degrading to the cause. Most agreed, though, with one soldier who commented that a "Negro can fall from rebel shot as well as me or my friends, and better them than us."

Initially the black soldiers received a great deal of verbal abuse, but they never responded to the racial slurs, causing an officer from Pennsylvania to remark that since the blacks had been used to the lash, vocal comments did not seem so bad to them. In time the racist attitudes softened. In the Department of the South, the white regiments worked closely with their black counterparts, and soon the men began to realize that former slaves could make fine soldiers. By April 1863, an officer who doubted the African Americans had changed his mind and called the 1st South Carolina "as efficient a regiment I believe as there is in the Union Army."[25]

By May 1863, the two African-American South Carolina regiments were prepared to join Gillmore's attack against Charleston and a third was being organized, but they were not the only black regiments being readied for the campaign. Another regiment was on its way, coming from Massachusetts, with its ranks made up predominantly of free, Northern blacks: the 54th Massachusetts.

The creation of a black regiment had been the dream of Massachusetts Governor John A. Andrew. A fervent abolitionist, Andrew had long called for the enlistment of African-Americans, and when the Emancipation Proclamation was issued, he received permission from the War Department to enroll blacks from Massachusetts into the army.

Andrew's zeal had blinded him to one small detail that nearly wrecked his plans before they got underway. Massachusetts had a very small black population, and after six weeks of recruiting, there were only one hundred men on the regiment's roles. Undeterred, the governor engaged the prominent abolitionist, George L. Stearns, to raise recruits. Bankrolled by wealthy Bostonians and backed by African-American leaders including Frederick Douglass, Stearns opened offices throughout the Northern states and sent recruiters into Canada and Federally occupied regions of the South. It was even claimed by one wag that he had recruiting offices in Egypt. Soon, enough men were raised to outfit not only the 54th but also a second black infantry regiment, the 55th Massachusetts and eventually the 5th Massachusetts Cavalry regiment.

To officer his regiment, Governor Andrew sought out idealistic men dedicated to ending slavery who had some military experience. Andrew's choice for colonel was Captain Robert Gould Shaw of the 2nd Massachusetts Infantry Regiment. After a day of deliberation, the twenty-five-year-old officer accepted the command. Shaw had all the needed attributes to lead a regiment like the 54th. He was an idealist, but he also realized that determined efforts were required to secure an idealistic end. Educated in Switzerland and Harvard, Shaw was described as "simple, direct, earnest true mind and character . . . revolted at . . . injustice or cruelty."[26]

When the war started, he was living in New York and was a member of the city's famous 7th New York Militia regiment. With them, he had marched to Washington in April 1861 and set up camp inside the Capitol in the House of Representatives Chamber. Though the 90-day regiment did not see any action, Shaw did manage a brief audience with President Lincoln. After the 7th New York was mustered out of service, Shaw was commissioned a second lieutenant in the 2nd Massachusetts and participated in the battles of First Winchester and

Antietam. At Antietam he was wounded during the fighting in the East Woods.

He was not an active abolitionist but shared those views about slavery. His main mission was to train a regiment capable of showing the nation that black soldiers could and would fight. This was the task Shaw set for himself, and though he would take time off to marry Anne Haggerty of New York, he never wavered from his appointed mission.

Joining Shaw were other officers who realized the importance of their assignments. Their average age was twenty-three, and all were eager to be part of the new experiment. From March until late May companies were formed and trained. It was hard work, but the men were dedicated to their task. By the end of May the regiment was ready, and on May 28, 1863, the 54th received its colors, then marched through Boston to the waterfront where the transport *Demolay* waited to take the unit south.

It was estimated that more than twenty thousand persons turned out to see the regiment. Among the crowd were numerous abolitionists, including Frederick Douglass whose two sons, Charles and Lewis, were sergeants in the regiment. Even the pacifist-poet John Greenleaf Whittier watched the regiment, momentarily giving up his vigil for peace for one hour. The sight of the African-American soldiers moved him deeply.

As the troops moved past William Lloyd Garrison's home, the great abolitionist stood on his balcony, his right hand resting on a bust of John Brown. As the 54th marched over the spot of the Boston Massacre, where Crispus Attucks had fallen eighty-eight years earlier, they broke into song, treating the crowd to a stirring rendition of "John Brown's Body." At the wharf they boarded the *Demolay* and began their voyage to the Department of the South.[27]

Colonel Shaw and his black soldiers were on their way to Port Royal where they would join the African-American regiments of Colonels Higginson and Montgomery. The officers and men of the three units were in sharp contrast. The Massachusetts regiment was primarily composed of free blacks, many having lived in the North for several generations. Before volunteering for the military, they had had occupations much like their white counterparts. A breakdown of Company A reveals that thirty-five percent of the soldiers had been farmers and twenty-four percent laborers. Other occupations included seamen, blacksmiths, hostlers, teamsters, and butchers. Most could read and write and only one reported being born in a slave state.

Because of the makeup of his regiment, Shaw did not have to take on any extra duties such as being father figure and teacher to his men.

Unlike Higginson, he did not have to direct his men in the rudiments of living in a free society. He did, however, realize that the 54th was there to prove the African American's fighting ability. To accomplish this, he knew he would have to fight resentment and racism to keep his regiment from being turned into an armed unit of laborers. For many this would have been a difficult task, but with the 54th's high profile and Shaw's political connections, he found ways around military bureaucracy and short-sightedness.[28]

On the other hand, the South Carolina regiments were exclusively made up of former slaves who had no experience living in a free society. Most were volunteers, joining to fight for their freedom and to liberate relatives still held by their former masters. Others from the Port Royal area, however, remembering Hunter's heavy-handed recruiting for the 1st South Carolina, would sometimes have to be conscripted forcibly. As Montgomery wrote:

> Finding it somewhat difficult to induce the Negroes to enlist, we resolved to the draft. The negroes reindicate their claim to humanity by shirking the draft in every possible way; acting exactly like *white men* under similar circumstances: Hence, I conclude, they are, undoubtedly human. The only difference that I notice is, the negro, after being drafted does not desert; but once dressed in the uniform with arms in his hands he feels himself a man; and acts like one.[29]

Montgomery's statement also reveals his opinion toward African-American troops. Though a renowned antislavery man, he was not a reformer. To him the enemy was slavery, which had to be destroyed at any cost and by any method. The question of black equality was never an overriding issue for Montgomery, only the utter extermination of slavery.

Higginson, on the other hand, not only wanted to end slavery, but also uplift the slaves. Acceptance as an equal, Higginson believed, would only come after educating the slave in the ways of a free society. Higginson and his regiment were active participants in the educational, political, and economic experiments going on at Port Royal. Besides military instructions, the men of the 1st South Carolina attended school and learned lessons from Northern missionaries who were determined to help them and their families bridge the gap from slavery to citizenship.[30]

Shaw did not have to concern himself with such matters. He was not on a religious crusade like Montgomery, nor did he need to conduct educational seminars. His men had already experienced freedom and were now trying to prove themselves as soldiers. They needed an opportunity to fight.

The 54th Massachusetts arrived at Port Royal on June 3, 1863, and proceeded to Beaufort. The next morning the regiment disembarked, marched through the town, and made camp in an old cotton field. In Beaufort was the 2nd South Carolina, which had returned from a raid up the Combahee River. There, with the aid of a spy ring organzied and operated by former slave Harriet Tubman, Montgomery's men had destroyed some of South Carolina's largest rice plantations and freed nearly eight hundred slaves. The liberated slaves were housed in the Baptist Church where the men were urged to join the army, and with Tubman's help, Montgomery gained 150 volunteers.[31]

During his first day ashore in South Carolina, Colonel Shaw was met by Colonel Higginson. Together they dined and discussed the qualities of African-American troops. Shaw worried that his men, untried as they were, would flinch at combat, but Higginson assured him that black troops would respond well on the battlefield. As Higginson later wrote: "that, doubtless, removed all his anxieties, if he really had any."

Other soldiers looked over the new arrivals and most were impressed. One officer from Pennsylvania called them a fine body of men, well drilled and more intelligent than the South Carolina Negroes but did not think they were as good in their morals.[32]

Shaw and his men remained in Beaufort only a few days. Within a week they were transported to St. Simon's Island, Georgia, where they joined Montgomery's 2nd South Carolina and became part of Montgomery's campaign to eradicate any evidence of slavery from the Southern coast. These raids, which were carried out by both white and black troops, were designed to destroy all military and public property along the coast and carry off as many slaves as possible. Montgomery, most likely with Hunter's tacit blessings, took the missions one step further by burning "every palatial residence of slave holders and their machinery, crops," but he spared all slave huts.[33]

These blows not only struck at the heart of slavery by destroying the cash crops and carrying off slaves, they also placed the black soldiers and their officers in severe peril, for as yet, the Confederacy did not recognize the North's use of African-American troops. Hunter was a declared outlaw, and a Presidential Proclamation, which was later made law by the Confederate Congress, declared that all slaves captured in arms against the Confederacy should be turned over to the state authorities and dealt with by state laws. Free blacks and whites serving with the African-American units would also be turned over to state authorities. At best, former slaves would be returned to slavery, at the worst they and their free comrades could be put to death for leading a slave insurrection.

Under such circumstances the African-American regiments undertook dangerous raids along the Southern coast. Those led by Colonel Higginson had always refrained from destroying private property, but Montgomery took it upon himself to exterminate all evidence of slavocracy so, in the war's aftermath, whites would not have any reason to return to their property and instead abandon the land to their former slaves. Montgomery did his work well, and soon after the raid along the Combahee River, protests from both Confederate and Northern officials forced General Hunter to reprimand his crusading officer. Hunter sent instructions to Montgomery to cease burning homes and household goods; however, Hunter did say that Montgomery could reopen his campaign if the enemy carried out its threats against the black regiments and their officers. Then, with the war degenerating to a "barbarous and savage conflict," Hunter believed the North would be justified in carrying out attacks on civilian property. But until the South acted first, Montgomery was to refrain from his usual style of warfare.[34]

Hunter's orders did not reach Montgomery in time to soften the commander's attack on Darien, Georgia. On June 10, 1863, five companies from the 2nd South Carolina, eight from the 54th Massachusetts under Colonel Shaw, and a section of artillery were loaded on transports and under the protection of gunboats moved up the Altamaha River toward Darien, Georgia. Montgomery had a particular interest in attacking the town. It was not only filled with useful livestock and lumber, but before the war, an officer currently serving in the 2nd South Carolina had been run out of town for his Union views, losing all his property. An object lesson was on Montgomery's mind.

As the flotilla approached Darien, the Union gunboats drove off Confederate pickets. The troops landed and entered the town, which contained rows of cotton warehouses. After driving Rebel pickets out of the town, detachments from each regiment were ordered to break into houses and collect food and anything else that might be useful in camp. The soldiers led by their officers carried out a controlled, but very thorough, plundering of Darien. The action horrified Shaw, but Montgomery assured the young colonel that he would take all responsibility and justified his deed by saying that since the black troops were outlaws under Confederate law they were not bound to the regular rules of warfare. To Montgomery he was redressing the wrongs caused by slavery. Before leaving, Montgomery had his regiment with one company from the 54th set fire to the town. Montgomery personally set the torch to the last building.

The Darien expedition pitted the realistic Kansas Jayhawker against an idealistic New Englander. Shaw was outraged by having to participate in such activities and immediately began writing letters to Governor Andrew and others to help him free the 54th from such duty. Governor Andrew, disturbed by the mission assigned his pet regiment, wrote Hunter asking why the Massachusetts soldiers had been used in such a manner. Hunter replied to the governor, pointing out that Montgomery's raids were important to the cause since they were intended to: ". . . compel the rebels either to lay down their arms and sue for restoration to the Union or to withdraw their slaves into the interior, thus leaving desolate the most fertile and productive of their counties along the Atlantic seaboard."[35]

Hunter considered the raids honorable work and did not take the 54th away from Montgomery, but Shaw's men were never again used in such a manner. In late June, after General Gillmore relieved General Hunter, the African-American regiments were transferred to Port Royal, where they camped on St. Helena Island. Here they were under the overall command of Brigadier General Strong. Shaw and Strong soon became friends. The two discussed the role of black troops, and Shaw was quite happy to discover that Strong wanted to use his regiment in the coming campaign. Shaw wrote Governor Andrew that Strong was anxious to do all he could for the regiment and "will no doubt give the black troops a chance to show what stuff they are made of."

By early July, General Strong and the white regiments on St. Helena began boarding transports and sailing north, and though Shaw enjoyed the festivities of the Fourth of July, celebrating with the local African Americans and their Northern teachers, he became concerned that the 54th had been forgotten. On July 6 he wrote Strong respectfully expressing his concern about being left behind. Though Strong did not reply, Shaw soon had his answer when on July 8 the 54th and the 2nd South Carolina boarded transports and joined the expedition off Charleston.[36]

Gillmore was nearly ready to launch his attack. By July 3, the masked batteries on the northern tip of Folly Island were complete, and reports from his chief scout, the intrepid Captain Lewis S. Payne of the 100th New York, were encouraging. Working at night, Payne had scouted all the channels, creeks, and shores of the Confederate-held island. He had landed on Morris Island several times, once spending the daylight hours hidden in the marsh observing the Confederates. His ventures provided Gillmore's staff with needed information concerning the enemy works and the general lay of the land. With Payne's reports, and batteries readied, Gillmore awaited only the support of the navy before starting his attack.[37]

The death of Foote had thrown the navy's timetable off. It had been hoped that the new flag officer would arrive about the same time as Gillmore, but from necessity, Welles ordered Du Pont to cooperate with Gillmore. Du Pont acknowledged the orders, but refused to initiate any relations between the two services. Fear of another reversal kept him from doing anything. If there was to be any joint operation, the first overtures would have to come from the army.[38]

At first, Gillmore did not make contact with the navy. Instead he went about his own preparations, expecting the navy to approach him. When it became obvious that assistance was not coming, Gillmore complained to General Halleck about Du Pont's inactions. Gillmore reported that he thought it possible to land on Morris Island without the navy, but that protection by the ironclads was necessary to keep the Confederate gunboats from cutting off the landing forces. Finally, after wasting valuable time, Gillmore went to see Du Pont. Much to the general's surprise, Gillmore found Du Pont willing to support the army as long as the navy's role was limited. Gillmore left the meeting impressed by Du Pont's zeal and energy, and was looking forward to the attack.[39]

Actually, Du Pont was merely putting on a front for the general. Upset by having to help Gillmore, Du Pont was appalled at the assistance asked by the army. He was requested to send one monitor into the narrow Stono River, while the rest were to engage the enemy works on Morris Island, primarily Battery Wagner. The idea of attacking earthworks frightened Du Pont, for he felt it was suicidal to ask the monitors to take on such positions. His apprehensions were calmed when he learned that his replacement was on his way south, and it was with relief that he ordered his captains to prepare for the arrival of Rear Admiral Dahlgren. If disaster came, as he strongly suspected, Du Pont wanted no part of it.[40]

The new commander of the South Atlantic Blockading Squadron had had an unusual career for a naval officer. Dahlgren had joined the navy in 1826 and had served until 1846, when declining eyesight forced him to take a leave of absence. Five years later his eyesight recovered, and Dahlgren was given a position in the ordnance depot at the Washington Navy Yard. While serving there, Dahlgren invented three types of boat howitzers and a class of heavy ordnance capable of firing both shot and shell. Dahlgren's soda-water-bottle-shaped smoothbores helped to make the United States Navy the finest armed navy in the world.

Dahlgren was described by a fellow officer as being "never an approachable man, over six feet tall in height, very slender, severe and sallow visage, wore old fashion black stock necktie, he looked more like a minister of the Gospel than a navy officer." Though not an impressive figure, Dahlgren did have the energy and the outlook of a fresh commander, unhindered by past reversals.[41]

When he arrived on July 4, Dahlgren immediately met with General Gillmore. Gillmore was anxious to get started, and though unfamiliar with the waters and his officers, Dahlgren agreed to the army's time-table. Officially taking over on July 6, the new commander had less than three days to prepare for the assault on Morris Island.[42]

Gillmore's plan called for two diversions to draw the Confederates from Morris Island. One was to be made by Colonel Thomas W. Higginson's 1st South Carolina Regiment, which was to proceed up the South Edisto River on armed transports in an attempt to cut the Charleston and Savannah Railroad at Jacksonborough. The second diversion was to be carried out by General Alfred Terry's division. Terry's men were to be carried into the Stono River on transports and landed on the southwestern shore of James Island. Here they were to feign an attack, but in no way was he to jeopardize his command.

The main assault was to be made by Seymour's division against Morris Island, with Strong's brigade leading the way. The attack on Morris Island was a dangerous undertaking. Gillmore originally planned to attack at night, having one force land at the southern end and the other between Batteries Gregg and Wagner. In this way the Union commanders hoped to seize the Confederate works opposite Folly Island and Battery Wagner at the same time. The attack was to be covered by the newly built Union batteries and the ironclads. The date set for the attack was July 9, and the only thing that stood in Gillmore's way was the Confederate defenses.[43]

The Confederates had not been idle since the April ironclad attack against Fort Sumter. When it became apparent that the Northern soldiers on Folly Island were not going to join in a general assault on Charleston, General Beauregard realized that he had some time to increase his defenses before a new attack was started; however, the general had to work under a steady reduction of manpower.

Due to Confederate campaigns in other theaters, Beauregard was ordered by Secretary of War James Seddon to send units away from Charleston and Savannah. In April, two brigades under Brigadier

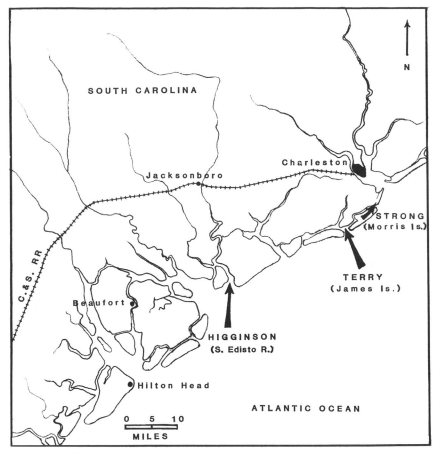

Map 8: Planned Union assaults for July 9, 1863

Generals John R. Cooke and Thomas L. Clingman were sent to North
Carolina, while in early May, the brigades of Brigadier Generals States
Rights Gist and William H. T. Walker were sent to reinforce Vicksburg.
A short time later, Brigadier General Nathan G. Evans' brigade also
entrained for Mississippi. By June, Beauregard's department had been
reduced by 10,000 men. It nearly lost more when, during a May
strategy session in Richmond after the Battle of Chancellorsville,
General Lee suggested that Beauregard be brought north with men
from North and South Carolina to threaten Washington, while Lee
invaded Pennsylvania. Though the latter move was never carried out,
the reductions that had taken place would affect the Confederates
ability to defend Charleston.

Beauregard and South Carolina officials protested the transfer of the five brigades, but Seddon was unmoved. The secretary of war was convinced that the Northerners were reducing their forces in South Carolina to reinforce positions in North Carolina and the Army of the Potomac. Seddon did try to calm the protests by pointing out the importance of Vicksburg and that the "near approach of your sickly season and the present sultry weather give added confidence of no serious danger of attack on Charleston."

With his remaining forces, Beauregard continued to prepare his defenses. Stationed in and around Charleston under the immediate command of General Ripley were some 2,600 infantry, 3,800 artillery-men, and 550 cavalrymen. Every unit was from South Carolina—the Palmetto State—and among their ranks were a large number of Charlestonians. Though most had seen action in previous attacks against Charleston, their experiences were limited to fighting from behind breastworks where the artillerymen did most of the work. Still, since the men were from South Carolina, they were fighting on familiar ground and had that extra incentive given to soldiers fighting for home and family. Morale was high and motivation strong.[44]

To help defend the city, Beauregard amassed as many pieces of heavy ordnance as possible. He also directed the Charleston Arsenal to continue converting older smoothbore guns into rifles. Added to this growing pool of ordnance were two massive 11-inch Dahlgrens taken from the sunken *Keokuk* in a remarkable salvage operation. Besides the two valuable cannon, the Confederates also found on the *Keokuk* a signal book, and with it the key to breaking the Federal code.[45]

The additional guns made Charleston's harbor defenses even more formidable. Because of this, Beauregard and Ripley suspected that Morris Island would be the target of the new attack. As early as April 1863 Beauregard wrote: "The James Island line is their best; but that is also very strong. I think it's more probable they will move from Stono Inlet along Folly Island, thence Morris Island, to endeavor to take Fort Sumter a'la Pulaski; but they may find that to be a piece of Folly."[46]

Even though Beauregard predicted an attack on Morris Island, he still retained the majority of his men on James Island, which was seen as the key to the city. Here were placed some 1,200 infantry, 1,500 artillerymen, and 150 cavalrymen. Scattered around the harbor at Fort Sumter, Sullivan's Island, and Castle Pinckney were 200 infantry, 1,300 artillerymen, and a handful of cavalrymen. In the city was the district's reserve consisting of the locally raised 450-man Charleston Battalion. If needed, Citadel cadets and militia could be called up.

This left on Morris Island 650 infantrymen, 350 artillerymen, and 26 cavalrymen.

By the set strategy, the forces guarding Charleston were to stall and slow any enemy attack. The Charleston Battalion, with any units that could be spared from other areas, would be quickly sent to the threatened sector. At the same time, reinforcements would be rushed to the city using the railroad. The Confederates were counting on the courage and fighting ability of their men and the strength of their fortifications to hold on until help arrived. At the predicted point of attack, however, the Confederates had not yet completed their defenses.[47]

In the months leading up to the Federal assault, orders went to General Ripley to finish the works planned for the southern tip of Morris Island. An appeal went out to local slave owners calling for 2,500 slaves per month to build the fortifications, but the slave owners did not respond. Already stung by the raids of Higginson and Montgomery and fearing that more of their valuable property would run off or be injured, they withheld their slaves. In March, the Confederates received only 400 slaves and later the number dwindled even more. In April, 350 arrived; May, 80; and in the critical month of June only 40 slaves reported for work.[48]

Without the necessary slaves, the Confederates had to use more and more soldiers as laborers. This resulted in another problem. At Charleston, the engineers reported to General Beauregard, the department commander, but the infantry were directly under Brigadier General Ripley, the Charleston district commander. Since the engineers who designed and oversaw the construction of the forts were of lower rank than the infantry officers who commanded the working parties, the engineers could not order the soldiers to do the work. They could only give suggestions to the officers in charge of the work details. Sometimes the engineers' instructions were ignored or altered, and on other occasions, frustrated engineers failed to appear. By late May, only seven guns were in position. There were no magazines or communication trenches connecting the batteries. The footpaths and rope ferries connecting James and Morris islands were not finished. The battery at the mouth of Vincent's Creek had only its pilings set, and the covering batteries planned for Black Island had not been started.[49]

Such pettiness and inefficiency in the face of a coming attack infuriated General Ripley. On June 1, he removed the engineers and ordered Captain John C. Mitchel of the 1st South Carolina Artillery to take over and finish the batteries. With the engineers removed from activities at Light-House Inlet, Mitchel organized working parties from the 21st and 25th South Carolina Infantry Regiments, and in a short time was completing the batteries. By June 14, the works were far enough along that the Confederates were able to provide covering fire so that munitions from the blockade runner *Ruby*, which had run aground in Light-House Inlet, could be saved.

Mitchel continued in charge until June 21, when Beauregard ordered the construction turned back to the engineers. Though sympathetic to Ripley's situation, Beauregard did not want a precedent set wherein any infantry officer could order about the engineers, and to protect their standing in the department for the sake of future operations, Beauregard ordered Ripley to stay out of the engineers' affairs.[50]

However, by the time the engineers returned to Morris Island, the Confederate defense was almost set. Even though the batteries on Black Island and at the mouth of Vincent's Creek were not finished, the works on Morris Island were nearly complete. On the island's southern tip, huddled around the ruins of the old lighthouse, which now served as a signal tower, were eleven detached batteries supported by a line of rifle pits at Oyster Point. The batteries mounted three 8-inch navy shell guns, two 8-inch seacoast howitzers, one 24-pounder, one 30-pound Parrott, one 12-pound Whitworth (unmounted), and three 10-inch mortars. The guns, built into the small hillocks, were unevenly distributed, and though not connected, they could give formidable opposition to an enemy landing if supported by a large infantry force.

In early July, the works were manned by 220 artillerymen of companies I and E of the 1st South Carolina Artillery under Captains Mitchel and J. Ravenel Macbeth and a detachment of Company H, under Lieutenant Edward D. Frost. The infantry support was provided by 400 men of the 21st South Carolina Regiment commanded by Major George W. McIver and 50 men from Company D, 1st South Carolina Regiment, under Captain Charles T. Haskell.[51]

Farther down the island, nearly three miles north of Light-House Inlet, was Battery Wagner. By July, Captain Langdon Cheves was supervising the final touches to the battery's construction. Cheves had completed everything except the cutting of a canal in front of Wagner that would place a water barrier between the battery and any enemy siege works that might approach the work. Even without the canal, Wagner was formidable.

An irregular fortification, built of earth revetted with palmetto logs, the battery offered a strong seafront, mounting a 10-inch Columbiad, a rifled 32-pounder, and a 32-pound smoothbore to any naval attack. Learning from past mistakes, the Confederates built heavy traverses

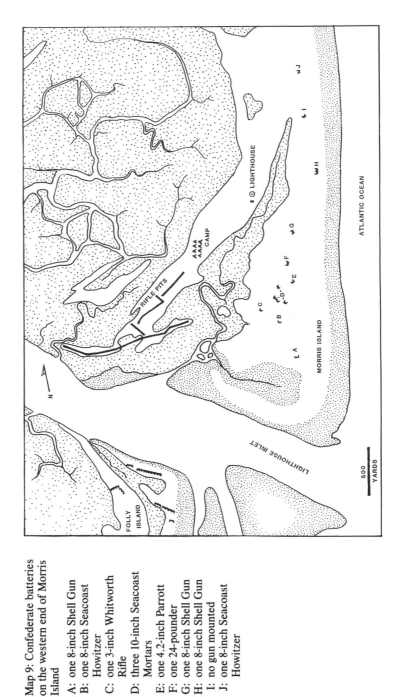

Map 9: Confederate batteries on the western end of Morris Island

A: one 8-inch Shell Gun
B: one 8-inch Seacoast Howitzer
C: one 3-inch Whitworth Rifle
D: three 10-inch Seacoast Mortars
E: one 4.2-inch Parrott
F: one 24-pounder
G: one 8-inch Shell Gun
H: one 8-inch Shell Gun
I: no gun mounted
J: one 8-inch Seacoast Howitzer

that protected the guns and gunners. Connecting the land and sea fronts was a large salient, one face of which commanded the ship channel while the other provided a crossfire on the land front. From this salient ran an earthen wall that stretched entirely across the island. Arranged for howitzers and infantrymen, the battery's garrison could concentrate a killing fire on anyone charging up the beach. At the end of the land front was another, smaller salient that also provided flanking fire. From here the western wall ran for about 300 feet along Vincent's Creek before cutting back across the island to form Wagner's gorge wall. The gorge wall was nothing more than an infantry trench, but attacks from this direction were not expected.

In front of Wagner was a deep moat designed to fill with water at high tide. Inside the battery, built into the seaface, was a huge 30-by-100-foot bombproof capable of housing 900 men. On the west side of the parade were some lightly constructed wooden quarters for the officers and medical stores.

With three guns on the seaface and six guns landward, Battery Wagner was manned by 107 artillerymen of Chichester's and Mathewes' artillery companies and 212 men of the 21st South Carolina, all under the commander of Morris Island, Colonel Robert F. Graham.[52]

Three-quarters of a mile north of Battery Wagner on Cummings Point stood Battery Gregg. Named for Brigadier General Maxcy Gregg, who had been mortally wounded at the Battle of Fredericksburg, the work was designed to fire on vessels approaching from the south in the main ship channel. Battery Gregg was not expected to fight off infantry attacks and was manned by only thirty men under Captain Henry R. Lesesne of Company H, 1st South Carolina Artillery. Battery Gregg did, however, control the wharf where all reinforcements and supplies had to land.

In all, Colonel Robert F. Graham had a force of 665 infantrymen, 330 artillerymen, and 26 cavalrymen to defend Morris Island. He hoped to be able to stop the Federals from landing, but if not, he could fall back to Battery Wagner and try to hold on until help arrived.[53]

It was apparent that an attack was coming. Anticipation of the Union assault was not based on guesswork. A Confederate observation balloon had reported a large number of transports in the roads at Port Royal. Also, on the night of July 8, Captain Haskell had taken a scouting party up Folly Creek and had spotted enemy launches and some construction on Folly Island. At the same time, intercepted messages alerted the Confederates that barges and cutters were being readied off Folly Island. These reports confirmed the Confederate suspicions. Colonel Graham immediately placed his men on alert and wired his superiors that an attack "on this point is imminent." Ripley passed the warning on to Beauregard who quickly began to implement the Confederate plan. Troops were ordered to stand ready while others were immediately ordered to board trains for transportation to Charleston. Directions were also left sending the first infantry battalion to reach the city to Morris Island. (See appendix, tables 2 and 3.)[54]

Chapter 3

THE INITIAL ASSAULT

Aim low and put your trust in God.
Brigadier General George C. Strong

While Graham watched for signs of attack, General Gillmore readied his army. Mass and firepower, two powerful elements of warfare, were possessed by Gillmore, but he did not use them. Instead, he split his army and did not strike Morris Island with his full force. Gillmore had nearly always been an engineer. The majority of his career had been spent teaching engineering, designing and constructing fortifications, and emplacing artillery. The exact science of engineering had real answers to problems, but on the battlefield, answers could not always be found using hard science and mathematics. His brief sojourn as a division commander in Kentucky had not prepared him for running an independent campaign.

The unknown facing Gillmore was the strength of the Confederate forces defending Charleston. Though he had no exact figures, Gillmore was convinced that he was outnumbered. For this reason he tried to mask his attack on Morris Island and stop enemy reinforcements from reaching Charleston by planning two diversions. To stop Confederate forces from Savannah from reaching Charleston, Gillmore ordered Colonel Higginson to take a portion of the 1st South Carolina up the South Edisto River and cut the Charleston and Savannah Railroad. At the same time, to pull Confederate attention away from Morris Island, Gillmore directed Brigadier General Terry to proceed into the Stono River and land his 5,260-man division on James Island. The attacks were to occur simultaneously with the assault on Morris Island. By

Gillmore's precise mind, the diversions would allow his men to quickly seize Morris Island. In reality he was weakening his mass and spreading thin his firepower.[1]

With more than fifty percent of his force committed to the diversions, Gillmore, supported by the navy, planned to capture Morris Island using a two-pronged night attack. One force was to land between Batteries Gregg and Wagner, while the other assaulted the southern end of Morris Island. For the attack, Gillmore assembled a number of barges in the Folly River on the north side of Folly Island, while at Port Royal, Dahlgren readied a flotilla of launches and cutters.

On July 7, Dahlgren ordered the tug *Dandelion* to debark from Port Royal with the assembled boats and proceed with "great secrecy" to Folly Island. The *Dandelion*, along with the tug *O. M. Petit*, became mother ships to a flock of naval launches. Armed with the Dahlgren boat howitzer, a bronze weapon designed by Dahlgren, the launches were capable of providing an effective cover fire for the landings. The entire force was commanded by Lieutenant Commander Francis M. Bunce, who made his flagship on the launch from the gunboat *Pawnee*.[2]

While waiting for the navy, the army's contingent was organized for action. Commanders ordered regimental cooks to prepare three days' rations for the men. On July 8, the soldiers of Strong's brigade were put through rigorous final inspections. At the same time, a white flannel strip was sewn on the left sleeve of every soldier so that friend might be distinguished from foe in the night attack.[3]

As the soldiers readied themselves for battle, other necessary provisions were being carried out. Surgeon John J. Craven established a field hospital on Folly Island about a half mile from the batteries. Other medical preparations included the arrival of Clara Barton on board the steamer *Canonicus*. The well-known nurse had been in the Department of the South since April 1863, when she came to Hilton Head to visit her brother David, a departmental quartermaster, and to escape the petty politicians and officers who interfered with her work in Virginia. She had been warned by friends that it was a "bad omen" for her to go any place because as she later stated: "I have never missed of finding the trouble I went to find and was never late."[4]

However, at Hilton Head Clara Barton found a garrison she described as being "too few to fight and too many to be killed." Much of her time was spent in the company of officers from the 67th Ohio, with whom she wrote poetry and rode about the island. On one such ride she came upon a group of soldiers who made some comments that made her realize she had given way to too much happiness and had to return to her sterner duties. She may have left the department had not

General Gillmore arrived and set things in motion. She considered Gillmore a commander who "acts more than he talks," and before Gillmore left for Folly Island, he dined with Clara Barton and issued her a pass allowing her to work on Morris Island. In early July, she joined the forces leaving Hilton Head, determined to put her pass to good use by returning to her self-appointed mission.[5]

At nightfall of July 8, as Clara Barton and additional supplies were leaving Hilton Head, the men on Folly Island marched to barges waiting in the Folly River. The loading was long and tiresome. For almost the entire night Strong's men waited in silence, some in boats, some on shore. The anxiety of battle compounded with frustration as the men quietly cursed the delays. Finally, toward dawn, word was passed that the attack had been called off. Disgusted, the tired soldiers returned to their camps.[6]

Gillmore had canceled the assault because the naval launches, delayed by a heavy squall, had not reached the rendezvous point on time, and his engineers had failed to cut sufficient passageways through the Confederate obstructions in the Folly River. Even if the navy had arrived, the landing parties would have been stalled by the obstructions, and a gigantic traffic jam of barges and launches would have resulted. As his engineers went to work clearing the obstructions, Gillmore made plans to proceed with the attack the following morning.[7]

While the assault on Morris Island was put off for one more day, Terry's movement went ahead as scheduled. Placed on vessels of various quality, troops from Port Royal were brought to Stono Inlet, and though one artilleryman reported that his ride "was a case of bumpety bump, with the expectation of finding the boat going to pieces and sinking at any moment," all of the vessels survived the passage. Early on the morning of July 9, the transports joined other troop carriers and warships under the command of Commander George B. Balch at Stono Inlet. Underway after noon, the vessels moved up river. The gunboat *Pawnee* led the way, followed by the monitor *Nantucket*, gunboat *Commodore McDonough*, mortar schooner *C. P. Williams*, and thirteen transports. Lobbing shells onto James and Johns islands, the warships provided protection as elements of the 104th and 52nd Pennsylvania infantry regiments came ashore at Legare's Landing on Battery Island. Wading through waist-deep mud, the Union soldiers reached solid ground, drove off Confederate pickets, moved on to Sol Legare Island, and seized the causeways that connected Sol Legare Island to James Island. (See appendix, table 4.)[8]

The opportunity now existed for Terry to land the rest of his division and advance onto James Island. Such a bold move could have pushed aside the defending Confederates and established a Union position on the inner regions of Charleston Harbor. Terry, however, hesitated. General Gillmore had ordered his subordinate not to commit his men to battle and Terry obeyed. No more troops landed on the ninth, and those on Battery and Sol Legare Islands kept in close contact with Balch's warships in case the Confederates attempted a counterattack.

With the lead elements of Terry's division safely ashore, Gillmore worked with his officers to revise the attack on Morris Island. The new plan was less complicated and therefore less dangerous than the originally planned night assault. Since the Union batteries overlooking Light-House Inlet had been partially unmasked, it was feared that the Confederates had been forewarned. Because of this, the two-pronged night assault was dropped. Unwilling to risk men in a boat attack in the creeks that ran along Morris Island, the Union commanders decided to strike a concentrated blow on the southern end of Morris Island. Hoping to employ superior firepower from their batteries and ships, the officers thought they could land Strong's brigade at daylight directly under the Confederate guns and then overrun the enemy's positions and take the entire island. The battle between Folly and Morris islands would depend largely on cannon power and ability of the opposing artillerists. In this realm Gillmore and Dahlgren had complete confidence. (See appendix, table 5).

Though the Federal forces remained on alert all day and security was kept tight, some Union artillerymen from Company D, 3rd Rhode Island, decided they wanted more than their usual fare of hardtack before the battle opened. Not wishing to face death without a square meal, three sergeants raised fifteen dollars and one of them, Sergeant Edward W. Hamilton, ran the guard and travelled five miles to the nearest sutler where the only thing available was unmarked canned goods. Buying up the sutler's stock, Hamilton hurried back to the batteries, again avoiding the pickets and rejoined comrades. The hoped for feast never occurred. Once opened, the cans were found to contain spoiled asparagus, and the men went to bed hungry. However, the asparagus did not go to waste as the sergeants placed the cans inside their cannon so to pass them over to the enemy in the opening volley.[9]

On the evening of July 9, the Union movement proceeded according to plan. At 9 P.M., Strong's brigade again marched to the north side of Folly Island where the boats were waiting. This time all the vessels were ready and the obstructions removed. With four companies of the 7th Connecticut in the lead vessels, followed by the 6th Connecticut, Strong's brigade proceeded up the river. Ill-skilled at handling the cutters, the men did not row in unison, causing one soldier to remark later that it was as if there were "forty different tides running in as many directions." Silence was kept, the only noises were hushed officers' voices, the muffled oars, and an alligator occasionally plunging into the water. By early morning on July 10, the flotilla reached Light-House Inlet and positioned itself behind the tall grass lining the waterway. Lieutenant Commander Bunce stationed his armed launches across the inlet, waiting for daylight when the attack would begin. The soldiers did not rest. A slight breeze and the current in the Folly River required that they row continuously to maintain their vessels' positions. While doing this many of them pondered the task ahead, disliking the prospect of facing Confederate batteries in open boats.[10]

While Strong's men waited at Light-House Inlet, Dahlgren prepared his monitors for battle. His vessels were all veterans of the April 7 attack, but now increased armor protection added to their decks and turrets improved them further, though only Dahlgren's flagship, the *Catskill*, was completely altered and she was the only monitor permitted to venture close to the Confederate works. The rest were under orders to stay off and avoid any point-blank exchanges. As the warships left for battle, they steamed past the watery grave of the ironclad *Keokuk*, a casualty of Du Pont's unsuccessful attack and a grim reminder of the ability of the Confederate artillerists.[11]

On shore, activity began at 3:00 A.M. when Gillmore was awakened by his aides. They moved to the batteries where Gillmore joined Seymour, the commander of the assault. Dawn approached; in the next hour the Union commanders busily finished their preparations. Nearly 2,500 men of Strong's brigade were in boats. Another 1,350 men and a battery of light artillery remained near the batteries, ready to follow the initial landing force. Another 1,450 men were held in reserve. The army was ready, awaiting daylight. (See appendix, table 5.)[12]

As morning neared, General Seymour impatiently walked among the Union batteries. It was crucial that the Union guns open fire first and immediately gain the surprise needed for the landing. At 4:15 A.M., Seymour directed his guns unmasked. It was too dark for the gunners to make out their targets, but Seymour hoped by the time the obstructions were cleared sufficient light would be available. In less than an hour the batteries were unmasked. The Confederate works were visible, and at 5:08 A.M., Seymour gave orders to begin firing.[13]

The morning of July 10 was fair, there was no breeze and the air was hot. Though expecting an attack, the Confederates had not broken their routine. No extra men had been posted, and the soldiers at the batteries had started to eat breakfast when Seymour's thirty-two rifled guns and fifteen mortars interrupted. As the first shells fell on their positions, the Confederate drummers sounded the long roll and artillerymen rushed to their guns, while the supporting infantry of the 21st and 1st South Carolina hurried to rifle pits in front and to the right of the batteries. Though it was morning, the extreme heat forced most of the Confederates to go to battle stripped to the waist.[14]

The duel between the batteries continued for more than an hour with neither side gaining an advantage. The Union soldiers in boats waited for Strong's signal to move forward. As they watched the contest, the men saw something that caused them to disregard their orders to maintain silence: the appearance of the monitors on the Confederate flank. Soon, they erupted into cheers as the navy added its weight to the contest.

Onboard the *Catskill*, Dahlgren was leading the monitors *Nahant*, *Montauk*, and *Weehawken* into action. As previously arranged with Gillmore, the rear admiral was moving in to flank the Confederate batteries. At first, only the *Catskill* came close to Morris Island, but soon the commanders of the other monitors, recognizing that their vessels could withstand the concussion of Confederate shots, ignored their orders and closed with the enemy. Using primarily shrapnel and grapeshot, the monitors fired their loads at great elevation so metal balls and fragments scattered over hundreds of yards, ripping through the Southern batteries.[15]

The effect of the monitors' guns on the battle was seen plainly by the Strong's men. The fire of the Confederate batteries, now enfiladed by the ironclads, tapered off and became erratic. Noticing this, the Union soldiers cheered even more loudly, finally drawing the attention of the Confederate gunners. Their position revealed, Lieutenant Commander Bunce maneuvered his armed cutters toward Morris Island and began to return fire. By now all available artillery pieces had entered the fight. The noise of the bombardment was so great that it was heard at the Union base in Port Royal, more than fifty miles away.[16]

From the beginning of the attack, the Southern cannoneers kept up an effective exchange with their Northern counterparts. Throughout the bombardment, the Confederate artillery commander, Captain John C. Mitchel, ran from gun to gun, encouraging his men, but once flanked by monitors and boat howitzers, the accuracy of the Confederate batteries began to tail off. The artillerymen, however, did manage to lob a few shells toward the launches. One vessel was sunk, and General Strong's lead boat came dangerously close to being destroyed. Anxiety mounted in the barges as the men felt helpless to answer the

Confederate shells. One soldier remarked that he did not mind being killed or drowned; it was the possibility of both that bothered him, as he was wedged in so tight that he could "neither pray, fight nor swear."[17]

Slowly, the Union soldiers, through bursting shells, worked their boats nearer and nearer. Leading the way was the 7th Connecticut, followed by the 6th Connecticut, 3rd New Hampshire, 76th Pennsylvania, 9th Maine, and four companies of the 48th New York. As the distance to Morris Island shortened, the Federals found that the Southerners could not depress their guns enough and their shells were whistling harmlessly overhead, but just as they escaped the cannon fire, the Confederate soldiers in the rifle pits began a rapid fusillade.

Still, Strong ordered his men ashore and all the regiments, except Colonel Chatfield's 6th Connecticut, obeyed. Instead of landing, Chatfield veered his regiments' boats into Light-House Inlet, and taking

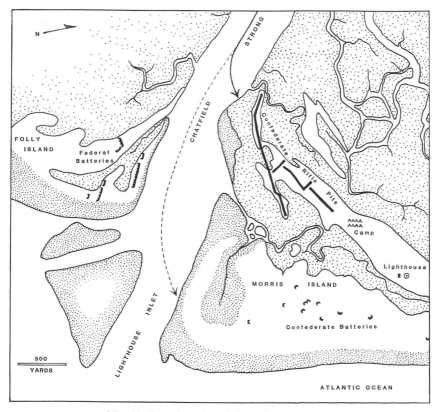

Map 10: Assault on Morris Island, July 10, 1863

advantage of the Confederates' inability to depress their cannon, led his regiment toward the ocean.

While Chatfield's men were pulling away, Strong directed the rest of his units against the rifle pits. First ashore were skirmishers armed with seven-shot Spencer rifles. Then, regiment after regiment, with bayonets fixed, clamored out of their boats, formed in knee-deep mud and began wading inland. Strong, anxious to join the fray, leaped from his boat before it landed and disappeared under the water, leaving only his hat floating on the waves, but he soon surfaced, reached shore, stripped off his waterlogged boots and began directing the attack. Pausing to fire volleys, the Northerners continued to press on, and soon the lead regiment, the 7th Connecticut, reached the rifle pits where they engaged in heavy hand-to-hand fighting. The Confederates, led by such officers as Captain Haskell, fought hard, but as Haskell went down with a mortal wound, the defense suddenly collapsed and the Southerners began a hurried retreat.[18]

The quick departure of the Confederate infantry was caused by the appearance of Chatfield's 6th Connecticut in the batteries above them. Having slipped under the enemy's guns, Chatfield had landed his men above the batteries and charged the rear and flanks of the Confederate works. For a short time, the artillerymen resisted, but muskets and bayonets soon overwhelmed ramrods and spikes. The batteries were taken, and the Union soldiers pushed on to surround the rifle pits. Seeing disaster and probable surrender, the Confederate commanders ordered a retreat—but it soon became a rout. As Chatfield and Strong united their forces, a number of Confederates were taken prisoner. Those who managed to escape the envelopment streamed toward Wagner under artillery fire from the monitors and the naval howitzers which had been taken off the launches and brought ashore; and though they probably did not notice, the Confederates also received shells from their former artillery pieces which were now manned by the versatile soldiers of the 7th Connecticut.[19]

As the Southerners fled, they crashed into reinforcements from the 7th South Carolina Battalion and the 20th South Carolina who had been rushed to Morris Island. Landing at Cummings Point as the Union attack progressed, the first two companies ran nearly the entire length of the island, arriving in time to be swept back into Battery Wagner by their retreating comrades. Realizing that his position at Light-House Inlet was lost and not wishing to risk his command any further, Colonel Graham formed the rest of the reinforcements inside Wagner while he rallied and reorganized the men fleeing toward the battery.[20]

While the morning's events demoralized the Confederates, the

Northerners were elated. Strong, mounted on a mule, and Chatfield, waving a captured Confederate flag, directed their men to follow the fleeing enemy. The soldiers were inspired by the discovery of newspapers in the captured works telling of Union victories at Gettysburg and Vicksburg. Lieutenant Colonel John Bedel of the 3rd New Hampshire ran among the advancing soldiers with a newspaper in one hand and his hat in the other, crying "Vicksburg captured: Great victory at Gettysburg!" The men responded by cheering and charging towards Wagner.

But even this news could not push the exhausted men to greater exertions. The heat was becoming unbearable, and the Union soldiers found themselves dodging solid shot from Brooke rifles mounted on Fort Sumter's barbette wall. The Brooke shots killed some Union soldiers, and a near miss buried the officers of the 3rd New Hampshire in the sand, wounding Lieutenant Colonel Bedel. As the column reached Wagner, the battery opened, scattering the leading Federals with a terrible storm of grape and canister. The attacking force could do no more; its momentum was blunted. The exhausted men halted, most falling in the sand to rest. Commanders quickly organized a picket line across the island and awaited orders.[21]

While the rest of the Federals were ferried from Folly to Morris Island, the Northern monitors followed the retreating Confederates. Already the battle was beginning to affect the men inside the iron ships. On monitors only the sailors serving in the turret or pilothouse had the luxury of seeing sunlight or breathing fresh air. Those below decks served in an environment that was dark as the blackest night, having only lanterns for light. They also had no idea how the battle was progressing. Hits were hardly noticed, while near misses sounded like "screaming demons" as they passed overhead.

When in action, the men and officers below deck would strip off everything except pants and shoes as they passed powder and shot from the magazine to the turret. Though ventilators were suppose to clear the ship of smoke, they actually served as conduits which carried the smoke throughout the vessels, causing an officer on the *Weehawken* to comment that during an engagement the air "is so thick in a few hours you can cut it."

Once the Southerners were driven from their batteries, the commanders of monitors allowed their men to open hatches and come on deck to get some fresh air before they engaged Battery Wagner. The break was greatly appreciated by the men who were covered with soot and nearly exhausted. As the monitors approached Wagner, the sailors returned below decks, and except for a break for lunch, the ironclads kept up a steady bombardment until nightfall, giving the army time to consolidate its position.[22]

Gillmore was jubilant about the day's work; though his men had failed to take all of Morris Island, they had captured three-fourths of the island and he was confident that the remaining Confederates could be easily dealt with in the morning. He had watched the attack from the base of the lookout tower behind the Folly Island batteries. When the southern end of Morris Island was secure, Gillmore and his staff crossed over to inspect the victory.[23]

The landing on Morris Island had been a great success. The execution of the attack was faultless, the coordination between the artillery and navy was perfect, and Chatfield's improvised flanking movement brilliant. Union casualties had been only fifteen men killed and ninety-one wounded, while the Confederates lost nearly three hundred men, eleven artillery pieces, and nearly all of their equipment. The haste in which the Confederates had evacuated their position was evident. The Northerners found rice still being cooked in kettles, bread in the oven, and watermelon on the table. (See appendix, table 6.)[24]

Gillmore placed his aide, Major William S. Stryker, in charge of the Confederate camp and prisoners. Among the captured were some "high-bred" Charlestonians, including the mortally wounded Lieutenant John Stock Bee, son of William C. Bee, president of a blockade-running company, and Captain J. Ravenel Macbeth, the son of Charleston's mayor. Stryker was drawn to the two enemy officers and found Macbeth tending to the dying Bee. Sensing a chance to escape, Macbeth requested permission to go to the newly establish Union field hospital for brandy to give to Bee and asked Stryker to assign to him as a guard "a rather weak looking soldier." Stryker, not fooled by Macbeth's ploy, directed a sergeant and three other men to escort the Confederate, saying: "if he tries to escape shoot him." Later, before being exchanged, Macbeth admitted to Stryker that he had intended to escape had not Stryker assigned the extra guard.[25]

Though not a strategic surprise, the Federal assault had tactically caught the Confederates off guard. Unlike the attacks on Hatteras and Hilton Head, the army did not sit on transports waiting for the navy to clear the way; the soldiers landed while the bombardment was in progress. As the men rushed ashore, the navy and supporting land batteries shifted their fire farther down the island and the monitors concentrated on Battery Wagner. The attack reflected Gillmore's confidence in the destructive power of his guns.

Besides the innovative application of artillery, the Federals also made good use of the bayonet. On this day the bayonet was employed effectively in the brisk hand-to-hand fighting in the rifle pits and batteries, but its success may have blinded Gillmore to the bayonet's weakness against a better prepared enemy.

If Gillmore's attack had any flaw it was his failure to utilize fresh units for an attack against Wagner later that day. Though nearly three regiments were quickly transferred to Morris Island after the battle, they were not used to pursue the Confederates. Instead, the pursuit was handled by the same regiments that had carried out the boat assault, and by then, they were too worn out to push on and capture Battery Wagner. If Gillmore had used the men from his second wave and reserve more effectively, he could have completed his victory, but by delaying, he gave the Confederates time to regroup and prepare.[26]

On the naval side, Dahlgren had also learned some lessons. Even though most of his monitors had not been completely modified, they were capable of dueling with the Confederate works. In future operations against Wagner, there would be no restrictions placed on the ironclads; however, during the fourteen-hour engagement, heat and exhaustion had taken their toll. Many of the coal passers and firemen fainted. All the sailors were weakened by the conditions as the monitors were proving to be hot boxes in the summer weather.[27]

While the Northerners rejoiced in their success, the Confederates inside Wagner feverishly tried to prepare their defenses. In the fight, Colonel Graham had lost one-third of his effective force, with only 57 of the 142 artillerymen from the batteries escaping to Wagner. Among the casualties were many important artillery officers. Captain Charles T. Haskell and Lieutenant John S. Bee had been killed. Captain J. R. Macbeth and Lieutenant J. Guerard Heyward had been captured. The loss of these young Carolinians was a severe one.[28]

Another crucial loss occurred in Battery Wagner. When the attack had started, Captain Langdon Cheves, one of Wagner's designers and the current chief engineer of Morris Island, immediately began to ready the battery for an assault. As Cheves went about his duties, word reached him that his nephew, Captain Haskell, had been killed. Though badly shaken by the news, Cheves continued with his work as Wagner was now heavily engaged with the monitors. While moving across the parade field toward the battery's magazine, Cheves was instantly killed by shell fragments when a monitor shell skipped over the battery wall and exploded.[29]

Besides the loss of vital officers, Graham also found himself with a badly crippled and fatigued command. He had no fresh troops. The reinforcements, having run nearly a mile from Cummings Point, were disorganized and tired, but morale was remarkably good. These men were native South Carolinians, many from coastal regions around Charleston. They realized that not only a battle, but homes and families were in jeopardy. They reformed inside Wagner and positioned themselves on the ramparts to resist any further assaults.

While the men in Wagner waited, the Confederate high command continued to bring reinforcements to Charleston and distribute them to the threatened districts. On the morning of July 9, the increased Union activity on Folly Island and the appearance of warships in the Stono River caused General Beauregard to place his department on the alert. Later that day, after the Federals landed on Battery Island, Beauregard wired Major General William Henry Chase Whiting, commander of Wilmington, North Carolina, to rush a regiment to Charleston. In his own department, Beauregard directed his quartermaster to ready the railway for transportation of eleven hundred men. At the same time, the 7th South Carolina Battalion was ordered to Morris Island along with some companies from the 20th South Carolina.

After the Union attacks on July 10, another flurry of telegrams was sent. Additional aid was requested from Wilmington, and that same day Whiting entrained Brigadier General Thomas L. Clingman's brigade, which was followed a short time later by two regiments under Brigadier General Alfred H. Colquitt. The commander at Savannah, General Hugh W. Mercer, also responded, sending by train the majority of Brigadier General William Booth Taliaferro's brigade. The governor of South Carolina mustered the state militia, and Brigadier General Johnson Hagood was ordered to Charleston to take command of James Island.

Before noon on July 10, trains carrying the lead elements of Taliaferro's brigade began arriving at St. Andrews depot across the Ashley River from Charleston. The 32nd Georgia was immediately sent to James Island, while a mixed command of Georgia infantry companies under Colonel Charles H. Olmstead was readied for deployment to Morris Island.[30]

The reinforcements from Savannah might have been delayed if Gillmore's diversion sent into the South Edisto River had accomplished its mission. The expedition, under Colonel Higginson of the 1st South Carolina Infantry, left Beaufort on July 9 with 250 men from his regiment and a section of artillery from the 1st Connecticut Battery onboard the transport *Enoch Dean*, the tug *Governor Milton*, and the armed steamer *John Adams*. The following morning, the small force brushed aside a section of the South Carolina Washington Artillery and cut through the obstructions on the South Edisto River. After sending men ashore to destroy a rice mill and pick up fugitive slaves,

Higginson attempted to push on to the railroad bridge but the receding tide made it impossible to continue. The *Enoch Dean* ran aground under heavy enemy artillery fire. The *Governor Milton* pulled the *Enoch Dean* to safety, but then ran aground on the pilings herself. The *Governor Milton* had to be abandoned, with her two field pieces. Higginson's force returned to Port Royal the next day, having failed to destroy the important railroad bridge.

One participant summed up the expedition: "We destroyed a few hundred bushels of rice, burned the mill, captured a lieutenant and two men, brought off two hundred contrabands and their baggage, lost two men and had several wounded. I got a hundred pound note of 1776 and other Continental money from the Morris House." However, the Union diversion missed its prime objective, and the railroad tracks to Charleston continued to carry men and material.[31]

While the attack on the Edisto had been designed to stop Confederate troops from reaching Charleston, the Union landing on James Island was intended to keep the Confederates from sending reinforcements to Morris Island. Again, Gillmore's diversion failed to interrupt the Confederate distribution of forces. Arriving troops were evenly divided between the two threatened points until July 12, when Beauregard felt Morris Island to be secure. Neither diversion accomplished its mission, and both deprived Gillmore of needed forces for the attack on Morris Island. The assault on Battery Wagner had to be postponed, and as a result, the Confederates were given a reprieve.[32]

While the Northerners were finished for the day, the Confederates continued to work. Around midnight on the tenth, General Hagood, the department's designated troubleshooter, arrived in Charleston and was immediately given command of James Island. At the same time, under the cover of darkness, Colonel Olmstead's command was transported by steamer to Morris Island. Rushed from Savannah, the force was comprised of eleven companies—four from Olmstead's 1st Georgia, four from the 12th Georgia Artillery Battalion under Lieutenant Colonel Henry D. Capers, and three companies of the 18th Georgia Infantry Battalion commanded by Major William S. Basinger; a total of 460 men.[33]

Olmstead's Georgians increased Wagner's garrison by nearly a third, and they were soon incorporated into Colonel Graham's defense. To help protect the land-front, additional Rains torpedoes (land mines) were placed before Wagner's southern face. Outside the battery, Graham placed Major James H. Rion and 150 men of the 7th South Carolina Battalion and the 20th South Carolina in shallow rifle pits located on a sand ridge in front of the battery. The rest of the men were distributed along Wagner's walls. The artillerymen stood by their cannon with shell, stands of grape and canister at the ready. Graham commanded a total of roughly 1,770 men. Expecting an attack, Graham kept his men at their posts; if there was to be any sleeping it would be on the ramparts.[34]

The Northern soldiers were also having a difficult time resting. The pause in the fighting had given the Federals a chance to examine their new position. Morris Island seemed a poor trade for Folly Island, but they were nearer to Charleston. The night did not pass easily for the Union soldiers. Most knew that Battery Wagner would be assaulted in the morning.[35]

At 2:30 A.M. on July 11, General Strong called on Lieutenant Colonel Daniel C. Rodman of the 7th Connecticut, and after a brief consultation, the two agreed to make the 7th Connecticut the attack's forlorn hope. Before daylight, Rodman, under the cover of a dense fog, led the four companies of his regiment forward to the picket line, marching along the firm sand exposed by the low tide. The bells of the fleet were heard to the east, and farther inland, voices from the Confederate outposts. Five hundred yards from Wagner, the 185 men halted. Behind the 7th Connecticut were two more regiments from Strong's brigade, the 76th Pennsylvania and the 9th Maine.

Strong accompanied the Connecticut troops to the front where he ordered them to rush the battery with bayonets, not pausing to fire until they reached Wagner. Urging his lead regiment, Strong ordered, "Aim low and put your trust in God. Forward the Seventh!"[36]

The Union soldiers advanced in silence to within twenty-five yards of the Confederate rifle pits when a volley of rifle fire struck the Federals. The Southerners then pulled back, pausing to fire two more times before they scurried down the beach past Wagner's ocean wall and into the battery. The 7th followed closely, but instead of pursuing the retreating Confederates down the beach, Rodman led them directly at Wagner.

Inside the battery the Southerners on the ramparts held their fire until their comrades had vacated their front. Then the artillery opened with canister and grape, followed by a compact volley of rifle fire.[37]

Rodman's men, who were already in Wagner's moat, escaped the initial eruption, and instead, the blast crashed into the following regiments which had not kept the proper interval behind the attack's spearhead. Stunned, the Pennsylvania and Maine soldiers stopped, but the Connecticut troops moved on, plodding through the water in the moat and up the exterior wall. The men tried to enter the battery, but were thrown back. A few individuals worked their way around to the

Map 11: Battery Wagner, July 11, 1863

A: No gun mounted
B: No gun mounted
C: 32-pounder rifle
D: 10-inch Columbiad
E: 32-pounder smoothbore
F: 8-inch Seacoast Howitzer
G: 42-pounder Carronade
H: 8-inch Shell Gun
I: 8-inch Shell Gun
J: 32-pounder Carronade
K: 32-pounder Carronade
L: 32-pounder Carronade
M: 10-inch Seacoast Mortar

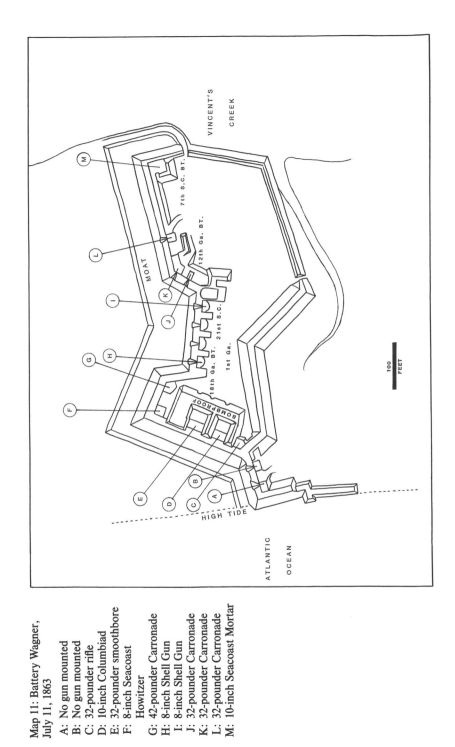

seafront and managed to infiltrate the gun chambers, but the majority of the regiment remained on the exterior slope.[38]

Trapped on Wagner's wall, the Connecticut regiment was decimated. When the men tried to move forward, they were either shot or blown to bits by grenades. Caught in a deadly enfilade fire, the 7th could not advance. Rodman became frantic as he saw his command being destroyed. He gave the retreat order but recalled it when he saw the regiments behind his own trying to move forward, but the help never arrived. Unable to reform properly beyond the defile, the regiments were battered back; only a few individuals reached the battery. When the Confederates saw the Union regiments fall before their fire, they were able to concentrate their attention on the remains of the 7th clinging to the parapet. The situation became desperate. Most of the regiment's officers were disabled. Finally, the wounded Rodman, lying on the parapet, again ordered a retreat, this time adding "every man for himself."[39]

The dash back across the ditch to the Union lines proved deadlier than the initial rush. Many chose to stay where they were rather than risk the run. Those who survived the retreat streamed through the reserve regiments (the 3rd and 7th New Hampshire). Strong met his men with tears in his eyes crying "my fault" over and over.

The attack had been a disaster. The 7th Connecticut lost nearly one hundred men, and the next morning only eighty-four enlisted men and four officers appeared at roll call. Total Union casualties numbered at least 339 men; the Confederates suffered only six dead and six wounded (See appendix, table 7.)[40]

The failure of Strong's attack shocked the Union high command. The official reason given for the repulse was the failure of the following regiments to properly support the Connecticut soldiers. By falling behind the lead regiment, the Pennsylvania and Maine troops caught the full fury of the Confederate fire and were stopped in their tracks. Alone, the 7th Connecticut lacked the momentum and force needed to take Wagner.

In reality, the attack never had a chance. The Northerners, so overconfident from their success the day before, made no special preparations, thinking a quick bayonet assault would easily overrun Wagner. Even though Gillmore's artillery train was nearby, there was no artillery bombardment preceding the assault, and no covering fire was given to the attackers. Only three regiments were used, and as a result, the defenders actually outnumbered the attackers. Overconfidence had cost the Federals dearly.

Immediately after the repulse, as the routed soldiers streamed back,

General Strong ordered his reserve regiments to build a defense line across Morris Island. These works were intended to resist Confederate counterattacks, but the following day, Gillmore expanded their function.

Realizing that more preparation would be needed before the next attack, Gillmore took Strong's line of breastworks and began laying out breaching batteries so his artillery could pulverize Wagner. Gillmore named himself the department's chief engineer and placed himself at the head of all engineering operations. On his personal staff served Colonel Edward Wellman Serrell, the English born commander of the 1st New York Volunteer Engineers, and the regiment's major, James F. Hall. Actual field command went to Captain Thomas Benton Brooks, a tough civilian engineer also from the New York Engineers. Brooks' top assistants were first lieutenants Charles R. Suter and Peter S. Michie, both recent graduates of West Point and members of the U.S. Army Corps of Engineers.[41]

On July 12, the engineers began construction of four breaching batteries. Armed primarily with the siege guns and mortars from the Folly Island batteries, the batteries were called O'Rorke, Reynolds, Weed, and Hays. The first three were named for Union officers killed at Gettysburg, while Hays was named in honor of an officer captured at Chancellorsville. The first guns were mounted on July 15, and the batteries were completed on the following day. Also, on July 16, Gillmore ordered Colonel Serrell to seek out a location for a battery in the midst of the marshes that separated Morris Island from James Island.[42]

Construction of the batteries was difficult. The Union soldiers worked on twelve-hour shifts, both night and day. If not on fatigue duty, the men were in rifle pits 525 yards in front of the batteries. The Confederates responded with artillery fire from Battery Wagner, which Gillmore tried to control with sharpshooters.

At first, the Federal sharpshooters, located on the second floor in an abandoned house along Vincent's Creek, were able to sweep Wagner's interior. Their fire wounded and killed a number of Confederates, including Captain Paul Hamilton Waring, a staff officer who was struck down inside Wagner while conversing with General Taliaferro. The Northern sharpshooters so bedeviled the garrison that finally a group of five men decided to take matters into their own hands, and on July 17, four officers and one sergeant, led by Lieutenant Thomas Tutt, decided to sneak out and burn the house. Though such an expedition was forbidden by standing orders, Captain Hansford Dade Duncan

Twiggs used his authority as a staff officer to pass himself and his four comrades out of Wagner.

Armed with rifles, the men moved through the sand dunes bordering Vincent's Creek. As they neared the building, they were spotted by the eight sharpshooters on the second floor of the house but were able to avoid the enemy fire and quickly rushed past the house and entered it on the opposite side. Once inside, a general fusillade broke out with the Northerners firing at their assailants down a narrow stairway. Lieutenant Tutt attempted to charge up the stairs but was pulled back by his comrades. Tutt then ordered the house set on fire, starting with the stairway. With the flames reaching the upper story, the Southerner's moved out of the building and began firing at the sharpshooters as they ran out the door and jumped from the windows. Both sides fired wildly while the Northerners scrambled back to their lines.

Though pleased with their action, the small band of Confederates soon realized that the entire Union command was now alerted. Bullets whizzed about the men, some passing through their clothes as they ran to cover behind a nearby sandridge. Their new position placed them even closer to the Northern line, and while some considered surrender, Lieutenant Tutt refused and continued to discharge his weapon at the enemy. As the Federals began moving toward them, the cannon in Battery Wagner opened, and soon a artillery duel broke out, which allowed the Southerners to race to safety.

Back at Wagner, the men quickly separated and returned to their commands. Though the results had proven favorable, Captain Twiggs was placed under arrest for allowing the men to leave the battery; however that night, while sleeping in the guard house, he was released.[43]

The small skirmish had silenced the Northern sharpshooters, but the Northerners had a more effective way to silence Wagner: the Union navy.

Before starting the batteries, Gillmore asked Dahlgren to keep up a covering fire on Wagner so his soldiers could be spared the concentrated fire from the Confederate battery. Dahlgren accepted the assignment, using his ironclads to "pepper away at Wagner." The shelling proved effective, but the sailors suffered for it. The firerooms of the monitors averaged 140 to 160 degrees in the hot South Carolina weather. One officer commented that: "These monitors are hot beyond all reason. The air is foul; the officers and crew are black from head to foot with smoke and ashes carried in the confined air, and there is no way to get fresh air; in fact they [the crews] nearly smothered."[44]

Dahlgren was eager to do all he could to assist Gillmore. The rear admiral kept in constant communication with both Generals Gillmore and Seymour over the plan of operations. He even attempted to organize three battalions—two of sailors and one of marines—for shore duty. Off Charleston, Dahlgren concentrated twenty-one warships, including four monitors, the *New Ironsides*, and the powerful wooden frigates *Wabash* and *Powhattan*. At Light-House Inlet, the *Commodore McDonough* was stationed, and in the Stono, the *Pawnee, Huron, Marblehead,* and the *C. P. Williams* protected Terry's division. Three more monitors were undergoing final improvements at Port Royal and would be available to Dahlgren in time for Gillmore's next assault on Battery Wagner (See appendix, table 9.)[45]

Confederate reaction to the Union lodgement on Morris Island was one not of despair but dedication to the long struggle ahead. Charleston newspapers called for an immediate counterattack and referred to the assault in historical and Biblical terms. The Yankees were viewed as Vandals and Philistines. References were made to the Persian attack on Athens, with Gillmore being seen as a new Xerxes. The *Daily Courier* declared that "Should Charleston fall, life will no longer be worth living."

President Davis viewed the landing as a "serious act." He realized that the South could ill afford to lose Charleston. Besides its value as a blockade-running port, the South had to retain the city as a symbol and rallying point. The Confederacy had already lost Vicksburg, and the reports from Gettysburg confirmed another devastating loss. If Charleston fell, the South would have a third major defeat, which would greatly affect the nation's ability and will to fight. For the well-being of the nation, Charleston had to hold.

Preparations were made for a long fight. After consultation with Beauregard, Mayor Charles Macbeth requested that all women and children leave the city, and he temporarily closed all businesses. At the same time, to head off a possible revolt, all free male Negroes, mulattoes, and mestizoes were ordered to register with the police.

While the mayor was handling the civil matters, Beauregard and his staff took additional measures to block the Federal advance. By July 10, two thousand infantry and 250 artillerymen had arrived at Charleston, while requests for help were sent to Richmond and Wilmington. The initial reinforcements were deployed throughout the harbor, with the bulk of the forces going to James and Morris islands.[46]

On July 11, Beauregard began to prepare for the inevitable. Fully aware that the Northerners planned to reduce Fort Sumter, Beauregard sent instructions to the fort's commander, Colonel Alfred Rhett, to ready his position for a bombardment. Rhett was told to strengthen the fort's gorge wall by filling it with sand and other material. The sally-port was ordered closed, and a new entrance started on the western face, away from Morris Island. Colonel Rhett was also directed to prepare for the withdrawal of the majority of Sumter's heavy guns.[47]

While work started on Fort Sumter, General Ripley journeyed to Morris Island and visited Battery Wagner. He found the garrison jaded, but in good spirits. Although preparations for evacuation had been made, Ripley did not believe them necessary. Instead, he suggested that additional works be built that would assist Wagner in holding off the Federal advance. Acting on Ripley's report, Beauregard ordered his chief engineer, Colonel David Harris, to build a zigzag coverway from Gregg to Wagner, to construct additional mortar and rifled batteries at Cummings Point east of Battery Gregg, to add obstructions in the creeks near Wagner, and to place additional torpedoes in front of the battery. Of these planned works, only the obstructions and torpedoes were added. The Confederates did not have the labor or material to strengthen both Morris and James Island at the same time.[48]

On July 12, Beauregard called a meeting to discuss the situation at Charleston and to decide on a defense plan for Morris Island. Among those attending the council were Generals Beauregard, Ripley, Tali-aferro, and Hagood, and Beauregard's chief of staff, Colonel Thomas Jordan. The state of South Carolina was represented by Governor Milledge L. Bonham and Confederate Congressman William Porcher Miles. Greatly concerned over the Federal position on Morris Island, they hotly debated the possibility of launching a counterattack. With nearly 1,500 men arriving from Wilmington, it was proposed to send reinforcements to the island at night and strike at the enemy before they became well entrenched. Though the plan was dangerous, they were willing to take the risk, believing that Southern fighting ability would overcome greater numbers; however, they did not have enough vessels and the idea was dropped.

Because they lacked the ability to throw the Northerners off Morris Island, it was agreed that Battery Wagner had to be held until the harbor's inner ring of works was given substantially more firepower; since it was only a matter of time before the Federals would rip apart Fort Sumter with their land-based artillery, the fort could no longer be the center of Charleston's defense. Instead, Sumter would be replaced by a new circle of fire anchored on the batteries of Sullivan's Island and Fort Johnson. The majority of Sumter's guns were to be removed to these points and Sumter would be given only enough armament to ensure its defense. Its power to stop enemy ships would soon be destroyed, but since it was a symbol of the Confederacy, all agreed that it would be held at all costs.[49]

While the harbor defenses were being rearranged, the Confederates planned to fight as long as possible on Morris Island. The longer Battery Wagner held, the more time the Confederates had to perfect their new fortifications. To give Wagner's defenders some assistance, plans were made to construct works containing heavy guns along James Island's eastern shore. These new batteries would take over as a flank defense for James Island and support Wagner; however, long range shelling could not stop any determined advance on Morris Island, and it would ultimately be the garrison of Battery Wagner that would have to give the Southerners the needed time to complete their works.[50]

To help the defenders of Morris Island, Beauregard and his advisers decided to send to the island four 12-pound howitzers, two 32-pound howitzers, fresh troops, and a new commander, Brigadier General William Booth Taliaferro.[51]

After the meeting, Beauregard, still not willing to give up some sort of counterattack, wrote Commander John Randolph Tucker, flag officer of the Confederate naval squadron at Charleston, proposing an attack by the navy. Beauregard suggested reinforcing the station's two ironclads, the *Chicora* and *Palmetto State*, with the unarmoured ram *Charleston*, the blockage runner *Juno*, and any other available vessels and use them in a night attack against the Northern monitors. By arming the vessels with spar torpedoes (explosive devices that detonated when thrust against the side of an enemy vessel) Beauregard thought the possibility of driving a torpedo into at least one of the monitors was good, and if the Union fleet could be driven away, the Union army would be cut off and would either have to abandon their position or be captured.

Since Beauregard had no authority over Tucker, he could only suggest the plan. The attack never took place; Tucker, who was an aggressive officer and fully backed the use of spar torpedoes, simply did not have the men or vessels to carry out such an operation. The *Palmetto State* and *Chicora* were little more than floating batteries that probably could not survive long outside the harbor. Though the *Charleston* had more efficient engines and was a better seagoing vessel, it would be at least a month before her armor was in place, and to send the ship into battle without an iron shield was suicide. The use of confiscated blockade runners like the *Juno* was a possibility, but the ships, though very fast, were too frail to be effective warships. Tucker also lacked sailors for such an attack. Instead, all the navy could do was stay on the defensive inside the harbor and send torpedo-armed rowboats against the enemy, and though five attempts were made in the next week, none reached their targets.[52]

With the navy and army unable to provide any offensive help, the men on Morris Island were forced to look to their own resources. With additional guns, a fresh garrison, and a new commander in Brigadier General William B. Taliaferro, the Confederates prepared to meet their enemy.

Morris Island's new commander, General Taliaferro, was a Virginia-born, Harvard-educated lawyer who had arrived with his brigade on July 10 from Savannah. An experienced commander, he had served under General Thomas J. "Stonewall" Jackson in the Valley Campaign, the Peninsula, Antietam, and Fredericksburg, commanding a regiment, brigade, and division. Never an admirer of Jackson, Taliaferro had often criticized his eccentric superior. When he was denied promotion to major general, Taliaferro demanded a transfer from the Army of Northern Virginia. Sent to Beauregard's department, the proud aristocrat was given command of a brigade at Savannah. A proven fighter and a resourceful officer, Taliaferro found himself in a difficult position on Morris Island.

Arriving at Wagner on July 13, Taliaferro discovered his new command in the midst of a constant bombardment from the Union navy. His garrison, for the most part, consisted of the same force that had repelled the July 11 assault. The two 32-pound howitzers had arrived and had been mounted on the land front while two 12-pound howitzers were positioned outside the fort to sweep the beach. The other two field pieces had been left at Battery Gregg to guard against possible small boat attacks. The light artillery was commanded by Captain William L. DePass and manned by detachments from his own artillery company and Company A, 1st South Carolina Artillery. These reinforcements and additional cannon raised the garrison's spirits, but the new artillery pieces and men could do nothing to silence the Union ironclads.

Battery Wagner could reply to the ships with only one 32-pound rifle, a 32-pound smoothbore, and a 10-inch Columbiad. The Columbiad was the only gun capable of injuring the ironclads, but its effectiveness was limited.

In bombarding Battery Wagner, the monitors would steam slowly toward the shoreline, revolve their turrets, and fire, skipping their round shells across the water so they would land inside the battery. The noise of the ricocheting shells caused the defenders to think more cannons were being fired than actually were. At first, the Confederates were quite curious about the monitors. Colonel Olmstead described a monitor off Wagner as having deliberate movements and insignificant in appearance. "The deck almost level with the water, and the little black turret giving small promise of its hidden power for attack." However, the same officer wrote that all curiosity ended when the men were introduced to a 15-inch shell.

Besides the monitors, Dahlgren also employed the *New Ironsides* against Wagner. The Confederates feared the *New Ironsides* more than any other warship. The massive ironclad would release broadsides in rapid succession causing a storm of shells to fly about Wagner. The shells sometimes would bounce into the interior of the work, bury themselves, and explode. Others would simply roll into the battery, while some were timed to burst in the air, showering fragments down on the garrison.[53]

For all the shelling, the navy was not Taliaferro's main concern. What worried him more was what Gillmore might be planning. The Union works were hidden from Taliaferro's view by sandhills. To discover the intentions of his opponent and to raise morale, he organized a reconnaissance. The probe was to be headed by Major James Henry Rion of the 7th South Carolina Battalion with a force of 150 men.

At midnight on the thirteenth, Rion, a Canadian-born, Charleston lawyer, moved his command out of Wagner, and after advancing about three-quarters of a mile, they encountered Union outposts. Quickly driving in the enemy pickets, the Confederates moved on until confronted by a line of rifle pits. Confused by the action and unable to see in the darkness, the Federals in the rifle pits opened fire without waiting for their pickets to pass from their front. Musket fire lit up the night as the Union soldiers fired into their own men and at the Confederates. Rion's soldiers returned fire, but when Northern field guns joined the action, he ordered his men to retire. Once back in Wagner, it was discovered that twenty-seven men were unaccounted for. Taking a small search party, Rion again journeyed down the island. While gathering up his lost men, Rion found the enemy rifle pits abandoned with numerous dead Union soldiers lying in the shallow ditch. Before dawn the Confederates returned to Wagner after finding twenty-four of their missing comrades.

The sortie had been successful. Rion brought back two prisoners, and his casualties were eleven men wounded and three missing. From the prisoners, Taliaferro learned that a number of heavy guns and mortars were being mounted against Battery Wagner. The information warned of an ensuing bombardment and infantry attack. Since Beauregard needed the majority of his troops to defend James Island, Taliaferro had to prepare with the resources on hand. To strengthen his position, the commanding general ordered his rifle pits in front of Wagner enlarged and deepened; however, besides these improvements, Taliaferro could do little except wait.[54]

Beauregard was informed of Gillmore's activities on Morris Island and intended to aid the island when he could, but his main concern was Terry's division on James Island. From the incoming troops, Beauregard had sent forty-seven hundred to James Island where they were put under the command of General Hagood. Unlike Morris Island, the Confederates on James Island were in a position to launch a counterattack.

Since the initial landing on July 9, General Terry had been very careful in deploying his division. Over the next four days, he cautiously disembarked the remainder of his force. Refusing to bring on any conflict, Terry carefully placed his fifty-two hundred men across the southeastern portion of Sol Legare's Island under the protection of the guns of the naval vessels and transports.

For the first few days, there was no combat except some long range shelling by the navy's gunboats. Slowly, Terry expanded his position, shifting the 10th Connecticut across a small causeway onto James Island toward Grimball's Landing. At the same time, he allowed his men to picket the northern end of Sol Legare's Island near Legare's Plantation at Rivers' Causeway. On occasion, men from Colonel Shaw's 54th Massachusetts were assigned to picket duty. Shaw was worried over the Confederate response to having African-American soliders on their front, but he was relieved to find that his men had no trouble with the enemy pickets, the only action being the usual exchange of words between the two sides, though as one officer of the 54th noted, the rebels could not tell the color of the pickets and called the black troops "flat headed Dutchmen."[55]

From July 10 to 15, Terry's division worked to improve its position while battling the heat, rain, and mosquitoes. The old Confederate causeway to Cole's Island was repaired, should it be needed as a retreat route. A battery of light artillery, the 1st Connecticut Battery, was landed, and Terry maintained constant communication with the navy to make sure its support would be available.[56]

By July 15, Terry's force occupied a line from Grimball's Plantation on the Stono River to Legare's Plantation on Big Folly Creek. Though well-guarded and supported by warships, the Federal defenses did not deter the Confederates who were organizing an attack.

After carrying out a reconnaissance, Hagood learned that the Northerners had posted a regiment, the 10th Connecticut, in an exposed position near Grimball's Landing on the Stono River. Seeing an opportunity to strike the enemy, General Hagood laid plans to cut off the Federals at Grimball's and trap them against the Stono River. The plan was not a simple one. For it to work, Confederate artillery under Colonel James D. Radcliffe had to drive off the Union gunboats guarding the Union regiment at Grimball's, while infantry led by Colonel Carleton Way held the enemy in place. At the same time, a brigade commanded by Brigadier General Alfred Colquitt would advance from Secessionville, across Rivers' Causeway, onto Sol Legare's Island, through the Federal pickets, and then back to the mainland via Grimball's Causeway. In doing this, Colquitt would bring his force behind the Union regiment at Grimball's, cutting off their line of retreat. For the attack Hagood assembled thirty-two hundred infantrymen, cavalrymen, and artillerymen. Though it was a complicated plan, Hagood felt his men and commanders were capable of carrying out their assignments.[57]

At dawn, July 16, four Confederate Napoleon cannon opened on the gunboats *Pawnee* and *Marblehead* from a hidden battery. The cannoneers directed their fire at the *Pawnee,* the larger of the two vessels. The narrow confines of the Stono made it impossible for the warships to bring any guns to bear, and before they could escape, the *Pawnee* received some forty hits. Though the Confederate guns were too light to seriously damage the warship, they did force the *Pawnee* and the *Marblehead* to drop down river where they joined the *Huron* off Battery Island. As the warships pulled away, General Colquitt's brigade came out of Secessionville and began to move onto Sol Legare Island.[58]

On this morning, three companies of the 54th Massachusetts were on picket duty at Rivers' Causeway, while the rest of the regiment was encamped slightly to the rear. With little warning, Colquitt's men charged over the causeway and crashed into the 54th's outposts. Immediately, Colonel Shaw readied his regiment, while the men of the 10th Connecticut quickly abandoned their camp and equipment and left Grimball's Landing.

The Confederate swept into Shaw's outposts where vicious hand-to-hand fighting took place. Unwilling to retreat, the African Americans fought hard, but were soon pushed aside by the larger Confederate force. Around an abandoned house, one company of the 54th was cut off and overrun by the cavalry that followed Colquitt's infantry. To escape the gauntlet of sabres, some men surrendered, others fought to the death, while a few ran into the marsh, willing to risk drowning over

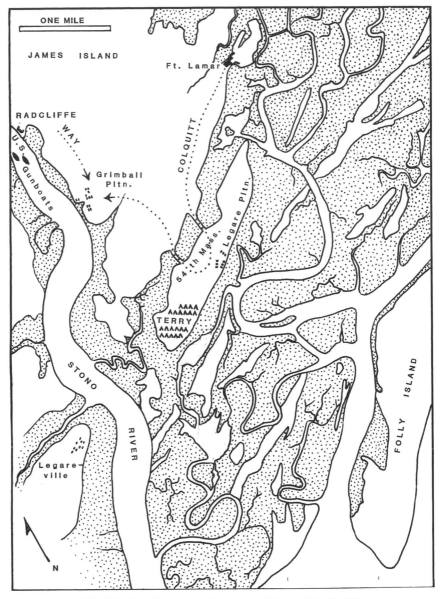

Map 12: Confederate assault on James Island, July 16, 1863

being taken prisoner. In the deep marsh mud, the soldiers stumbled into oyster beds; the sharp shells slashing their bodies.

In the fighting at Rivers' Causeway, the African-American soldiers fiercely resisted the Confederates until overwhelming numbers forced them back, but their sacrifices had not been in vain. While struggling hand-to-hand with the enemy, the men from the 54th had given the 10th Connecticut enough time to pull back onto Battery Island, and by now, Terry's division had been alerted.

As his battered pickets rejoined their regiment, Shaw directed long-range volleys at the advancing Confederates until ordered by General Terry to pull back and join the rest of the division in a new battle line across Battery Island. The Connecticut Battery was rushed to the front, while supporting fire came from the gunboats *Pawnee, Marble-head,* and *Huron* in the Stono, and the transports *Mayflower* and *John Adams*, located in Big Folly Creek.[59]

Braving the Federal guns, the Confederates came on. The Marion Artillery and its four Napoleons dueled with the Connecticut artillery-men, but Colquitt only feigned an assault. Instead of attacking, the Confederates cleanly broke off the engagement and moved across Grimball's Causeway, off Sol Legare Island, and toward Grimball's Landing. To the Northerners, it appeared that their artillery had turned the Confederates, but Colquitt was merely following the prearranged plan and soon linked up with Colonel Way's force near Grimball's Landing, discovering that their quarry had already slipped away.[60]

Initially, it seemed the assault had accomplished little. The Union force on Sol Legare Island was still intact and dangerous; however, the attack had proven the efficiency of the Confederate forces in the Charleston area. By carrying out three separate but coordinated move-ments, Hagood's command had driven off Federal gunboats and car-ried out a dangerous maneuver in the face of massed artillery fire. Although the Union force at Grimball's was not cut off, Hagood did accomplish his mission. The maneuver had drawn Gillmore's attention to James Island, and when reports came in that the Confederates had attacked with nearly ten thousand men, Gillmore decided to withdraw Terry's division.[61]

Before leaving James Island, the 54th reoccupied its lost camp. A number of the men who had been missing were found hiding in the marsh. They reported that the Confederate cavalry had taken many black prisoners. Reports circulated that when officers were present the prisoners received humane treatment, but sometimes, when authority was lacking, the African-American soldiers were bayoneted and shot by Southern infantrymen. Some Union officials suspected that many of the dead African Americans had been mutilated, but on closer examination, it was found to be the work of fiddler crabs. The 54th had taken the brunt of the attack and suffered the heaviest casualties, forty-three of the forty-six Union losses.

The 54th received praise for its work. Officers and privates of other regiments, complimented the 54th's performance. Later in the day, men from the 10th Connecticut made a special trip to the Massachusetts' bivouac to personally thank the African-American soldiers. Especially gratifying to Shaw was a message from General Terry stating that the commanding general was "exceedingly pleased with the conduct of your regiment. They have done all they could do." Even the Confederates complimented the African Americans. After the battle, the *Charleston Courier* commented that the blacks had fought better than the whites, which the newspaper reasoned was because the blacks did not believe that the Confederates would take them prisoner.

The Confederates had taken captives, and Beauregard did not know what to do with them. He wrote the inspector general of the Confederacy, General Samuel Cooper, asking for instructions. While he waited on a reply, the African-American prisoners were placed in the Charleston jail.[62]

Back on James Island, Shaw worried about his missing men, but like Beauregard, the young colonel had other matters on his mind. On the afternoon of the sixteenth, the 54th was pulled off the front line and mail was distributed. At this time, word of the unsuccessful attack on Wagner reached the men. Shaw discussed the attack with his second-in-command, Lieutenant Colonel Edward N. Hallowell, saying that if another attack on Wagner took place, he would volunteer the 54th to lead the assault. At the same time, Shaw also commented that he did not believe that he would survive the regiment's next engagement.[63]

Before the day was over, the Federals began making arrangements to leave James Island. Terry's foresight in repairing the causeway paid off. Only Stevenson's brigade, the artillery, and the wounded were taken off by the transports. The rest were marched at night to Cole's Island in the midst of tremendous thunderstorms. Shaw described the withdrawal in a letter to his wife, writing:

> My regiment started first at 9½ p.m. Not a thing was moved until after dark. . . . It thundered and lightened and rained hard all night and it took us from 10 p.m. to 5 a.m. to come 4 miles. Most of the way we had to march in single file along the narrow paths through the swamps. For nearly ½ mile, we had to pass over a bridge of one, and in some places, two planks wide without a railing and slippery with rain; mud and water below, several feet deep and then over a narrow dike. By the time we got over, it was nearly daylight. . . . I have never had such an extraordinary walk.

Reaching Cole's Island on the morning of July 17, Terry's exhausted men dropped onto the sand and fell asleep, but they were not allowed to rest long. Some regiments were immediately transferred to Folly Island where they marched another six miles to Light-House Inlet before stopping. Others, like the 54th Massachusetts remained exposed on Cole's Island with little food until that evening when they were transferred to a small steamer and taken to Folly Island where preparations were underway to continue the campaign.[64]

Chapter 4

THE GRAND ASSAULT

Led into Wagner like a flock of sheep.
Colonel Haldimand S. Putnam

From Battery Wagner, the Confederates could see the Federals constructing siege batteries. Anticipating an early assault, Beauregard kept his engineers and artillerymen busy. As the Confederate commander summed up the situation to the Confederacy's adjutant and inspector general, Samuel Cooper: "Contest here is now one of engineering. With sufficient time, labor and long range guns, our success is probable, owing to plan of defense adopted. Otherwise, it is doubtful in proportion to the lack of those three elements."[1]

To help defend Morris Island, the Confederates, using steamboats and rowboats operating at night, carefully changed the island's garrison. By July 17, Taliaferro had a new force under his command. The reinforcements were composed of the 31st and 51st North Carolina Infantry regiments, five companies of the Charleston Battalion and Georgia artillery detachments from Companies B and K, 63rd Georgia and Company D, 22nd Georgia Artillery Battalion. Also stationed on Morris Island were twenty-six cavalrymen from the 5th South Carolina Cavalry serving as couriers. In all, the island's garrison numbered more than 1,800 men, with 1,620 stationed within Battery Wagner.

Wagner's armament consisted of eleven cannon and one mortar on the land front, two heavy guns on the seaward side, and two field pieces stationed near the beach. Battery Gregg contained three heavy seacoast guns and two field pieces. With such a force, Taliaferro felt his garrison could give a good account of itself in the coming battle. (See appendix, table 13.)[2]

Unaware of the Confederate preparations, Gillmore's engineers continued their construction of the siege batteries. The works were completed on July 16, and that same day Gillmore met with Dahlgren to work out the plan of attack. The rear admiral readily agreed to add the squadron's guns to the bombardment, but he thought Gillmore "too sanguine." Dahlgren did not like the general's overconfidence and thought Gillmore underestimated Battery Wagner, but Gillmore was sure that after a day's bombardment, an infantry assault could easily overrun the bastion.

By Gillmore's plans, the artillery was to open fire on July 17, and with the navy, keep up a bombardment until sunset when the infantry would rush the battery. Rain, however, forced postponement of the attack until the next day.[3]

Early on the morning of July 18, Federal artillerymen readied their guns. The bombardment was scheduled to start at 9:00 A.M., but early morning squalls moistened the Union batteries' powder, so instead of opening with its total force, the cannonade began slowly and built its intensity. Offshore, the navy, who had kept their powder dry, began the bombardment as five wooden gunboats from long range deliberately aimed their pivot guns against Wagner. In time, as new powder charges were brought forward, the army's batteries joined the barrage.

At 11:30 A.M., Dahlgren, on the monitor *Montauk*, led the monitors *Catskill, Nantucket, Weehawken, Patapsco*, and the ironclad frigate *New Ironsides* to a position twelve hundred yards off Wagner. The ironclads anchored and soon began using their massive Dahlgren and Parrott guns on Wagner's sand walls. As the tide rose, Dahlgren instructed his vessels to move closer. The monitor's smoothbore guns, using round shells that weighed more than three hundred pounds, were fired on a horizontal plane and ricocheted off the water into the battery, while the rifled guns were fired with enough elevation to hit Wagner's sand walls.

Though the monitors fired the largest shells, the most imposing warship was the *New Ironsides*. This vessel, which entered the battle flying the sunken *Keokuk's* pennant, had the ability in a single broadside to launch one thousand pounds of explosive shell against an enemy. Near the *New Ironsides*, Dahlgren kept boatloads of marines to use as a landing party. The rear admiral, however, did not want to commit these men directly to battle, as they numbered only 280 and were commanded by three "very young first lieutenants."[4]

By noon, all of the Federal artillery, on land and sea, was in action.

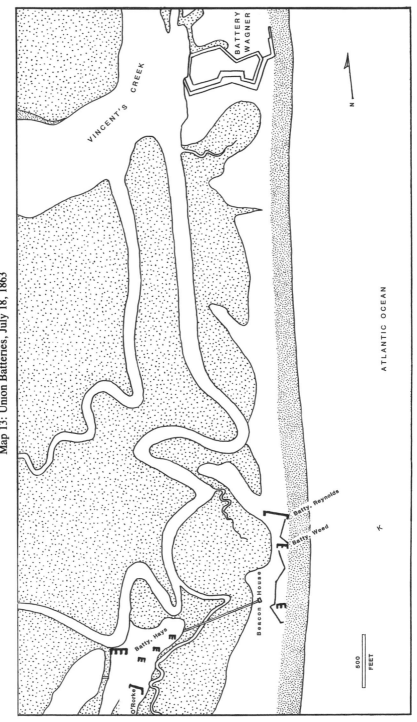

Map 13: Union Batteries, July 18, 1863

VINCENT'S CREEK

BATTERY WAGNER

N

ATLANTIC OCEAN

Batty. Reynolds

Batty. Weed

Beacon House

Batty. Hays

O'Rorke

500
FEET

Projectiles screamed at Wagner at a rate of nearly one every two seconds. Taliaferro estimated that more than nine thousand shells were poured into the battery, creating a deadly crossfire. As Gillmore watched from a sandhill through his lorgnette, huge clouds of sand were blown into the air. Gigantic craters appeared as the Federal guns mutilated Battery Wagner, while dense sulphur clouds engulfed the rapidly firing Union batteries. From the seaward side great jets of water shot upwards from the skipping shells. To the men watching, it seemed that Wagner was being buried in a mass of iron fragments which they believed no one could survive.[5]

Wagner's appearance was one of almost total submission. The bombardment demolished the wooden quarters on the parade ground, driving all except the Charleston Battalion and the gun detachments into the bombproof. Some of the Charleston Battalion found refuge in rice caskets sunk into the sand outside the battery, which provided some safety from the shower of shells. Part of the battalion remained in the work along with the artillerymen, crouched behind the parapet. At first, the artillerymen attempted to return the fire, but the shelling's intensity soon forced them to cover their cannons with sandbags. The only reply against the land batteries came from the garrison's lone mortar, which fired one round every hour.

On the seaward front, the Confederate gun chambers were better protected. Here, the artillerymen dueled with the ironclads using a 32-pounder and a 10-inch Columbiad. The 32-pounder could only dent the enemy's iron plates, but the Columbiad's heavy shot could cause some damage. For a time, the Confederates kept up the uneven duel until the tide rose, then the monitors moved to within three hundred yards from Wagner, where their fire dismounted the Columbiad.[6]

With their main seaward weapon knocked out of the fight, the artillerymen found refuge inside Wagner's bombproof, while gun crews from other Confederate works tried to counter the bombardment. Cannon from Fort Sumter, Battery Gregg, and batteries on James Island, firing at extreme range and with limited ammunition, tried to disrupt the bombardment, but little was accomplished. The only damage was done by the batteries on James Island, which managed to place some shots near a Union battery whose men were showing off while wearing dress uniforms as they worked their guns. Their joke, however, soon backfired when Confederate shells struck the marsh surrounding the work, splattering the men with mud.[7]

While the Northern gunners believed their shells were ripping Battery Wagner apart, in actuality little damage was done to the battery or its garrison. The sand fort was able to absorb the punishment and protect its garrison. There were few casualties inside Wagner. Only eight men were killed, most by concussion, and twenty wounded. Among those knocked unconscious was Captain Hansford D. D. Twiggs, who was now back on staff duty after the raid against the enemy sharpshooters. Taken to the bombproof, Twiggs was soon revived by some strong, hundred proof "medicine."

Though most escaped injury, the threat of death was constant. The men outside the bombproof were always in danger. A near miss buried Taliaferro up to his knees in sand while others were constantly dodging shells and fragments. One soldier described the scene as being the "grandest and most fearful storms ever rained upon a battery on this continent. The air was filled with a bursting storm of iron, whose solid masses and fragments buried themselves in nearly every foot of the devoted fort."

To give a steadying example, Major David Ramsay of the Charleston Battalion sat in a chair behind the parapet calmly reading a newspaper. Ramsay seemed oblivious to the passing shells. When necessary, he would help carry wounded into the bombproof, but always he returned to his seat and his reading.[8]

During the height of the bombardment, Wagner's flag was shot away. The Union soldiers, thinking the battery had surrendered, ceased fire and began to cheer, but when the smoke cleared, Engineer Captain Robert Barnwell was seen standing on the rampart defiantly holding a battle flag. Immediately, the Federal guns resumed firing, but by this time Major Ramsay, with Sergeant William Shelton, a Provost Flinn of the Charleston Battalion, and Lieutenant William E. Readick of the 63rd Georgia, had replaced the garrison flag. Taliaferro would later compare these men to the Revolutionary War hero Sergeant William Jasper, who reset the flag of Fort Sullivan during a British attack against Charleston.[9]

In the afternoon, Colonel Harris, the department's chief engineer, came from Charleston in a small boat and ran the gauntlet of shells from Cummings Point to Battery Wagner. Once at the battery, Harris immediately began assisting the defenders. His expertise was badly needed. The Union shells were filling in passageways and gun chambers. Though the Confederates tried to keep the battery serviceable, the work was exhausting. At 3:40 P.M., Taliaferro signaled General Ripley in Charleston to "Please relieve me & staff broken down." But no relief could be sent. Later in the afternoon enemy fire began tearing apart the sand and timber roof over the main magazine. Taliaferro feared his position would soon be "blown into the marsh," but night

came and the bombardment ended before the magazine was pene-
trated.[10]

Shortly after sunset the firing stopped. Gillmore, confident that his
artillery had reduced Battery Wagner, quickly sent a message to
Dahlgren indicating that he was preparing to send in the infantry.
Dahlgren pulled his vessels back and waited. His ships had fired more
than nineteen hundred shells into Wagner. With night falling and the
Federal assaulting column massing on the beach, Dahlgren ordered his
vessels to cease firing to avoid hitting any soldiers. For the rest of the
night, the sailors remained silent witnesses to the growing drama being
played out onshore.[11]

Unknown to the Northern leaders, the Confederates, using the code
book taken from the *Keokuk*, had broken the Union code and had been
reading the Federal messages since the start of the campaign. At 4:45
P.M., the Confederate signalmen intercepted the following message
from Gillmore to Seymour: "Keep your infantry under arms; the men
must remain in line. The island is full of stragglers. Send a staff officer
to brigade commanders. How large is your supporting column?"

This order, coupled with the earlier message to Dahlgren, warned
the Confederates of the coming attack. Word was rushed to Beauregard
in Charleston, who immediately ordered General Hagood and the 32nd
Georgia from James Island to Morris Island.

Taliaferro, at his post in Battery Wagner, did not need any forewarning; he reasoned that the bombardment had been in preparation for an
assault. With it done, he expected an immediate attack. The men in
the bombproof, who had suffered through eight hours of confinement
in stifling quarters without any food or water, were given a blessing by
a Catholic priest, then they hurried to their assigned positions.

The artillerymen dug their guns out of the sand and double-shotted
them with grape and canister. The squadron of couriers found places
along the wall with the infantrymen, and the two companies of the 31st
North Carolina at Battery Gregg were rushed to Wagner.[12]

Taliaferro positioned his men carefully. Three companies of the
Charleston Battalion were stationed from the sallyport on Vincent's
Creek to the center of the work. The center was held by the 51st North
Carolina; a portion of the 31st North Carolina was assigned to the
seaward salient, and two companies of the Charleston Battalion
manned the seaward wall. At the main sally port Taliaferro planned to
station the two companies of the 31st North Carolina as soon as they
arrived from Battery Gregg. The remainder of the 31st North Carolina
was placed on Wagner's interior where it could serve as a reserve
force. Manning the battery's guns were artillerymen from Companies

H and I, 1st South Carolina; Company A, 1st South Carolina Artillery; and Companies B and K, 63 Georgia, plus a small detachment from D Company, 22nd Georgia Battalion. Outside the fort, on the beach, stood a detachment of artillery from Company A, 1st South Carolina Artillery, under Captain William L. De Pass and Lieutenant T. Davis Waties with two 12-pound howitzers.

All the units took their positions except the 31st North Carolina. The majority of the 31st refused to leave the bombproof, and their officers could not persuade them otherwise. Only a part of this regiment was in position when the attack came.[13]

To the south, the Federals were making their final preparations. Near evening of the eighteenth, the 54th Massachusetts was transferred, along with Stevenson's brigade, from Folly to Morris Island. Once ashore, Shaw and the regiment's adjutant, Lieutenant Garth Wilkinson James, reported to General Strong. At headquarters, Strong informed

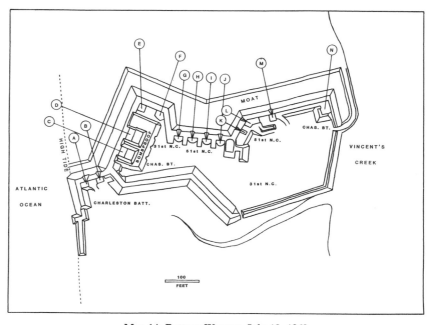

Map 14: Battery Wagner, July 18, 1863

A: 12-pounder Howitzer	H: 32-pounder Howitzer
B: 12-pounder Howitzer	I: 32-pounder Howitzer
C: 10-inch Columbiad	J: 8-inch Shell Gun
D: 32-pounder	K: 32-pounder Carronade
E: 8-inch Seacoast Howitzer	L: 32-pounder Carronade
F: 42-pounder Carronade	M: 32-pounder Carronade
G: 8-inch Shell Gun	N: 10-inch Seacoast Mortar

Shaw of the coming attack. Remembering Shaw's letter requesting that the regiment be assigned to his brigade and knowing the young colonel's desire to place his regiment alongside white troops in a position for glory, Strong offered Shaw the honor of leading the assault. Both men knew the 54th had been without food or rest, but this did not stop Strong from offering or Shaw from accepting the lead position. Shaw ordered Lieutenant James to bring the regiment from its present position with Stevenson's brigade to the head of Strong's column, while Shaw had supper with General Strong and Edward L. Pierce, a reporter for the *Boston Tribune* and former missionary to the freedmen in the Port Royal area.[14]

Though Strong had offered the spearhead to Shaw, the 54th had been chosen to lead the assault in an earlier meeting between Seymour and Strong. The fact that the regiment was tired and hungry held little consequence. All of the Union regiments in the campaign had been active up to this point.

The decision to put the 54th in the lead was not made lightly. The use of African-American soldiers was fraught with danger. If a commander refused to use them as front line troops, he would be attacked by abolitionists and politicians who favored their use. On the other hand, if a commander used them too aggressively and they suffered heavily in battle, then the officer would be accused of using them as cannon fodder, or worse yet, as a shield for white troops. For career-minded officers, black troops were a two-edged sword.

Shaw's regiment presented Gillmore and Seymour with a difficult problem. The officers knew the government expected them to give the unit a major role in the campaign, but on the other hand they did not want to appear to use the regiment callously. Undoubtedly, Shaw's friendship with Strong and his written request to have his regiment reassigned to Strong's command played an important role in placing the 54th at the head of the column, but also, the Federal commanders truly believed that their bombardment had devastated Wagner, and nearly all expected an easy victory. By placing Shaw and his men in front, they were giving the regiment the opportunity to achieve its destiny with a minimum loss of life.

Such logic could help explain a report that came out seven months after the battle, during the testimony of Nathaniel Paige, a special correspondent of the *New York Tribune*, before the American Freedmen's Inquiry Commission in February 1864 at New Orleans. Paige, who claimed to have overheard a conversation between Gillmore and Seymour an hour before the attack was launched, stated that Seymour and Gillmore ridiculed the African-American soldiers and decided to put them in the lead in order to "dispose" of them. Paige quotes Seymour as saying: "Well I guess we will let Strong lead and put those damned niggers from Massachusetts in the advance; we may as well get rid of them one time as another. But I would give more for my old company of regulars than for the whole damned crowd of volunteers."

Paige's testimony implied that Seymour wanted to use the 54th Massachusetts as a shield for the following white troops, with the intent of killing off the African-American soldiers. He also called Seymour a racist and a coward. Paige's story, however, does not hold up. Seymour was not a coward, and though he was a devoted "McClellan man" and shared some of the former Northern commander's political views, he had also spoken to freedmen at Port Royal during camp meetings where he promised to fight for them and their children. By the time Paige reportedly saw the two officers, the attack had already been worked out with General Strong. The decision to lead with the 54th Massachusetts was made by Seymour and Strong, not by Seymour and Gillmore. If anything, Seymour and Gillmore saw the assault as an opportunity to politically dispose of the African Americans by allowing them to spearhead Strong's assault. As Seymour wrote four months after the attack and three months before Paige's testimony: "It was believed that the Fifty-fourth was in every respect as efficient as any body of men; it was one of the strongest and best officered, there seemed to be no good reason why it should not be selected for this advance. This point was decided by General Strong and myself."[15]

Gillmore was confident of success no matter what regiment was in the lead. He told Seymour that only Strong's brigade would be needed but agreed to have the full division drawn up. Gillmore had faith in the power of his guns, but this was not Fort Pulaski. Wagner did not have brick walls that could be smashed and sent flying about the work's interior. The pounding taken by Wagner would have destroyed masonry redoubts, but it only disfigured the battery's earthen wall and interior. The garrison had been untouched, the landward artillery was undamaged, and the crews uninjured. One regiment had been shell-shocked, but this did not detract from the earthwork's defense. Designed to cover itself, Wagner, even without the 31st North Carolina, remained formidable.

Gillmore and many of his officers believed that "the fort was reduced and helpless, and its garrison's spirit broken." Gillmore expected an easy victory. Seymour and Strong anticipated some resistance, but none that could not be quickly overcome. Colonel Haldimand S. Putnam, commander of the second brigade, did not agree. Putnam, a

West Point graduate and a former engineer, thought the Union soldiers were going into Wagner "like a flock of sheep," but his opinion was overruled. Before the attack, Putnam commented bitterly that "Seymour is a devil of a fellow for dash."[16]

At dusk Gillmore ordered Seymour to ready his division. Word was passed to General Strong, who with Shaw rode together toward the front. Before rejoining his regiment, Shaw took leave of the general and hurried back to brigade headquarters where he left certain letters and papers for his family with Mr. Pierce should anything happen to him. He then overtook his regiment and with Lieutenant Colonel Hallowell, moved the 54th Massachusetts from its position west of the batteries toward the beach. Behind them came the rest of Strong's command, followed by Putnam's and Stevenson's brigades. As Putnam's brigade passed the batteries, the bombardment ceased.

The 54th Massachusetts was the strongest regiment in the Union force. The other regiments had large sick roles, reducing their effective forces by nearly thirty percent, or 90 to 150 men. In the first brigade only the 54th, with its 650 men, was large enough to be drawn up in two lines two men deep, with one wing of five companies or one battalion in front followed by a second wing of five companies in the rear. The following regiments formed in either a column of companies or in line by regiment.[17]

For the attack, Shaw instructed his second in command, Lieutenant Colonel Hallowell, to take the state flag and direct the second battalion while Shaw positioned himself in the center of the lead battalion with the national standard. Rifles were loaded, but they were not capped. The assault was to be a simple bayonet rush. No plans of the battery had been given to officers, nor were they supplied with any tools to cut away obstructions. There were no artillerymen to assist in working any captured artillery and no engineers to lead the way. The bayonet was all.[18]

The men of the 54th were uncharacteristically quiet as they waited on the beach. The soldiers were ordered to lay down until the time came to attack. During this period, Shaw smoked cigars and paced in front of the regiment while other officers talked in hush voices. During the respite, the regiment's adjutant, Lieutenant Garth Wilkinson James, known as "Wilkie," approached the commander of A Company, Captain John Appleton. Commenting on the significance of the coming charge, Lieutenant James said to Appleton: "We have the most magnificent chance to prove the valor of the colored race now," and as he spoke he accidently discharged his revolver into the sand which immediately brought a look of disapproval from Colonel Shaw. Chagrined, James added: "I would not have had that happen for anything."

As the officers and men gazed at Wagner, the monitors could be seen pulling out to sea. In the east, a sea fog began to rise, which contrasted the bright sunset in the western sky. Occasional couriers rode along the beach, carrying orders to the nearly sixty-four hundred men behind the 54th. Confederate batteries continually shelled the massing Union soldiers. Their shots would bound and roll along the ground for hundreds of yards. When one entered the Union ranks, the soldiers would move aside, allowing the shot to continue on.[19]

The lull was finally broken when General Strong appeared in their front mounted on a large grey horse. The men remained on the ground while the fully uniformed general addressed his troops. In a short, quick talk, Strong told the African-American soldiers that he too was a Massachusetts man and knew that they would uphold the state's honor. He then asked if there was anyone who thought they would be unable to sleep in the fort that night. A chorus of noes answered his question. He then called the color-bearer forward. This day the flag was carried by Sergeant John Wall, a former student from Oberlin, Ohio. Strong asked who would pick up the flag if the color-sergeant fell. Many shouted out yes and then Shaw, who stood nearby, removed his cigar and said "I will," to which the regiment responded with cheers. Finally, Strong ordered the men to keep their files and ranks and as one veteran recalled, to go in and "bayonet every mother's son of them."[20]

Finishing his encouragement, Strong left to join the rest of his brigade. Colonel Shaw moved along the front of his regiment. The advance was to start at 7:45 P.M. He had been through bloody fighting before. At Antietam, Shaw's life was saved when a bullet struck his watch. This night he wore the rank insignia of colonel and carried papers of identification. Shaw had always been reserved with his men, but not tonight. The regiment was chosen to lead the assault on a city that rivaled Richmond as a symbol of the South. The nation would be watching his regiment. The young colonel addressed his soldiers: "Now I want you to prove yourselves men." Shaw walked to the front and center of the 54th and called it to attention. He gave his final orders: "Move in quick time until within a hundred yards of the fort; then double quick and charge," he paused, "Forward."[21]

The men moved in the darkness under fire from the distant Confederate works. Wagner remained silent. With five companies in front and five in the rear, the men tripped through shell craters and over the abandoned Confederate rifle pits on their way toward Wagner. Soon they reached the defile, where the marsh cut across the island toward the ocean. Attempting to retain their formation while going through this narrow corridor, men on the ocean side were forced to wade knee deep in the water while others had to wait until their comrades had passed through before moving on. Coming through the defile, the regiment shifted back to the left, and now, with only a hundred yards to go, the order was given to charge.

Immediately, Taliaferro ordered his men to fire. An observer watching from a signal tower on Folly Island saw the work become a continuous streak of fire. Canister and musket balls tore through the Union ranks. Great numbers of the regiment were lost between the defile and the moat. The noise and flashes from the Confederate guns were so heavy one officer thought a thunder and lightning storm had swept onto the battlefield. Volleys from Wagner cut into the attackers with such intensity that one bullet struck the sword of Lieutenant Richard H. L. Jewett driving it back into his head. The Confederate howitzers outside the fort, one commanded by Lieutenant Waties and the other by Captain De Pass, cut huge gaps into the attacking formation. The effect of the Confederate fire was devastating. Both Lieutenant Colonel Hallowell and Lieutenant Wilkie James were wounded and the color-bearer, Sergeant Wall, fell into a shell crater. Unable to go on, Wall called for someone to take the national colors, and they were soon gathered up by Sergeant William C. Carney.

For a moment, the Confederate fire stalled the 54th, but then, led by Shaw, the remaining soldiers charged into the moat and through the one foot of water. Part of the regiment veered off to the right toward Wagner's seaward salient, but the majority followed Shaw against the battery's center. As they moved up the slope more men were lost, including Sergeant Major Lewis Douglass who went down with a painful wound. Casualties were so thick that bodies in the moat resembled stepping stones. But still they came on. Captain Appleton recalled that as they reached the crest of the parapet he looked back and saw a "sea of bayonets" surging up the slope and into the battery.

Among the first to reach the crest was Colonel Shaw who called out: "Onward boys! Onward boys!" Those remaining followed, some jumping down into the gun chambers where they came to grips with the Confederates who came out almost eagerly to meet the invaders. In the darkness flashed bayonets, handspikes, and swords. Infantrymen clubbed at each other with their rifles, while the artillerymen swung their heavy rammers. For a brief moment, Shaw remained on the parapet swinging his sword calling to his men, then, as bullets ripped into his body, he collapsed forward onto the parapet.[22]

Even with their commander dead, the black soldiers continued to fight on, but silhouetted on the parapet, they suffered heavily. Sergeant Carney, carrying the national colors, climbed the wall and joined the men still struggling to enter the fort, but with them, he was soon forced back onto the embankment where he planted the colors and though wounded, kept up the fight.

To this point the 54th had used only their bayonets. Now, forced back into the ditch, the remaining officers opened with their revolvers and the men capped their muskets. The soldiers clung to the exterior slope, seeking vantage points from which to fire on the Confederates. Seemingly outraged by the presence of the African Americans, the Southerners fought furiously; some, following the example of Wagner's artillery commander, Lieutenant Colonel John C. Simkins, leaped onto the rampart. The Confederates seized the 54th's state colors, but were unable to take the national flag.

The fighting was fierce. More and more Confederates came forward, grappling with the African-American soldiers. Fierce individual fights took place as battlers dueled all along the parapet. For a brief while, all the pent-up anxieties, hatreds, and emotions of more than two hundred years of racism exploded on Wagner's walls. Lieutenant Colonel Simkins was cut down, but other Southern officers replaced him, recklessly leading their men.[23]

The 54th fought on, but the regiment was being decimated. The remaining officers armed themselves with muskets and joined in the savage fighting alongside their soldiers. Command soon fell to Captain Luis Emilio who realized the seriousness of the situation. Without help the regiment could not hold its position. Emilio looked out in the darkness for the following regiments, but they were not in sight. To retreat would mean running through the gauntlet of Wagner's fire, but without support the regiment would be sacrificed. Emilio held as long as he thought possible, but when De Pass's artillery moved forward from the beach and began to sweep the 54th's position with canister, Emilio decided to salvage what he could and ordered his men to retreat.[24]

Most of the soldiers obeyed and broke from the slope, but others chose to remain rather than risk the return. A few, led by Captain Appleton, worked their way along the embankment and joined the fight in the seaward salient, but most followed Emilio across the moat and back to the Northern lines. The fugitives ran into elements of Union forces formed down the beach, causing more confusion and disorganization. Once out of Wagner's range, Emilio gathered all the men he could find and formed a line in some rifle pits. Here, the fragments of the regiment waited in case they should be needed again. One of the last men to reach the new position was Sergeant Carney, who had crawled away from Wagner. Although wounded four times, he still retained the national flag. For his actions, Carney would become the first African American to receive the Medal of Honor.[25]

Emilio thought the 54th had hit Wagner unsupported; but in the dark and confusion of battle, he had not seen that the following regiments, the 6th Connecticut and the 48th New York, had attacked the battery.

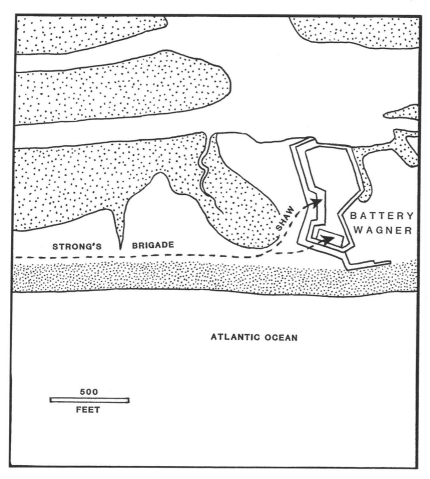

Map 15: Assault on Battery Wagner by Strong's Brigade. The 54th Massachusetts hit in the center of Battery Wagner while the 6th Connecticut and the 48th New York struck Wagner's seaward salient. The 3rd New Hampshire, the 9th Maine and the 76th Pennsylvania attacked the battery's center after the first three regiments had been repulsed.

The first regiment behind the 54th Massachusetts was the 6th Connecticut. Veterans of the July 10 small boat landing, the regiment had been the original choice to lead the assault until the position was given to Shaw's regiment. Unlike the 54th, the Connecticut regiment formed in column by companies. Into the growing darkness, led by Colonel Chatfield, the 6th followed the Massachusetts soldiers and then, as Wagner opened, charged forward. Battling through a hail of musketry and artillery fire, Chatfield directed his men to the right of the 54th at the point in Wagner's wall where the salient met the land face.

Like the lead regiment, the 6th Connecticut swept down into the moat and up onto the parapet. Here, where only a portion of the 31st North Carolina had taken its position, the Connecticut soldiers leaped down into the battery and moved among the passageways near the main bombproof. In the darkness, they grappled with the Confederate defenders. The regiment's color-bearer was killed, and those who attempted to pick up the national flag were also struck down, their bodies falling on the standard. To save the colors, Captain Frederick B. Osborn pulled the flag from under the bodies of his fallen comrades.

Though inside the battery, the men from the 6th Connecticut were unable to exploit their advantage. Colonel Chatfield went down with a mortal wound, and soon the regiment lost its momentum. Like the 54th, it was driven back to Wagner's exterior slope and eventually forced to retreat across the bodies of their own dead and wounded.[26]

While the men from Massachusetts and Connecticut were struggling against Wagner's garrison, the 48th New York came forward and joined the battle. Like the 54th Massachusetts, the men of the 48th were also on a personal crusade. Raised by an ex-clergyman, the Reverend James H. Perry, who tried to recruit only men of piety for his command, the 48th was nicknamed "Perry's Saints." Their mission was to carry on a holy war against the Confederacy, and now at Wagner, the "Saints" were meeting their greatest test.

The 48th drove directly into Wagner's seaward salient with five hundred men and sixteen officers. Though weakened by the previous assaults, the Confederates met the New Yorkers with extreme determination. One Northern officer felt that the presence of the black soldiers had caused the enemy's "self defense to be converted into brutal ferocity." Charging up the wall of the salient, the Federals were met by Wagner's fearsome sea coast howitzer, an iron artillery piece whose eight inch mouth spewed forth destruction with every blast. Courage and Christian piety were not enough for the 48th to enter Wagner. By the time the regiment retreated one half its men and fourteen of its sixteen officers were lost.[27]

While the men from the first three regiments were fighting and dying, the final three regiments from Strong's brigade were mysteriously held back. Though no explanation has ever come to light, for some reason Strong and Seymour did not commit the first brigade all at the same time. It is possible the commanders thought that only three regiments were needed to overrun Wagner, or they did not want to congest the narrow and darkened battlefield until the lead units had reached their objective. Whatever the reason, Strong's final regiments did not advance until Federal soldiers were seen fighting on the battery's walls.

Led forward by General Strong and accompanied part of the way by General Seymour, the 3rd New Hampshire, the 9th Maine, and the 76th Pennsylvania moved out into darkness toward the flashing guns. As they neared Wagner, Seymour realized that the lead regiments had entered the battery. Strong and his men were sent on, while Seymour sent a courier to Colonel Putnam ordering him to bring his brigade forward. As Strong's final regiments made their charge, Seymour's aide returned, reporting that Putnam, acting under orders from General Gillmore, refused to advance. Confused, Seymour sent his aide back to repeat the order, but by now the Federals had been forced out of Wagner, and the advantage was lost.[28]

While Seymour was repeating his command for Putnam's brigade to advance, the 3rd New Hampshire led the remaining regiments of the first brigade toward Wagner. Its commander, Colonel John H. Jackson, a veteran of the Mexican War, brought his men forward with his usual command of "Come." When the regiment reached the defile, Colonel Jackson found the area choked with retreating men. He halted the regiment and sent Lieutenant Colonel John Bedel ahead to determine if an advance could be made across the marsh. In the darkness, Bedel became confused and joined some men rushing Wagner, where he was captured.

When Bedel did not return, Colonel Jackson moved his regiment through the defile, and soon the men from New Hampshire came under a rain of shot, canister, grape, and shell. One survivor reported that the "guns and bayonets seemed to suffer (if indeed they could suffer), and many parts of the muskets were shot away and the bearer left unharmed."

The enemy's well-directed fire tore severe gaps into the ranks of the 3rd New Hampshire and the following 9th Maine and 76th Pennsylvania. The crowded defile also broke up the regiments' formations causing them to charge Wagner in small units, thus severely reducing their hitting power. Colonel Jackson was struck down by a shell fragment, but a now dismounted General Strong led the brigade's survivors on to Wagner, where they attempted to rush over the battery's walls in the same area where the 54th Massachusetts had struck. For a brief period, the Federals struggled up the battery's slope only to be sent tumbling back into the moat. Strong soon realized the hopelessness of the situation and decided to retreat. To give the order, Strong stood on the embankment, and while doing so received a mortal wound from a grape shot in his thigh.[29]

As the remnants of Strong's brigade streamed back to the Federal lines, fifteen to twenty minutes of comparative calm drifted over the battlefield. Throughout the initial assault, the second brigade commander, Colonel Putnam, had kept his men lying down. When Seymour's first order reached him to advance, Putnam refused, citing a directive from General Gillmore, but no such order has ever been found. Putnam had been against the attack from the start, and it is possible that an overconfident Gillmore had told the commander that his men would not be needed, and Putnam interpreted this as an order. However, when Seymour's second command reached him, Putnam readied his brigade.

Putnam ordered his men up from the sand. The regiments, the 7th New Hampshire, 100th New York, 62nd Ohio, and 67th Ohio, were already formed by battalions into a giant column. On horseback, Putnam rode to the head of his formation and gave the order to advance. While moving toward Wagner the brigade halted twice; once to allow the survivors of the 54th Massachusetts to move through its ranks and again to let the rest of Strong's brigade to pass to the rear.

Accompanying the second brigade was General Seymour. The division commander realized the early advantage had been lost when he had been unable to provide reinforcements to his lead units once they entered the battery. Now as the second advance began, he ordered Stevenson's brigade, his third and final brigade, to follow Putnam's men. Seymour wanted to be sure that this time there would be enough support and manpower should his troops gain a foothold inside Wagner.

Putnam led his brigade against Wagner's seaward salient. Again the Confederate artillery responded with a storm of shot that filled "the air like the drops of a summer shower." One soldier believed that the Confederate shells were bigger than hogsheads. A member of the 100th New York recalled that "the grape and canister from the enemies guns dealt death and destruction in our ranks" and that all around men were "falling, screaming with pain and crying to God to forgive their sins." All of the regiments took severe casualties and the 67th Ohio lost seven of eight color-bearers during the rush. Colonel Putnam had his horse killed, and a shell burst wounded General Seymour. As Seymour was carried from the field, he repeated the call for Stevenson to come forward, but unknown to Seymour, General Gillmore had ordered the third brigade not to move.[30]

Spearheaded by the 7th New Hampshire, Putnam's men drove toward Wagner's left. Like a great wave, the second brigade overlapped both sides of the seaward salient. Confederate fire broke the portion of the Federal column that hit the salient's southwest angle, but those on the right continued on into the earthwork where the Confederates, thinned by the previous attacks, were unable to stop the Union troops. Charging over Wagner's wall, the brigade's survivors seized the salient, while elements of the 67th Ohio captured two seaward gun chambers. Joined by black and white survivors from the first brigade who had remained on Wagner's exterior slopes, the Northerners tried to push on, but soon found themselves in a cul-de-sac.

By a fluke in its design, Wagner's southeast salient formed a fort within the battery. The roof of the main bombproof, which bisected the salient's neck, was six feet higher than the parapet. The rise afforded protection for the Federal soldiers, but also deterred any advance. The Union soldiers, exhausted and unnerved by their rush into Wagner, took advantage of the position to escape enemy fire, but in so doing, all momentum and organization was lost.

In vain, officers tried to rally their men, but their orders, pleas, and threats were often lost among the cries of wounded and the noise of battle. Confusion reigned throughout the area. No two men of one regiment stood together, and no officer could find a command. Colonel Putnam, delayed but not hurt when his horse was killed, entered the area and tried to organize his command before the Confederates had time to counterattack.

General Taliaferro was well aware of the threat posed by the Federals. Not knowing how disoriented his enemies were, Taliaferro feared that the Northerners would soon fashion their own fort inside Wagner. The Confederate commander immediately ordered his men to form a line across the neck of the salient and called for someone to explore the enemy's position. Lieutenant James Campbell of the Charleston Battalion volunteered. Campbell climbed onto the parapet and, seeing the confusion below him, ordered the Northerners to surrender. Instead, two Federals lunged at Campbell with bayonets but missed their target, then Campbell found himself being grabbed around the leg and pulled down into the salient.

When Campbell did not return, Taliaferro called for volunteers to

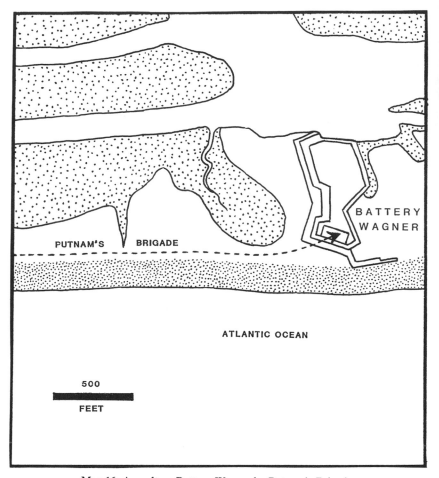

Map 16: Assault on Battery Wagner by Putnam's Brigade

rush the Federals. Men of the Charleston Battalion and the 51st North Carolina came forward. Led by Major Ramsey, the counterattack was stopped not by Putnam's men but by the fire of the 31st North Carolina, which was finally emerging from the bombproof. Confused and with no knowledge of the situation, the North Carolinians unleased a volley into their own men, mortally wounding Ramsey and stopping the counterattack.

While Taliaferro again tried to organize a strike against the Federals, the Confederates moved artillery into position to sweep the salient. Captain DePass and his two howitzers from outside the battery were placed to fire from the seaward side while Colonel Harris completed the crossfire by positioning another piece inside the fort. The men working DePass's howitzers were no longer the original crews. Nearly every man of the first detachment had been killed or wounded, so during the battle, DePass had to rush forward a new detachment from Battery Gregg.

The artillery raked the Federals, and Putnam, who had determined that he would either hold or die in the salient, tried to send some men against the field pieces. Three officers and some men responded, but their way was blocked by a crowd of soldiers, some wounded, others paralyzed by fear. Before a path could be made, a discharge of cannon fire killed two of the officers and a number of the soldiers and forced the survivors to seek cover.

With his artillery doing effective work, Taliaferro ordered Captain William H. Ryan of the Charleston Battalion to lead another rush against the Federals. With men from his command and the 31st North Carolina, Ryan charged the Federal position. Resistance was weak, but in the darkness, it was sufficient. Captain Ryan was killed and his men forced back. Refusing to stop, Taliaferro brought more men forward and ordered them to keep up a constant fire on the Union soldiers.

Unknown to the Confederates, their artillery and musketry were causing chaos within the salient. The number of wounded and dead was constantly increasing. Putnam, with help from Colonel Dandy of the 100th New York and other officers, attempted to lead an attack over the bombproof, but few men responded. While trying to urge his men to follow, Putnam was killed and Dandy wounded. By now every regimental commander was killed or wounded, and command fell to Major Lewis Butler of the 67th Ohio. With only 350 men and two other officers left uninjured and no reinforcements in sight, Butler realized he could not hold. The regimental colors were sent out first, then Butler directed a final volley over the bombproof before leading the survivors out of Wagner.

Not all of the Federal soldiers followed Butler. Fearing the deadly belt of fire outside the battery more than prison camp, a number of unwounded men remained behind. Those who stayed were soon captured when General Hagood and the 32nd Georgia arrived at Wagner. Two companies from the reinforcements were immediately sent along the rampart, sealing off the escape route and capturing the remaining Northerners.[31]

The recapture of the salient ended Taliaferro's greatest fear. If Northern reinforcements had reached Putnam's men and solidified the position, Wagner would have been untenable. However, the third

Union brigade, Stevenson's, which could have exploited the break-through, never entered the battle. Though twice ordered forward by General Seymour, it had been held back by Gillmore's command until the commanding general learned the results of Putnam's attack. When word reached Gillmore that elements of the second brigade had taken a portion of the battery, he allowed Stevenson to advance, but quickly countermanded the order when Gillmore learned of Putnam's death. The third brigade was the last organized force on Morris Island besides the artillerymen. If this brigade was broken, there was nothing to resist a counterattack. Gillmore, not wishing an even greater disaster, re-fused to commit Stevenson's men.

On the battlefield Stevenson found Captain Emilio and the remnants of the 54th Massachusetts. The African-American soldiers were the only Federal regiment to reform after being repulsed. Emilio and his soldiers wanted to join the third brigade in another attempt on Wagner, but with the advance called off, Stevenson praised Emilio and his men for their spirit and then ordered them to the rear.

Though denied a chance to attack Wagner, Stevenson's soldiers began carrying out dangerous but vital work. A defense line was drawn up to protect the Union batteries from any counterattack, and search parties were organized to look for wounded still lying on the battlefield. Stevenson, well aware of the Confederate regulations that considered black troops and their officers criminals, ordered his men to be especially alert in searching for wounded survivors from the 54th Massachusetts. Stevenson also sent forward three companies of the 97th Pennsylvania to reconnoiter Wagner to see if any Federals were still holding out in or near the work. These men returned shortly, reporting that the Confederates were in full possession of the battery.[32]

By 1:00 A.M. on July 19 the battle had ceased. Though the firing had stopped, the tragedies of the night were far from finished. The broken Union troops streaming to the rear found drunken artillerymen barring the way. The artillerymen had been ordered to check any straggling. This they tried to accomplish with liberal use of their pistols and swords. It was reported that: "A colored man was sure to be cut down and a white man, unless wounded, was not suffered to pass unmo-lested." Toward the end of the battle, as the flow of men increased, the disillusioned artillerymen were carried away along with the mob. When the last Union soldier had surrendered in Wagner, Confederate soldiers slipped over the walls and stripped the Union dead of valua-bles. Nature also added to the horrors: the tide came in, drowning many of the wounded who lay on the beach.[33]

Throughout the night, men from Stevenson's brigade found themselves not only searching for wounded but also policing the ambulance drivers, who in their haste ran over and killed their fellow soldiers. Once loaded, they returned to their lines on the run, injuring the men inside. Officers on the scene soon issued orders placing guards on every ambulance with instructions to shoot the driver if he went faster than a walk. The order was later approved by General Stevenson, who had his soldiers work all night retrieving the wounded, with some intrepid men crawling as far as Wagner's moat to look for fallen comrades.[34]

One ambulance on which guards were not placed was operated by Clara Barton. She had been on Morris Island since the fourteenth and had established a camp on the southern end of the island, about a mile north of the lighthouse. All through the terrible night of the eighteenth and all the next day, she worked at comforting the wounded. Among her patients were many of the officers that she had so gaily rode with on Hilton Head a few weeks before. With the doctors, Clara Barton forwarded the wounded to a field hospital near Light-House Inlet where, because the Federals feared an enemy counterattack, they were immediately placed on small steamers and sent to Stono Inlet where they were transferred to the hospital ship *Cosmopolitan* and taken to hospitals at Hilton Head and Beaufort.[35]

Throughout the night, the Confederates remained at their posts, not interfering with Union details gathering the wounded. Once it was known that the Federal assault had been turned back, General Ripley, who had been at Fort Sumter since July 11, called Taliaferro to Sumter to report on the night's action. Taliaferro turned command over to General Hagood and then proceeded to meet with his district commander.

Unknown to Ripley and Taliaferro, Beauregard had issued instructions to send the 20th and 21st South Carolina regiments to Morris Island for a predawn counterattack. Fortunately for both sides, transportation was not available, and the plans were scrapped. The inability of the Confederates to transfer the regiments kept a night of death and misery from becoming worse.[36]

Morning revealed what Wagner's concentrated fire had done:

"blood, mud, water, brains and human hair melted together; men lying in every possible attitude, with every conceivable expression on their countenances; their limbs bent into unnatural shapes by the fall of twenty or more feet; the fingers rigid and outstretched, as if they had clutched at the earth to save themselves; pale beseeching faces, looking out from among the ghastly corpses with moans and cries for help and water, and dying gasps and death struggles."[37]

The bodies were three deep in the salient. Putnam was found to have fallen on his back, hiding the ghastly wound in the back of his head. The features on his face were calm as his eyes stared at the cloudless sky. All along Wagner's front, the bodies of the dead had been so covered by burnt powder that it was difficult to tell black soldiers from white. Shaw, his body reportedly pierced by seven bullets, was thought to be a mere boy lying on the parapet among his men. Colonel Harris called the scene "pitiless" and was especially moved by the conditions of the dead and dying black soldiers, whom he angrily declared had been placed in front to serve as a shield to the white troops. Such a conclusion seemed logical to Harris because the 54th had not been supplied with any means to scale the sand walls or spike the guns.[38]

The attack had devastated the Northern regiments. Of the 5,000 Federals who attacked Battery Wagner, 1,515 became casualties with 246 men killed, 890 wounded, and 391 captured. The 54th Massachusetts lost forty-two percent of its men, while the "Saints" from the 48th New York suffered more than fifty percent casualties. The 7th New Hampshire lost eighteen officers, the most of any regiment in the war for a single battle. The Union division commander was wounded, both brigade commanders killed or mortally wounded, and every regimental commander was killed or wounded. Losses in the officer ranks were extremely heavy. Among the dead and mortally wounded were General Strong and Colonels Shaw, Putnam, and Chatfield. An officer from the 48th New York aptly summed up the assault when he commented that Wagner had been the "gate of Hell."

In comparison, the Confederates suffered light casualties, numbering only 222 men. Six Southerners were listed as prisoners, including Lieutenant Campbell, who was carried out of Wagner's salient by the retreating Federals. The heaviest losses for the Confederates came from the artillerymen who worked the field pieces on the beach and the 51st North Carolina. The garrison did, however, sustain some critical deaths among its officers, including Lieutenant Colonel Simkins, Major Ramsey, and Captains William T. Tatum and William H. Ryan, brave men whose experience and leadership would be missed in the coming weeks.[39]

On the morning of July 19, while both sides were recovering from the fight, the Federals sought a truce to bury the dead and care for the wounded. The Confederates agreed, but would not allow the Union soldiers to come within their lines. Wagner had been roughly treated, and Beauregard did not want the enemy close enough to inspect the damage. In some ways July 19 was almost as deadly and confusing for the two sides as the night of the eighteenth. Neither the Federals nor the Confederates had enough doctors to handle the wounded. Union surgeons quickly processed their patients and placed them on transports for Hilton Head and Beaufort where the facilities were better.

Even though ordered to keep the Union stretcher-bearers from entering their lines, the Confederate and Union enlisted men mixed freely. Soldiers, who hours earlier had been attempting to kill each other, now talked amiably, "cracked jokes and made cuts at each other." For a moment the war was set aside, but both armies knew that in a short time they would again become bitter enemies.[40]

Beauregard, who had been made aware of the presence of wounded African-American soldiers, ordered special care for all Union wounded, regardless of color. Every available doctor from Charleston was sent to Morris Island where they found that the close-range firing had produced ghastly wounds which resulted in one amputation after another.

Details are sketchy, but reports indicate that only the bodies of Confederate officers were sent to Charleston. The remaining Confederate dead were hurriedly buried behind Wagner, while the Union dead, including officers, were placed in front of the battery. Due to the extreme heat, the burials were carried out as quickly as possible. The Confederates interred the dead in the easiest manner possible, caring little if they placed blacks, whites, officers, and enlisted men in common, mass graves.

While the burials and medical operations were going on, the Confederates discovered that a Federal assistant naval surgeon, John T. Luck, had somehow wandered within their lines. Though enlisted men passed freely between the pickets, Luck, who had been sent ashore by Dahlgren with other surgeons to assist Gillmore's doctors, was quickly seized and soon made to work with the Confederate doctors. Surgeon Luck was later released, and from his testimony would come one of the battle's most infamous legacies.

Surgeon Luck would later claim that while tending the wounded he fell into conversation with General Hagood and the two discussed the disposition of Colonel Shaw's body. According to Luck, Hagood declared that he had known Shaw before the war, but since Shaw had commanded black troops, Hagood stated that: "I shall bury him in the common grave with the Negroes that fell with him." In a short time, the Northern press would take Luck's unsubstantiated story and alter Hagood's supposed words to: "I buried him with his niggers."

Many years after the war, Hagood wrote that he had never known Shaw, but had seen his body on the morning of July 19. He remembered a naval surgeon who had been captured, but denied talking to him about Shaw. Hagood also pointed out that there were no special orders given regarding the burial of Federal troops.

From other accounts, however, it is known that Hagood had given specific instructions concerning Shaw's body. In a post-battle meeting presided over by General Hagood, it was decided by Wagner's principal officers that they would return all bodies asked for, except Colonel Shaw's. As Colonel George P. Harrison Jr. of the 32nd Georgia recalled, the Southerners were quite bitter to the commanders of black troops and felt no obligation to treat them in accordance to military customs. Hagood assigned Harrison the duty of burying Shaw. As Harrison wrote, a deep and wide trench was dug in front of Wagner and Shaw's body was laid "there without roughness and with due respect," and then the burial detail "placed on his body twenty of the dead blacks whom he had commanded."

While the burial of dead continued, the doctors completed their emergency operations, and the wounded prisoners were sent to hospitals in Charleston. Beauregard initially made certain that both the black and white wounded were placed together. Conditions in the hospitals were bad. The Charleston doctors, lacking medicines because of the blockade, did what they could. The doctors were aided by some uninjured Union prisoners who served as orderlies.

The unwounded prisoners were divided by race, the whites being placed in a warehouse, while the blacks were put in the city jail and Castle Pinckney. Beauregard still did not know what to do with the black prisoners. He again wired General Cooper for clarification on the status of the African-Americans and asked for instructions. While awaiting a reply, Beauregard, along with his opponent, evaluated the situation.[41]

For the South, Battery Wagner and its garrison had done their job. The North was stopped from seizing the rest of Morris Island, and time was gained to complete the work at Fort Sumter, strengthen the defenses on Sullivan's Island, and finish the new defenses on James Island. Beauregard realized the Federals would either have to quit the island, launch another assault, or open siege operations. The latter seemed most likely. The battle would soon become one of engineering skill and determination.

To most Northerners, little immediate good seemed to have come from the attack. Gillmore was not criticized at the time for placing the 54th Massachusetts regiment in front, and many observers thought "prejudice was down," because of the regiment's excellent showing. The 54th was not the first African-American unit to perform well under fire. Black units had been carrying out efficient operations along the

Southern coast and in Mississippi, Louisiana, and Kansas long before the 54th took the field. Over a month before the attack on Battery Wagner, two African-American regiments with some black officers undertook an unsuccessful assault on the Confederates at Port Hudson, but this was a western battle, fought by western soldiers who had no political patrons. It did not gain the publicity and notoriety caused by the near destruction of the 54th and the death of Colonel Shaw.

The 54th had been groomed from the start by its organizers and recruiters to act as heroes in order that they become models for their race. Newspaper reporters and politicians followed their every move. If they had broken and run at Wagner, the whole experiment of using black troops in combat would have been compromised, but this did not happen. Because of the regiment's fine showing, the attack was hailed as proof that African-Americans could fully participate in military operations. The 54th lost more than forty percent of its men and fourteen of its twenty-two officers, but the losses were not as important as the performance of the regiment, which fought like a veteran unit and reformed after a terrible mauling.[42]

The battle served as a symbol to the abolitionists and others who championed the cause of African-American troops. In a short time, Colonel Shaw and his men became national heroes. They would be immortalized in speeches, poems, editorials, drawings, and paintings. Such comments—"buried with his niggers"—only served to heighten their reputation. Their immortal charge set an example. The Federal government, which had been closely watching the conduct of its new soldiers, increased the enlistment of men of African descent. Before the war ended, nearly two hundred thousand African-American soldiers had served in the Union army. The impact of these men on the Northern war effort cannot be overestimated. The South, already outnumbered on the battlefield, found their enemies even more numerous and determined. After the assault on Battery Wagner, a new face was added to the war from which there was no turning back.

Besides its importance to the cause of black troops, the attack on Battery Wagner was also a turning point in military technology. In his planning, General Gillmore had tremendously underestimated the sand battery. In February 1862, Gillmore destroyed Fort Pulaski's brick walls with rifled artillery, but Battery Wagner was not Pulaski. The Federal artillery was quite capable of crushing a masonry work, but it could only disfigure Wagner's earthen ramparts. At Pulaski, Gillmore had ended the era of masonry fortifications. At Wagner he opened the era of trench warfare.

The bombardment of Battery Wagner was one of the largest in the war and was executed perfectly. The coordination between the Union army and navy was excellent. Wagner's earthern walls, though badly plowed up, could not be knocked down. The well-protected Confederates were able to survive with few casualties. When the advance came, the majority of the Southerners were ready and able to resist the attack.

Gillmore and his commanders were so overconfident that their artillery could destroy Wagner they failed to properly outfit their troops. No scaling ladders or trenching tools were supplied. The officers seemed to have no conception of the lay of the land or construction of Wagner. Many of the regimental leaders did not even know that the defile in front of Wagner existed.

Overconfidence, poor preparation, too much space and time between units, and the confusion caused by a night assault all led the Federals to suffer one of the war's greatest disasters. If they had kept the bombardment up for a longer period of time, they might have compromised Wagner's magazine and forced either a devastating explosion or an evacuation. If they had attacked during the daytime, the navy could have kept up a covering fire and stopped reinforcements from reaching Wagner. If the attacking regiments had been provided with equipment to enter the fort and been accompanied by engineers and artillerymen, they might have gained and held a portion of the battery, but these things were not done. As it was carried out, the attack was doomed to failure. It should never have taken place.

Though the repulse was one of the greatest Northern catastrophies of the war, Gillmore and Dahlgren, unlike Hunter and Du Pont, refused to turn back. The officers noted their mistakes and tried to learn from them. Since the direct assault had failed, new tactics were soon agreed upon, and the campaign for Charleston continued.[43]

General Pierre Gustave Toutant Beauregard, commander of the Department of South Carolina, Georgia, and East Florida. (National Archives, Washington, D.C.)

Colonel David B. Harris, chief engineer for the Confederate Department of South Carolina, Georgia, and East Florida. (Valentine Museum, Richmond, Virginia).

Brigadier General Johnson Hagood, district and brigade commander during the Morris Island campaign. Hagood also commanded Battery Wagner. (Library of Congress, Washington, D.C.)

Brigadier General Roswell S. Ripley, Charleston District commander during the Morris Island campaign. (Library of Congress, Washington, D.C.)

Brigadier General Stephen Elliott, commander of Fort Sumter during the September 8, 1863 night assault on Fort Sumter. (U.S. Army Military History Institute, Carlise, Pennsylvania.)

Brigadier General Alfred H. Colquitt, brigade commander and a commander of Battery Wagner. (Valentine Museum, Richmond, Virginia.)

Brigadier General Thomas L. Clingman, brigade commander and a commander of Battery Wagner. (National Archives, Washington, D.C.)

Brigadier General William Booth Taliaferro, commander of Battery Wagner during the July 18, 1863 assault. (Virginia State Library, Richmond, Virginia.)

Captain John H. Gary, killed at Battery Wagner August 13, 1863. (South Caroliniana Library, Columbia, South Carolina.)

Captain Robert Pringle, killed at Battery Wagner August 21, 1863. (South Carolina Historical Society, Charleston, South Carolina.)

Colonel Lawrence Keitt, commander of the 20th South Carolina Infantry Regiment. Keitt commanded Battery Wagner and was in charge of the evacuation of Morris Island. (South Caroliniana Library, Columbia, South Carolina.)

Lieutenant John Stock Bee, killed on Morris Island during the July 10, 1863 attack. (Gibbes Art Gallery, Charleston, South Carolina.)

Rear Admiral John Dahlgren, flag officer of the South Atlantic Blockading Squadron. (Library of Congress, Washington, D.C.)

Major General Quincy A. Gillmore, commanding general of the Department of the South. (U.S. Army Military History Institute, Carlise, Pennsylvania.)

Major General Truman Seymour, division commander in the Department of the South. Truman was wounded during the July 18 attack on Battery Wagner. (U.S Army Military History Institute, Carlise, Pennsylvania.)

Major General Alfred H. Terry, division commander in the Department of the South. (U.S. Army Military History Institute, Carlise, Pennsylvania.)

Brigadier General Israel Vogdes, comman-
der of Folly Island and a division in the
Department of the South. (U.S. Army Military
History Institute, Carlise, Pennsylvania.)

Brigadier General George C. Strong,
brigade commander in the Department of
the South. Strong was mortally wounded
during the July 18 attack on Battery
Wagner. (U.S. Army Military History
Institute, Carlise, Pennsylvania.)

Colonel Edward Serrell, colonel of the
1st New York Engineers. (Library of
Congress, Washington, D.C.)

Clara Barton, who served as a nurse on
Morris Island. (Library of Congress,
Washington, D.C.)

Colonel Robert G. Shaw in civilian clothes. (U.S. Army Military History Institute, Carlise, Pennsylvania.)

Colonel Robert G. Shaw, colonel of the 54th Massachusetts. He was killed during the July 18 attack on Battery Wagner. (U.S. Army Military History Institute, Carlise, Pennsylvania.)

Colonel John L. Chatfield, colonel of the 6th Connecticut. Chatfield was mortally wounded during the July 18 attack on Battery Wagner. (U.S. Army Military History Institute, Carlise, Pennsylvania.)

Colonel Haldiman S. Putnam, brigade commander in the Department of the South. He was killed during the July 18 attack on Battery Wagner. (Author's collection.)

Chapter 5

THE SIEGE BEGINS

*Send more limes, rum and sugar and a little water
we'll hold for another day.*
Colonel Lawrence M. Keitt

The defeat of July 18 weighed heavily on General Gillmore. His second failure against Wagner had convinced Gillmore that the enemy outnumbered him at least two to one in infantry and five to one in artillery. Still, when Admiral Dahlgren offered to land soldiers behind Wagner should another assault be launched, Gillmore momentarily considered the plan, but only if the landing force was made up of naval personnel. When faced with this prospect, Dahlgren begged off, reporting that he had few marines and fewer blue jackets available for land service.

Since the force at hand was not strong enough for another attack, Gillmore sent word to Halleck, writing that he would continue the campaign and, if reinforcements were sent, victory would be guaranteed. Otherwise, Gillmore promised to strengthen his position and begin carrying out a siege against Battery Wagner. A siege operation, which consisted of building zig-zag trenches protected by batteries of artillery against an enemy position, was a laborious and time consuming task, but without reinforcements, it was the only reasonable option left to Gillmore.[1]

On July 19, orders were sent to Major Thomas B. Brooks to take the trench established by Stevenson's brigade and prepare a position from which to open siege lines. Brooks went about his task quickly and efficiently. Work parties headed by the 1st New York Engineers and served by infantrymen soon created the siege's first parallel. Initially, the line was built for defense. Emplacements for siege and field guns and mortars were constructed. Traverses were established between the guns and the parapet arranged for infantry fire. A palisade of sharpened stakes was placed in front of the line, and in time, Requa batteries and wire entanglements were added.[2]

The wire entanglements were constructed by setting stakes deeply in the ground, in groups of five, forming a quincunx. The wire was strung tightly among the stakes, making an effective obstacle against any attacking force. This was one of the first appearances of wire obstructions on such a scale. The entanglements were the forerunners of the barbed-wire barriers that would appear on future battlefields.

Another innovation being perfected was the Requa battery, a predecessor of the machine gun. These batteries were constructed by the Billinghurst Company of Rochester, New York, and were intended to replace the short-range field guns in defensive positions. They consisted of twenty-five rifle barrels arranged horizontally and attached to a field carriage. Operated by three men who fed in a clip consisting of twenty-five cartridges, the gun was effective up to thirteen hundred yards and a good crew could fire 175 shots per minute. The engineers, impressed by these accurate and efficient weapons, placed them liberally among their trenches.[3]

The defense measures placed into the first parallel were opening on Morris Island a new type of warfare. The engineers and artillerymen—the technicians of war—were taking control. The infantryman remained a vital element, but only in so far as his ability to use the new weapons. The impersonalization of modern warfare emerged. The industrial revolution was spreading to the battlefield. On Morris Island, the men who had seen war as flag-waving charges watched as the new professionals took over. Shovels began to replace the rifle and the individual soldier was becoming lost amongst the mass firepower and trenches provided by the artillery and the engineers.

General Gillmore excelled in this style of warfare, and he did not remain in his depression long. Two days after the assault, while the engineers were busily strengthening the trenches, he announced his new plans for taking Battery Wagner and destroying Fort Sumter. Siege lines were to push on towards Wagner, and at the same time, breaching batteries would be constructed and Fort Sumter battered into submission.

To continue, Gillmore needed the navy. He communicated with Dahlgren, who agreed to assist. The navy commander was anxious to keep up the attack; however, he sensed that Gillmore had lost some of his confidence, noting that the general was often preoccupied with small details.

One concern that was not minor was the army's ever-decreasing strength. Gillmore, with good justification, was uneasy over his ability to defend his position from a possible Confederate counterattack. So far, the fighting on Morris Island had cost his army nearly sixteen percent of its effective force while another fourteen percent of his men were on an ever-increasing sick roll. Gillmore was also concerned about the ability of his other posts to repel enemy attacks. At Port Royal, a number of regiments were due to be discharged from service, and with Dahlgren bringing the majority of his vessels to Charleston, Gillmore was concerned over a Confederate attack, especially against his main supply base on Hilton Head Island. To protect this vital center, he felt obliged to dispatch the survivors of the 6th Connecticut back to Port Royal.

Dahlgren tried to ease Gillmore's concerns over manpower by increasing the navy's commitment to the campaign. The steam frigate *Wabash*, with her 635-man crew, was brought from Port Royal to assist in the operations. The vessel was kept out of action, but her crew was put to work. Detachments from the *Wabash* relieved men onboard the monitors, manned the nightly picket boats that watched the main ship channel, and provided a 170-man unit to serve two 5-inch Whitworth cannon recently taken from a captured blockade runner, and two 8-inch Parrotts, which Dahlgren loaned to the army for duty on land.

Dahlgren realized that the campaign would be long and that he would need additional men to keep his squadron up to strength. He wrote Secretary of Navy Welles asking for additional seamen and marines and also urged the secretary to use his influence to gain reinforcements for Gillmore. Dahlgren was anxious to end the affair on Morris Island because the longer the Federals were held up by Battery Wagner, the longer the Confederates had to perfect their seaward defenses. If the campaign dragged on too long, the flag officer feared his monitors would be unable to force their way into the harbor.[4]

Dahlgren was correct. For every day that Battery Wagner held, the longer the Confederates had to rearrange and strengthen their harbor defenses; however, initially the Southerners were not sure if they could hold Wagner.

During the days after the attack, the Confederates worked to restore Battery Wagner to fighting trim. Though the battery had survived the July 18 bombardment and attack, it needed extensive repairs and renovations before it could withstand a prolonged siege. The barracks and storehouses had been destroyed, cannon disabled, and the slopes and inclines plowed up.

Some repairs were carried out on July 19, while the two sides observed a truce to bury the dead and care for the wounded, but the next day the Federals opened a heavy bombardment against the battery. During the action Sergeant Samuel A. Tynes of the Company A, Lucas Artillery Battalion, was struck down while bravely manning his gun. The wound was mortal, and when Tynes' commanding officer, Captain John Gary, expressed his concern, Tynes replied that it was far better that he and not Gary had been wounded. Four days later, Sergeant Tynes died, and in time, a battery would be named for him on the Stono River, the only Charleston position ever named for an enlisted man. Captain Gary would continue to serve in Battery Wagner, but on August 13, less than a month after the death of Tynes, Gary would also be killed during a bombardment, and in time, he too would have a battery named in his honor.

The bombardments kept the Confederates from repairing Wagner during the day; however, at night, when the enemy's fire was reduced and not very accurate, Wagner's garrison busily replaced woodwork and enlarged and strengthened bombproofs and magazines. Still, the men were limited in what they could accomplish, but then they gained valuable time when the Federals stopped their bombardment to exchange prisoners.[5]

On July 21, during a lull in the firing, a flag of truce appeared from the Union lines. General Hagood, still commanding Wagner, sent his aide, Captain Carlos Tracy, to meet the flag. In the dunes between the lines, Tracy met General Vogdes, who had come forward to arrange a prisoner exchange, but before any details could be discussed, the fleet, unaware of the army's flag of truce, resumed firing. Tracy abruptly ended the conference and hurried back to Wagner.

When informed about the request, Hagood sent word to Beauregard asking for guidance. Beauregard instructed Hagood to proceed with an exchange, but on no account was he to enter into any discussion about African-American prisoners.[6]

The next day another flag appeared and again Tracy walked into no man's land to meet Vogdes. The Federal officer was cordial and apologetic, explaining that the flag of truce had been violated the day before because Gillmore had failed to inform the navy about the cessation of hostilities. Satisfied with the explanation, Tracy agreed to a parlay, and soon the two officers were joined by General Hagood.

As a sign of good faith, Vogdes opened the meeting by offering to return the body of Lieutenant Bee for that of Colonel Putnam. Hagood agreed, and as the dead officers were carried between the lines, Hagood and Vogdes began to discuss the exchange of living soldiers. Since the Federals had already sent their able-bodied prisoners north, an agreement was worked out concerning the wounded. Because the Confederates held more wounded prisoners, Vogdes told Hagood that the Confederates could decide who was to be traded. Hagood, relieved that the issue of black prisoners had not come up, agreed. The time for the exchange was set for 10:00 A.M., July 24, and would take place between ships off Morris Island.[7]

For the rest of the twenty-second and all of the twenty-third, the Union batteries and vessels refrained from firing on Battery Wagner, giving the Confederates time to continue their repairs. Also on the twenty-third, General Taliaferro returned to Wagner and relieved Hagood as the island's commander; however, on the twenty-fourth, the Union batteries, along with four monitors, the *New Ironsides*, and four gunboats, opened fire on Battery Wagner. The bombardment ripped at Wagner's sand walls. The 10-inch Columbiad, just recently remounted, was disabled and soon light was seen through the roof of the bomb-proof. At the same time, the enemy's shells tore at the roof of the main magazine. Again, as on the eighteenth, Taliaferro considered evacuating his position, but then at 10:00 A.M., a Confederate vessel was seen coming out of the harbor and moving toward the Union squadron.

The ship was the recently impressed blockade runner *Alice*. Seized by the Confederates at the start of the campaign, the sleek sidewheel steamer was now serving as the Southern truce vessel and was still commanded by her civilian captain, James Eagan. On board were 105 wounded Union prisoners under the supervision of Colonel Edward C. Anderson and Chief Quartermaster J. Motte Middleton. Also accompanying the prisoners was Bishop Patrick N. Lynch from the Cathedral St. Finbar. Serving as stretcher-bearers were members of the Charleston Fire Department.

As the *Alice* neared Wagner, a shot from the *New Ironsides* exploded near the vessel's bow, but the *Alice* continued on. The Federals soon stopped their bombardment, and Dahlgren's flagship, the monitor *Weehawken*, halted the *Alice*. The rear admiral held the Confederate vessel for forty-five minutes until the Union hospital boat, the *Cosmopolitan*, under the command of Gillmore's provost marshal, Lieutenant Colonel James F. Hall, arrived.

The two vessels came alongside each other, and a plank was thrown over from the *Cosmopolitan*. Surgeon John J. Craven, the officer in charge of the North's hospitals on Folly and Morris Islands, crossed over and made arrangements with Colonel Anderson for the exchange.

Since the Southerners held more prisoners, it was agreed to parole the difference. Forty captured Confederates, five surgeons and assistant surgeons were traded for 104 Union wounded (one had died on the way out). Throughout the exchange, Anderson and Motte were pressed by Federal officers for information about the captured blacks, but all overtures were resisted.

While the exchange was going on, Union officers, including Gillmore's aide Major Stryker, looked over the blockade runner, noting that the ship still carried part of its British cargo of munitions destined for Confederate armies. He also recorded that the *Alice*'s English crew "dressed in height of fashion" and made a point of "talking loudly of the superior intellect of southern chivalry."

The truce stopped all active operations and allowed the Union soldiers and sailors operating against Battery Wagner a chance to relax. Men on the monitors came on deck to get some air, while Rear Admiral Dahlgren gazed longingly on the *Alice*, a blockade runner that had often eluded his warships. Later, the flag officer wrote to Secretary of the Navy Welles requesting such vessels for his squadron.

While the Northerners took advantage of the lull to rest, the Confederates in Wagner quickly organized work parties and began removing the powder from the threatened magazine. Taliaferro, though, did not believe that Wagner could be held and called on General Ripley to evacuate the battery and Morris Island. Then, much to Taliaferro's surprise, the bombardment was not renewed and the garrison was able to complete their repairs, so that by the end of the day Wagner was considered secure.[8]

Though the exchange had not included the African Americans taken prisoner at Wagner, their fate was far from settled. The Confederates, who refused to exchange or even mention the fate of the blacks to the Federals on the *Cosmopolitan*, knew that the military had already handed the prisoners over to the state of South Carolina for trial. On the other hand, the Federals held certain Southern prisoners, including Captain Macbeth, the son of Charleston's mayor, at Hilton Head as possible hostages in case the Confederacy carried out retribution against the African-American soldiers.

In all, the South controlled about eighty prisoners from the 54th Massachusetts. The wounded were treated in hospitals, while the rest were either confined in Castle Pinckney or the Charleston jail. The day after the attack on Wagner, Captain William H. Peronneau, Pinckney's commander, reported to headquarters that the prisoners in his charge were willing to submit to state laws and go to work on Confederate defenses. Though no reasons were given, some of the men could have been genuinely disillusioned with their service, while others, knowing the probable result if placed on trial, were trying to head off execution. Whatever their motivations, all of the men, along with the surviving wounded, joined their comrades in the Charleston jail. Placed in a large octagon tower, the remaining seventy-three soldiers awaited their fates.

By Confederate law, the men were to be given over to South Carolina authorities for trial, and by existing South Carolina acts, there was no such thing as black soldiers. Either the men were free blacks leading a slave revolt or slaves in rebellion. For the former, the penalty was death, for the latter, it was either reenslavement or execution. To the men of the 54th it seemed that the verdict of death had already been decided on when the state erected a gallows in the jail yard before their trial began.

Yet many Confederate officials, including General Beauregard and Secretary of War James Seddon, realized that any execution would cause retaliation against Confederate prisoners. President Lincoln, in an effort to defend the North's black soldiers, had issued a proclamation on July 30, 1863, declaring that the African Americans were covered by General Order 100 which stated that "for every soldier of the United States killed in violation of the laws of war a Rebel soldier shall be executed and for every one enslaved by the enemy or sold into slavery, a Rebel shall be placed at hard labor. . . ."

Such statements helped convince Beauregard that the South would have to change its policy toward African-American prisoners. Though he and his officers considered the use of black troops an affront to the South, the commanding general did realize that the war had taken another step, and they reluctantly had to recognize the legitimacy of the North's "Sable Arm."

At first, Beauregard and his staff tried to retain the African American soldiers as prisoners of war since none were former South Carolina slaves, but the governor, the prewar radical Milledge L. Bonham, pressed the matter, and on July 29, Beauregard was ordered by Secretary of War Seddon to turn the prisoners over to state authorities. Even so, Beauregard did not remove himself entirely from the case and directed his aide, Brigadier General Thomas Jordon, to watch the proceedings, and he also assisted in finding a suitable defense attorney.

Governor Bonham established a commission that interviewed twenty-four black prisoners. The resulting report stated that all but one were disillusioned with their military service and roundly complained about lack of pay, poor leadership, and their being used as a shield for white troops during the attack on Wagner. None of the men was a former South Carolina slave, but four of the twenty-four had been slaves. These were Privates George Counsel, Henry W. Worthington, Henry Kirk, and William H. Harrison. Counsel and Worthington had been born in Virginia, while Kirk and Harrison were Missouri natives. Since these men were former slaves who had been captured fighting against the Confederacy, Bonham decided to use them in his test case, and on August 7, preparations were started to form a court.

The man assigned to defend the African-American soldiers was Nelson Mitchell, a respected member of Charleston's legal profession. The case was a difficult one. Mitchell would not only be defending his clients' legal and military rights, he would be challenging Southern social and cultural beliefs. Many in South Carolina wanted the captured black soldiers tried and summarily executed because their use by the North struck at a basic tenet of Southern life—it openly challenged the Southern belief that whites were superior to blacks. If African Americans were accepted by the Confederacy as soldiers, then Southerners might eventually be forced to accept them as social and political equals. The *Charleston Mercury* declared that blacks were altogether a different class and their use as soldiers was an uncivilized act that had to be met with severe retaliation. The paper demanded that Lincoln's threat be ignored and that the South Carolina legal system carry out its appointed mission.

The trial was held on September 8, 1863, in the Police Court for the Charleston District. South Carolina was represented by the state Attorney General, Isaac W. Hayne, who was assisted by Alfred Proctor Aldrich, while Nelson Mitchell, assisted by Edward McCrady, handled the defense. Mitchell argued that even though the men had been born slaves, they were now legitimate soldiers of the United States, protected by the rules of war. As such, the Charleston Police Court did not have the legal right to try them as rebelling slaves. After a three-day trial, the court agreed with Mitchell's arguments and ruled that it had no jurisdiction. The court then directed the provost marshal to have the prisoners "re-committed to jail and the governor be informed of the actions of the court."

Another version of what went on in Charleston was related after the war by Daniel States, a prisoner from the 54th, taken during the attack on Wagner. In his story, which is not backed up by South Carolina records, two prisoners, Sergeant Walter A. Jeffries and Corporal Charles Hardy, were chosen as the defendants. Enlistment records reveal the two as free-born blacks. Jeffries was a native of Cincinnati, and Hardy was born in Philadelphia. Both were prisoners with States in the Charleston jail.

By States's account, Jeffries and Hardy were interviewed by Mitchell, who was friendly and kind to the soldiers, and upon the completion of the case came to the jail late at night and called up to Sergeant Jeffries: "All of you can rejoice. You are recognized as United States soldiers."

States's story does not match existing records, but it is interesting to note that men in his version were free blacks who conceivably were put on trial to test the portion of the Confederate law that viewed free blacks serving in military units as being provocateurs leading a slave revolt. If any white officers from the 54th had been captured, they too may have faced a trial.

In later accounts, the story of the trial would become highly romanticized by reporters and writers. Nelson Mitchell would become a Northern hero who sacrificed his property and public standing to serve the captured African Americans. These stories were not true. Mitchell was not ostracized by his fellow citizens during or after the trial.

The results of the legal proceeding ended a difficult situation for the Confederacy and headed off any retaliation. Closely watched by the government and military officials, the case ended for the war what Secretary of War Seddon called a question "so fraught with present difficulty and danger."

Though the Confederacy was forced to accept the African Americans as soldiers, the South still lacked clear guidance on what to do with prisoners who were escaped slaves. The North expected them to be treated as any other prisoner and be eligible for exchange, but the South still considered them property and as such returnable to their owners. Lincoln's proclamation and threat of retaliation kept the Confederacy from sending the men back to slavery, but they were often held in separate jails and refused exchange. Because of this, the Lincoln government ended most prisoner exchanges. The near-total ban on trading captured soldiers was kept up until the end of the war, and though it sentenced thousands of men to death in camps both North and South, it also deprived the South of desperately needed manpower.

The African-American prisoners in Charleston, both freemen and former slaves, were kept in Charleston for nearly eighteen months as government and state officials tried to determine who should take responsibility for their imprisonment. Finally, in December 1864, the survivors were sent to the prisoner of war camp at Florence, South Carolina. Here, in the last month of the war, Corporal Hardy and Privates Worthington and Harrison would die. In death they joined their legal counsel, Nelson Mitchell, who died in February 1864.[9]

While Beauregard kept track of the legal proceedings in Charleston, he also worked to prepare his command for continued operations around Battery Wagner and Morris Island. For the moment, the reinforced sand battery keyed the Confederate defense. Beauregard knew that eventually Gillmore would construct breaching batteries to destroy Fort Sumter. To negate this, Beauregard had to alter his harbor defenses. Guns from Fort Sumter would be sent to new positions on Sullivan's Island, while on James Island new defense lines were started overlooking Morris Island and along the Stono River.

To help him accomplish his plans, Beauregard, like Gillmore, called for additional help. Brigadier General Nathan George "Shanks" Evans' brigade returned from Mississippi, and the final two regiments of Brigadier General Alfred H. Colquitt's brigade from Wilmington were sent to Charleston, as well as additional heavy guns and mortars. To support the army, the Confederate navy sent detachments of sailors to Charleston from Wilmington and Savannah. These men served on ironclads and manned small boats that picketed the harbor and shuttled troops between islands.

Besides the reinforcements, Beauregard also consolidated the engineering offices at Charleston. At the start of the campaign, the engineers operating around Charleston were directed by Colonel Harris, who commanded both the War Department Engineers (army officers) and Major William H. Echols' state engineers (civilians and state officers). Harris initially reported to General Ripley, the district commander, but after the attack on Wagner, the engineers were placed directly under Beauregard's command. Later in the siege, Major General Jeremy F. Gilmer, chief engineer of the Confederacy, arrived in Charleston at Beauregard's request and added his expertise as Beauregard's second-in-command. Considered by many to be the best engineer in the Southern army, Gilmer was described as "a tall sallow dignified man and with the exception of his erect military carriage has more of the air of a student than a soldier."

The war at Charleston was coming down to labor, material, and engineering skill. Since the Confederates were short of material, it was often up to the engineers to make up the difference with skillful work. On James Island new, well-protected batteries were built between Fort Johnson and Fort Lamar, which contained powerful guns that could flank the Northern siege lines. At Fort Sumter guns were removed and replaced with dummy cannons called Quaker guns. The lower rooms of the gorge wall were filled with sand and cotton bales; the second tier casements were sealed off and filled; a new sally-port was constructed away from Morris Island, and the gorge wall was covered with sandbags. The artillery pieces removed from Sumter were sent to Sullivan's Island and placed in new fortifications bearing on the main ship channel.[10]

For the Confederate engineers to finish their projects, Battery Wagner had to keep the Federal forces occupied. If it fell before the works were completed, the Northern ironclads would be able to force their way into the harbor, or Gillmore could land his men on James Island and march on Charleston. Every day that Wagner held, the stronger the Confederate defenses became.

To hold Gillmore in check on Morris Island, the Confederates developed a defensive scheme that allowed them to maximize their advantages and yet protect the defenders. Battery Wagner's firepower was increased on the land side by the addition of two siege howitzers and an 8-inch mortar, while the seaward battery received another 10-inch Columbiad and a 32-pound rifle. The garrison was to be kept at 1,200 men. 1,000 infantrymen, 180 artillerymen, and various support troops such as signalmen and couriers.

During the day, Wagner's ramparts were patrolled by a small guard of infantrymen. Out in front, about one hundred yards from the moat, fifty to one hundred men were positioned in rifle pits which ran along a sand ridge that extended from the marsh to the beach. At Wagner's seafront, artillerymen stood ready to duel with Federal ironclads, while others watched the landfront for enemy activity. About seven hundred men were kept in the main bombproof while the rest of the garrison was stationed behind the battery inside rice caskets that were sunk into the ground.

At night, a basic routine was developed. An additional one hundred men joined the soldiers in the rifle pits, while another one hundred watched both the marshes and the beach between Wagner and Gregg for small boat attacks. Inside Wagner, men worked in the quartermaster and commissary sections and supplied working parties for Wagner's chief engineer. These work crews joined gangs of slaves in carrying out essential repairs. Divided into two shifts, one group worked from sundown to midnight, and the other from midnight to sunup. The remainder of the infantrymen remained on guard along with the post's artillerymen. At Battery Gregg, detachments kept up a watch for enemy activity and repaired any damage caused by enemy fire.[11]

The work of the engineers was essential to Wagner's survival. They were constantly replacing sandbags, revetting gun chambers, making and positioninig gabions, and cleaning passageways. In carrying out their assignments, the engineers not only used the detachments from Wagner's garrison but also employed slaves requisitioned from local

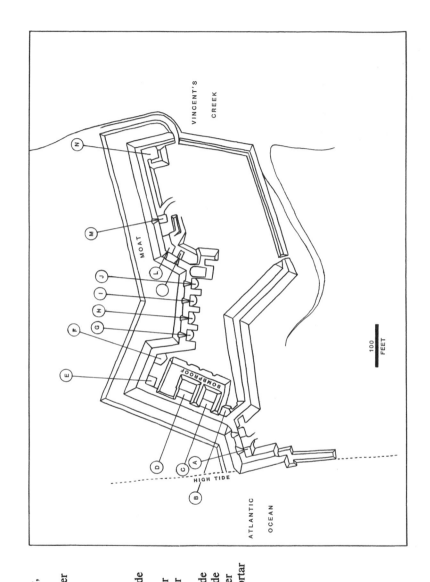

Map 17: Battery Wagner, July 25, 1863

A: 8-inch Siege Howitzer
B: Disabled
C: 10-inch Columbiad
D: 32-pounder
E: 8-inch Seacoast Howitzer
F: 42-pounder Carronade
G: 8-inch Shell Gun
H: 32-pounder Howitzer
I: 32-pounder Howitzer
J: 8-inch Shell Gun
K: 32-pounder Carronade
L: 32-pounder Carronade
M: 8-inch Siege Howitzer
N: 10-inch Seacoast Mortar

VINCENT'S CREEK

MOAT

BOMBPROOF

HIGH TIDE

ATLANTIC OCEAN

100 FEET

plantations. Though slaves were used more extensively at Fort Sumter and on James Island, those sent to Wagner carried out important and necessary work.

Because of their value, the engineers were very careful in their use of slave labor; if too many were injured, the owners would refuse to honor further drafts. Though there were a number of free blacks in Charleston, their use was severely limited because the majority of them held positions vital to the war effort. Many worked in the shipyards and machine shops, made up volunteer fire brigades, and were crew members abroad the Confederate quartermaster vessels. A few individuals even served on the city's ironclads.[12]

The duty on Morris Island was demanding and dangerous for all concerned, and to keep the defenders as fresh as possible, the Confederates established a system that continually rotated the island's garrison. The infrantry was replaced about every third day, while the artillerymen served slightly longer. The movements were under the overall supervision of Charleston's chief quartermaster, Motte A. Pringle, who coordinated the transportation of men and material throughout the harbor. For Morris Island, the journeys took place at night, but because of limited transportation, the exchanges were far from smooth or complete, with some lasting over two evenings. The safest method was to have the replacements congregate at Fort Johnson and then be taken to Cummings Point in small boats operated by the navy. However, when the Northern vessels threatened an attack, the sailors would be recalled to the ironclads and then the quartermaster department had to take one of its small steamers directly to Cummings Point, where they provided an easy target for the Union ships and land batteries. Though his mission was dangerous and his vessels were constantly breaking down, Major Pringle was always able to maintain connections with Morris Island and keep the island's defenders properly supplied.[13]

Command of Morris Island was rotated about every five days. Headquarters was at Wagner, where the commander directed the defense of the battery. The task was grueling. The commanding officers had to supervise all facets of the island's defense, and they had little time to rest. Generals Beauregard and Ripley made frequent visits to Morris Island, and Colonel Harris often came to Wagner to direct the engineering work. Beauregard realized that this operation was something new in modern warfare. For both posterity and his own place in history, Beauregard ordered all his commanders to keep daily journals.

Throughout the siege, the Confederates used only their most reliable

troops and best commanders on Morris Island, and many of these men
and officers were South Carolinians. The Confederate command
counted on high morale to counteract the difficult circumstances.
Typical of the Confederate spirit at Wagner was Colonel Lawrence M.
Keitt's reply on August 3 to Beauregard's telegrams concerning the
battery's ability to hold out during a heavy bombardment. Keitt told
his commander: "Send some more limes, rum and sugar and a little
water, we'll hold for another day."[14]

Possibly the most important element in Wagner's defense was the
artillery. The guns on the land front were mostly carronades and
howitzers placed to stop infantry assaults by sweeping the land approach with shell, grape, and canister. The howitzers in Wagner varied
from the stubby 8-inch siege howitzers sent out after July 18 to the
longer seacoast howitzers. The carronades were obsolete ship cannons
pressed into service by the Confederates to serve as howitzers, a duty
for which they were well suited.

Together with two 8-inch naval shell guns, the howitzers and carronades were used to disrupt the enemy's work parties. During the first
portion of the siege, the Confederate artillerymen were able to work
their pieces during the day, but as the Federals aligned more artillery
and increased their fire against Wagner, the Southern gun crews were
often driven into the bombproof and their cannon disabled. Eventually
the Southerners had to limit their cannon fire to night actions and use
only the 10-inch and 8-inch mortars during the day.

On Wagner's seaward side, the Confederates used two 10-inch
Columbiads and a rifled 32-pounder to challenge the Union fleet. It
was an uneven battle. The seaward battery was rarely at full strength
as the Union ironclads were constantly disabling and dismounting the
guns.

The Confederate artillery suffered from poor and obsolete material.
Many guns had damaged parts and incorrect elevating screws. Car-
riages were old and showed the signs of constant use. Fuses were often
defective. Because of splits in its cheeks, the 10-inch mortar could be
used only for very slow firing. Many of the guns were castoff, oddities,
or were at the end of their serviceable life. The original 10-inch
Columbiad supposedly had fired twelve hundred times before July 18,
an incredible service life for any gun of that era. The second Columbiad, sent from Fort Sumter, was thought to have had an equally
impressive history.[15]

One of the most important units stationed at Wagner was the
sharpshooters. Early in the siege, it became apparent that the Confederate artillery was vulnerable to effective enemy counterbattery fire

and usually could not operate during the day, so to harass the Federals, Wagner received a special detachment of sharpshooters. These men were not ordinary sharpshooters—they were armed with the deadly British Whitworth rifle, a specially bored weapon that had a thirty-three-inch barrel and a fourteen-and-one-half-inch telescopic sight on the left side of the stock. Accurate up to eighteen hundred yards, the weapon was deadly in the hands of an expert rifleman.

How the Whitworth rifles came to Charleston is unknown; possibly they were a gift of a blockade-running company stationed in the city. At the start of the campaign, there were about twenty rifles in the Charleston area, and as early as July 19, Beauregard suggested that Whitworths be used in both Fort Sumter and Battery Wagner. A short time later, General Hagood organized a special detail from the 21st South Carolina and had them instructed in the use of the rifles. For the first part of the siege, these men operated at Wagner, and later, men from Company F, 8th North Carolina, took over. The sharpshooters became celebrities. Excused from fatigue duty, they rested in the bombproof or the sandhills when not firing on the Union trenches or ironclads. The men could always be distinguished from the rest of the garrison by their one black eye caused by the rifle's recoil.[16]

Other important units on Morris Island included the ordnance, commissary, quartermaster, and medical departments. The ordnance department kept the battery's magazines in order and supplied the garrison's men and artillery with their ammunition. The commissary and quartermaster detachments, stationed at Cummings Point, looked after the troops' feeding and transportation. The commissary bureau fed the garrison, and though the meals often arrived cold, the men never suffered from a lack of food. The medical department kept a hospital in Wagner's bombproof under the care of a chief surgeon, usually the senior surgeon of one of the garrisoning regiments, with assisting surgeons on hand.[17]

Another important section was the department's signalmen, which consisted of seventy-six men under Captain Frank Markoe. They maintained the harbor lights, set up a signalling system used by transports and blockade runners, and were stationed around the harbor sending and receiving messages. Using their own code, dispatches were sent by wig-wagging flags during the day and torches at night. Since the Confederates had broken the Northern code, one important part of Markoe's command was a detachment of twelve men who did nothing but read enemy communications.

On Morris Island, the signalmen, consisting of one sergeant and five soldiers, were stationed at Cummings Point. To send messages to

Charleston, the men stood on top of Battery Gregg, often under fire from the Union guns. No one was killed during this work, but some were wounded.[18]

Since the island's headquarters was located at Battery Wagner, all messages that were sent or received at Battery Gregg had to be taken between the two works. This task was carried out by the island's couriers stationed at Cummings Point. The detachment normally consisted of one sergeant and ten cavalrymen. For their use, ten mounts were kept on the island. Originally from the 5th South Carolina Cavalry and later from the 4th South Carolina Cavalry, the men were stationed in a small bombproof where they awaited messages. When a communication was received, the courier next in line would be sent to Wagner. To reach his destination, the horseman had to ride down the beach for three-quarters of a mile under constant fire from naval vessels. As the lone horseman neared Wagner, land-based artillery as well as Northern sharpshooters would join the turkey shoot. There was no cover. The courier rode at top speed, clinging to the back of his mount. The horses knew the run so well that the riders just turned them lose. There was no pause until they reached Wagner's sally port. Sometimes a courier was kept in Wagner to carry the reply, but if not, the original courier again braved the enemy fire on a return run.[19]

The rides of the couriers were often watched by the island's garrison. It was one of the few bits of action that the men saw. For the most part, the Confederates carried out a passive defense. Although sorties were possible, none was ever attempted. Instead, Beauregard and his commanders added other defensive measures designed to delay the Federal advance and strengthen Wagner's defenses.[20]

One project adopted by the Confederates centered around the use of torpedoes. A fairly new weapon in warfare, a torpedo was a powder-filled canister designed to blow up on contact with the enemy. For the most part, the Confederates had placed their torpedoes in water to stop Northern vessels from entering the harbor; however, it soon became apparent that they could be employed on land, and in late July, Captain M. Martin Gray, the head of Charleston's torpedo office, began laying out torpedoes in front of Wagner. The devices were usually made of artillery shells that were buried in the sand and covered by a board that sat on the shell's contact fuse. When sufficient pressure was placed on the board, it was forced down on the fuse and the shell exploded. The torpedoes were spaced over an area of about 100 to 150 yards in front of Wagner with a small path left to allow the Confederates to reach their rifle pits.[21]

Besides the torpedoes the Confederates also sent out to Battery

Wagner some three thousand pikes that had been discovered in the city's arsenal. The pikes, probably left over from the War of 1812, were used as a trou-de-loup (boards with spikes protruding) in the battery's ditch, forming a wall of sharp spikes that would have to be cut through before an attacker could reach Wagner's parapet. Along with the pikes and torpedoes, Wagner's garrison also received a large supply of shotguns, whose effect against attackers at short range would be devastating. The shotguns had been found in the Charleston Arsenal by the department's chief of artillery, Colonel Ambrosio J. Gonzales, who realized their value to Wagner's defenders.

Colonel Gonzales was one of a number of unique individuals who made up the Charleston garrison. A Cuban-born intellectual turned revolutionary, he had taken part in a number of failed coups to free Cuba from its Spanish overlords before settling in the South and marrying into the Elliott family. Gonzales viewed Cuba as part of a greater Southern Confederacy and enthusiastically backed the South in its war for independence. In April 1861 he joined Beauregard's staff as a volunteer aide. When Beauregard was transferred to Virginia, Gonzales remained at Charleston. Though not a trained soldier, his versatility made him a popular officer and his advice was often followed.[22]

While the Southerners concentrated on perfecting their defenses, there were a few opportunities for them to strike at their foes. One occurred in early August when the Confederates moved to eliminate harassing Federal pickets.

Throughout the campaign, pickets and scouts of both sides operated in the salt marshes that separated Morris Island from James Island. These men watched enemy movements and reported the construction of batteries. The Northern scouts, led by the now-legendary Captain Payne, had became so bold that every night they would row out to an observation post at the unfinished marsh battery near Cummings Point. From here, Payne observed Confederate vessels arriving at Morris Island. Whenever he sighted an enemy ship, Payne fired off rockets alerting the Federal batteries to open fire, driving off the Confederate steamers. Payne's work not only disrupted boat movement, but also embarrassed the Confederate leaders who could not understand how a Yankee could operate so freely in the Southern marsh. On August 3, after two nights of having his boat operations interrupted, Beauregard directed his commanders to eliminate the pesky Federals.

At Fort Johnson the following night, General Ripley brought together a mixed unit of sailors and infantry to attack the Union pickets. Under the command of Captain Martin Henry Sellers of the 25th South

Carolina and transported on boats from the ironclad *Chicora* under Lieutenant Commander Alexander F. Warley, the Confederates surprised Payne and his men at the site of the marsh battery. In a short, brisk fight, the Southerners drove off one boat and captured another. Among their wounded prisoners was the famous Captain Payne.[23]

The next evening, the Confederates won another, though unexpected, victory—this time over the enemy's naval pickets. Like the Northern army, the Union navy also manned a number of picket boats in the waters around Charleston. Besides operating in the rivers and streams, the navy placed armed launches in the main ship channel where, under the protection of a monitor, they watched for enemy warships and blockade runners. On the night of August 5, a launch commanded by Mate Edward L. Haines spotted a blockade runner near Cummings Point. Believing help was near and expecting an easy capture, Haines moved to take the ship.

The vessel observed by Harris was the blockade runner *Juno*, which like the *Alice* and other blockade runners had been pressed into duty by the Confederate navy. Armed with a spar torpedo and manned by regular seamen under the command of Lieutenant Philip Porcher, CSN, the *Juno* was on her nightly watch when called on to surrender by Haines, who emphasized his point by firing his boat howitzer at the Confederates. The shell missed its mark, and Porcher quickly turned the *Juno* and rammed Haines' boat. Stunned by the attack from what they thought was a passive blockade runner, the Federals tried to board the *Juno*, but Porcher, calling the engineers from below deck, met the boarders with a volley of small arms. Outnumbered and without any support, Haines and most of his men surrendered while eight managed to swim back to other Federal boats.

The captured Northerners and their launch were taken into the harbor where they were transferred to the ironclad *Chicora* and then sent on to Charleston. While being escorted into captivity, one of the captured sailors was heard to remark: "This comes from placing an officer in charge of a boat who gets you into trouble, but can't get you out."[24]

Although the Confederate actions caused Gillmore and Dahlgren to pull in their pickets and raised Southern spirits, they hardly hindered the Union's effort on Morris Island. The Confederates knew that the North was going to continue the campaign. Using a balloon from Fort Johnson, the Confederates could see first hand the enormous resources that the North was bringing to bear against Battery Wagner.[25]

Chapter 6

THE SIEGE CONTINUES

Charleston is too important to be lost when so nearly won.
Major General John G. Foster

While the Confederates fully expected the campaign to continue, there were some major doubts on the Northern side. Even though Gillmore had begun preparations to build breaching batteries and open a siege against Wagner, the general was hesitant to push on without reinforcements. In dispatches sent after the July 18th attack to General Halleck, the North's commander-in-chief, Gillmore requested that eight to ten thousand veteran troops be sent to his department. Halleck found Gillmore's letters highly annoying, especially after the artilleryman's optimism before the campaign began. If Halleck had had his own way, no troops would have been sent and the campaign probably would have ended, but then other parties intervened.

The unexpected help came from the navy. When Admiral Dahlgren wrote Secretary of the Navy Welles for more marines, the rear admiral commented on Gillmore's depression and the army's need for reinforcements. Dahlgren expressed concern that the entire campaign might be called off if no additional troops were sent.

The dispatches reached the secretary on July 26, and after reading them, Welles immediately sent Gustavas Fox to confer with Halleck, but the commander of the army refused to discuss the situation. Welles, puzzled and angered at Halleck's action, took Dahlgren's dispatches and hurried to see President Lincoln.

In his meeting with the president, Welles pushed for a continuation of the campaign and suggested that troops from the Army of the

Potomac be sent to Gillmore. Lincoln agreed, and within two days, Halleck, under direction from the president, dispatched reinforcements.

Halleck reluctantly ordered ten thousand men to the Department of the South. One contingent, organized into a two-brigade division under the command of Brigadier General George Henry Gordon, was made up of eleven regiments, eight of which were Gettysburg veterans from the XI Corps, Army of the Potomac. The other half of the reinforcements consisted of five thousand men in three brigades from Major General John G. Foster's command in North Carolina. Among the troops from Foster included a brigade of African-American soldiers, consisting of the 1st, 2nd, and 3rd North Carolina, and the 55th Massachusetts. Also sent south was the 3rd United States Colored Troops, a regiment of African Americans that had been formed in Philadelphia.

In writing Gillmore to inform him about the reinforcements, Halleck took the opportunity to chastise his commander:

> You were distinctly informed that you could not have any additional troops, and it was only on the understanding that none would be required that I consented to your undertaking operations on Morris Island. Had it been supposed that you would require more troops, the operations would not have been attempted with my consent or that of the Secretary of War.

But Halleck was in a minority within the high command. Most wanted to see the campaign continued in the hopes that it would bring Charleston under Federal control. As General Foster, who gladly sent men to the crusade, wrote to Gillmore: "Charleston is too important to be lost when so nearly won."[1]

By the first week of August, the three brigades from North Carolina arrived on Folly Island along with the 3rd USCT (United States Colored Troops). They were joined on August 15 by General Gordon's division. With this help, Gillmore began to take a firmer hand in his operations. The rest of the 7th Connecticut was brought from St. Augustine and, along with other units, was assigned to the artillery.

The new arrivals were pleased to be part of the campaign. It was said that on one transport every officer and soldier was "happy to be able to have a slap at Charleston." One officer commanding the African-American troops in the 55th Massachusetts wrote:

> It will be perfectly jolly if we can have a hand in the taking of Charleston. How the Southern female population in that city would

hate to pay proper respect to the colored soldiers from Massachusetts. Colored soldiers any how would be pretty bitter there, but when they combine the unpleasant properties of being colored and coming from Massachusetts it would be unbearable.[2]

The reinforcements were bivouaced on the western end of Folly Island, in an area called Camp Seymour. Within days, the veterans of Gettysburg and the inexperienced troops from North Carolina, both black and white, were crossing to Morris Island to work in the trenches. Immediately, the men learned the harsh reality of war on the little barrier island. The summer heat was nearly unbearable, causing one to write: "We are really near the hotbed of secession and a confounded hotbed it will be for us if the sun comes down as it is doing today." The newcomers were also introduced to Confederate cannon fire and sharpshooters, which soon proved deadlier than the sun.

The engineers put the soldiers to work on the siege lines and new breaching batteries that were located on a portion of Morris Island that protruded into the swamps west of the parallels. As with the Confederates, the Federals soon settled into a routine that would continue throughout the siege.[3]

A revitalized Gillmore reviewed all work. His main field engineers were Colonel Serrell, the recently promoted Major Brooks, and Lieutenant Michie. Colonel Serrell was in charge of the overall operation, but he gave free rein to his subordinates working in the trenches and on the breaching batteries, while he concentrated on Gillmore's pet project, the marsh battery.

The most difficult task fell to Major Brooks, who supervised the siege lines that ran directly toward Battery Wagner. Under constant enemy fire, Brooks had to build sapping trenches and supporting batteries. For this duty, he oversaw large fatigue parties which were led by skilled engineers from his own regiment, the 1st New York Engineers.

To provide men for Brooks, brigade camps were set up on Morris and Folly islands. General Terry commanded Morris Island. His division, made up of veterans from the July 10 and 18 attacks, provided the majority of the work details. Units were rotated so that regiments would serve three days in front of Wagner doing fatigue or guard duty, one day in camp, and another day doing picket or fatigue work away from the front lines.

Folly Island was garrisoned by General Vogdes' division, which was made up of the three brigades from North Carolina and General

Gordon's division. Men from these units served a 24-hour tour of duty on Morris Island, then returned to Folly Island.[4]

The soldiers on Folly Island escaped the rigors experienced by their comrades on Morris Island. Though occasionally the Confederates would lob shells into their tents from a work on James Island, nick-named "Battery Crossfire," the men established comfortable quarters. By locating their camps near the ocean, the Federals were able to enjoy the breeze and swim in the salt water, which one officer claimed "was worth at least two doctors and several medicine chests to us."

Another officer, serving with the 55th Massachusetts, had one of his privates detailed as his personal chef. The man was so versatile that he could cook a meal of oysters and then conduct a prayer meeting. However, his employer had mixed reviews about the nightly services and commented that: "though in reality I like to hear the men singing and praying, yet I must confess, an hour and a half of it every night within fifteen feet of me does now and then grow rather tedious."[5]

In the evening, soldiers from Folly Island would be shifted to Morris Island by small steamers or a scow pulled by ropes where they were organized into either fatigue parties or the grand guard. Those assigned to construct the trenches split into three working parties, numbering from one hundred to five hundred men. Enlisted men from the 1st New York Engineers made up one third of the fatigue units, while the rest came from infantry regiments. Commanded by an engineering officer, each group worked an eight-hour shift; the first started at 4 A.M., with reliefs at noon and 8 P.M. As with the Confederates, orders between the engineers and laborers were transmitted through the infantry officers. The amount and quality of work done depended on the harmony between the engineers and line officers; however, Brooks often complained that officers from the infantry regiments would not accompany their men into the trenches, causing discipline to suffer. The result was less work being accomplished. Many officers refused to report for fatigue duty, forcing Brooks and his engineers to continually request work parties from specific regiments that had officers who were willing to accompany their men into the front lines.

Duty in the trenches was physically draining. Three-fourths of the work was done at night and nine-tenths of it under enemy fire. Troops loudly complained about being used as common laborers. Prisoners were taken from the guardhouse and used in the trenches, but they would often escape their guards and return to camp. African-American units were employed a great deal, doing slightly more than one-half of the fatigue duty. Only the veteran 54th was ever considered for grand guard duty, but because the attack on Wagner had so reduced its officer corps, the regiment was kept on fatigue duty with the other black regiments. Such treatment soured many officers and soldiers from Wild's African Brigade, who often expressed their desire to return to North Carolina; however, though the men grumbled about being laborers, they worked hard, which was somewhat astonishing since the soldiers were receiving at least three dollars less a month than their white comrades.

The reason for this inequity in pay dated back to the 1862 Militia Act, a bill passed by Congress to push the hesitant Lincoln government toward the recruitment of black troops. The act overrode the 1792 Militia Act which had barred men of African descent from serving in the army and militia. Besides opening up the army and militia to African-American soldiers, the bill also authorized the government to enlist African Americans for the construction of entrenchments, camp service, or other labor and set pay at ten dollars a month.

When first enlisted, the War Department had promised the South Carolina and Massachusetts African-American soldiers the standard pay for privates of thirteen dollars per month, but Congress, evoking the 1862 Militia Act, only authorized ten dollars for privates and three dollars less for all enlisted ranks. Reaction to the decrease in pay varied. Certain regiments accepted the ten dollars while the 54th and 55th Massachusetts, officers and men alike, refused all pay until the inequity was righted. In Colonel Higginson's 1st South Carolina, the paymaster ignored the regulations and gave out thirteen dollars a month until ordered to stop. To make up for the overpayment, the regiment saw its pay reduced to seven dollars. The regiments' officers vehemently protested the pay inequity, and as Congress and politicians debated, the African-American soldiers continued to labor, fight, and die on Morris Island.[6]

Conversion of the breastworks that contained Battery Reynolds into a defensive parallel was accomplished in relative safety. Though physically demanding, the line was far enough away from Confederate positions to escape any disruptive fire. At the same time, Major Brooks directed the construction of breaching batteries and an improved road from Light-House Inlet to the first parallel.

On the moonlit evening of July 23, Major Brooks directed his men to open a second parallel on a low ridge 480 yards in front of the first parallel and 870 yards from Battery Wagner. The approach and the second parallel was made by a technique known as the flying sap. In this operation the fatigue party formed a long line with each man carrying a cylindrical wooden, woven basket measuring three feet in length and two feet in diameter known as a gabion. Transported in the gabions were a shovel and an axe. The gabions were carried to a particular point and then placed upright in the sand. After using the axe to clear away any roots, earth was shoveled into the gabions. Once filled, additional dirt was thrown over the top of the gabions to form a natural slope with the ground. When finished, the men then received two more gabions and repeated the process.

Beginning from the right center of the first parallel, the engineers cut a zig-zag trench across Morris Island. Though the back and forth movement increased the amount of work needed to reach the site of the second parallel, it provided the working parties with the greatest amount of protection since it never provided the enemy with a direct shot down the trench.

Throughout the night, work parties, numbering nearly five hundred men from the 4th New Hampshire and the 1st New York Engineers, labored in the trenches. By daylight, they had zig-zagged across 480 yards, built across Morris Island a parallel ten feet thick and 175 yards long, constructed a battery mounting six howitzers, implanted seventy-five yards of inclined palisading and sixty yards of wire entrenchments, and started a large bombproof. The only portion of the work that Major Brooks found regrettable was that the bombproof was constructed in the center of an old graveyard that had one time served a plague hospital. Later, Brooks would discover that one of Morris Island's prewar nicknames was "Coffin Island."

Immediately, the parallel was occupied by an advance guard that included sharpshooters and men manning Requa batteries and howitzers. Over the next few days, the engineers provided the soldiers with splinter-proofs, keeps, and latrines. They then went on to build traverses and began revetting the parallel with sandbags, fascines, and smaller gabions called sap fagots. Cut board lumber was then brought in and used to construct gun platforms and to line the interior of the bombproofs and magazines.[7]

One unique element in the second parallel was the surf battery. The work was constructed to the right of the parallel, on top of a crib work located at the low water mark. Connected to the second parallel by a musketry parapet that extended from a Requa battery, the surf battery was surrounded by water at high tide. Containing two howitzers, it was positioned to thwart any enemy attack along the beach.[8]

The work on the siege lines not only required a tremendous amount of labor, it also demanded a huge stockpile of supplies. To make sure the engineers never ran out of needed equipment, the Northerners organized a special detachment to make siege material. Since Morris Island had been cleared of all wood, save two trees, the details were stationed on Folly Island where they worked night and day turning wood from saplings, trees, and bushes into 1,429 gabions, eleven sap rollers, 162 fascines, and 302 sap fagots. To supplement this output, Major Brooks also established workshops at Beaufort and Hilton Head.

At Hilton Head was located a vast engineer depot which provided finished products that were brought to Morris and Folly islands. This included items made of iron and cut board lumber that was manufactured at steam-powered sawmills. The completed items were then placed on board quartermaster vessels that kept up a constant shuttle between Hilton Head and the islands off Charleston. Larger vessels docked at the Stono Inlet end of Folly Island, while light drafted ships were used to transport munitions directly to Morris Island. As the siege went on, Brooks developed a depot at Light-House Inlet where he placed the steam derrick *Dirrigo*, which removed cargo from supply vessels. The engineers also operated on Morris Island a steam pile driver. Later, steam condensing machines were brought in so salt water could be converted into fresh drinking water.[9]

An indispensable item used throughout the siege was the common sandbag. By an account kept by the engineers, 46,175 sandbags were expended on Morris Island. Laid as headers and stretchers, usually in English or Fleming bond, the sandbags were used to revet parapets and embrasures, form loopholes for sharpshooters, fill gabions, and cover splinterproofs, magazines, and bombproofs. Empty bags were even used to transport shot and shell to the batteries. Because of the fineness of the sand used in the bags, the Federals kept the bags damp to keep the sand from escaping. With careful use, Major Brooks believed the sandbags could last four months before disintegrating.

Though placed extensively throughout the siege lines, sandbags were found inadequate when used for revetting the embrasures for heavy artillery. The blast from the guns often burst the sandbags. To overcome this problem, Major Brooks improvised by removing iron plates from the blockade runner *Ruby*. The plates from the iron-hulled derelict were fashioned into embrasure linings that withstood the firing of the cannon and effectively kept sand from clogging the openings.[10]

After perfecting the second parallel, Major Brooks, in the first week of August, was directed by Gillmore to open a third parallel 330 yards in advance of the second and only 540 yards from Wagner. Again the flying sap was used to reach the designated site, but a different and quicker method was used to establish the new parallel.

With the enemy in rifle pits only sixty yards away, the engineers, with pickets in front, crept to their positions carrying no arms. They held a short-handled shovel in their right hands and a rope in their left. The men were placed at intervals of six feet. When the head engineer decided on the parallel site, the rope was dropped and the men went down on their knees and quietly shoveled sand onto the rope. By morning the engineers had completed a trenchline that was soon expanded into a completed siege position.[11]

Though the Federals managed to accomplish a remarkable amount of work, the strain on the soldiers was tremendous. Temperatures during the last days of July ranged to well over 100 degrees, making it difficult to sleep even after a night of exhausting work. Enemy fire from Fort Sumter and James Island often proved disruptive. The 7-inch Brooke rifles mounted on Fort Sumter's barbette wall could fire the length of Morris Island, landing shells in Union camps. On July 25, the Confederates opened fire from newly built Battery Simkins, located on a sand spit near Fort Johnson, with 10-inch Columbiads and a 6.4-inch Brooke. From this point on, the Union soldiers were increasingly subjected to flanking fire from James Island as the Confederates continued to strengthen and build new batteries bearing on Morris Island.

The cannon on James Island and Fort Sumter was bothersome, but the most dangerous fire came from Battery Wagner. When Wagner opened, it could stop all work. On July 28, fire from the battery stampeded the teams of twenty-three loaded wagons. Some two weeks later, cannon fire caused the African-American troops operating in front of Wagner to break and run. Brooks felt this occurred because there were not enough officers in the trenches as the unit had only one lieutenant on duty with 175 men.[12]

The most constant danger to the Union soldiers was the Confederate sharpshooters. During the day, no one within a thousand yards of Battery Wagner could expose himself without becoming a target for the men operating the deadly Whitworth rifles. The Southerners would fire at every opportunity, watching for any movement that indicated a human presence. Union artillerymen found that the Confederates watched the six-inch square portholes through which the cannoneers viewed the flight of their projectiles. Whenever one darkened it immediately attracted a Whitworth bullet. In time, as their trenches neared Wagner, the Federals sometimes caught a glimpse of their assailants, and one Confederate sharpshooter was described as being very dark complexioned. Nicknamed the "nigger" sharpshooter, it was reported that he could hit the arms of cannoneers through embrasures, and it was certain death if any soldier exposed himself in the trenches. On one occasion a young Union sharpshooter, no more than seventeen, entered into a duel with the infamous Confederate, but in the midst of the fight, when the young soldier placed his eye to a port hole, he was struck dead.[13]

At the beginning of the siege, the North's sharpshooters were unable to challenge the Confederates. To rectify this problem and disrupt the enemy, Major Brooks asked General Gillmore to disband the existing sharpshooters and to form a new and more efficient company. Gillmore approved the recommendation and a search for the most accurate shooters in the Union army began. In a short time, the sixty best marksmen were organized into a company of sharpshooters under Captain Richard Ela of the 3rd New Hampshire. Among the regiments turning out men for service as sharpshooters was the 54th Massachusetts, which would have made Ela's unit one of the first integrated forces in the army.

By August 3, the troop, armed with Springfield rifles, was ready for service. On a typical day, the sharpshooters took their positions before daylight, carrying with them rations and one hundred rounds apiece. By evening, both the food and ammunition would be gone. Initially the Federals were at a disadvantage dueling with the longer-ranged Whitworth rifles, but as the Union lines pressed closer to Wagner, the Union sharpshooters, whose rifles had an effective range of six hundred yards, were able to compete on nearly equal terms with the Confederates. In time, both sides gained respect for the other's ability.[14]

While the majority of the fatigue parties were used to construct the siege lines, other important duties included the establishment and completion of the breaching batteries. For this work, Lieutenant Peter S. Michie supervised hundreds of men who labored to build fortifications designed to mount the war's heaviest artillery. Positioned behind the siege lines, the engineers enlarged and improved Batteries Weed and Reynolds, while new works were constructed around Batteries O'Rorke and Hays on the spit of Morris Island that stretched into the marsh toward James Island. The fortifications, known as the left batteries, were outfitted to contain heavy Parrott guns which were directed against Fort Sumter's gorge. Later, as the siege lines zigzagged to the third parallel and beyond, additional breaching batteries were also located in the second parallel.

Going into these works were seacoast mortars and Parrott rifles. The cannon, which weighed from 9,700 to 27,500 pounds, were shipped to Morris Island from Hilton Head. Because of the weight of the guns, the vessels could only enter Light-House Inlet at high tide. Once landed, the cast iron monsters were placed on sling carts—giant wheels

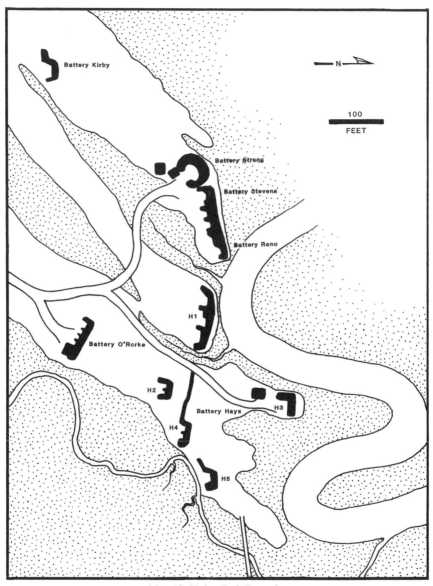

Map 18: Union Left Batteries

Battery Hays had five parts. For the July 18 attack H1 mounted seven 30-pound Parrotts, H2 mounted two 20-pound Parrotts, H3 was not yet constructed, H4 mounted two 20-pound Parrotts, and H5 mounted two 20-pound Parrotts. For the August 17 bombardment H1 mounted seven 30-pound Parrotts, H2 had no armament, H3 mounted one 8-inch Parrott, and H4 and H5 had no armament.

connected by a shaft from which the cannon were suspended. For the heaviest guns more than one hundred men had to be detailed to pull the sling cart to the batteries, a distance of more than two miles.[15]

Protecting the work parties was a unit of soldiers known as the grand guard. This detachment, numbering close to five hundred men, protected the engineers and the fatigue details from any enemy sorties. Often stationed in shallow trenches between the forward parallel and Battery Wagner, the men in the grand guard served a twenty-four-hour tour, combatting heat, exposure, and enemy fire. Duty in the grand guard was looked upon with apprehension by Northern soldiers. Any unguarded movement attracted a sharpshooter's bullet or artillery fire. One group of soldiers, from the 85th Pennsylvania, made the mistake of gathering into a small area that was seen by the enemy. In a short time, a mortar shell from James Island exploded over the men, killing seven and mortally wounding the other two. As one observer reported: "The parts of their bodies, clothing, equipments, and broken guns were scattered in all directions."

Even troops located inside bombproofs were in danger. One night, a Confederate 10-inch shell crashed into a splinter-proof shelter in the second parallel that was serving as the grand guard's headquarters. The shell badly wounded the guard's commanding officer, Colonel Joshua B. Howell. The fifty-six-year-old Howell, the popular commander of the 85th Pennsylvania, who now commanded a brigade in Terry's division, was knocked senseless by a shell fragment. Pulled from the wrecked bombproof, most thought he had been killed, and Howell recalled that he heard great lamenting from his soldiers as he was carried away. Howell soon recovered and, much to the joy of his men, returned to his command; however, as a reminder of his near brush with death the Colonel kept a piece of the Confederate shell.[16]

The need for constant vigilance on the part of the grand guard made it essential that veteran troops with proven officers be used. Throughout the siege the majority of the men used in the grand guard came almost exclusively from the white regiments. The 54th Massachusetts was considered for use with the guard, but because the unit had lost so many officers and the other African-American units were relatively untried, the Union commanders preferred to use the older and proven white troops.[17]

Elsewhere, guard duty was not so hazardous. On Cole's Island and other points where the picket lines of the two sides came in contact, a cordial relationship developed. Discussions and meetings took place between the soldiers on duty, and such items as tobacco, coffee, and newspapers were exchanged, but these scenes took place away from Morris Island, where the fighting went on without any break.[18]

While the work continued on the siege lines and batteries, Gillmore took time for other projects that he hoped would assist his campaign. One such scheme centered on the use of calcium lights—the military version of the limelight—to illuminate Cummings Point. Gillmore hoped the lights would reveal the night movements of enemy transports. If the lights worked, then artillery fire could be used to drive off Southern reinforcements. When first employed, the lights were placed in the left batteries, some three thousand yards from Cummings Point, but the distance proved too great, and they eventually were turned on Battery Wagner, making it difficult for the Confederates to carry out their nightly repairs. Later during the siege, Gillmore relocated the searchlights on boats off Cummings Point, effectively covering Battery Gregg and the troop landing area.

Besides the calcium lights, Gillmore also ordered incendiary shells, commonly called "Greek fire." Two types of "Greek fire" were received. One was made by Robert Parrott for use in his cannon, while the other was known as Short's Solidified Greek Fire. In both cases an incendiary material was placed inside a special shell that was designed to explode over a target and start a fire.[19]

Gillmore planned to use his "Greek fire" in a battery specifically built to shell Charleston. Shortly after the July 18 attack, Gillmore instructed Colonel Serrell to explore the possibilities of constructing a battery in the marsh between James and Morris islands. By one account, Serrell gave the duty to a young engineer lieutenant who, after examining the salt marsh, declared the project could not be done. Serrell informed the doubting engineer that nothing was impossible and to requisition any necessary materials. A short time later, Serrell received a request for twenty men eighteen feet tall for work in the marsh. At the same time another request was sent to the department's surgeon asking him to splice three six-foot men together to make the needed eighteen-footers. The requests did not amuse Serrell, and he soon replaced the young officer.[20]

True or not, Colonel Serrell did take over the project and, with assistance from Lieutenant Michie, developed a plan for one of the most unique batteries ever constructed. After seventeen days of personally trudging through the marsh and carrying out tests, Serrell developed a design that Gillmore approved, and on the evening of August 10, the engineers, supported by fatigue parties from the 7th New Hampsire, began work.[21]

The battery was built in two parts. The parapet was constructed first. For its foundation, sheet pilings were driven into the marsh by use of a hand, lever-operated driver. On top of the pilings was bolted a three-sided grillege of logs two layers thick. The grillege surrounded three sides of a rectangular area where the gun platform was to be located.

Placed on the grillege were thirteen thousand sandbags, weighing more than eight hundred tons. The sandbags were carried to the battery by the men of the 7th New Hampshire over a plank causeway two to four feet wide and seventeen hundred yards long. The journey took the men over an hour to complete and many fell off the slippery boards into the marsh. The men from New Hampshire complained that they felt "like a church steeple," as they walked over the planks, attracting the fire of Confederate batteries on James Island.

Once the parapet was completed, work began on the gun platform. Here, Serrell's careful calculations came into play. The platform had to support the weight of a 24,000-pound gun and carriage while not disrupting the parapet. To accomplish this, Serrell did not connect the parapet to the platform. Instead, he designed the battery so its two parts floated on the marsh in equilibrium. To construct the gun deck, the engineers packed down marsh grass, canvas, and sand in the rectangular area formed by the parapet. Then on top of this base they placed a close-fitting plank platform.

The Confederates, from positions on James Island, dimly watched the Northerners working nightly in the marsh and on occasion would lob shells toward the working parties. To confuse the enemy, Serrell had a mock battery established to the south of the real battery. At the same time, log-booms were placed in the surrounding creeks and armed launches watched for any Confederate attacks. During the day, the working parties went back to their camps and rested while a squad of soldiers armed with seven-shot Spencer rifles garrisoned the empty battery. Though the guards suffered under long-range bombardments from Southern artillery, the men remained hidden and made no hostile motions except to attack their rations.

While operating in the marsh, the Northerners managed to complete their tasks with little interference from the Confederates. Serrell and the engineers pushed the project toward completion as quickly as possible. The soldiers providing the labor found the work hard, and since they did not understand the reason for the work, they often contemptuously referred to the project as the Marsh Croaker, Mud Lark, and Serrell's Folly.

By August 17 the battery was ready for its armament. First the 8,000-pound iron carriage was ferried out to the site, then the huge,

16,300-pound, 8-inch Parrott was taken from the wharf at the southern end of Morris Island and placed on a specially prepared boat. Positioned over the keel, the Parrott weighed the vessel down so that it floated with only five inches of freeboard. The trip to the battery was slow, with water constantly being pumped from the boat, but before daylight, the Parrott was successfully landed and placed on the platform. Four days later, the gun was mounted. Serrell's calculations had been accurate. The downward pressure from the mounted gun did not disturb the parapet, and soon the battery was readied for action.

The battery's garrison was a detachment of the 11th Maine Infantry under Lieutenant Charles Sellmer, who had served nine years in the regular artillery and had attended the artillery school at Fort Monroe before the war. Sellmer's detachment had been called up from Fernandina, Florida, on July 22 for service in the siege lines and, after a few weeks operating mortar batteries, they were assigned to take over Gillmore's marsh battery. On August 21, Sellmer and his men took charge of the work, which was now referred to as the "Swamp Angel," a name given the battery by a member of the 3rd Rhode Island Artillery. The next evening, Sellmer supervised the unloading of shells, powder cartridges, primers, and other needed implements. While Sellmer readied his gun, engineer Captain Nathaniel Edwards took compass readings on St. Michael's church steeple in downtown Charleston for night firing. Whenever Gillmore was ready, the Swamp Angel was prepared to fire into Charleston.[22]

While the Union army prepared for the bombardment and readied the marsh battery, the Federal navy continued its close support. Throughout the weeks following the attack on Battery Wagner, Rear Admiral Dahlgren continually assisted Gillmore's operations by shelling Wagner and employing numerous picket boats in the channels and creeks about Morris Island. At the same time, the Navy watched for blockade runners and any forays by Confederate ironclads. The work was difficult and gruelling for both men and vessels. Ships were constantly suffering mechanical difficulties and had to be sent to Port Royal or north for repairs. Illness also took its toll with hundreds of sailors on the squadron's sick rolls. The 150-man crew of the screw steamer *Marblehead* was so infected with scurvy Dahlgren had to send the ship north.

While Dahlgren worried over the condition of his wooden vessels, the situation on the monitors was worse. Because of their never-ending operations, the monitors were in constant need of repair. Their smokestacks were riddled and all had holes in their decks. The bottoms of the vessels became fouled, reducing their speed. The *Nahant*, which

Dahlgren briefly stationed at Wassaw Sound, Georgia, to watch the Savannah-based Confederate ironclads, could barely make three-and-one-half knots. Dahlgren, reluctant to weaken his squadron, tried to carry out some maintenance off Charleston, but the work was piecemeal at best and rarely could the ships be brought up to full strength. Dahlgren was eventually forced to shuttle his monitors, two at a time, to the Navy's repair facilities at Port Royal, where more extensive work could be accomplished.[23]

Besides repairs, Dahlgren also worried over the physical deterioration of the monitors' crews. Temperatures over 100 degrees Fahrenheit inside the iron hulls was often a more formidable enemy than Confederate shells. Crews were frequently close to suffocation, and any chance to escape the interior of the vessels was quickly taken. On one occasion, a navy engineer, who appeared on the deck of a monitor without his full uniform, was reprimanded by the vessel's officer of the deck. The engineer, speaking for all of the men serving inside the iron hull, replied that "they did not wear uniforms in hell."

To ease matters, the ironclads' crews were given a twenty-five percent pay increase and special ice rations. The squadron's chief surgeon went so far as to order a ration of whiskey issued to the sailors serving on monitors. Though much appreciated by the crews, the whiskey order was quickly overturned by William Whelen, the navy's chief of the Bureau of Medicine and Surgery. Instead, Whelen sent instructions directing the sailors to take a swim each morning followed by drinks of strong coffee. He also urged that iced tea and coffee be issued during the day and a swim taken each evening. To combat thirst, the men were to be given a mixture of oatmeal and water and the crews were told to change their clothing as often as possible.[24]

Dahlgren also found his officers affected by the conditions. Two of his monitor captains had become ill, and other senior officers refused to take over the ironclads, thus forcing the rear admiral to give command of the vessels to less experienced commanders. The flag officer was also having difficulties with Captain Stephen C. Rowan, commander of the *New Ironsides*. Dahlgren found Rowen to be against any attacks on the harbor forts, especially if they involved his ship. Though Dahlgren privately expressed displeasure with Rowan, he was unwilling to call for the officer's removal.

Other problems plagued Dahlgren. Major Jacob Zeilin, commander of the 502-man marine battalion serving on Morris Island, reported that his men were incapable of operations on land because they were not accustomed to living ashore, not properly trained, and "out of sorts, sick and intractable." Word also reached Dahlgren that the

Laird Rams—British-built Confederate ironclads—might soon be coming in his direction.[25]

Concerns over enemy ironclads, sick marines, manpower shortages, and vessel maintenance were all reported by Dahlgren in his dispatches to Secretary of the Navy Welles. The rear admiral called on the secretary to send more sailors, warships, and ironclads. Welles immediately began gathering up needed reinforcements. Two hundred sailors were sent and another two hundred promised. Marines, taken from Northern posts and receiving ships, arrived and, after being reinforced by men from the squadron, were sent ashore for duty on Morris Island. Welles also instructed Dahlgren to make greater use of "contrabands," freed slaves living within the Union lines.

By early August, the promised help was arriving. Detachments of sailors joined the squadron, the monitor *Passaic* returned, and the monitor *Lehigh* was enroute. Additionally, mortar schooners, mounting 13-inch seacoast mortars, were sent. The sailing brigs *Bainbridge* and *John Adams* were dispatched to Charleston so their crews could be used as replacements. The *John Adams* arrived safely but the *Bainbridge* was lost in a gale before reaching Port Royal and disappeared with all but one of her nearly 100-man crew.[26]

With reinforcements arriving, Dahlgren continued to support the army, while at the same time he prepared his vessels and crews for the next stage of the campaign. Soon Gillmore's breaching batteries would be ready to batter down Fort Sumter's walls, and once this was accomplished, the monitors would be run into the harbor. For what he hoped would be the campaign's final operation, Dahlgren concentrated off Charleston the ironclads *New Ironsides*, *Montauk*, *Weehawken*, *Nahant*, *Patapsco*, *Passaic*, and *Catskill*, plus eight gunboats. Dahlgren met Gillmore and worked out plans as the land batteries were nearing completion. The rear admiral agreed with all of Gillmore's proposals, but commented that the general again seemed too "sanguine."[27]

If Gillmore appeared overconfident, he was putting on a good front. The strain of command was wearing on the army commander. Sickness and exposure to the South Carolina heat had worn him down. Though he heard no criticism from his subordinates, he did react strongly to detracting comments from newspaper reporters.

Early in the campaign, reporters and photographers swarmed over Folly and Morris islands, sending back daily reports about Gillmore's activities. To Gillmore these men were a nuisance. They also disgusted many of the Union officers by printing false stories of Confederate atrocities and angered Gillmore by reporting details of military operations and the names of units serving on Morris Island. To stop this, the Union commander issued General Order Number 66, which forbid the giving of any information by soldiers, officers, and civilians in the Department of the South to friends or the press which could possibly aid the enemy. Any violation of this order was to be met with the "severest punishment known to military law."

Still, information leaked through, causing Gillmore to order the arrest of Colonel John H. Jackson, commander of the 3rd New Hampshire. Jackson, who had been wounded in the July 18 assault, had gone back to New Hampshire to recover and recruit for his regiment. On the way home, he had been interviewed by a reporter in Boston. Though Jackson gave out no vital news, the story infuriated Gillmore, who, upon seeing the article, had Jackson arrested. The chagrined colonel was ordered to Washington, where, after an interview with Secretary of War Stanton, he was released.

Though Stanton found no fault with Jackson, he did sympathize with Gillmore's plight and directed the general to arrest all correspondents on Morris Island and confine them at Hilton Head until the campaign was completed. Stanton gave Gillmore the authority to take possession of the mail and to open all letters suspected of conveying military information. Gillmore was also given the power to deal with the offenders as he saw fit. The campaign was nearing its final stages, and Gillmore wanted no interference as he prepared to destroy Fort Sumter.[28]

Chapter 7

THE BOMBARDMENT OF
FORT SUMTER

They have ruined my beautiful fort.
Colonel Alfred Rhett

By mid-August, the Federal troops, under General Gillmore's critical eye, had turned the southern end of Morris Island into a massive ordnance complex, with heavy cannon arrayed against Fort Sumter and Battery Wagner. Never comfortable with handling troops in the field, Gillmore was now operating within his element. The building of batteries and the placement of guns and coordinated fire were procedures in which Gillmore excelled. There was probably no better officer North or South who could handle cannon like the Ohio-born artillerist/engineer. Yet, for all his planning and work, Gillmore found there were components he could not control.

The cannonade was scheduled to open on August 14, but in test firing their guns, the artillerists discovered that the Parrott-rifle powder cartridges were defective, forcing a two-day delay as they were re-mixed and repacked. By the time the cartridges were ready, Gillmore had taken sick and the attack was rescheduled for August 17.[1]

Gillmore's planned bombardment had little in common with the Confederate attack of 1861. The war was outgrowing the limited concepts of the men who had been in Charleston two springs before. This time the guns were positioned about two miles from Fort Sumter, and no smoothbores were used. Even the little Blakely rifle, which had been employed to such advantage in 1861, would have been discarded in 1863 as being too small. The new machines of destruction on Morris Island were ushering in a modern, more potent, age of warfare.

154

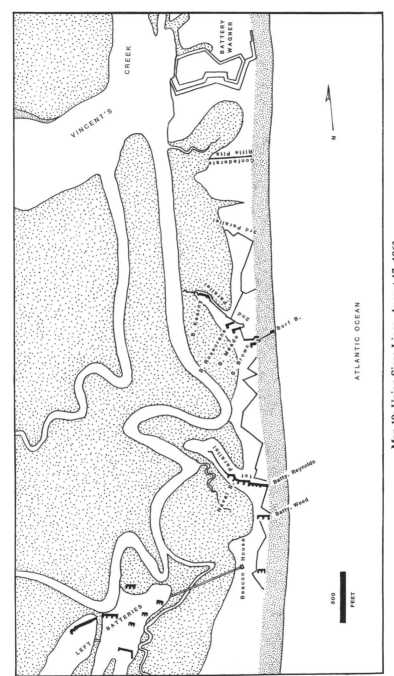

VINCENT'S CREEK

BATTERY WAGNER

N

Confederate Rifle Pits

3rd Parallel

B. Kearny
Rosecrans Parallel
B. Meade 2nd
B. Brown
Surf B.

ATLANTIC OCEAN

1st Parallel
Java B.
Batty. Reynolds

Batty. Weed

Beacon House

LEFT BATTERIES

500
FEET

Map 19: Union Siege Lines, August 17, 1863

Arrayed against Fort Sumter was the war's largest concentration of heavy ordnance. Positioned in twelve batteries were thirty-eight guns, which in one volley were capable of flinging more than three thousand pounds of metal. Each gun had its own deadly mission. Directed against Sumter's masonry walls were two 10-inch mortars, nine 6.4-inch and six 8-inch Parrotts, two British-made, 5-inch Whitworth cannons taken from the captured blockade runner *Princess Royal*, and one monster 10-inch Parrott which could fire shells weighing nearly 250 pounds. The rest of the guns, seven 4.2-inch Parrotts, ten 10-inch mortars, and three coehorns were to concentrate on Wagner, while three 4.2-inch Parrotts zeroed in on Battery Gregg. (See appendix, table 18.)[2]

For additional support, the navy promised to add the weight of its guns. Two monitors, the *Patapsco* and the *Passaic*, were to pepper away at Fort Sumter with their 8-inch Parrott guns, while the rest of the ironclads, backed by long-range firing from the wooden gunboats, were to sweep Battery Wagner and keep its garrison in the bombproofs and away from their artillery pieces.[3]

The Federals left no detail to chance. The batteries were to operate with clockwork precision. Like a giant factory that continuously turned out shot and shell, Gillmore and his men seemed to personify the efficient, mechanical North. Each battery had three shifts. Those working the larger guns firing on Fort Sumter worked four hours on and eight hours off, while the men operating the lighter siege guns served twelve hours on and twenty-four off. The batteries of Parrotts concentrated against Sumter were to maintain fire from daylight until dark, while the mortars and siege guns kept up a constant fire both day and night.

Each artillery piece was given a specific rate of fire. The 6.4-inch Parrotts were to fire every five minutes, the 8-inch Parrotts every eight, while the 10-inch Parrott was to fire once every ten minutes. After each shot, the bore was sponged with water to extinguish any burning material. To prevent the ever-present sand from affecting accuracy, the projectiles were greased and oil was kept on hand to sponge the bore after every third or fourth round. After twenty rounds, the guns were to be washed out and allowed to cool.[4]

At 5:00 A.M. on August 17, 1863, the first 8-inch shell from a gun in Battery Brown began its flight toward Fort Sumter. Immediately, the entire line of batteries joined in. Within two hours Dahlgren directed his ironclads down the channel and into action against Wagner. Once the Confederates had been driven into their bombproofs, the wooden gunboats came into range and added their guns to the increasing crescendo.

The Federal guns fired both shells and solid shot. Initially landing against Sumter's brick walls, the solid projectiles smashed and crumbled the fort's masonry. Also extremely effective were the percussion shells that exploded on impact, shattering bricks and scattering bits of deadly masonry throughout the fort. But as the bombardment went on and Sumter's walls were reduced to rubble, both the percussion shells and solid shots lost their effectiveness as their target turned from hard to soft. Eventually, the Federals armed their shells with timed fuses that exploded in or over their target.[5]

The officer in charge of Gillmore's batteries was Colonel John Wesley Turner, a West Point graduate and prewar artilleryman who had served early in the war as a commissary officer in Missouri under General David Hunter and later in New Orleans under General Benjamin Butler. Turner eventually rejoined Hunter in the Department of the South, and on Gillmore's arrival he was given the dual position of chief of staff and chief of artillery.

Turner not only supervised the operations of his gunners, he also carefully recorded how his guns performed. He and Gillmore knew that this was more than a bombardment of a Southern stronghold. It was also the world's first major use of heavy rifled artillery.

It did not take Turner long to evaluate the performance of certain cannon. He quickly realized that the British-made Whitworth rifles were nearly useless. Operated by sailors in the Naval Battery, their rounds did not take to the weapons' rifling, their shells exploded prematurely, and the solid shots rarely reached their targets. On the other hand, the Parrotts were models of efficiency. Turner wrote that: "The precision of the Parrott rifles were remarkable, probably excelling any artillery ever before brought on to the field in siege operations."[6]

Not only were the guns a fine example of Northern workmanship, but the accuracy of the Federal guns served as a potent testimony to the skill of the Federal cannoneers. Throughout the bombardment, hit percentages averaged seventy-eight percent. Even on August 18, when a severe gale flooded the trenches with two feet of water and high winds swept over the sand dunes, the Union guns were hardly affected. The artillerymen merely waded through the water, adjusted their aim for wind deflection, and continued firing, recording hits that day on eighty-seven percent of their shots.[7]

The most effective Federal cannon was the monster 10-inch Parrott whose 250-pound shells battered huge openings through Sumter's walls. The gun, mounted in a battery named for General Strong, was manned by a detachment from the 7th Connecticut under the command of Captain Sylvester Gray. Veterans of the July 10 landing on Morris Island and the July 11 assault on Battery Wagner, Gray and his soldiers were now serving as artillerymen for the Northerners' largest gun. During the first few days of the bombardment, the 10-inch Parrott shells travelled the two-and-a-half miles to Sumter in eighteen seconds, crushing masonry and crumbling casemates. The firing was also felt on Folly Island, as one officer claimed that the sea island vibrated every time the gun was fired.

For the first few days of the bombardment, the giant Parrott proved to be the most accurate gun in the Federal arsenal. Then, on August 20, a shell exploded prematurely near the cannon's muzzle, blowing off the extreme eighteen inches of the barrel. Undaunted, Gray had his men chisel off and file down the rough edges and resume firing. The missing eighteen inches had no effect on the gun's accuracy, and as one wag commented "The American Eagle is a fine bird, but he cannot beat the Ten Inch Parrott."[8]

Prematurely exploding shells were a constant problem for the Federal artillerists, but the durable Parrott guns were able to withstand a number of these explosions occurring in their barrels and keep operating. During the week-long bombardment, no Parrott gun was disabled, and Turner and his men took every precaution to keep the guns in service. With every hit, the artillerymen could see the results of their work, and many commented on the hot time that was obviously being experienced by the Southerners. The infantrymen who had built the batteries and helped mount the guns, which had nicknames like "Baby Walker," "Whistling Dick," and "Brick Driver," also viewed the work of their comrades, many climbing trees on Folly Island to watch and cheer every time bricks flew into the air. One soldier commented that it was a great pleasure to hear "our guns putting the question to old Sumter 'what went ye out of the Union for?' "[9]

While the Confederates were expecting the bombardment, their preparations were incomplete. When the attack commenced, engineers inside Fort Sumter were supervising a work force of just under five hundred slaves who were working to strengthen the fort by filling in casemates with sand, piling sandbags along the exterior of the gorge wall, and constructing new bombproofs, traverses, and blindages. Though a number of the fort's guns had been removed, Sumter still contained an armament of thirty-eight cannon and two mortars. The majority of the guns—including some of the largest in the Confederate arsenal—were located on Sumter's barbette. These cannon, though in an exposed position, were considered essential in warding off a naval assault. Because of this, the Confederates faced a dual dilemma. If they left the guns, located on top of Sumter's vulnerable brick walls, the cannon could be blown off their perch by concentrated artillery fire. On the other hand, if the guns, which could fire down on enemy vessels, were removed, then the Federal ironclads might be able to force their way into the harbor. For the moment, the Confederates gambled that the reinforced walls would hold against Gillmore's guns.

It did not take long for the Confederates to realize that they had

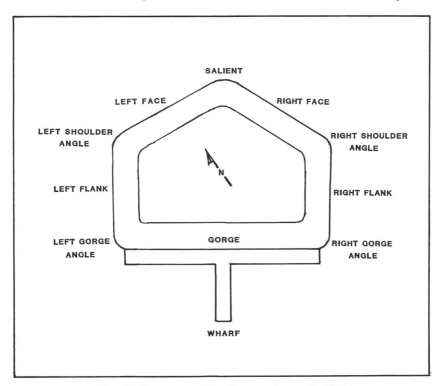

Map 20: Armament of Fort Sumter, August 17, 1863

Left Flank Barbette: two 10-inch Columbiads
Left Face Barbette: two 10-inch Columbiads, two 8-inch Columbiads, four 42-pounders
Left Face First Tier Casemates: two 8-inch Shell Guns
Right Face Barbette: two 10-inch Columbiads, five rifled and banded 42-pounders
Right Face First Tier Casemates: two 32-pounders
Right Flank Barbette: one 11-inch Dahlgren, four 10-inch Columbiads, one 8-inch
    Columbiad, one rifled 42-pounder, one 8-inch Brooke
Gorge Barbette: five rifled and banded 42-pounders, one 24-pounder
Salient Second Tier Casemates: three rifled and banded 42-pounders
Parade: two 10-inch Seacoast Mortars

vastly underestimated the power of the Parrott rifled-cannon. On August 17, the bombardment's first day, nearly seven hundred enemy projectiles smashed into Fort Sumter. The magazines were partially exposed, the hospital threatened, and numerous cannon disabled. On the eighteenth, nearly all the guns on the gorge, west and northwest walls, were out of action. By the nineteenth, a hole was punctured through the gorge wall allowing the Federal shells to pass into the fort. The next day, the gorge wall began to collapse.

Shots came fast at Sumter; timbers caved in and arches crumbled. Bricks were smashed into powder and sand bags blown apart. One by one, the barbette guns were dismounted, so by the end of the bombardment, only one, the 11-inch Dahlgren that had been spirited from the sunken *Keokuk*, remained serviceable on the east wall. Sumter's destruction devastated its commander, Colonel Alfred Rhett, who plaintively told a fellow officer: "they have ruined my beautiful fort."[10]

But Rhett and his command had little time for melancholy. To survive, every effort had to be given to repair and renovation. The garrison soon discovered that the rubble, formed by the destroyed walls and barracks, could be covered with sand and transformed into a new, stronger parapet. Each night, the garrison and its slave work force emerged from bombproofs and swarmed over the ruins, creating a second Fort Sumter from the remains of the first. The work was difficult and gruelling. Few could sleep in Sumter. The gangs of slaves had to be constantly watched and forced to work. The garrison, exhausted from daytime duties, would also join in with what little strength they had left. Yet, through the skilled direction of engineers and sheer determination, the Confederates were able to transform Sumter and remove vital equipment.

At night, when the Federal guns slowed their fire, the men created new traverses and bombproofs. Guns were remounted while others removed for shipment. Under the cover of darkness, small steamers would arrive and were loaded with shells, thousands of pounds of powder, all types of artillery gear, and any cannon that could be pulled out of the rubble. During the day, the garrison stood ready, while the slaves were kept in bombproofs. The artillerymen were constantly exposed to enemy fire and flying debris, but few were injured. During the bombardment only three men were killed and another thirty-five wounded. Casualties among the slaves were unreported, but probably mirrored that of the garrison. Near misses and miracle escapes were an everyday event. On the twenty-third, one shell-burst slightly wounded Colonel Rhett and four of his officers just as they were sitting down to lunch; while on another occasion, two slaves, Frank and

Wallace, had the post doctor write their master asking that they be removed from the fort as soon as possible since they had been hurt by flying bricks and at one point, as the note recorded, "Frank was struck dead for a while but is now recovered." The message ended with the plea: "Please send for us as soon as you can."[11]

Relief for the garrison and the fort was not available. Confederate batteries along the eastern rim of James Island tried to interfere with the bombardment and on occasion managed to send a shell into the Northern batteries killing and wounding some of the artillerymen, but the shelling was little more than a nuisance. The Southerners realized that their response was extremely limited against the breaching batteries which one described as "Pro-di-ge-ous."[12]

On August 22, toward the end of the bombardment, Generals Beauregard, Ripley, and Gilmer and Colonel Harris visited Sumter. After viewing the ravaged structure, the officers agreed that even though the fort was still defensible, its days as an artillery platform were over. Plans were laid to remove the remaining guns and artillerymen and turn the fort over to infantrymen. A few cannon, deeply nested within the casemates, would be left, but all that could be recovered from the ruins would be sent away and repositioned throughout the harbor. Since guns in Sumter could no longer cover the passageway through the harbor's obstructions, it was decided to switch the opening to the Sullivan's Island side of the channel, where it could be guarded by Fort Moultrie and its adjoining works. By the new defense plan, Sullivan's Island became the main bulwark against any naval assault, but Sumter still played a vital role, because if the fort should fall, the Federals could then use it as a base to open a hole in the obstructions which would allow the dreaded monitors to enter Charleston Harbor.[13]

Though the Confederates had correctly surmised the basic Union plan, their worries over an immediate naval assault were unfounded. Throughout the week-long bombardment, Gillmore insisted that the ironclads keep up a constant fire on Battery Wagner. These tactics kept Wagner's garrison from interfering with the siege guns, but they also exhausted the Northern sailors. Rear Admiral Dahlgren realized the strain being placed on his men, but as usual, complied with Gillmore's request.

When the bombardment opened on August 17, Dahlgren readied his six monitors. Specific orders were given for shelling Wagner and Gregg, while the monitors *Passaic* and *Patapsco* were to engage Fort Sumter. The *New Ironsides* was to assist, as circumstances warranted, at the discretion of its commander, Captain Rowan.

Before going in, Dahlgren was asked by his fleet captain, George W.

Rodgers, for permission to command his former vessel, the monitor *Catskill*. Rodgers, whose extended family had had a long association with the United States Navy and, with his cousins, Christopher Raymond P. Rodgers and John Rodgers, had participated in Du Pont's assault on Charleston, was a brave and resourceful officer. He had managed to avoid the political in-fighting over the monitors and Du Pont's removal, and in mid-July 1863, he had left the *Catskill* to become Dahlgren's fleet captain. But Rodgers was never comfortable in the staff position, and when it seemed that a strike might be launched into Charleston Harbor, he received Dahlgren's blessing to take command of the *Catskill*. Thankful for the opportunity, Rodgers told his commander that today he would go in the *Catskill* and "next time with you." With this said, Dahlgren took his position in the pilothouse of his flagship, the *Weehawken*, while Rodgers transferred to the *Catskill*.

Underway by 6:35 A.M. on the seventeenth, the monitors caught the incoming tide, and following the *Weehawken*, they moved up the channel and engaged Battery Wagner. Once in position, the vessels settled into the dull routine of loading, firing and loading and firing. Inside the *Catskill*'s crowded pilothouse, Captain Rodgers and four others were waiting for Dahlgren to order an advance up the channel. The helmsman, Oscar W. Farenholt, was leaning against the wheel, dozing, when he was suddenly awakened by an enemy shot crashing into the pilothouse roof. Interior plates suddenly flew off, instantly killing Rodgers and the vessel's paymaster, Josiah G. Woodbury, who had been serving as a signal officer. Two others were wounded, and the ship's wheel broken. Miraculously, Farenholt escaped any injury. Immediately, the *Catskill*'s next ranking officer, Lieutenant Commander Charles C. Carpenter, who had been superceded that morning by Rodgers, pulled the monitor out of action to transfer the dead and wounded to the tug *Dandelion*. The wheel was repaired, and Carpenter, whose life may have been spared by Rodgers replacing him in the pilothouse, returned the *Catskill* to battle. It was not until noon, when the squadron broke for dinner, that Dahlgren learned of the death of his fleet captain and friend. When the monitors resumed their attack late that afternoon, their flags stood at half mast.[14]

For the rest of the bombardment, the navy continued supporting the army, but no movement was made toward the obstructions. Monitors fired on Batteries Gregg and Wagner and occasionally certain monitors would add the weight of their 15- and 11-inch Dahlgrens and 8-inch rifles against Sumter's walls. Like the land-based artillerymen, the sailors found that their shells and shots made deep impressions on Sumter's brickwork. In a short time, the naval gunners opened gaps in the fort's seaward walls and revealed Sumter's inability to defend the channel.

While the monitors worked against Batteries Gregg, Wagner, and Fort Sumter, the ironclad frigate *New Ironsides* was used exclusively against Wagner. With its broadside of eight heavy guns, the huge ironclad alone could silence Wagner. An effective gun platform, Gillmore constantly requested use of the *New Ironsides* off Wagner, and Dahlgren would always comply.

Of all the Northern warships, the one most feared by the Confederates was the *New Ironsides*, which seemed impervious to shot and shell. The ship was so infamous that John Fraser and Company, the Confederacy's largest blockade-running firm, offered a bounty of $100,000 to anyone who sank the *New Ironsides*, while the Charleston firm offered only $50,000 for a monitor. Since cannon fire seemingly had no effect on the *New Ironsides*, another method of destruction had to be found.

General Beauregard felt he had the perfect solution in the army's recently completed torpedo boat. Named the *Torch*, the little vessel was a converted wooden gunboat that had been renovated for use as a torpedo boat by Captain Francis D. Lee. The ship was outfitted with a secondhand engine and had a dual-prong spar mounted in the bow with each arm holding a deadly torpedo. Because of the money involved, Beauregard and Lee were able to secure the services of James Carlin, a well-known captain of blockade runners. If the venture proved successful, Carlin proposed to purchase the *Torch* for use as a privateer.

On the night of August 20, Carlin took the *Torch* toward the Union vessels lying off Morris Island. A stop was made at Fort Sumter where a guard of eleven artillerymen under Lieutenant Eldrid S. Fickling was taken on board, then Carlin guided his vessel out of the harbor. Just after midnight, as the Confederates approached the *New Ironsides*, Carlin lowered his double-loaded spar and began maneuvering the *Torch* into position. Hailed by the Federals, Carlin kept up a series of evasive replies while he prepared to ram home his torpedoes. To avoid being caught in the ironclad's anchor chain, Carlin stopped the engine, and for a few minutes, the little vessel floated alongside the North's most powerful warship. Once clear of the chain, Carlin ordered the engine started, but the machinery failed to respond. Carlin, fearing he would soon be boarded, continued his misleading replies to the hails from the *New Ironsides*. Finally, the engine started and the Confederates pulled away, while the Federals fired blindly into the darkness. For a moment, as he steered the *Torch* back to Fort Sumter, Carlin considered attacking a nearby monitor, but he quickly concluded that "it would almost be madness to attempt it." Once back at Charleston, Carlin returned to the less dangerous profession of blockade running and urged General Beauregard to turn the *Torch* into a transport.[15]

Though the Confederates considered the *New Ironsides* to be the kingpin of the Federal squadron, Dahlgren felt that the warship's commander, Captain Stephen C. Rowan, purposely kept his vessel from fully participating in the squadron's actions. Though never criticizing Rowan in public, Dahlgren privately wrote cutting comments about Rowan's lack of aggressiveness.

Dahlgren's relations with Rowan reflected the rear admiral's personality. A renowned technician who dealt with naval ordnance before the war, Dahlgren had never been part of the navy's cliques, which dominated naval politics. Because of his ordnance work, Dahlgren rarely had an opportunity to exercise authority which denied him opportunities to develop a command presence and friendships within the navy's officer corps. His promotions came from his expertise with ordnance and not from sea duty. This lack of experience with his peers often haunted him in his relations with his officers and the army. While an aggressive and confident commander would have asserted himself more, Dahlgren refrained from exerting authority over troublesome officers such as Rowan, and while he would bitterly complain about Rowan and others in his correspondence and journal, he avoided confrontations.

Though many in his command supported him, Dahlgren was suspicious about the loyalty of certain subordinates. Indeed, some of the older naval officers viewed Dahlgren as an inexperienced sea commander who owed his position to his friendship with President Lincoln and ability to play the social/political games of Washington, D.C. For years, while other officers were earning their rank through extended and often dreary sea duty, Dahlgren was stationed at the Washington Navy Yard enjoying the amenities of shore duty in the nation's capital. These conflicts, both perceived and real, placed a strain on Dahlgren's ability to take firm control over his command.

Dahlgren's lack of command experience, combined with a tremendous ego, also affected his relations with the equally prideful Gillmore. While the campaign dragged on, these two war mechanics lost track of the jointness of their venture, which, with the successful bombardment of Fort Sumter, seemed ready for a climax.[16]

The ending of the bombardment was supposed to signal the ironclad attack; however, Dahlgren was not ready for an all-out assault. His crews were tired, most of his monitors had mechanical problems, and two monitors were down to one serviceable gun. Still, Dahlgren realized that he had to do something, and plans were made for a night reconnaissance to test the offensive power of Fort Sumter. On August 21, Dahlgren led the monitors past Wagner and toward Sumter, but the civilian pilot on the *Catskill* refused to cooperate, and without him, the ship ran aground. Disgusted, Dahlgren rescheduled the movement for the following evening.

The next night found the tide uncooperative, and it was not until 3 A.M. on the twenty-third, the day Gillmore ended the bombardment, that Dahlgren was able to bring the *Weehawken, Nahant, Montauk, Passaic,* and *Patapsco* to within eight hundred years of Fort Sumter. The monitors opened on Sumter and soon attracted heavy fire from Fort Moultrie. Dahlgren observed that Sumter was "pretty well used up"; managing only two or three shots in its own defense. At sunrise, Dahlgren withdrew his vessels to their berths off Morris Island where he noted that Captain Rowan was still holding the *New Ironsides* out of any close action, causing Dahlgren to bitterly comment in his journal that "Rowan is terribly careful about that vessel."

Dahlgren decided to rest his crews before making any serious attempt to pass through obstructions. He was satisfied with the progress against Sumter, but as long as the fort remained armed, the navy could not cut an opening in the barrier and the flag officer was unwilling to risk his ironclads in a dash over the obstructions. Reports came in daily that the Confederates were laying torpedoes in the main channel; and Dahlgren refused to move until an opening had been cleared. To do this, Fort Sumter would have to be completely silenced or occupied. Dahlgren thought that within two days Gillmore's guns would render Sumter untenable and, with his crews rested, he could send in boats to open a path for the ironclads through the torpedoes and other obstructions.[17]

The rest given to the men on the monitors was long overdue. Because of the aborted action on the twenty-first, the ironclad crews had been up for two days, and when they finally did engage on the twenty-third, their exhaustion was reflected in that night's poor marksmanship against Fort Sumter. As the surgeon of the *Nahant* wrote: ". . . we were all exhausted from having been up two nights in succession with a fight intervening. A more used up, dirty faced crowd than our officers I never saw. Downes, [commander of the *Nahant*] looked as peaked as an old nail, & had a dreadfully unclean mug. . . . But the misery must have thawed him . . . he treated all of his officers to some splendid whiskey."[18]

Though the navy had not yet launched its grand assault, the Northern bombardment, had effectively ended Fort Sumter's mission as an artillery platform guarding the harbor's entrance. Besides this, the destruction of the fort had also ended its guardianship of Battery Wagner and, conversely, the attack had proven that Wagner could not protect Sumter from a ruinous bombardment. While shot and shells flew over the earthwork, the men inside Wagner quickly learned that any help from Sumter's powerful rifled cannon was over. Throughout the week, Wagner's garrison had to fight its own battles against the enemy's batteries, ships, and sappers.

Left to their own accord, the men at Wagner resisted the best they could. Though Fort Sumter had been the principal target of the bombardment, Battery Wagner had received its share of attention. When the Northern guns opened on August 17, Wagner was commanded by Colonel Lawrence Keitt who found the fire of the light Parrotts and mortars annoying, but soon realized that the greatest danger came from the Union ships where his means of resistance was limited.

On August 17, Wagner's seaward guns, under the battery's chief of artillery, Captain Robert Pringle, stood at full strength: two 10-inch Columbiads and a 32-pound rifle. When the monitors came into range, Pringle's guns dueled with the ironclads, but the enemy fire became so accurate that Keitt ordered the artillerymen to seek cover from the barrage. When the monitors pulled away for lunch, Pringle and his men returned to their positions. So, when the ironclads approached Wagner later that afternoon the Confederates reopened the fight. By the end of the day, the chassis of one of the 10-inch Columbiads had been destroyed. Undaunted, Pringle continued the fight the following day, but again his command was overmatched and soon the 32-pound rifle was damaged, limiting the Southern response to a lone 10-inch Columbiad.[19]

With little interference from Wagner's seaward guns, the monitors were able to blanket Wagner with shell fire. By ricocheting their shots off the water, the Northerners were able to send their giant spherical shells skipping into the battery. No spot was safe within Wagner. On one occasion, Wagner's chief engineer, the Virginia-born Captain J. Morris Wampler, sat down in a sheltered area to write his family. Wampler wrote: "My dear wife and child," when a projectile bounded over the wall and instantly killed him. On the same day, another shell landed in a seaward gun chamber, disabling the entire crew. Any men venturing outside the bombproofs risked death or injury. As casualties mounted, most of the garrison was forced into the bombproof or the sand dunes behind the battery for safety.

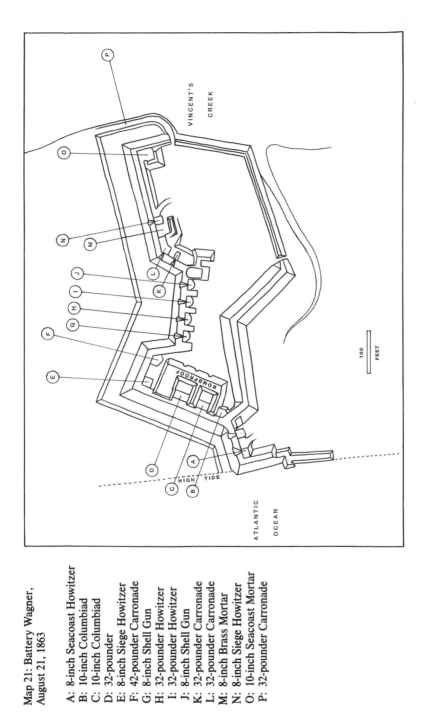

Map 21: Battery Wagner,
August 21, 1863

A: 8-inch Seacoast Howitzer
B: 10-inch Columbiad
C: 10-inch Columbiad
D: 32-pounder
E: 8-inch Siege Howitzer
F: 42-pounder Carronade
G: 8-inch Shell Gun
H: 32-pounder Howitzer
I: 32-pounder Howitzer
J: 8-inch Shell Gun
K: 32-pounder Carronade
L: 32-pounder Carronade
M: 8-inch Brass Mortar
N: 8-inch Siege Howitzer
O: 10-inch Seacoast Mortar
P: 32-pounder Carronade

Still, certain essential tasks had to be done, and much of the work was fearlessly carried out by Wagner's engineers. Through the extraordinary work of Captain John W. Gregorie, Wampler's replacement, and Colonel Harris, who stationed himself at Wagner throughout this period, the Confederates were able to keep the enemy guns from endangering the battery's bombproofs or magazines. At the same time, Colonel Keitt called for the establishment of a signal station in Wagner to communicate with the James Island batteries, and in a short time, work parties built a position on Wagner's west wall. From here, the Southerners could help direct supporting fire from James Island. Though in exposed positions, signalmen manned the tower day and night and miraculously sustained no casualties.[20]

Keitt was relieved on the night of August 20 by General Hagood, who encountered similar difficulties. The 10-inch Columbiad remained the only seaward gun, and the landward guns were in poor condition. Still, Hagood tried to slow the Union siege work and interfere with the bombardment by using his sharpshooters, available cannons, and mortars.

Hagood's tactics worked well, and effective counter-fire from Wagner's 8-inch seacoast howitzer and one of the 8-inch shell guns was directed against the enemy lines, but in doing so, the Southern artillerymen exposed themselves to enemy artillery fire. Against the enemy ironclads, Captain Robert Pringle continued to operate his lone gun. It was an uneven contest for the Confederates, who could watch the huge projectiles from the time they left the monitor's turret—"presenting the appearance of a rapidly enlarging disc." The monitor shells would skip two or three times before reaching Wagner. One projectile struck a school of mullet on its last rebound and flung a fish into the battery. It was immediately picked up by Pringle, who remarked that the enemy had just provided his supper; however, the brave captain, who had survived earlier duels with the monitors, was struck down by the next shell and killed.

For all their work and bravery, the Southerners could only slow the Northerners, who were still zig-zagging their trenches toward Wagner. On the evening of August 21, a rush by Colonel Dandy's 100th New York succeeded in establishing Union pickets within twenty yards of the rifle pits. Hagood, realizing this threat had to be driven back, immediately organized a sortie with men from the 25th South Carolina. Before dawn, the Southerners, led by Lieutenant Colonel Olin M. Dantzler, struck at the Federals before they could dig in, driving back the New Yorkers. Even though Hagood had saved his rifle pits,

Dantzler's men were unable to press on, and by the next morning, the Federals had established a fourth parallel.[21]

Besides being unable to stop the bombardment of Sumter and the siege lines, the men in Wagner suffered another frustration when they were unable to interfere with Gillmore's marsh battery as it began firing shells into Charleston.

Why Gillmore erected and used this battery has never been fully explained. In his official report, Gillmore states that the battery was built to drive shipping away from the city's wharves, and at other times, the whole episode seems to take on the atmosphere of a giant experiment in engineering and artillery firing.

By existing rules of warfare, Charleston was a legitimate target. It was an armed camp. There were fortifications in the city. It was home to a number of munition plants, and its wharves served blockade runners who carried war supplies.

But the reasons ran even deeper. To Northerners, Charleston was the symbol of rebellion. It was there that South Carolina officials voted for secession and started the inevitable march toward war. The firing on Fort Sumter, which started the conflict, only increased the North's belief that Charleston was a city of fire-eaters who deserved punishment. For most Northerners, Charleston's destruction seemed just retribution.

The Northern military also wanted redemption. Their impotence during the 1861 Fort Sumter crisis had deeply wounded the pride of many officers. If they could reduce Charleston like the Romans had reduced Carthage, so much the better.

Gillmore was well aware of these attitudes and shared them. He also had a personal motive for firing on the city. His well-laid-out plan had gone awry. He had seen his army shattered on the sands of Morris Island and his own physical condition reduced as the campaign sapped his confidence and energy. Revenge, for the blood of his soldiers, his countrymen, and himself, was also an important factor in his construction and use of the Swamp Angel.

On August 21, in the midst of the firing on Fort Sumter, Gillmore received word that the marsh battery, located seventy-nine hundred yards from Charleston, was completed and ready to fire. While the soldiers from the 11th Maine, who made up the gun crew for the marsh battery's 8-inch Parrott, completed their final preparations, Gillmore sent a message by way of Wagner to Charleston, demanding that General Beauregard immediately evacuate Morris Island and Fort Sumter or Charleston would be fired upon. The note reached Confederate headquarters at 10:45 P.M. Beauregard was not present and since the message was unsigned, it was returned for verification.

At 1:30 A.M., August 22, Lieutenant Charles Sellmer, aiming his gun by the compass reading taken on St. Michael's steeple, fired the first round into the city. Before dawn, the Swamp Angel would send sixteen shells into Charleston, with ten containing either Short's or Parrott's "Greek fire." The resulting flames were clearly seen, and some sharp-eared soldiers heard the bells and whistles of Charleston's firemen.[22]

Since the Confederates had ignored Gillmore's note, not believing it was official, no forewarning was given, and the first explosion caused everything from pandemonium to disdainful disgust. At the Charleston Hotel, the British illustrator and journalist Frank Vizetelly was reading a description of the battle of Waterloo when the first shell crashed into the city. Vizetelly quickly moved into the hallway where he found the corridors filled with terrified patrons who were rushing about in the scantiest costumes. As he described the scene: "One perspiring individual of portly dimensions was trotting to and fro with one boot on and the other in his hand, and this was all the dress he could boast of." When another shell exploded, Vizetelly gleefully commented that the entire crowd went "down on their faces every man of them in tobacco juice and cigar ends and clattering among the spitoons."

While the bombardment continued, Vizetelly joined two Austrian military observers at the Mills House Bar. Here, he spent the rest of the evening making bets where the next shell would land. As one of the Austrians described the game: "We could hear the whiz of the shells before they passed over our heads, and I bet the Englishman [Vizetelly] a thousand to one that the next shell would not hit us. He took the odds, forgetting that if he won he would be unable to collect his wager, and of course I won my dollar."

Farther down the peninsula from Vizetelly and the Mills House Bar, Williams Middleton was also reacting to the enemy shelling. Middleton, an extremely wealthy plantation owner and avowed Yankee-hater, lived in a large home on the city's Battery where he constantly observed the action on Morris Island from his veranda. When the first shells came into the city, Middleton was in bed, ignoring the enemy fire, then just before he was about to drop off to sleep a neighbor woke him to tell him that the "Yanks were shelling the city." As he described the scene to his wife, Middleton wrote: "As if I did not know it! Can you conceive of anything more absurd? I told him that I felt much obliged to him for taking so much trouble, but that I thought that all we could do was to let them shell and be damned." He then went on to assure his wife that he was perfectly safe. "Little or no damage has been done and not a soul hurt. As soon as they begin our batteries all open upon them and soon make it too hot for them to continue their deviling which is intended I expect for effect in the Yankee news market."[23]

The next morning at 9 A.M., Gillmore's note, now signed, again reached General Beauregard's headquarters. This time the general was present and an enraged Beauregard sent an immediate reply. The Confederate general considered the firing on the city an act of desperation and barbarity. He wrote: "I am surprised, sir, at the limits you have set to your demand. If, in order to attain the bombardment of Morris Island and Fort Sumter, you feel authorized to fire on this city, why did you not also include the works on Sullivan's and James Islands, nay, even the city of Charleston, in the same demand?" The evacuation of Morris Island and Fort Sumter was refused. The Confederate commander finished by indicating that unless he were given time to evacuate the city's noncombatants, he would use the "strongest means of retaliation. . . ."[24]

Beauregard's demand to allow citizens to leave was backed up by similar requests from foreign consuls. In his answer to Beauregard, Gillmore gave the Confederates one day to clear the city. At the same time, the Federal commander took the opportunity to lecture the Confederates on Charleston's role as an armed camp and munition site, pointing out that it was a legitimate military target and, since the campaign had been going on for forty days, the civilians and military should have known that a bombardment was inevitable.

Throughout the next night, the Swamp Angel remained silent. The gun had slid out of position and had to be moved back into place. During this time, the Union battery came under constant shelling from Confederate mortars, and although the Southerners' aim was accurate, their fuses were too long and the shells would land and bury themselves in the mud before harmlessly exploding.

Undeterred by the enemy guns, Sellmer and his men resumed firing on the evening of August 23, again using shells filled with Parrott's or Short's Greek fire. On this night many of the shells exploded in the gun, and after the sixth round, Sellmer found the cannon barrel to be moving in the breech-band. Sellmer had been warned that the Parrott was not a new gun and the exploding shells obviously shortened its life. Afraid that the piece would soon burst, Sellmer tied two lanyards together and positioned his men outside the battery, so if the gun exploded its crew would be shielded from the blast.

With the extended lanyard, Sellmer continued to operate the

cannon. After each shot the gun crew would reenter the battery, load the gun, set the primer, and attach it to the lanyard. The men then took cover as Sellmer, pulling on the lanyard, fired the gun. After thirteen more rounds, Sellmer, thinking that the Swamp Angel was still safe, decided to ignore his precautions and stood by the gun to check the time on his watch by the flash of the discharge. On this shot, the breech of the Swamp Angel exploded, throwing the gun onto the parapet. Lieutenant Sellmer and three others were injured, but not seriously, and the Swamp Angel's final shot, the thirty-sixth fired at Charleston, continued on to its target.[25]

The Swamp Angel was not replaced during the Morris Island operations, though later a siege gun was located in the Marsh Battery, which was eventually replaced with two mortars. Gillmore later explained that he expected no battlefield victory from the shelling, but felt that valuable artillery techniques were learned. The Swamp Angel accomplished a number of things. It was the first known firing of an artillery piece using a compass reading, and the distance covered by the Swamp Angel's shells was farther than any previous military bombardment.

Gillmore also gained the dubious distinction of being one of the first generals to bombard a civilian center in the hope of achieving a military end. As happened in later years, the shelling of Charleston fueled the defender's hatred for their enemies and provided them an even greater determination. Many civilians had already left the city before the campaign had begun and those that remained merely moved from the city's lower regions to areas out of range of the Federal guns. The city's manufacturing and industrial work continued, and all maritime activity was shifted up river.

In some ways, the Swamp Angel reflected Gillmore's frustration. Though he took satisfaction in shelling the birthplace of the war, Gillmore realized that it was an empty attempt to hurt an enemy who was proving far more resourceful than he had expected.

Besides the tenacious Confederate defense, Gillmore was upset over the navy's unwillingness to run the obstructions. The Union general felt that his work was done, and yet the campaign dragged on. In an act of rashness, Gillmore ordered six hundred men picked from Brigadier General Adelbert Ames's brigade for a night boat attack on Fort Sumter. When General Gordon, Ames's immediate superior, learned of the proposed assault, he unofficially wrote Gillmore, convincing him that the attack would be suicidal as long as the Confederates held the northern portion of Morris Island. Gillmore, realizing his mistake, called off the operation, but his frustration over the conditions on Morris Island was obvious. His bombardment had mutilated Sumter, but the navy would not act. His shelling of the city had resulted only in insults, and the siege of Wagner still dragged on.[26]

With the bombardment of Fort Sumter ended, the Federals turned their full attention to Battery Wagner. On August 21 the fourth parallel was established 350 yards from the battery; however, Union sappers found themselves in a very difficult position as the Confederate rifle pits, some 150 yards in their front, effectively covered their entrenchments. At the same time, the Confederate artillerymen, firing from James Island at ranges of three thousand to four thousand yards, were sending shells into the Federal works.

For the next three days, Major Brooks directed his fatigue parties in strengthening the new parallel and protecting it from the enfilading fire. At the same time, he continued to advance the sap. Working mainly at night with laborers supplied by the 3rd United States Colored Troops, Brooks fortified his position and extended the line to provide a jumping off point for an assault on the rifle pits.

At dusk, on August 25, the Federals were ready to launch their assault. In the forward trench were men from the 3rd New Hampshire. As the time for the attack approached, Brooks directed concentrated fire from coehorns, 8-inch mortars, and Requa batteries against the rifle pits. The Confederate defenders—men from the 54th Georgia— were in the process of being relieved by a detachment from the 61st North Carolina when the action began. Anticipating an attack, the Southern commanders kept both units in line; however, the orders to advance never reached the New Hampshire soldiers, and as one later expressed it: "the movement didn't move." Instead, a spirited exchange of small arms fire resulted between the two sides. In the end, Brooks was forced to cancel the assault. That evening he wrote that August 25 had been "the saddest day of the siege." To Brooks the Confederates seemed to be retaining their fighting edge while the Northern soldiers, "resting from the labor and excitement of demolishing Sumter, . . . do not yet take much interest in the operations against Wagner."[27]

The Confederate rifle pits that were holding up Major Brooks' operations had been greatly expanded since the early days of the siege, when they were merely small "rat holes" that provided protection for the individual pickets, and the Confederates were planning to even make them a greater obstacle. Captain John T. Champneys, Wagner's chief engineer from August 23 to 30, had made preparations to lengthen and enlarge them into a regular fortification. If this could be accomplished, Champneys believed the Federals could be stalled and eventually forced to make a major assault to take the new line. But

Map 22: Union Siege Lines, August 23, 1863

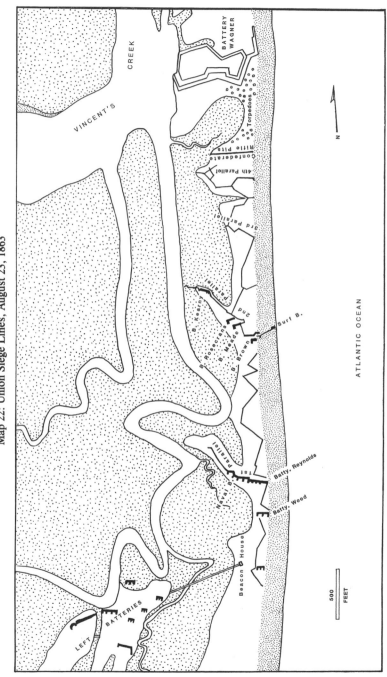

BATTERY WAGNER

VINCENT'S
CREEK

Torpedoes
Confederate Rifle Pits
4th Parallel

3rd Parallel

Parallel
B. Kearny
B. Rosecrans
B. Meade
B. Brown
2nd

Surf B.

1st Parallel

Naval B.
Batty. Reynolds

Batty. Weed

Beacon House

LEFT
BATTERIES

ATLANTIC OCEAN

N

500
FEET

Champneys' work was hindered by the lack of tools and sandbags. Before he could get underway, the Federals launched another assault.

Not wishing to give the Confederates time to prepare, General Gillmore immediately sent word to General Terry ordering him to take whatever means necessary to capture the rifle pits. Terry quickly readied the 24th Massachusetts and the 3rd New Hampshire from General Stevenson's brigade. At nightfall, the regiments, numbering some four hundred men, were moved forward. The Massachusetts regiment had been designated to make the rush while the 3rd New Hampshire was held in reserve. Each man in the assaulting column from the 24th Massachusetts had two shovels strapped to his back to rebuild the rifle pits once they were taken. Since the 24th was General Stevenson's old regiment, Terry allowed Stevenson to accompany them. At 6 P.M., the Requa batteries in the fourth parallel opened fire, sending out sheets of bullets and covering the attackers as they jumped from their trenchline and headed toward the enemy.

The Confederates, eighty-six men from the 61st North Carolina, got off one volley before they were overrun. Many of the men were trapped in the trench, while others, not wishing to risk the torpedoes planted between the rifle pits and Wagner, quickly surrendered. Only nineteen escaped. Immediately, the Union soldiers began to improve their newly won position, some forcing their Confederate prisoners to dig for them. One soldier reported that he dug so fast he blistered his hands while another was knocked senseless, when, in a rush to dig out the trench, the man next to him accidently struck him in the head with a shovel.

Inside Battery Wagner, Colonel George P. Harrison, Jr., the post's commander, was furious and began to organize a counterattack to retake the rifle pits but was persuaded from the venture by his fellow officers. Harrison did order artillery fire on the Union soldiers, but by now, the Confederate rifle pits were being formed into a fifth parallel and the final advance on Wagner was ready to begin.[28]

With the fall of the rifle pits, the Confederate high command realized that the Federal siege lines would soon cross the remaining two hundred yards of sand between them and Battery Wagner. But the time gained so far by Wagner's tenacious defense had been well used by the Southerners. The fortifications on James Island were becoming stronger each day. On Sullivan's Island, new batteries were built and armed with guns removed from Fort Sumter. To help man the new positions reinforcements arrived in Charleston. Among the incoming troops was Nathan "Shanks" Evans's brigade of veteran infantrymen which, with the fall of Vicksburg, was not longer needed in Mississippi. Additional cavalry was transferred to the Charleston area and seamen from Richmond and Savannah were brought in and placed on board the city's warships. By late August, General Beauregard had positioned around Charleston thirty-three hundred artillerymen and ninety-six hundred infantry.[29]

In addition to his increased manpower, Beauregard also directed his subordinates to strengthen Charleston's harbor defenses. Engineers placed heavy rope cables across the main channel, from which ran hundreds of smaller ropes, three-quarters of an inch in diameter and fifty feet long. The ropes were designed to foul the propellers of enemy warships. Among the ropes, just below the surface, were torpedoes poised to explode upon contact with ships' hulls. The new explosive devices were built and put in place by Captains M. Martin Gray and Francis D. Lee. To assist these officers and improve his torpedo program, Beauregard brought to Charleston Major Stephen Elliott, a resourceful ordnance officer who had experience using torpedoes.

Major Elliott had started the war as the commander of the Beaufort Volunteer Artillery Company and was later made the ordnance officer for the Third Military District. While holding this position, Elliott distinguished himself in the Battle of Pocotaligo and in attacks against Northern gunboats. When not in the field, Elliott experimented with torpedoes and, on at least one occasion, launched explosive devices against Federal vessels in St. Helena Sound. In mid-July, after the Federals had landed on Morris Island, Beauregard's chief of artillery, Colonel Gonzales, who was married to Elliott's cousin, requested the young officer as his assistant, and by early August Elliott was transfered to Charleston. Sent to James Island, Elliott was given the task of floating torpedoes down the Stono against enemy vessels stationed at the mouth of the river.

Also in August, Brigadier General Gabriel James Rains, the Confederacy's best torpedo expert, arrived to take over the torpedo bureau from Captain Gray. Devoted to his study of explosives, Rains was described by one observer as

> a most comical looking person . . . medium height, with a short, quick, jerky way of walking, and a most peculiar expression of face, the eyes and mouth of which are incessantly in motion. A great torpedo man . . . is a perfect monomaniac on the subject and talks of nothing else. I saw him get one innocent and confiding young man in a corner and I am certain he torpedoed him for at least two hours.[30]

Besides bringing in torpedo experts, Beauregard did everything possible to secure additional heavy artillery. Cannon were requested from all over the South. Damaged guns were repaired and out-of-date weapons were rifled and banded in the Charleston workshops. Beauregard also used his influence to gain the use of two British-built 12.75-inch Blakely rifled-cannon. The two guns, the largest ever used by the South, had been run through the blockade by John Fraser and Company for the Confederacy on the former commerce raider *Sumter*, now named the *Gibraltar*. The cannon were so large that they could not fit below decks and had to be positioned in the cargo holds muzzle up, giving the *Gibraltar* the appearance of having three smokestacks. The *Gibraltar* carried the guns to Wilmington, North Carolina, in late June 1863, and immediately, the city's commander, Major General William Henry Chase Whiting, made plans to use them at Wilmington; however, Beauregard's influence proved too formidable, and Whiting soon succumbed to pressure from government officials and shipped the guns to Charleston. They were eventually mounted on the city's battery where their 650-pound shots and 450-pound shells were expected to stop any ironclads that survived the run past Sullivan's Island.[31]

With their new fortifications, guns, and men, the Confederates stood stronger in late August than they had in early July when the Federal attack began. Battery Wagner had done its job, but the Confederates were not quite ready to abandon Morris Island.

To hold Morris Island as long as possible, the Southerners continued to place their best troops in Battery Wagner. With the Federals so close, duty in the battery was extremely hazardous, and sometimes not all the dangers came from the enemy. On the night of August 30, troops destined for Morris Island were brought to Fort Johnson where they were usually placed on navy launches and rowed to Cummings Point; however, on this night, the navy, fearing an attack by the Northern ironclads, was unable to furnish the needed boats and sailors. As a result, Major Motte A. Pringle, the quartermaster in charge, was forced to take the sidewheel steamer *Sumter* from Fort Johnson to Morris Island. Since the night was foggy, Pringle believed the movement would be hidden from the Union batteries and warships.

The exchange of troops went smoothly. The 27th and 28th Georgia Regiments landed, and the 23rd Georgia and 20th South Carolina were picked up, but when Pringle was ready to return to Fort Johnson, he discovered that the tide had gone out and to reach safety, he ordered the ship's civilian captain, James R. Riley, to take the *Sumter* around Fort Sumter and into the harbor by way of the main channel.

Though Pringle did not suspect any danger, the Confederate commander at Fort Moultrie, Major Robert De Treville, had his garrison sleeping by their guns waiting for the same ironclad attack that the

Confederate sailors were watching for. When lookouts at Moultrie sighted the vessel, the artillerymen opened fire. Terrified, the soldiers on the *Sumter* tried to signal their comrades while at the same time a small boat was sent ashore to stop the firing. Still, before anything could be done, four shots hit the *Sumter*, sinking it on a shoal near Fort Sumter. Miraculously, only two men were killed and another wounded. The dazed soldiers were at first placed in Fort Sumter and then eventually transferred to Sullivan's Island. In the after-action reports, Pringle blamed Moultrie's commander for being trigger happy, while Major De Treville blamed Pringle for bringing his vessel into the main channel without any forewarning. Though Beauregard placed responsibility on Pringle, any action against the quartermaster was waived because his service up to that time had been exemplary. To stop any more incidents from happening, the Confederates quickly adopted a system of signals which allowed their vessels to communicate with the harbor forts.[32]

Even with the loss of the *Sumter*, the Confederates were able to keep up their rotation of units in Battery Wagner. Every evening the garrison was turned out to their battle positions to watch for any enemy attacks while the garrison's engineers tried to repair the battery. During the last days of August, at least two hundred men using one thousand sandbags were required every night to keep Wagner in fighting trim. The work was extremely hazardous as the Federals illuminated the fortification with calcium lights, forcing the Southerners to stay in the shadows to avoid attracting enemy fire.

During the day, the majority of the garrison was kept in the bombproof. Though a large structure capable of housing nearly one thousand men, it was extremely uncomfortable, and sleep was nearly impossible. The enclosure was sweltering and its doors had to be kept shut to keep exploding shells from sending fragments throughout its interior. The bombproof also housed Wagner's hospital, so the soldiers were unwilling spectators to many crude operations. Those stationed outside the bombproof also found Wagner an unpleasant place. Enemy shells hitting behind the battery landed in the Confederate burial ground and continually dug up dead soldiers.[33]

Whenever possible, Wagner's garrison tried to disrupt the siege. The most efficient work was done by the sharpshooters, who by now had turned in their long-range Whitworth rifles for quicker-firing Enfield rifles. But as the Northern trenches grew closer, it was discovered that Union artillerymen could use their cannons as effectively as the Confederates handled their Enfield rifles. Whenever the Confederates fired their landward guns during the day, the embrasure would have to be closed immediately or Union cannon shells would come whistling through the opening. Once, when the Confederates failed to cover up, a bolt from an 8-inch Parrott slammed into the muzzle of an 8-inch siege howitzer, breaking the piece and driving its remains onto the parade. Besides zeroing in on artillery pieces, the Union gunners would often direct their shells at individuals, especially anyone moving between Wagner and Gregg. On one occasion, Colonel Rhett, dressed in the customary white uniform of the officer of the day at Fort Sumter, was inspecting Morris Island from Sumter's ruined parapet when the Union gunners chose him for a target. The projectiles came so close that Rhett had to duck to avoid incoming shells that exploded seconds later over the parade ground.[34]

While the shells from the Federal guns were dangerous, what the men in Wagner feared most were the bursting mortar shells, especially those fired by the small coehorn mortars whose projectiles would silently arc down into the battery. To protect themselves, the Confederates soon developed the art of dodging shells, and whenever a mortar shell was spotted, the men would immediately: "pop down to mingle with the fiddlers and the sand crabs."[35]

Confederate retaliation against the Federals was severely limited, and with the loss of the rifle pits, the Southerners realized that the campaign was nearing its end. Major General Gilmer correctly summed up the situation when he commented that: "As long as the contest is one of work and shooting at long range, no people can beat the infernal Yankees."[36]

Staged photograph taken after the fall of Battery Wagner showing the construction of a siege line and a sap roller. (Library of Congress, Washington, D.C.)

General Gillmore with map and staff on Morris Island. (Library of Congress, Washington, D.C.)

Naval battery in the siege lines. Manned by sailors from the USS *Wabash*, the photograph shows the two British manufactured 5-inch Whitworth guns. (Library of Congress, Washington, D.C.)

Turret of the USS *Catskill*. Note the 15-inch and 11-inch Dahlgren guns. (Library of Congress, Washington, D.C.)

The 10-inch Parrott gun after the explosion blew off part of its barrel. (Library of Congress, Washington, D.C.)

A Requa battery. Note the soldiers holding the cartridge that contains 25 metallic cartridges. (Library of Congress, Washington, D.C.)

Northern ordnance depot on Morris Island. (Library of Congress, Washington, D.C.)

Northern campsites on Morris Island. (Library of Congress, Washington, D.C.)

Northern bombproof with Confederate torpedo (land mine). The photograph was taken after the siege. (Library of Congress, Washington, D.C.)

Landfront of Battery Wagner, photographed after its capture. (Library of Congress, Washington, D.C.)

Entrance to Battery Wagner's main bombproof. Soldiers from the 54th Massachusetts Regiment are seen on left. (Library of Congress, Washington, D.C.)

The Swamp Angel after its explosion. Note the two-plank causeway leading to the battery. (Library of Congress, Washington, D.C.)

Two 6.4-inch Parrott rifles on Battery Stevens. The photograph was taken after the fall of Battery Wagner. (Library of Congress, Washington, D.C.)

An African-American regiment drawn up in Beaufort, South Carolina. (U.S. Army Institute of Military History, Carlisle, Pennsylvania.)

Chapter 8

THE CAMPAIGN ENDS

There is no more interesting a spot as Morris Island.
Clara Barton

The seizure of the Confederate rifle pits placed the Federals in position to begin their final approach against Battery Wagner. Major Brooks quickly turned the former Confederate defense line into a well-fortified siege parallel by emplacing Requa batteries and 8-inch mortars. At the same time, Brooks tried to push the siege lines forward with a flying sap, but enemy fire was too severe, and he reluctantly had to employ the slower but safer sap roller.

The sap roller was a giant, sand-filled, wooden, woven basket that was nine feet long and four feet in diameter. Used much like a portable breastwork, the sap roller weighed about a ton and was moved forward by using sap hooks and two strong levers twelve feet in length. Operated by a sapping brigade, which consisted of eight artificers and two noncommissioned officers from the engineers, the sap roller was slowly pushed forward a few inches at a time. Behind it, men quickly dug a shallow trench approximately four feet wide and two feet deep using axes and short handled shovels. Though difficult to maneuver and time consuming, the roller did provide adequate protection for the men as they worked their way across the final stretch of sand between them and Battery Wagner.[1]

Besides being forced to use sap rollers, Major Brooks found his operation being slowed by the presence of enemy torpedoes. On the night of August 26, as work was being done around the fifth parallel, a corporal from the 3rd USCT hit and exploded a torpedo. Killed instantly, the soldier was flung through the air and landed on the plunger of another torpedo. The incident was seen by many men in the trenches, including Major Brooks, but when the body was discovered the next morning by the new fatigue details, it was reported that the Confederates were placing the bodies of African-American soldiers over the torpedoes as decoys. Eventually, the story reached Northern newspapers where it was embellished to have the black soldier tied to the torpedo.[2]

The torpedoes caused a number of injuries to the fatigue parties and forced the Northerners to make a careful examination of the ground before they moved the sap rollers. More than sixty torpedoes were found; they comprised three types which Major Brooks carefully recorded. The first, of which the Federals found twenty, were made of 24-pound cannon shells that were encased in a cylindical tin box. The bottom of the box rested against a percussion fuse placed in the shell. The box was then buried in the sand with the fuse side pointing up, so when any pressure, such as a footfall, was made against the box, the shell would explode.

The second and most common form was made of ten-gallon wooden kegs, the ends of which were extended by conical additions. This particular shape was manufactured for marine use, and these were usually found floating in the harbor, but they were also used on Morris Island. For detonation on land, each keg had a plunger that when forced downward exploded the torpedo. Sometimes the plunger was covered by a board or attached to a three-armed piece of iron. If someone stepped on the board or one of the arms, the pressure would instantly set off the torpedo.

The third form, of which but three were found, consisted of large 15-inch navy shells. These torpedoes, probably unexploded shells from the monitors' 15-inch guns, were buried in the ground and were detonated by a plunger device that was covered by either a board or attached to the three-armed metal device used with the wooden kegs.

Though the torpedoes were liberally scattered among the sand, most were found along the beach, the logical approach of an attacking party. Initially, the Union engineers tried to explode the torpedoes by directing the sharpshooters to hit the plungers. This proved unsuccessful, so they either had to carefully defuse the torpedoes or, as they did with the wooden devices, drill a hole into the kegs and pour water into them.[3]

Besides the torpedoes, the Union soldiers were harassed by enemy sharpshooters and cannon. As the final zig-zags drew closer to Wagner, the enemy cannon fire became deadlier, with the Confederate artillerymen taking special delight in firing at the Federals during meal times. To protect themselves, the Northerners stationed men to watch for enemy activity. These lookouts would yell out the name of the enemy battery so their comrades could take cover. When the cry "Cover Johnson!" or "Cover Gregg!" was heard, the men would stop work and scurry for a sheltered area. If the incoming shells were from mortars, the lookouts would add "mortar" to their warnings. When the men knew that a mortar shell was coming, they would stay hidden until after the explosion to allow all the fragments from the shell to hit the ground. With such advance notice, the Federals were able to keep their casualties low; however, Major Brooks noted that the men would often fling themselves face down on the ground, taking no precaution to cushion their heads against the effects of concussion. Because of this, many a soldier who escaped shell fragments found himself dazed and injured.

The safest time to work in the trench lines was at night, when the flight of the shells could be seen by their burning fuses; however, there was no forewarning when Wagner's guns fired. Before notice could be given, the shells exploded among the men. After Wagner's fire and the mortar shells, what Union soldiers feared most were the Brooke rifles. The Federals erroneously referred to these guns as Whitworth cannon, and called their shells "lightning train."[4]

In the final days of the siege, the Union soldiers not only had to be aware of Confederate shells, but also their own. With the siege lines so close to Wagner, the shells from the Union batteries and ships presented a constant danger. Though the Northern gunners took extra care in aiming their pieces, they could not stop shells from tumbling or exploding prematurely. When this happened, casualties occurred in the forward trenches. One of the worst accidents happened on August 30, while Lieutenant Colonel Henry A. Purviance of the 85th Pennsylvania was commanding his regiment in the forward trenches.

The 85th had returned to grand guard duty at sunset on August 29, and Purviance placed himself in the front lines with his soldiers. This was Purviance's custom, and his men respected him for sharing their hardships. As the lieutenant colonel stated: "My headquarters are with my men. I have the same shelter during rain and storm that my men have."

One day after Purviance accompanied his regiment into the siege lines, the Pennsylvanians came under severe fire, not only from Wagner but also from their own gunners. In the early afternoon, a Federal shell exploded directly over Purviance, and its fragments carried away the back of his head, passed through his body, and ripped open his right arm. The men from his regiment were not allowed to remove the body of their beloved commander and, instead, remained at work while four companies of the 104th Pennsylvania escorted Purviance's remains to the dock for shipment north.[5]

The wounds inflicted by the shells were not clean, and if death did not come instantly, the soldiers often died while being dragged to the hospital. If they reached the hospital, amputation nearly always resulted. Though surgeons did their best, recovery from shell wounds was not common. Assisting the doctors on Morris Island was the future founder of the Red Cross, Clara Barton. She was deeply moved by the suffering and by the fact that so many men were dying on an island unknown to the rest of the nation. In late August, as the number of casualties increased, she wrote that there could be no more "interesting a spot in the face of the globe at this moment as Morris Island."[6]

When off duty, the men on Morris Island tried to find relief from the rigors of the campaign. Some would climb the sand dunes and watch the panorama of the battle below them. One such observer wrote that when the Union batteries fired in volleys the whole island would shake and the batteries would be covered with white smoke, then a "peaceful interval came, when strange stillness of the ordnance seemed like stopped heartbeats of the siege. The soft rush of the surf and the chirp of small birds in the scant foliage could be heard."[7]

The only relaxation available to the men was surf bathing. Daily, the beach of Morris Island would be crowded with off-duty soldiers. Many camps were located within a hundred yards of the beach, so each morning and evening the men could enjoy the water and the breeze off the ocean.

But even the ocean could not cure all the ills. The camps were uncomfortable and crowded. Tents were useless on the loose sand, so wooden platforms were built 18 inches off the ground and canvas tents stretched over them for cover. Only with experience could one sleep or relax. During July and August temperatures soared over 100 degrees, and the slightest breeze, though comforting, would cause sand to fly like a blizzard, which the soldiers termed a "Carolina snow storm." The sand affected everything: the men's clothing, food, and equipment. Fleas were a nuisance and the island was infested with rats. On occasion, large crabs would crawl inside the men's blankets, awakening them rudely, and on one day, much to everyone's misery, a "plague of locusts" struck Morris Island. As a soldier of the 85th Pennsylvania wrote: "I think this is the meanest place that I was ever in."[8]

Still, the soldiers worked on. The food was not bad, and commanders made certain the troops in the trenches received hot meals while on duty, though there were the usual complaints, especially over the hard crackers given to the men, which in reality were sandwiches because of the "fat worms inside." Unfortunately, for some the discovery was not made until after they had "supped on the horrors." Others thought that the crackers, which were termed hardtack, should be given to the artillery because "there could be no doubt of them penetrating Sumter."

The water on Morris Island was "abominable." To avoid salt water, wells were dug away from the beach. They varied in depth from four to eight feet and used one or two barrels for cribbing. The wells did not last long. After one day a green scum covered the top of the well and within a few days the men would be forced to dig a new well. Once, when a well went bad on a company from the 7th New Hampshire, the men decided to dig deeper to rid the well of its "bad smell and taste." After digging one more foot, they found the well was dug over a soldier's grave. The next morning the entire company reported sick and was given a ration of whiskey before returning to work.

To help ease the pain of drinking the water, many soldiers ran it through charcoal filters or mixed it with molasses. Also, doctors on Morris Island issued rations of whiskey every morning and evening. Though forbidden by military regulations, the doctors got around the rule by claiming that it was given to combat malaria. Though appreciative, soldiers complained that the rations issued were in "harmless quantities."

Camp routine was nearly forgotten by most regiments. When not on duty, the men were allowed to do as they pleased; however, on Folly Island some commanders insisted on constant drilling. The 1st North Carolina, comprised of African Americans recruited near New Berne, North Carolina, carried out nightly formations along the beach even after the men had spent the entire day in the trenches.

One night, Charles B. Fox, of the 55th Massachusetts, was awakened at midnight by the sound of music and went out of his tent to see a brigade proceeding to Morris Island to relieve the grand guard. As he described the scene, Fox wrote:

At the head of the column was the finest band in the Department, and as they wound along the beach close to the water's edge, the dark lines moving in good order, the bright guns glistening in the moonlight, and the sweet music of the band falling gently on the ear, the scene seemed hardly a reality of this stern, matter of fact world. They played a march in which was arranged the tune "Tis Midnight

Hour," and nothing could have been more fitting or appropriate. It was a touch of the romance of war.[9]

Most units skipped all drill in hopes that rest would help the men's health, but even with the extra time to relax the Union soldiers suffered a high rate of illness. The monotony of the routine made men dull and spiritless. As the siege dragged on with no apparent end in sight, the soldiers went about their duties listlessly. As their mental and physical conditions weakened, so did their resistance to disease. The heat of the day and the chill of the night, poor rations, exposure, and crowded conditions coupled with homesickness, caused many to become ill. Malaria, ague, fevers, and scurvy swept through the camps. Since the campaign was still in progress, few furloughs were given. Rest areas behind the lines were impractical on the small island, and desertion, unless one was willing to go over to the Confederates, was impossible. When the men became ill under these conditions they had little will to recover, so diseases which were not usually fatal killed many.

One soldier who joined the sick rolls on Folly Island was Lieutenant Frank Heimer of the 144th New York. For nearly three weeks, Heimer suffered with an unknown ailment. Unable to eat, he became worse. The opium pills given to him by the regimental doctor had no effect, and as the days passed he listened to the Dead March being played throughout the camp as Union soldiers were laid to rest in a nearby graveyard. Convinced that he was going to die, Heimer decided that he did not want to be buried in the regimental cemetery where the shallow graves quickly became "water holes." Instead, he chose a dry location on a sand ridge underneath a live oak tree and made his friends promise they would bury him there. But before Heimer passed on, he discovered that another soldier had been interred in his chosen spot. Outraged by the loss of his burial plot, Heimer decided to live. He pulled himself across the island to a house site, procured a brick and a door latch, and then crawled to an oyster bed. Using the brick as a table and the door latch as a hammer, he broke open oyster shells and devoured the raw oysters for the rest of the day. The nourishment had the desired result, and in a short time, he recovered and returned to duty.[10]

By the end of August, it was not uncommon for twenty-five percent of a regiment to report sick each morning. On one day, the 24th Massachusetts had 250 men on the sick rolls and only 275 ready for duty. Illness varied among the different units. Major Brooks noted that the average sick for the artillery was 6.2 percent; engineers, 11.9 percent; African-American infantry, 13.9 percent; and white infantry,

20.1 percent, with the entire army during the siege having an average of 19.88 percent reporting ill each day.

The difference in illness between the white and black troops caused many observers to believe that the African-Americans were better suited physically for service in the deep South; however, this was not the real reason. Instead, the credit for better health among the black troops was due to their regiments having more conscientious officers, who made sure their camps were kept in order and clean.[11]

To treat the men, there were a number of brigade hospitals on Morris Island. Each hospital had a chief surgeon and all were under the supervision of the army's chief medical officer, Surgeon Samuel A. Green of the 24th Massachusetts. The principal medicine to combat any sickness was quinine and whiskey. Later in the campaign, when men became too ill for the brigade hospitals, they were sent to a convalescent camp at St. Augustine, where, when strong enough to travel, they were given furloughs and sent home.

Another type of medical care available on Morris Island came from the Sanitary Commission. Established early in the war by various women relief groups who wanted to provide for the soldiers, the Sanitary Commission worked to improve hygienic conditions and food, furnished ambulances, and staffed temporary tent hospitals. On Morris Island, the Sanitary Commission was best known for trying to supplement the diet of the soldiers with vegetables and fruit. They also served "beef tea" to the men in the trenches.[12]

The final relief organization on Morris Island was headed by Clara Barton. Working alone out of her tent, the dedicated philanthropist passed out food, wrote letters, and assisted the army surgeons. Though urged by many to leave Morris Island, she refused and remained steadfast in her work, but in time—like Gillmore, Dahlgren, Terry, and thousands of men—became very ill. Unlike the soldiers, she was sent to Hilton Head where she eventually recovered. While there, she wrote of her experiences:

I am singularly free, —there are few to mourn for me, and I take my life in my hand and go where men fall and die, to see if perchance I can render some little comfort as the wife or mother would if she could be there. —I know nothing of hospitals,—nothing of security, nothing of permanency, nothing of renumeration, but *give* all I have of time, strength and means—and give it directly to those who need, and reserve nothing to even help *sustain* an assistant if I had one. My own living on Morris Island all the time I was there and will be again when I return was what the soldiers call "salt junk"—old beef of such hardness and saltness as you never dreamed of, lean bacon, and hard crackers, both buggy and wormy—there was not a potato or other cookery vegetable on that island for weeks, —I sent General Terry one day, on hearing that he was sick, a tin dish of stewed dried peas and half loaf of soft bread, which had been sent me from Hilton Head, and he was so grateful that he came as soon as he could walk alone to thank me for them. —Genl Gilmore the day before I came away sent his waiter to me with a cracked tea cup to know if I could let him have a *little white sugar*—he was *dangerously ill* and could take no nourishment *if he had it.*

Vessels come constantly, but they could bring only guns, ammunition, and timber, while the men work *sixteen hours* in twenty four in the midst of fire and death to hold the enemy *back*,—twenty four hours, that he could not raise his head erect once, could only be relieved under the cover of darkness, and all this with a little piece of salt meat and four wormy crackers in his *pocket* and a canteen of warm water—and when wounded and brot in if I had a mouthful of soft or palatable food to give him, it looked brighter to me than gold, and no mouthful of it passed my lips—or even could until there was enough for *all.*[13]

After a brief stay on Hilton Head, Clara Barton returned to Morris Island, with a black woman as an assistant, and continued her work.[14]

By the end of August, conditions on Morris Island were becoming worse and sickness had reached such heights that Lieutenant Colonel Augustus C. Hamlin, medical inspector of the Department of the South, reported that unless Wagner fell soon, a third attack "would be more economical of life," than a continuance of the siege operations.[15]

For the moment, any thought of a third attack was out of the question. Gillmore, suffering from camp fever and depression, was hoping the navy would now move against the obstructions and enter the harbor. Gillmore felt that there was little more for him to do. His guns had destroyed Fort Sumter, and though he had his batteries keep up a desultory fire on the fort, he was unable to renew a full-scale bombardment because many of his heavy Parrott rifles were nearly used up. He knew that any more intensive firing would render them inoperable.

Much to Gillmore's disgust, the navy was not yet willing to enter the harbor. Dahlgren refused to risk his ironclads until a passage had been cleared through the obstructions. Ideally, for this to occur, Fort Sumter should be in Union hands; however, since the Federal guns seemed to have effectively silenced the fort, Dahlgren decided to have his men remove the obstructions. A plan was formulated where small boats manned by sailors would be sent in at night, and while monitors stood between the launches and the enemy's batteries on Sullivan's Island, the work parties would create an opening in the obstructions near Fort Sumter.

On August 26, Dahlgren organized groups of "smart seamen" who volunteered to go in on small boats armed with "tackles, straps, fish hooks, saws, augurs, chisels hammers and anything else deemed necessary to clear the obstructions"; however, from the twenty-sixth to the thirtieth, the navy was foiled by bad weather as thunderstorms swept the area. Then on the thirtieth, it was noticed that the Confederates had remounted some guns in Fort Sumter overlooking the obstructions. Dahlgren, realizing that his volunteers would be slaughtered by cannon fire from Sumter, cancelled his movement and called on the army to knock out the guns. Gillmore did not believe the report but dutifully had his batteries reopen the following day, and after firing more than six hundred projectiles at Sumter, Gillmore declared that there were no serviceable guns left and called on the navy to finish their work, though unknown to the general the 11-inch Dahlgren mounted on the barbette remained operable.[16]

But Dahlgren decided to postpone any advance until he polled his ironclad commanders for opinions. On the morning of September 1, he called a meeting to discuss future operations. Commander Thomas H. Stevens of the *Patapsco* was all for running right at the obstructions in full daylight and urged that the *New Ironsides* be placed in the lead. Such an audacious attack was ruled out, as Dahlgren reported that Captain Rowan, the commander of the *New Ironsides*, "had no taste for that." Instead, the officers agreed on a conservative plan where they would take their vessels in at night and test the strength of Fort Sumter and the obstructions.

That night, with the monitors leading, the squadron approached to within five hundred yards of Sumter. The one gun in Fort Sumter greeted the ironclads and soon it was joined by the Confederate cannon on Sullivan's Island. The monitors returned the fire, and as Dahlgren later reported, "the *Ironsides* came up, for a wonder, and fired." At dawn, the ironclads withdrew, having fired 245 shots and received seventy-one hits. One of the enemy shot had struck the base of the *Weehawken*'s turret and drove in a fragment of iron that fractured Fleet Captain Oscar C. Badger's leg. He was the third fleet captain lost to Dahlgren.

Though he found the Confederate defenses to be strong, Dahlgren hinted that he might continue the attack, but then, before any firm plans could be made, the rear admiral received a note from Gillmore asking for the navy's assistance against Battery Wagner. Dahlgren readily agreed, writing that though he was prepared to force a passage into the harbor, "General Gillmore is now ready for another movement and I propose to assist him first."[17]

By this time in the campaign, General Gillmore was feeling extremely frustrated. Though he had accomplished his primary mission of destroying Fort Sumter, he could not understand why the navy would not attack. He was also being pressured by his subordinates to complete the seizure of Morris Island. So by early September, after his ordnance chief, Colonel Turner, had replaced the worn Parrott guns, Gillmore made his final plans. Gillmore was motivated by the realization that Dahlgren was obviously seeking every possible excuse to avoid an all out attack, to prod the navy onward, Gillmore decided to bring the campaign to a climax by capturing Wagner and establishing breaching batteries on Cummings Point where the army could provide the navy with close in covering fire.

The Union soldiers welcomed Gillmore's new push. They too were ready to end the matter and rid themselves of the miserable life on Morris Island. They also shared Gillmore's opinion of the navy, which they felt was avoiding the final conflict. A rumor that quickly spread through the camps had Rear Admiral David G. Farragut arriving to take command of the fleet, but this was false. The men expected little from Dahlgren and his vessels. An infantry officer cynically wrote of the monitors: "One story is that the Rebs have a couple of men with revolvers (Colts Navy). One on Fort Sumter and the other on Fort Moultrie and that the Monitors are afraid to go up least their fire should sink them!"

For the final advance, tired but proven veterans were returned to work. The 85th Pennsylvania took up their familiar position in the grand guard while the African Americans of the 54th Massachusetts took over the fatigue details. The engineers wanted only the best units in the trenches as the campaign neared its end.[18]

As the Union lines pushed forward, Wagner came under an intensified and unrelenting bombardment. During the day, the Federals used their coehorn mortars to shower shells into the battery while from the sea the *New Ironsides* directed her broadsides against Wagner's main bombproof and magazines. The Confederate garrison was forced to seek refuge either in the sand dunes behind the battery or in the bombproof. Only a small band of sentries were kept on guard, but even these stalwart individuals were often forced to huddle behind protective traverses to avoid the metal fragments that whirled about Wagner.

During the bombardment, Union warships zeroed in on the Confederate wells located behind Wagner. The situation became so desperate that to relieve the garrison's thirst, officers had to call for volunteers to fetch water. These intrepid individuals covered themselves with canteens and then crawled to and from the wells under heavy enemy fire.

Night brought little relief as the Federals kept up their firing guided by the light from their calcium lights located not only in the siege lines but also on board a ship. In this way, the lights were able to illuminate Wagner from two directions, thus exposing more of the battery to an effective night fire. Still, the engineers managed to work in the shadows, and using large parties of soldiers and slaves, repaired the battery.

The Confederate response to the Federal bombardment was limited. The sharpshooters continued their work, often entering into personal duels with their counterparts in the Federal trenches. On one occasion, a Southern rifleman picked off his opponent and gleefully shouted "I got him," but before a moment had passed, he was struck in the shoulder and came tumbling down the wall.

Only at night could the landward guns be worked. During the day the cannon were usually kept covered with sandbags to protect them from being dismounted or broken up by enemy shot. The garrison did try to reply by using the 10-inch mortar and an ancient brass mortar which reputedly was a relic from the Revolution; however, since the Union lines were so close, shell fragments from these mortars often landed in Wagner. Some support came from the Southern batteries on James Island, but even these gunners would occasionally land a "friendly" shell inside the battery.[19]

As the Federal lines inched closer to Wagner, it became even more vital for the Confederates to keep up close communication with the high command in Charleston. Because the bombardment drove the signalmen from their post, the Southerners turned to the couriers to run messages between Batteries Wagner and Gregg.[20]

On the night of August 31, the final detachment of horsemen was sent to Morris Island. The squad consisted of Sergeant E. C. Holland and six privates from Company H, 4th South Carolina Cavalry. One of the new unit was Private John Harleston, who fell into conversation with one of the departing cavalrymen. The man's final words to Harleston were: "I thank God I'm getting away from this place. I tell you it is hell, hell!"[21]

Harleston, who was also known as "Pirate" because of his early war service on the privateer *Savannah*, soon understood the comment. Of the ten original horses, only five were left, and all of them had been wounded at least once. Before Harleston could get settled, he was called on to deliver a message to Battery Wagner. Advised to take the "flea-bitten Grey," which had recently lost its tail to a shell, Harleston mounted the veteran horse, gave it his head, and hung on as the Grey charged down the beach. With no guidance from its rider, the horse ran straight for Wagner. As the grey neared the sally port, it made a quick stop that sent Harleston forward and nearly head over heels to the ground.

This was the first of many trips made my Harleston between Wagner and Gregg. The couriers had their names placed on a list by their sergeant, each taking their turn on the dangerous ride. The grey that Harleston had ridden on his inaugural run was the best of the five horses. He always ran at full speed, was able to avoid shell craters, and was never frightened by enemy cannon fire.

On a typical run, a courier would come under fire from enemy monitors, the *New Ironsides*, land batteries, and sharpshooters. It was not uncommon for a rider and horse to disappear into clouds of sand thrown up by exploding shells. Yet for all the danger, only four horsemen were wounded in the last week of the siege.

After a successful run, the courier stayed in Wagner until another came up from Gregg. While in the battery, Harleston and his companions observed plaintive scenes of life and death. Throughout the day, the bulk of the garrison remained confined in the bombproof watching mangled wounded brought in for crude operations, while enemy shells exploding overhead caused sand to spill down on the troops, patients, and doctors.

On one occasion, a shell caved in the entrance to a small bombproof, trapping nearly forty men. A squad of Georgians immediately went to work to dig out their comrades before they suffocated. Because of the narrow confines of the bombproof's passageway, the captain in charge directed the soldiers to work one at a time, for five minutes each. When one man was slow to go forward, the captain called upon him to hurry, to which the man responded: "Yes, Captain soon as I get off this coat." While the soldier fumbled with his buttons, the captain stated: "Damned, I believe you are afraid." The coat was then pulled off and the man went forward, and before he could get very far, he was struck by a shell fragment and killed. Immediately, the captain replaced the fallen soldier and worked until the bombproof door was cleared.

Harleston had many narrow escapes inside Wagner, but his luck ran out when he was stunned by an exploding shell. Barely conscious, he was rushed to the hospital where Wagner's chief surgeon, Dr. William C. Ravenel, found him to be unhurt. When he awoke in the midst of amputated legs and arms, Ravenel offered the confused courier a brandy. Harleston accepted the treat and then discovered in one of his cavalry boots a brass sabot that had cut the leather but barely bruised his skin.[22]

The conditions viewed by Harleston were well known by the Confederate high command, who realized that Battery Wagner was quickly becoming untenable. During the first week of September, General Beauregard called meetings with his ranking officers to discuss the situation. A number of plans were put forward. Some called for an immediate counterattack, while another proposed the construction of a new work between Batteries Wagner and Gregg. Though these plans had some merit, the officers also prepared for evacuation, and requests were sent to Wilmington and Richmond for additional sailors to help man the needed vessels.

Though the Confederates discussed evacuating Morris Island, no such plans were made for Fort Sumter. Instead, they increased their commitment to the demolished fort. Since the post was no longer a viable artillery position, preparations were made to place an infantry command inside the ruined fort. A newcomer to the campaign, Major Stephen Elliott, was designated as the post's future commander.

Since early August, Major Elliott had been serving on James Island, working with torpedoes. He soon became a favorite of General Beauregard who chose him to take over Fort Sumter. Though he was already trained in artillery and civil engineering, Elliott was given additional instructions by Colonel Harris and Colonel Gonzales in the fine art of defense, so, when it became necessary to pull the artillerymen out of Sumter, Elliott would be ready to take over.

While Elliott received his training, the Confederates positioned their ironclads to support Fort Sumter. Throughout the last days of August and the first week of September, Captain Tucker and his three ironclads, the *Chicora, Palmetto State,* and the recently completed *Charleston* were kept on nightly patrols off the ruined fort, watching for small boat attacks. Tucker and his men also watched the enemy ironclads should they try to run the obstructions. Though the lumbering rams were no match for the monitors, Tucker planned to fight to the bitter end should the enemy enter the inner harbor.[23]

While the Confederates were discussing their options and preparing their new defenses, General Gillmore had already made up his mind to finish the affair. On the afternoon of September 2, Gillmore met with Dahlgren onboard the rear admiral's flagship, the *Philadelphia*, to gain the navy's support.

Gillmore's plan was a combination of brute force and guile. On September 4, the Federal land batteries and the *New Ironsides* would turn their guns on Battery Wagner. The bombardment would force the Confederates into their bombproofs and allow the Union sappers to push their trenches up to Wagner's moat. With his lines this close, Gillmore could then organize an assault that could be over Wagner's parapet before the Southerners could respond.

A second provision in Gillmore's plan called for a night landing against Battery Gregg, which would capture Cummings Point and trap Wagner's garrison. To assist in this attack and guard against any Confederate reinforcements from reaching Morris Island, Gillmore asked Dahlgren to send a monitor through the treacherous and shallow channel that ran between Cummings Point and Fort Sumter. Dahlgren disagreed with this and only consented to station two monitors on the ocean side of Cummings Point on the night of the attack.[24]

Without the monitor, Gillmore altered his plan and decided instead to only raid Battery Gregg. The sortie was to be undertaken by the "boat infantry," the army's pickets who served on barges in the creeks separating Morris Island and James Island. The army's maritime force was commanded by Major Oliver S. Sanford of the 7th Connecticut and was comprised of detachments from the 85th and 104th Pennsylvania, 3rd New Hampshire, and 7th Connecticut.

Added to Sanford's unit for the attack on Battery Gregg were one hundred men from the 100th New York. One of the officers assigned to the detail was Lieutenant Smith B. Stowits, who recalled that before he learned of the assignment, the regimental chaplain dropped by his tent to ask if Stowits could swim. When an affirmative reply was given the chaplain responded that "it was favorable," and then left without telling Stowits of his new mission.

Under the new plan, the men were to go in on the night of September 4, seize Battery Gregg, spike its guns, blow up the magazine, and then pull out before the Confederates could react. Gillmore wanted to use only army boats and personnel, but late on the afternoon of the fourth, he learned that he did not have enough oarsmen to carry out the attack. He asked Dahlgren to send on one hundred to two hundred sailors to assist the operation. Dahlgren agreed and also placed his own picket boats, four launches commanded by Lieutenant Francis J. Higginson, under army control.

On the evening of the fourth, Sanford assembled his force at the wharf near the left batteries and directed his vessels through the tidal creeks and into Charleston Harbor. As they approached Battery Gregg from the west, a boat was seen pulling away from Cummings Point. Sanford wanted to let the boat go and press on for Gregg, but Lieutenant Higginson, not use to operating under army control, ordered his men to pull for the enemy launch. Once alongside, a flurry of gunfire was exchanged before Higginson and his crew subdued the Southerners. Immediately, Major Sanford, fearful that the garrison at Battery Gregg had heard the gun shots, called off the attack.

Captured in the boat were twelve men, including a surgeon and the wounded Major Frederick F. Warley of the 2nd South Carolina Artillery Regiment. Warley, who had been serving as Wagner's chief of artillery, carried messages from Wagner's commander detailing the terrible conditions within the battery, but even this could not soothe the ire of Major Sanford who blamed Lieutenant Higginson for the expedition's failure. However, canceling the attack may have been a blessing in disguise as the Confederates had been expecting a Union attack either on Gregg or between the two batteries. The creek side of the island was well patrolled, and the garrison of Battery Gregg was on alert.[25]

Gillmore did not give up the idea of taking Battery Gregg and rescheduled the boat attack for the following night when it would coincide with the bombardment of Battery Wagner. By now, Colonel Turner had had time to rest his gun crews and replace worn and exploded cannon. The new bombardment was to be carried out by one 10-inch, four 8-inch, nine 6.4-inch, and ten 4.2-inch Parrotts; ten 10-inch and four 8-inch siege mortars; and three coehorns mortars. The 4.2-inch Parrotts were directed against Battery Gregg and the area between Wagner and Gregg. The larger Parrotts, with the exception of the two 8-inch Parrotts in Battery Brown, were to concentrate on Wagner's bombproof, while the guns in Battery Brown pounded Wagner's seaward salient. The mortars were to keep their shells arcing down on the entire battery, while the *New Ironsides* would fire on Wagner's seaward wall. The shelling was to be kept up for thirty hours at the end of which Gillmore planned a final assault.[26]

At 5:15 A.M., on September 5, the army batteries opened. A half hour later, the *New Ironsides* reached its position off Wagner and began firing. Though occasionally a monitor would join the ironclad frigate off Morris Island and toss a few shells at Wagner or Gregg, it was the *New Ironsides* which impressed Gillmore, writing that the vessel: "with astonishing regularity and precision, kept a constant stream of shells from her eight gun broadsides ricocheting over the water against the parapet of Wagner, whence, rebounding upward, they dropped nearly vertically, exploding in or over the work and searching every part of it."

Gillmore was equally pleased with the work of his own gunners who never slackened their fire night or day. He wrote that: "the spectacle presented was of surpassing sublimity and grandeur.'' The cannonade so subdued Battery Wagner's garrison that Federal sappers were able to push their trenches another 150 yards with no interference. Because of the excellent work of his artillerymen and fatigue parties, Gillmore decided to continue the bombardment for one more day so the engineers could further lengthen and improve the trenches for the final assault. The sappers worked on, and as they neared Wagner's moat, they were forced to dig through the mass graves of the Northern soldiers from the July 18 attack. By now, the only danger to the men in the trenches were short-falling or misdirected Union shells. To protect themselves and show their comrades their location, the engineers placed a large American flag at the head of the sap.

On September 6, the sappers reached Wagner's ditch. During the evening, Captain Joseph Walker of the 1st New York Engineers climbed down into the moat. In the midst of the bombardment he carefully examined Wagner's entire land front, making notes for the attack. He also removed about two hundred pikes from the battery's counterscarp to provide a passageway for the attacking column. With this accomplished, Walker crawled back to the siege line and directed his men to run the trench line along the crest of the moat and prepare it for occupation by the storming party.[27]

Gillmore entrusted the third assault against Battery Wagner to Brigadier General Alfred H. Terry. Dependable and careful, Terry prepared his forces. Using the information from Captain Walker, Terry armed his lead elements with axes to cut their way through the abatis. He also issued his officers maps of Battery Wagner which were drawn using information gained from Confederate deserters. Terry did not want a repeat of the July 18 attack where much of Seymour's division had become confused once they reached the battery.

Chosen to spearhead the assault was the 3rd New Hampshire and 97th Pennsylvania. These regiments were to be placed in the forward trenches, and when the signal was given, a forlorn hope of 100 picked New Hampshire soldiers, led by Captain James F. Randlett, would rush forward and seize Wagner's seaward bastion. Once this was accomplished, the rest of the men from the 3rd New Hampshire and 97th Pennsylvania would charge into the bastion, capture the sea wall and sally port and take up a position on top of the bombproof. From here the soldiers were to climb down into the battery and seal the entrance to Wagner's main bombproof, thus trapping the men inside.

Behind the lead regiments, Terry placed Brigadier General Thomas G. Stevenson's brigade, which was reinforced by the 4th New Hampshire and 9th Maine. By the plan, Stevenson's force was to

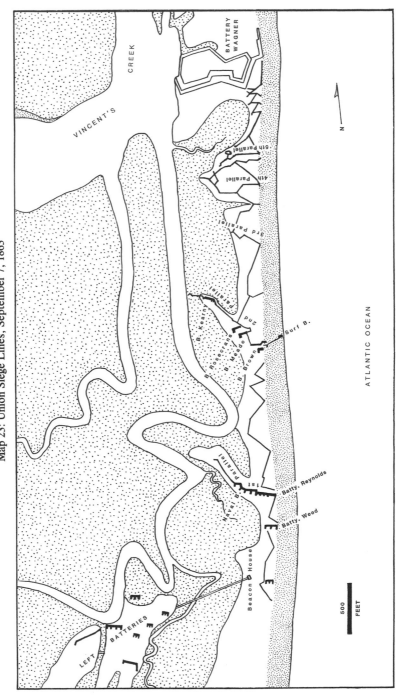

Map 23: Union Siege Lines, September 7, 1863

VINCENT'S CREEK

BATTERY WAGNER

6th Parallel

4th Parallel

3rd Parallel

2nd Parallel

B. Kearny
B. Rosecrane
B. Meade
B. Brown

Surf B.

1st Parallel

Batty. Reynolds

Batty. Weed

B. Naval

Beacon House

LEFT BATTERIES

ATLANTIC OCEAN

N

500 FEET

advance as soon as the lead units had entered Wagner. They were to move double-quick down the beach until they had passed Wagner, then form across the island and move into the battery.

To cover the rear of Stevenson's brigade and to stop any reinforcements from reaching Wagner, Colonel William W. H. Davis' brigade was ordered to follow Stevenson's men and position themselves across Morris Island facing Cummings Point. Terry kept Colonel James Montgomery's brigade of African-American regiments in reserve (See appendix, table 20.)

The attack was to occur 9:00 A.M. on September 7. To signal the assault, a large national flag would be waved at Beacon House, then the red banner flown on the *New Ironsides* would be hauled down, and the attack would begin.[28]

While the Federals were formulating their plans, the Confederates were preparing for the inevitable. On September 4, before Gillmore began his final bombardment, General Beauregard called a meeting to discuss the situation on Morris Island. Attending the conference were Generals Gilmer, Ripley, Jordan, Hagood, and Colquitt, and Colonel Harris. The Confederates realized it was a matter of only days before the Union sap reached the battery's ditch, and once Wagner fell, Morris Island would have to be evacuated. Not wishing to lose Wagner's garrison, evacuation plans were started.[29]

On Morris Island, Wagner's commander, Colonel Lawrence M. Keitt, unaware of the decision made in Charleston, continued to carry on. During these final days, Wagner's garrison consisted of the 27th and 28th Georgia Regiments, the 25th South Carolina, Companies D (Kanapaux's) and E (Johnson's) of the Palmetto Artillery Battalion, and Company A of the 2nd South Carolina Artillery Regiment.

When the Federal bombardment commenced on the fifth, Keitt realized his position was untenable. As the first shells began exploding in Wagner, he ordered the majority of his men into the main bombproof, leaving on duty only the artillerymen, sharpshooters, and pickets. On the seaward side, the two 10-inch Columbiads dueled with the *New Ironsides*, but their shots could not damage the seemingly indestructible warship.

On the land front, the Confederates tried to fight back, but the bombardment was too heavy. No one could stand near the parapet without being covered by sand. Men were forced to huddle behind the breastworks to escape the shells, and the sharpshooters found the fire so heavy they stopped bothering to aim when firing and instead held their rifles to the loopholes and pulled the trigger. During the bombardment one of the 10-inch Columbiads was dismounted while still loaded, its carriage on fire and the muzzle pointing at a magazine. Volunteers quickly rushed out and extinguished the flames, but as the day went on, more and more equipment was damaged and men killed and wounded. The number of casualties became so high that the litter bearers and surgeons soon fell behind in their work. To clear space in the bombproof, Keitt had the wounded that could be moved placed in the sand dunes behind the battery.[30]

About 4:30 P.M., on September 5, Keitt received a message from Charleston telling him that communications between Gillmore and Dahlgren had been intercepted and deciphered. The messages were about the rescheduled night attack on Battery Gregg. Keitt immediately sent the 27th Georgia, Kanapaux's artillery company, fifty men from the 25th South Carolina, and two field pieces to Gregg. All that night the Confederates waited and at about 1:30 A.M., Captain Henry Lesesne, Gregg's commander, observed fifteen to twenty barges nearing the battery. He immediately ordered one of Battery Gregg's 10-inch Columbiads to fire, and then the infantry and field pieces opened up. The Federals returned the fire, and after a brisk exchange, the Union boats withdrew. As soon as the skirmish ended, courier Harleston, who had been serving with the men in Battery Gregg, was sent to Wagner to tell Keitt of the victory.[31]

Though Harleston's dispatch was welcome news, the men in Wagner had no time to celebrate. Inside the battery, Harleston found that the fatigue parties were being shredded by the exploding shells. The enemy's three calcium lights were illuminating parts of the battery as if it was midday. In the darkness above the beams of the calcium lights, there could be seen the "lurid flashes of guns" and the shells could be "tracked by flaming fuses—the darting of Parrott shells, and curving arching mortars."[32]

The sixth of September dawned with gloomy prospects. Colonel Keitt, not knowing the fate of his garrison, instructed Doctor Ravenel and the post's quartermaster to carry all wounded to Cummings Point, regardless of shell fire. Keitt saw that during the night the enemy's sap had moved closer to Wagner's moat. Realizing that a sudden rush would gain the parapet before his men could emerge from the bombproof, Keitt redistributed his garrison. As a mobile reserve, he placed 325 men from the 27th Georgia, 28th Georgia, and 25th South Carolina among the sand dunes in Wagner's rear. On duty behind Wagner's parapet were 150 artillerymen and about 150 men of the 28th Georgia, while stationed in the bombproof were 350 men of the 25th South Carolina.

By 8:00 A.M., the soldiers in Wagner watched helplessly as the monitors *Passaic, Montauk*, and *Nahant* joined the *New Ironsides* and added their guns to the bombardment. In a short time the seaward salient became so treacherous that Keitt was forced to evacuate it. Passages soon filled with sand and the battery began to lose its form. The shelling was so intense that no work could be carried out, and at 8:45 A.M., Keitt sent his slave laborers into the sand dunes behind Wagner. Inside the bombproof, men from the 25th South Carolina watched surgeons perform amputation after amputation. A member of the regiment wrote his fiance of the experiences: "It would take a much better pen than my own to give you the faintest idea of the horrors of this place—the lower regions is perhaps but a singular picture, imagine anything that is truly terrible, and you will perhaps approach the idea."

Throughout the day, Wagner's garrison held on. Early in the afternoon, Colonel Harris and Captain Francis D. Lee, one of Wagner's designers, arrived at the battery. Lee replaced Thomas B. Lee as chief engineer, while Harris made a personal inspection of the situation for General Beauregard. The engineers, quickly realizing that the battery was indefensible, sent word to Charleston to begin the evacuation. The news was welcomed by Colonel Keitt who afterwards, in an act of bravado, informed Beauregard that unless the boats arrived soon, he would lead his garrison in a charge against the Federal lines. Beauregard, though, had no intention of letting the garrison be sacrificed in a suicidal charge, and by late afternoon, Keitt received detailed instructions for the abandonment of Battery Wagner and Morris Island.[33]

To cover the evacuation, Beauregard directed all available batteries and forts to concentrate their guns on Morris Island. Rowboats manned by sailors from the *Palmetto State* and other vessels were ordered to Cummings Point from which the island's garrison would be carried to waiting quartermaster steamers. To guard the transports, the navy stationed the ironclads *Charleston* and *Chicora* near Fort Sumter. If the enemy's warships should interfere, the sailors were instructed to turn away from the transports and pull for Fort Johnson. When the island was completely evacuated, the Confederate artillerymen in the neighboring works, signaled by either the exploding of Wagner's and Gregg's magazines or rockets, would open on Morris Island. The quartermaster vessels were placed under the direction of Major Motte A. Pringle, who wished to redeem himself after the *Sumter* debacle. The entire operation was under the supervision of Lieutenant Colonel Olin M. Dantzler of the 20th South Carolina.[34]

After dark on September 7, Captain Charles C. Pinckney, the district ordnance officer, arrived on Morris Island with equipment to destroy

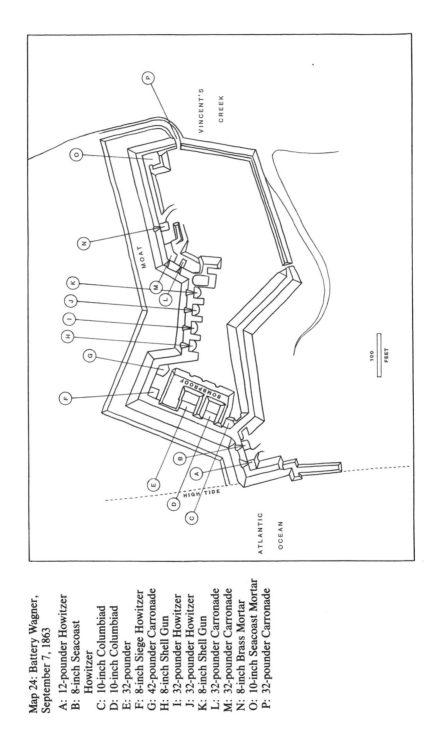

Map 24: Battery Wagner,
September 7, 1863

A: 12-pounder Howitzer
B: 8-inch Seacoast
Howitzer
C: 10-inch Columbiad
D: 10-inch Columbiad
E: 32-pounder
F: 8-inch Siege Howitzer
G: 42-pounder Carronade
H: 8-inch Shell Gun
I: 32-pounder Howitzer
J: 32-pounder Howitzer
K: 8-inch Shell Gun
L: 32-pounder Carronade
M: 32-pounder Carronade
N: 8-inch Brass Mortar
O: 10-inch Seacoast Mortar
P: 32-pounder Carronade

the cannon and blow up Wagner's and Gregg's magazines. Once Pinckney arrived, Keitt and his officers began withdrawing their men and equipment. To keep the enemy from learning what was going on, Wagner's 10-inch mortar maintained a steady shelling of the enemy siege lines, while the sharpshooters kept up a rapid fire.

The first men sent from Wagner to the embarkation spot at Cummings Point were the wounded. Then Lieutenant Robert M. Stiles took the slaves from the sand dunes and had them construct a line of rifle pits near Battery Gregg. Once done, the slaves were sent off with the ordnance and signal equipment. The 28th Georgia was then moved from Wagner and occupied the new rifle pits. Then, trying to fool the Yankees, Keitt brought the two companies of the 25th South Carolina from the sand dunes into Wagner in hopes that the enemy would think reinforcements were arriving.

While the "reinforcements" were marched in, four companies of the 25th South Carolina, the majority of the artillerymen, and one field piece left the battery. Next, Keitt removed the 27th Georgia and another field piece. After leaving the gun at the rifle pits, the Georgians continued on to Cummings Point where they waited until the garrison from Battery Gregg embarked, then they boarded the rowboats and left Morris Island. A short time later, the remaining men of the 25th South Carolina, except for those serving as sharpshooters, were pulled out of Wagner and sent to Cummings Point.

At 11:00 P.M., Keitt turned command of Wagner over to his chief of artillery, Captain Thomas A. Huguenin, and went to the rifle pits. From there Keitt ordered the 28th Georgia out of the defense line, and with the 25th South Carolina, the Georgians boarded boats and left the island. When word of the regiments' departure reached Huguenin, he dispatched all but twenty-five artillerymen and ten sharpshooters. At Battery Gregg, Keitt remained with Kanapaux's artillerymen and a few couriers, waiting for Huguenin, Pinckney, and their detachment.

The last duty left to Huguenin and Pinckney was the spiking of the guns and laying a slow fuse to Wagner's magazine. To accomplish this, the two officers led the artillerymen along the parapet among the sharpshooters, spiking the cannon. By the prearranged plan, Huguenin had fifteen minutes to complete his work, but the Union bombardment, the calcium lights, and lack of proper tools made it difficult to keep on schedule. Lacking the necessary rat tail files to drive down into the cannon's vents, Huguenin and Pinckney had to improvise with whatever material was handy. Also, since the enemy was so close, they had to be careful not to make too much noise when spiking the guns.

The Confederates deliberately carried out their mission, and by midnight, all the guns were disabled except for one 10-inch Columbiad. This piece Huguenin double-charged and prepared to burst as a signal to Keitt that all was done. After the massive cannon was rigged for destruction, Huguenin laid a fuse to the main magazine. When finished he ordered off the sharpshooters and artillerymen, leaving in Wagner himself, Captain Pinckney, Wagner's ordnance officer Lieutenant Edmund Mazyck, Lieutenant James A. Ross of the 25th Carolina, and Ordnance Sergeant John M. Leathe. Together they attempted to explode the 10-inch Columbiad. Huguenin, while pulling the lanyard, declared: "The last gun from Wagner, fire!" Nothing happened. They tried again, with no result. The men then tried to unspike another gun, but it too failed to fire. Huguenin realized that by now the enemy might suspect something, and gave up trying to fire the cannon. He lit the fuse to the magazine, watched it burn for half a minute and then with the rest hurried off to Battery Gregg.

At Cummings Point, Colonel Keitt anxiously waited for Huguenin and his party. With Keitt and the rear guard were four cavalrymen including Private John Harleston. The couriers, forgotten in the evacuation, had decided to find their own way off the island. Before they left, Harleston wanted to shoot the little grey horse that had served him and the cavalrymen so well, but he was stopped by another courier, and Harleston turned the horse loose hoping the Federals would take care of the animal. A skiff was then located, and they departed the island, leaving behind Keitt and a small rear guard who still waited for the men from Wagner.

By now, Keitt was beginning to believe that Huguenin's party had been captured, and with enemy barges spotted in Vincent's Creek, he ordered the fuse to Gregg's magazine lit. Minutes later, the men from Wagner, minus Huguenin, appeared. Believing that Huguenin, who had an injured knee, had been captured, Keitt ordered everyone into the boats. As they pulled away the limping Huguenin arrived on the beach. At first the captain thought he had been abandoned, then a launch appeared in the darkness and Huguenin waded out and was taken aboard. He was the last Confederate to escape Morris Island.[35]

Throughout the Confederate evacuation, the Federals' bombardment never slackened. By dawn of September 7, Gillmore had estimated that his heavy land guns had fired 1,411 projectiles, with 1,247 hitting Wagner and of these hits 1,173 struck the roof of the bombproof. This, plus the firing of the ironclads, allowed the Northerners to complete their preparations. By 1:00 A.M., while Huguenin and his party were trying to fire the final gun from Wagner, the Union regiments were occupying the forward trenches. Weaving their way through the siege lines, the soldiers passed by mortar batteries, sharpshooters, and fatigue parties made of the African-American soldiers from the 55th Massachusetts, who were still digging the forward lines. Also at the front stood the men of the 39th Illinois who were serving as the grand guard while Dahlgren's Marine battalion watched the beach. The lead elements were given axes and tools to spike the enemy cannon. Though well-prepared, the men were not anxious to attack Wagner. One regiment, the 85th Pennsylvania, had attended a church service before going forward where they were reminded by the chaplain that: "It is appointed unto man once to die." Another soldier, remembering only too well the bloody repulse of July 18, noted: "I hear that Wagner is to be assaulted tonight. I pity the poor boys who are to do it."[36]

While the final arrangements were underway, Confederate deserters began entering the Union lines and reported Wagner's evacuation. At first no one believed it, but the captured men were sent back to headquarters where Gillmore, at 11:15 A.M., informed Dahlgren that: "A deserter just in reports Wagner evacuated."

Other deserters followed, and while General Terry interviewed them, officers in the front line began to investigate the battery. Individuals from both the 3rd New Hampshire and the 39th Illinois slipped into Wagner and found it empty, and one Illinois soldier discovered the burning fuse leading to the magazine and cut it. While these men were reporting back to their respective commands, the officers operating the sap roller, with soldiers from the 55th Massachusetts, slid down the ditch and clamored up the parapet. One officer, Captain Wheelock Pratt of the 55th, wrote his wife that once they were inside Wagner, Lieutenant Michie of the engineers ran up to them "as tickled as a child with a new toy . . . he skipped about like a young calf—he caught me by the arm shaking me in his joy say 'the engineers have done it this time.' "

By 3:30 A.M., a portion of the 39th Illinois came into Wagner, followed by Randlett's two companies from the 3rd New Hampshire. Randlett's men, who had been designated as the attack's spearhead, quickly moved through the battery, and soon the rest of the regiment entered Wagner. Not lingering in the empty work, the New Hampshire soldiers quickly moved down the beach. At Battery Gregg they captured some tardy Confederate boats and extinguished the fuse leading into Gregg's magazine. By now, the Confederate batteries on James Island had opened an intensive bombardment that blanketed the northern end of Morris Island. But neither casualties caused by the Confederate fire nor the enemy torpedoes could dampen the enthusiasm of the Federal army. As word of the abandonment passed through the Union army, cheers went up. At 5:30 A.M., Gillmore signaled Dahlgren, "The whole of Morris Island is ours, but the enemy has escaped."[37]

After seizing Gregg, the Union soldiers returned to Wagner where they found marines lounging about the work like they had taken it. At dawn, the Confederates could see that their enemies had occupied Wagner. As Colonel Harris wrote: "the next morning, to our chagrin, could be observed the flag of a Massachusetts Regiment planted up on the ramparts of the glorious Battery Wagner."

Even so, the Southerners had much to be proud of. Only three boats and some fifty men were captured by the Union forces. The Southern evacuation, one of the largest of the war, was a great accomplishment. It was soured, though, by the failure of the magazines to explode. Still, the Confederates, unbeknownst to an overwhelming enemy only yards away, had withdrawn more than one thousand men.

Among those reaching safety was Private Harleston, who with his companions had been picked up by a transport. While onboard the vessel, Harleston found himself with some of the infantry that had garrisoned Wagner. One man, who recognized Harleston as a cavalryman, told him how he had watched and cheered the couriers. Then, on a more somber note, he added, "I have heard the preachers talk about Hell, a great big hole, full of fire and brimstone, where a bad fellow was dropped in, and I will allow it used to worry me at times, but gentlemen, Hell can't be any worse than Battery Wagner. I have got out of that, and the other place ain't going to worry me anymore."[38]

CONCLUSION

We have built one cemetery, Morris Island.
Clara Barton

The fall of Morris Island encouraged the Union commanders to make one final effort to capture Fort Sumter. By now both Gillmore and Dahlgren realized that the Confederate fortification had to be taken to clear the channel obstructions; however, by this point, the two officers ceased to fully cooperate with each other. The long campaign on Morris Island had strained the working relationship between Dahlgren and Gillmore and greatly affected the planned amphibious assault on Fort Sumter.

Both commanders felt that Fort Sumter was vulnerable. Its tall vertical walls no longer existed. Battered into rubble, the debris seemed to offer a ramp leading directly into the fort. But in this case, looks were deceiving. In the midst of the debris, the Southerners had fashioned a new fort with a new garrison. On September 4, three days before Wagner's evacuation, Colonel Rhett and his artillerymen had been withdrawn and replaced with infantrymen from the Charleston Battalion under the command of Major Elliott. In a short time Elliott and his garrison converted the ruin into a formidable position.

Admiral Dahlgren was the first to act. On September 7, he sent a note to Fort Sumter demanding its surrender. The Confederates responded by inviting Dahlgren to come and take it. The flag officer quickly made preparations for a small boat attack the following night. To assist the assault, Dahlgren directed Commander Edmund R. Colhoun to take the monitor *Weehawken* into Charleston Harbor via the

205

shallow channel running between Cummings Point and Sumter. Once in the harbor, the monitor was to sever Sumter's communications.

After daylight on September 7, Colhoun slowly guided the *Weehawken* through the narrow, treacherous channel dropping buoys to mark deep water. When he reached a point midway between Cummings Point and Fort Sumter, Colhoun anchored his vessel and waited for the tide to rise before continuing. Then about ten in the morning, Dahlgren developed second thoughts about sending a monitor on such a dangerous mission and ordered Colhoun to return, but as the monitor moved back through the channel, the ship grounded and held fast.

Throughout the day, the *Weehawken* resisted all efforts to break free. The Confederates watched, but did not suspect the monitor's plight. It was not until the following morning that Major Elliott realized the *Weehawken* was stranded and signaled neighboring batteries to open fire. To draw attention away from the vessel, Dahlgren quickly boarded the *New Ironsides* and with five monitors steamed up the channel and commenced a covering fire against Sullivan's Island. At the same time, the *Weehawken* began sending shells into Fort Moultrie. A shell from her 15-inch gun exploded a supply of ammuniton stored inside the fort. The resulting confusion and casualties temporarily silenced the Confederate guns and allowed Colhoun and his men time to eat breakfast. Once finished, the sailors returned to their guns and concentrated on Fort Sumter. On the afternoon tide, the monitor floated free and steamed away. Though the *Weehawken* was no longer part of his plan, Dahlgren refused to cancel the assault.[1]

Unknown to Dahlgren, General Gillmore also had organized a boat attack for the same night. The two commanders learned of each other's plans when word was passed between the two asking for support. Dahlgren requested the return of the navy's four launches, which had been serving with the army's amphibious unit, while Gillmore called upon the navy to place its force under army command. As the day wore on, additional messages were sent between Morris Island and Dahlgren's flagship, and in the end, the two officers refused to work together. An exasperated Gillmore finally signalled Dahlgren:

> You decline to act in concert with me or allow the senior officer to command the assault on Sumter, but insist that a naval officer must command the party. Why this should be so in assaulting a fortification, I cannot see. I am so fearful that some accident will take place between our parties that I would recall my own if it were not too late.
>
> I sent you the watchword by special messenger, who has returned.

We must trust to chance and hope for the best. No matter who gets the fort if we place our flag over it.[2]

Throughout the day, the two services went on with their preparations. Gillmore organized an attacking force of about five hundred men from the 10th Connecticut and the 24th Massachusetts under Colonel Francis A. Osborn of the 24th Massachusetts. The assault regiments were to be transported on barges manned by the oarsmen of the 7th Connecticut under Major Sanford. The army's assault called for the boats to exit the tidal creeks near Cummings Point and land on Sumter's gorge and left flank.

The navy's plan was more elaborate. Dahlgren ordered an attack force of five hundred marines and sailors assembled on launches which were to be towed toward Fort Sumter by the tug *Dandelion*. Once abreast of the fort, the launches were to be cast loose and their crews were to row to Fort Sumter. While certain designated vessels made a diversion against Sumter's right face, the rest were to land on the fort's right flank.

Though planned for the same night and at the same time, there was no coordination between the two forces. The commanders did agree to use the password "Detroit" should the two expeditions become entangled. Gillmore, fearful that the army and navy would end up attacking each other, gave Osborn strict instructions to turn back if the navy landed first.[3]

The operation was a disaster. The navy opened the battle, and even though the army's boat infantry were within striking distance, Colonel Osborn reluctantly obeyed orders and commanded his vessels to turn back. In the darkness, the navy officers in charge of the launches became disoriented and confused, and only one quarter of the landing force got ashore.[4]

Elliott and his men were ready and waiting for the Federals. Throughout the day the Confederates had been reading the Northern dispatches and knew an assault was coming. Forewarned, Elliott had his 300-man garrison positioned around Sumter's walls, outfitted as "sentries, grenadiers, turpentine-ballers and keg-flingers." When the first marines and sailors came ashore, Sumter's garrison opened a rapid fire and began throwing turpentine balls and grenades at the enemy. At the same time, the CSS *Chicora* along with batteries from Fort Johnson and Sullivan's Island began sending shells into the midst of attackers. Soon, the navy launches pulled off, and those men who had landed on Sumter's broken walls surrendered. As Major Elliott triumphantly wrote his sister: "My dear child, twelve first rate officers

Map 25: Small Boat attack on Fort Sumter, September 8–9, 1863

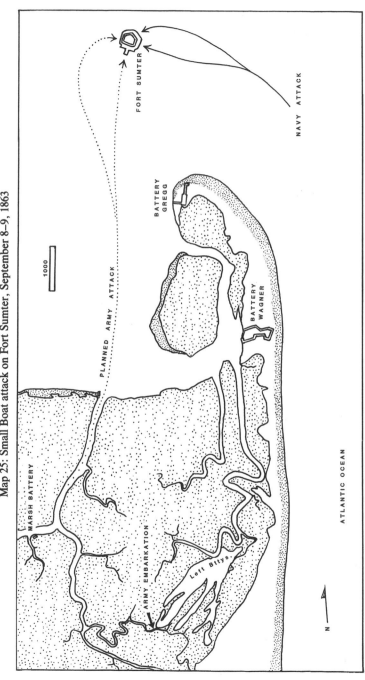

and about one hundred and fifteen or twenty splendid men bagged by 70 which was the whole force actively engaged. . . . Not the least satisfactory part of it is that not one of my men was touched."[5]

The small boat assault against Fort Sumter ended Gillmore's activities against Charleston. The army commander felt he had accomplished his assigned task: the destruction of Sumter as an artillery position. At the same time, his regiments were depleted and exhausted. For the army, the campaign was over.

To deliver his final report to General Halleck in Washington, Gillmore chose one of his staff officers, Major William S. Stryker. As he was packing his luggage, Stryker received a joking remark from his friend Captain Scollay D. Baker of the 9th Maine, who bid Stryker a safe trip. After completing his preparations, Stryker rode to Wagner to take another look at the battery that had cost "so much time and labor, so much blood and precious life." As he neared the work he saw a cart carrying the body of Captain Baker who moments earlier had given Stryker kind greetings and farewell. A cannon ball from Fort Johnson had severed Baker's head from his body.

With this grim memory, Stryker traveled on a steamer to New York, and from there he journeyed to the capital, pausing briefly at his parents' home in Trenton, New Jersey. A mere skeleton, "worn out with fatigue, and loss of blood from a slight wound, and malaria fever," Stryker was not recognized by his parents, who at first thought the emaciated stranger was an officer come to tell them that their son had been killed. But his sister was not fooled, and Stryker was able to enjoy nearly an hour with his family before boarding a train for Washington.

Once in the capital Stryker passed Gillmore's dispatches on to army headquarters. Before he had time to leave, Stryker was ushered into the presence of President Lincoln who met the young major in the East Room of the White House. For nearly ninety minutes the two men talked about the campaign. The president asked questions concerning the cannon used on Morris Island, the bombardment of Sumter, the monitors, the *New Ironsides,* and more. In the midst of the technical explanations, Stryker counted sixteen humorous stories that Lincoln interjected into the midst of their conversation, which put the major at ease and allowed him "to talk as long as he wanted." Stryker left the White House impressed by the versatility and knowledge of the president who seemed to absorb every detail about the campaign.[6]

While his aide was meeting with the president, Gillmore cared for his veterans. He immediately authorized furloughs and soon a relaxed atmosphere prevailed on Morris Island. For the first time in the campaign, ice sent south by the Sanitary Commission was distributed daily to the men. One novel sight for the soldiers was the appearance of women, nurses with the Sanitary Commission, which caused one officer to write after seeing one: "It was really luxurious to see her, and I took a second look."

Though the whiskey ration was discontinued, the food improved. An oven to bake soft bread was constructed, and the troops were able to discard their usual hardtack. The men found various ways to celebrate the campaign's end. Some African-American regiments held festivals and carried out races where groups of soldiers tried to outrun each other while pulling siege guns along the beach. But there were also somber moments as the men began to remove the bodies of their comrades from the mass graves in front of Wagner for reburial at the Beaufort cemetery.

To honor their fallen heroes, the Federals renamed the captured batteries. Wagner became Fort Strong, while Gregg was named for Colonel Putnam. At the southern end of Morris Island, the detached Confederate batteries were reformed into two new defensive works named Battery Purviance and Fort Shaw.

On September 15, Brigadier General Gillmore issued a congratulatory order to his command and the navy in which he thanked them for their courage, skill, and patient labor. A week later, Gillmore received his laurels when he was promoted to major general. To honor him, the navy placed bunting on their mastheads, the army fired a salute, and the men from the 47th New York presented the general with a monstrous eagle that they had captured on neighboring Seabrook Island. Two days later, September 24, a mass review of two infantry brigades, one white and one black, and three artillery brigades were led past Gillmore by the department's combined bands.

The parade, which lasted three hours, put a final end to the campaign. Soon, regiments began leaving for more comfortable camps at St. Augustine and Hilton Head. The army had completed its task, and though the artillerists were ready to use their guns at any time, the remaining work at Charleston was now in the hands of the navy; however, most soldiers did not believe the navy would continue the attack. As one officer noted: "There is a great deal of grumbling and swearing at the fleet that they do not now advance. . . . We will soon know whether the ironclads are of any value or not."[7]

Rear Admiral Dahlgren joined in celebrating Gillmore's promotion, but now the flag officer realized that the navy was now expected to take the lead and run into Charleston Harbor. As usual, Dahlgren wanted to avoid the dangerous task and tried to interest the army in new attacks against James and Sullivan's islands. Gillmore rebuffed the admiral and would not consider any new advances, to which Dahlgren noted that the general's promotion had proven a "sedative."

Dahlgren found himself in an uncomfortable situation. Even though Fort Sumter had been reduced and no longer served as an artillery position, it did anchor the Confederate line of obstructions that stretched from Sumter to Sullivan's Island. Without Sumter in Federal hands, the obstructions could not be removed. This meant that the navy would have to risk running the obstructions, which were known to be intertwined with torpedoes. Dahlgren and his commanders did not relish this task, but they dutifully went about preparing their ships for an assault.

It took more than a month for requisite repairs to be completed, but during that time, the Navy Department changed its position. In October, Welles wrote Dahlgren that the department could not risk its ironclads in a frontal attack against Charleston's defenses. Instead, the secretary of navy suggested that Dahlgren continue to support the army but avoid unnecessary risks. A relieved Dahlgren happily called off the attack. He again offered his assistance to the army, but by now Gillmore had reduced his forces around Charleston and was in no position to continue an overland campaign.[8]

To Gillmore and his command, the navy's failure to run the obstructions capped a bittersweet campaign. For two months soldiers had toiled and died on Morris Island. They captured their objectives and smashed Fort Sumter into rubble, but their accomplishments were negated when the navy refused to carry out the final strike. On the other hand, Dahlgren and his sailors believed that the army was still responsible for capturing Sumter, which would then allow the navy to clear the channel. Because of these disputes, the bitterness and mistrust that had become evident in the final weeks of the siege grew into a professional and personal feud between Gillmore and Dahlgren that would not end until Dahlgren's death in 1870. For all the work and cost in material and lives, there had been few results; the army and navy blamed each other for falling short of victory.[9]

The Federals had failed because the design had been flawed from the start. Since the Union leaders lacked the soldiers to carry out Seymour's plan of capturing both Morris and Sullivan's islands, they settled for Morris Island. This might have worked if not for the tenacious Confederate defense. If Gillmore and Dahlgren had taken Morris Island in one quick rush and destroyed Fort Sumter in the first weeks of July, they might have successfully run ironclads into the harbor. Instead, they were stalled by Battery Wagner for nearly two months, and Beauregard was able to readjust his defenses. By early September, new works on James Island opposite Morris Island were finished; the cannon removed from Sumter were placed on Sullivan's Island, and the harbor obstructions were laced with torpedoes.

Though the Confederates had stopped their enemies, the end of the Morris Island Campaign brought little rest. Work continued on new fortifications, and old ones were strengthened. The grim tradition of naming new batteries and forts after fallen comrades continued as Batteries Bee, Gary, Simkins, Tatom, Haskell, Ryan, Ramsay, Wampler, Waring, Pringle, Cheves, Tynes, and others became reminders of the costly fighting on Morris Island.

While the construction of new fortifications continued, Beauregard, fearing that the Northerners would bring new assaults against James Island or possibly John's Island, asked for and received reinforcements. In mid-September, Brigadier General George T. Anderson's Georgia brigade and Brigadier General Henry A. Wise's Virginian brigade arrived from Virginia, but they were not needed as the Federals did not resume their offensive. Left alone, the Confederates continued to perfect their defenses, which would never again be seriously tested by any sustained Northern attack.

The immediate results of the campaign were hardly decisive. In the respective departments little changed. The Union army, instead of being concentrated at Port Royal, was now centered on Folly and Morris islands. To meet this threat, the Confederates shifted the bulk of their troops to the Charleston area. But as before, the Union soldiers, supported by the navy, occupied the fringe islands, while the Confederates held the interior lines.

While the situation along the South Carolina coast was only slightly altered, the Confederates had gained some important political and strategic results. Though they had been forced off Morris Island, the South had gained a morally uplifting, strategic victory. A barrier island had fallen, but Charleston had held. After Gettysburg and Vicksburg, the South badly needed a victory. Throughout the summer of 1863, while the guns in other theaters remained quiet, Southerners watched the affair near Charleston with great anticipation. If Charleston was lost, the Confederacy would have been dealt a severe blow, not only militarily but also in confidence. By holding onto Charleston the defenders proved that the Northern legions could be stopped. The symbol of the Confederacy and secession was safe, and there was still hope of independence.[10]

The campaign also slowed down the North's naval planning. Throughout 1863, the only squadron of Union monitors was kept off

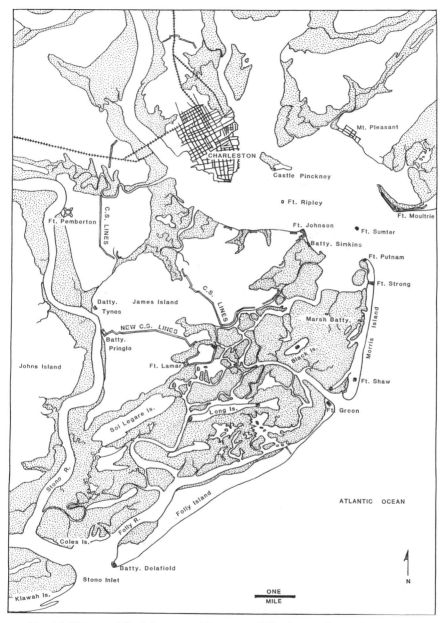

Map 26: Union and Confederate positions around Charleston, September 10, 1863

Charleston. Because of the stubborn Confederate defense, the vessels were occupied in South Carolina waters for more than a year, preventing their use against Mobile and Wilmington. The longer the monitors were held off Charleston, the more time the Confederates had to strengthen defenses at other ports. Northern campaigns against Mobile and Wilmington had to be postponed until additional ironclads were finished; this would not be until the summer of 1864 when an expedition was finally organized to attack Mobile. For the rest of the war Dahlgren continued to blockade the coast and use his monitors to watch Confederate ironclads at Savannah and Charleston, but his vessels never again threatened Charleston's defenses.

The attack on Morris Island did end Charleston's role as the South's premier blockade-running port. During the campaign, only a handful of runners risked coming to Charleston. Then, after the seizure of Morris Island, the combination of Federal batteries on Cummings Point and a line of picket boats supported by monitors just seaward of the harbor obstructions, effectively closed the port. From September 1863 until March 1864, there was no blockade-running activity at Charleston, but it did not affect the flow of supplies into the Confederacy, as Wilmington soon succeeded Charleston as the South's main blockade-running port. The transition was accomplished so quickly that there was no drop in imports or exports.[11]

While Dahlgren kept his vessels operating along the coast, watching for enemy blockade runners and ironclads, Gillmore moved the army's focus of operations away from Charleston and into Florida. In February 1864, a division under General Seymour occupied Jacksonville, Florida, but when it tried to move inland, it was met and defeated at the Battle of Olustee by some of the same Confederate units that had fought at Charleston.

A few months later, many of the men and officers were on the move again. In May 1864, troops from both sides were shifted to Virginia. Beauregard and soldiers from Charleston met Gillmore and men from the Department of the South at the Battle of Drewry's Bluff. During Grant's overland campaign against Richmond, General Stevenson was killed at Spotsylvania and Colonel Keitt died at Cold Harbor. Stephen Elliott left Fort Sumter and commanded a brigade from Charleston at Petersburg where he was badly wounded during the Battle of the Crater. General Seymour eventually entered Charleston, but he was taken there as a prisoner after being captured at the Battle of the Wilderness. He was exchanged in time to command a division in the Shenandoah Valley, at Petersburg, and in the Appomatox campaign where units that had served on Morris Island closed Lee's escape route at Appomattox Court House. In a final bit of irony, men who had not only survived Morris Island, but also the Richmond-Petersburg Campaign, again clashed with each other at Fort Fisher, the guardian of Wilmington, North Carolina, where many more died fighting over a sand fortification.

For the combatants left in the southeast, there were also more battles. In July 1864, under the overall direction of General John G. Foster, white and black Union forces tested the Confederates on James and Johns Islands outside Charleston, but the assaults were not pressed home, and the Federals pulled back. Then in the fall, while supporting Major General William Tecumseh Sherman's march through Georgia, Foster organized a strike from Hilton Head against Lee's old railroad defense line at a place called Gopher Hill. Turned back at the Battles of Honey Hill and Tulifinny, the Federal soldiers continued to press the Confederates along the railroad line until Sherman captured Savannah. In February 1865, while Sherman's men moved inland against Columbia, Gillmore was returned to command and with Dahlgren's reluctant support began maneuvering his troops toward Charleston. But, before they reached the city, the Confederates, with their communications threatened by Sherman's advance through the interior of South Carolina, evacuated Charleston.

Though the Morris Island campaign did not capture Charleston, the campaign bore a number of unique features. One of the most important aspects was the extensive use of black troops with white troops. Because of the close confines of Morris Island and the characteristics of siege work, the white and African-American troops were in constant contact. Major Brooks reported that "in no military operations of the war have Negro troops done so large a proportion and so hazardous fatigue duty, as in siege operations on this island." Realizing the uniqueness of the situation, Brooks asked his subordinates to comment on the African-American soldiers.

The replies were favorable. One officer reported that he never had a black desert or skulk from duty. He noted that they will: "endure, resist and follow." Another officer wrote that blacks had a greater appreciation of their duty and tended to work harder and longer than the white soldiers. The officers also noted a difference between the African Americans recruited in the North and those from the slave states. The former slaves lacked education and the aggressive spirit that the engineering officers felt requisite in a good soldier. However, they did point to the excellent showing of the 54th Massachusetts and suggested that these characteristics came from the debilitating conditions inherent to slavery and were not characteristic to African Americans as a whole. One officer noted that the Northern blacks had the same good qualities as the white soldiers and not all their bad qualities.

Racism did not die out in the Department of the South. Even after the campaign, both Generals Edward A. Wild and Gillmore had to issue orders forbidding the use of black soldiers as laborers to police the camps of white soldiers; but, because of the limited area of operation, white units observed the African Americans under battlefield conditions. As a result, many of these men came to recognize the blacks as comrades and often accepted them as fellow soldiers. One officer from the 55th Massachusetts felt the close confines of Morris Island forced the two races to accept each other. As he wrote: "The way the two kinds of soldiers affiliate is very astonishing and gratifying," and when he saw a white soldier share a tobacco plug with a black soldier, he commented: "If this is not living pretty close I should like to know what is."

The acceptance of African-American soldiers ranged from the level of common soldier all the way up the command. After the campaign, General Gordon wrote that the black troops faced the enemy with zeal and were cool and self possessed under fire. He felt that by their actions they should be used to the fullest against the enemy. By the time the campaign ended, the black troops had been accepted, allowing officers to integrate divisions and brigades, a practice not seen in other departments.

Because of the campaign, the Confederacy had to accept the North's use of the African-American soldiers. Though the Southerners continued to segregate the prisoners until 1864 and tried to hide their existence from their slaves, the question of black soldiers was settled. Even the radical newspaper the *Charleston Mercury* remained mute on the topic after the Charleston trials confirmed the legitimacy of African American troops.[12]

Besides giving the Northern leaders a stage to view the use of black troops, the campaign on Morris Island served as a showcase for tactical innovations. The use of new weapons and experimental techniques set the battle apart from others. Both land and naval developments occurred that proved invaluable to future military operations.

The Union navy made great advances in their understanding of ironclads. Du Pont's action of April 7, 1863 had injured the reputation of the monitors, and it took extended service off Charleston for the vessels to redeem themselves. Dahlgren started the campaign cautiously, but as the operations wore on, he took note of the monitors' ability to withstand enemy fire.

The damage done to the ironclads from July 10 to September 7 was not incapacitating, and the vessels proved durable. The only vessel sent north after the campaign was the *Passaic*, which required repairs on its turret mechanism that could be accomplished more efficiently at a Northern navy yard than at Port Royal. The monitors, though "not as good as new," still retained their fighting ability.

In writing Secretary Welles, Dahlgren noted that the protracted usage to which the monitors were exposed had resulted in holed decks, cannon worn out, side armor shaken, and tops of pilothouses crushed, but all were repairable, and no vital principal had been seriously damaged. (See appendix, table 21.)

The problems found during the Morris Island campaign were remedied in the next class of monitors, the *Canonicus* class. These ships had improved pilothouses, thicker deck and side armor, and a protective glacis to keep shot from jamming the turret. The new class was also armed with two 15-inch Dahlgren guns instead of the mixed armament carried by the *Passaic* class.

The *New Ironsides* also came under study during the siege and though many officers, including Gillmore, were impressed with the vessel, Dahlgren was not. The rear admiral wrote that though the ship was a powerful floating gun platform, her uses were limited. Her unprotected ends, deep draft, and inability to respond in a small channel made the ship difficult to handle in battle. Others believed the vessel was superior to the monitors due to her ability to take punishment and deal out a high volume of fire, and even Dahlgren had to admit that, when engaged, no ship could deliver a more powerful and rapid broadside. During the campaign, the *New Ironsides* was struck 154 times by cannon fire with no appreciable damage. She also fired 4,439 rounds as compared to a total of 3,585 for the eight monitors.

Under Dahlgren's supervision, the ironclad's ship-to-shore bombardments were incredibly accurate and devastating. The coordinated bombardments by the army and the navy were excellent. They covered amphibious landings and supported movements on shore. Many of the techniques of amphibious warfare against enemy-held beaches and ship-to-shore bombardments found their beginnings on Morris Island.[13]

Like the navy, the army learned from its experiences. Trench warfare with all its sophisticated methods of killing came to the forefront on the small island, and soldiers were forced to seek shelter in trenches, as the shovel and ax became important features of the battlefield.

New weapons and methods of land warfare that were improved in future campaigns came about on Morris Island. The Bellinghurst and

Requa battery, a forerunner of the machine gun, received its first major test on Morris Island; aerial reconnaissance from Confederate balloons saw service, as did search lights and wire obstructions. Rifled artillery's ability to pulverize masonry forts was proven. Earthworks were clearly shown to be the fortifications of the future, and trench warfare was recognized as an integral part of the battlefield. Artillerymen developed saturation bombardments, long range firing, shelling by compass readings, civilian bombardment, and coordinated land and sea cannonades.

The fighting on Morris Island should have served as a classroom to other Civil War commanders but, as with most wars, the experience gained was often ignored, and the lessons had to be relearned through more bloodshed and death.

Morris Island also slipped from public memory. For most, only the charge of the 54th Massachusetts was remembered, while the rest quickly faded as the war moved on to new battlefields. By the time the Southerners left Morris Island, the Chickamauga Campaign was underway, and soon, national attention would leave the South Carolina island and be riveted on northern Georgia.

But to the troops who suffered on the little island the campaign never could be forgotten. Both Gillmore and Beauregard praised their officers and soldiers for their bravery, endurance, courage, patriotism, and heroic gallantry. Congratulations were received from government officials, and Gillmore even issued four hundred medals to enlisted men who had exhibited "gallant and meritorious conduct."[14]

Morris Island was destined to be best remembered by those who fought there. An appropriate epitaph for the campaign was written by Clara Barton shortly after the siege had ended:

> We have captured one fort—Gregg—and one charnel house—Wagner—and we have built one cemetery, Morris Island. The thousand little sand-hills that in the pale moonlight are a thousand headstones, and the restless ocean waves that roll and breakup on the whitened beach sing an eternal requiem to the toll-worn gallant dead who sleep beside.[15]

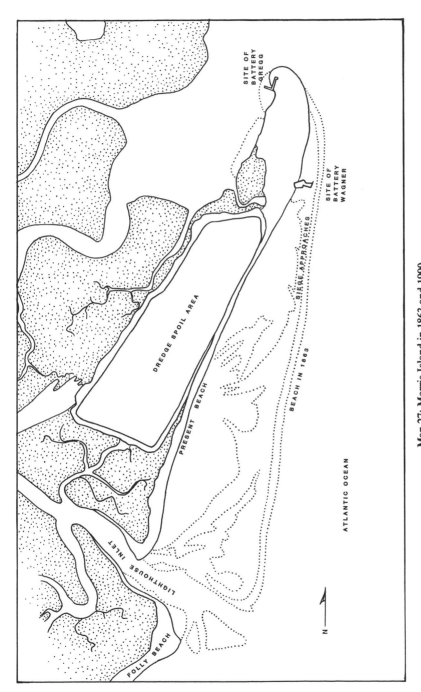

Map 27: Morris Island in 1863 and 1990

SITE OF
BATTERY
GREGG

SITE OF
BATTERY
WAGNER

SIEGE APPROACHES

BEACH IN 1863

DREDGE SPOIL AREA

PRESENT BEACH

LIGHTHOUSE INLET

FOLLY BEACH

ATLANTIC OCEAN

N

Appendix

THE ROLL OF BATTLE

Table 1: DEPARTMENT OF THE SOUTH, JUNE 30, 1863
Estimated Effective Strength

Brigadier General Quincy A. Gillmore

Folly Island: Brigadier General Israel Vogdes.
First Brigade (Colonel Haldiman S. Putnam): 4th N.H., Lt. Col. Gilman E. Sleeper, 450; 7th N.H., Col. Joseph C. Abott, 500; 62nd Ohio, Lt. Col. Clemens F. Steele, 500; 67th Ohio, Col. Alvin C. Voris, 470. Total: 1,920.

Second Brigade (Colonel Joshua B. Howell): 6th Conn., Lt. Col. John Speidel, 540; 39th Ill., Col. Thomas O. Osborn, 500; 100th N.Y., Col. George B. Dandy, 600; 85th Pa., Lt. Col. Henry A. Purviance, 480. Total: 2,120.

Not Brigaded: 1st N.Y. Engineers, Companies C and H, Major James E. Place, 270; 1st Mass. Cavalry, Co. I, Lt. Charles V. Holt, 65; 3rd N.Y. Artillery, Battery F, Lt. Paul Birchmeyer, 75; 3rd R.I. Heavy Artillery, 3 companies, Capt. Richard G. Shaw, 300; 1st U.S. Artillery, Battery C, Sergeant Michael Leahy, 50; 3rd U.S. Artillery, Battery E, Lt. John R. Myrick, 60. Total: 820 men. Total Folly Island: 4,860.

Port Royal Island: Brigader General Rufus Saxton.

Beaufort (Colonel William W. H. Davis): Infantry—115th N.Y., Col. Simeon Sammon, 500; 52nd Pa., Col. John C. Dodge, 610; 55th Pa., Col. Richard White, 500; 104th Pa., Lt. Col. Thompson D. Hart, 600; 1st S.C., Col. Thomas W. Higginson, 600; 2nd S.C., Col. James Montgomery, 530. Total infantry: 3,340. Artillery—1st Conn. Battery, Capt. Alfred P. Rockwell, 75; 3rd R.I. Heavy Artillery, Co. A, Lt. Edward F. Curtis, 100; 1st U.S. Artillery, Battery D, Lt. John S. Gibbs, 75; 1st U.S. Artillery, Battery M, Lt. Loomis L. Langdon, 75. Total artillery: 325. Cavalry and Engineers—1st Mass. Cavalry, three companies, Maj. Atherton H. Stevens Jr., 150; 1st N.Y. Engineers, Co. K, Capt. Henry L. Southard, 70. Total Cavalry and Engineers: 320. Grand Total Port Royal Island: 3,885.

Seabrook Island (Brigadier General Thomas G. Stevenson): 10th Conn., Col. John L. Otis, 450; 24th Mass., Col. Francis A. Osborn, 590; 56th N.Y., Col. Charles H. Van Wyck, 600; 97th Pa., Lt. Col. Augustus P. Duer, 530; 1st N.Y.

Engineers, Co. I, Lt. James H. Harrold, 70; 3rd N.Y. Artillery, Battery B, Capt. James E. Ashcroft, 75. Total Seabrook Island 2,315.

Saint Helena Island (Brigadier General George C. Strong): 7th Conn., four companies, Lt. Col. Daniel C. Rodman, 200; 9th Me., Col. Sabine Emery, 560; 54th Mass., Col. Robert G. Shaw, 760; 3rd N.H., Col. John H. Jackson, 550; 48th N.Y., eight companies, Col. William B. Barton, 420; 76th N.Y., nine companies, Col. De Witt C. Strawbridge, 470; Independent N.Y. Battalion, eight companies, Lt. Col. Simon Levy, 300; 1st N.Y. Engineers, Co. D, Capt. Frederick E. Graef, 70; 3rd R.I. Heavy Artillery, Co. C, Capt. Charles R. Brayton, 100; 1st U.S. Artillery, Battery B, Lt. Francis Reynolds, 50. Total St. Helena Island, 3,480.

Hilton Head Island (Colonel John Chatfield): 8th Me., Major John Hemingway, 500; 76th Pa., Company D, Capt. William S. Diller, 60; 174th Pa., Col. John Nyce, 400; 176th Pa., Lt. Col. George Pilkington 400; 3rd S.C., five companies, Col. Augustus G. Bennett, 250; 1st N.Y. Engineers, Cos. E and G, Col. Edward W. Serrell, 140; 1st Mass Cavalry, Company M, Capt. John G. Thayer, 50; 3rd R.I. Heavy Artillery, six companies, Col. Edwin Metcalf, 600. Total Hilton Head Island: 2,400.

Fort Pulaski (Captain John H. Gould): 48th N.Y., Cos. G and I, Capt. Anthony Elmendorff, 170; 3rd R.I. Heavy Artillery, Co. G, Capt. John H. Gould, 100; 1st N.Y. Engineers, Co. F, Capt. Samuel C. Eaton, 60. Total Fort Pulaski: 330.

Ossabaw Island: 47th N.Y., Major David A. Allen, 380.

Fernandina: 11th Me., Col. Harris M. Plaisted, 335.

Saint Augustine: 7th Conn., six companies, Col. Joseph R. Hawley, 380.

Grand Total Department of the South: 18,365.

Table 2: DEPARTMENT OF SOUTH CAROLINA, GEORGIA, AND FLORIDA, JUNE 1863
Estimated Effective Strength

General Pierre G. T. Beauregard

First District: South Santee River to the Stono River, Brigadier General Roswell S. Ripley.

First Sub-division, James Island (Colonel Charles H. Simonton): Infantry—25th S.C., 690; 20th S.C., seven companies, 500. Cavalry—5th S.C. Cavalry, three companies, 150. Artillery—1st S.C. Artillery, Company A, 80; 2nd S.C. Artillery, nine companies, 915; Palmetto Light Artillery Battalion, six companies,[1] 410; Lucas Heavy Artillery Battalion, three companies,[2] 240. Total: 2,985.

Second Sub-division, Sullivan's Island and Mount Pleasant (Colonel Lawrence M. Keitt): Infantry—20th S.C., three companies, 200. Cavalry—5th S.C. Cavalry, two companies, 140; Sparks Cavalry Company, 80. Artillery—1st S.C. Regulars,[3] 690; Santee Artillery Company, 75. Total: 1,185.

Third Sub-division, Morris Island (Colonel Robert F. Graham): Infantry—21st S.C., 615; 1st S.C. 50. Cavalry—5th S.C. Cavalry, detachment, 26. Artillery— Gist Guard Artillery Company, 55; Mathewes Artillery Company, 55; 1st S.C. Artillery, Companies E, H & I, 220. Total: 1,021.

Fourth Sub-division, Charleston and harbor forts (Colonel Alfred Rhett): Fort Sumter, Colonel A. Rhett, 1st S.C. Artillery, five companies, 475; Castle Pinckney and Fort Ripley: Captain William H. Peronneau, 1st S.C. Artillery, Company G, 75; Charleston: Lieutenant Colonel Peter Cheves Gaillard, 5th S.C. Cavalry, 150; Siege Train,[4] 275; Charleston Battalion, five companies infantry, one company heavy artillery, Company E, 460. Total: 885.

Total First District: 6,626.

Second District: Stono River to the Ashepoo River (Brigadier General Johnson Hagood): 7th S.C. Battalion 400; 6th S.C. Cavalry, 600; Rebel Troop Cavalry, 50; Stono Scouts, 50; Palmetto Light Artillery Battalion, Company F (Chestnut Artillery), 90; Marion Artillery Company, 90; Washington Artillery Company, 90. Total Second District: 1,370.

Third District: Ashepoo River to the Savannah River (Brigadier General William S. Walker): 11th S.C., 540; 3rd S.C. Cavalry, 700; 4th S.C. Cavalry, 700; Partisan Rangers, 100; Palmetto Light Artillery Battalion, Company A (Furman Artillery), 90; Beaufort Artillery Company, 90; Chestatee Artillery Company, 90; Lafayette Artillery Company, 90; Nelson Artillery Company, 90; Rutledge Mounted Rifles, Horse Artillery, 90. Total Third District: 2,580.

Fourth District: South Santee River to the North Carolina-South Carolina border (Brigadier General James H. Trapier): 1st S.C. Battalion, Sharpshooters, 250; German Artillery, Company A, 75; German Artillery, Company B, 75; 2nd S.C. Artillery, Company D, (Inglis Artillery), 75; Waccamaw Artillery Company, 75; 21st Georgia Cavalry Battalion, Companies A, B, C, D and E,

[1] The Palmetto Light Artillery Battalion was also designated the 3rd South Carolina Artillery Battalion.
[2] The Lucas Heavy Artillery was designated as the 15th South Carolina Heavy Artillery Battalion.
[3] The 1st South Carolina Regulars usually served as artillery and were later designated the 3rd South Carolina Artillery Regiment. The men on Morris Island, however, were serving as infantry.
[4] The South Carolina Siege Train was also designated the 18th South Carolina Heavy Artillery Battalion.

250; 5th S.C. Cavalry, Companies F and I, 100; Tucker's Cavalry, Companies A and B, 100. Total Fourth District: 1,000.

District of Georgia: Brigadier General Hugh W. Mercer.

Taliaferro's Brigade (Brigadier General William B. Taliaferro): 1st Georgia Volunteers, Companies G, H, I and K, 160; 12th Georgia Artillery Battalion, Companies A, B, D and F, 160; 32nd Georgia, 565; 54th Georgia, nine companies, 500; Jo Thompson Artillery Company, 60; Total: 1,445.

River Batteries (Colonel Edward C. Anderson): 1st Georgia Volunteers, Companies A and B, 100; 22nd Georgia Artillery Battalion, Companies A, B, C and E, 200; 29th Georgia, Companies A and G, 150; 30th Georgia, Company K, 50; Total: 500.

Fort McAllister (Major George W. Anderson, Jr.): 1st Georgia Company C, 50; 12th Georgia Artillery Battalion, Company C, 50. Total: 100.

Siege Train (Major George L. Buist): 12th Georgia Artillery Battalion, Company C, 50; 54th Georgia, Company A, 50. Total: 100.

Heavy Artillery: 1st Georgia Volunteers, Companies D, E and F, 150; 18th Georgia Battalion, three companies, 130; 22nd Georgia Artillery Battalion, Companies D and F, 100; 32nd Georgia, Company C, 60; 63rd Georgia, 750. Total: 1,190.

Light Artillery: Chatham Artillery Company, 100; Regular Georgia Artillery Company, 60; Terrell Artillery Company, 60; Total: 220.

Cavalary: 4th Georgia Cavalry, 730; 5th Georgia Cavalry, 750; 20th Georgia Cavalry Battalion, six companies, 350; 24th Georgia Cavalry Battalion, four companies, 250; Hardwick Mounted Rifles, two companies, 150. Total: 2,230.

Total District of Georgia: 5,785.

District of East Florida: Brigadier General Joseph Finegan.

Bayport (Captain J. C. Chambers): three independent companies, 150.

Camp Cooper, near Fernandina (Major Robert Harrison): 2nd Florida Cavalry, Company K, Captain F. J. Clark, 70; Milton Artillery, Company B, 70. Total: 140.

Green Cove Springs (Captain A. A. Ochus): independent company, 50.

Camp Finegan, near Jacksonville (Lt. Col. A. H. McCormick): 2nd Florida Cavalry, Companies B, C and F, 230; Partisan Rangers, four companies (2nd Fla. Battalion), 200; two independent companies, 100; Hilton Head Artillery, Company A, 70. Total: 600.

Fowler's Bluff and Cedar Keys: one company, 60.

Lake City: independent company, 50.

Palatka: 2nd Florida Cavalry, Company H, 70.

Tampa (Captain J. W. Pearson): independent company, 50.

Total District of East Florida: 1,170.

District of Middle Florida (Brigadier General Howell Cobb): 1st Special Florida Battalion, 200; 2nd Florida Cavalry, five companies, 250; Florida Cavalry Company, 50; seven independent companies, 350; 1st Georgia Regulars, 600; 64th Georgia, 500, Cobb Guards Artillery Company, 50; Echols Artillery Company, 50; Kilcrease Artillery Company, 50; Leon Artillery Company, 50; Georgia Siege Artillery, one company, 50. Total District of Middle Florida: 2,250.

Department Grand Total: 20, 781.

Table 3: CONFEDERATE TROOP DISTRIBUTION IN THE
CHARLESTON AREA, JULY 9, 1863
Estimated Strength

First Sub-division: July 10, 1863: Colonel Charles H. Simonton to July 10; Brigadier General Johnson Hagood, July 11–18.

Secessionville: 25th S.C., Lt. Col. John G. Pressley, 690; 20th S.C., Lt. Col. Olin M. Dantzler, seven companies, 500; 1st S.C.A. Light Battery, Capt. Francis D. Blake, 80. Total: 1,270.

Clark House: Palmetto Battalion, Co. D, Wagner Artillery, Capt. Charles E. Kanapaux, two 12-pounders, two Napoleons, 120; Palmetto Battalion, Co. G (DeSaussure Artillery), Capt. William L. De Pass, two 12-pounders, two Napoleons, 90. Total: 210.

West James Island Lines: Palmetto Battalion, Co. E, Capt. John D. Johnson, two Wiard guns, 50; Palmetto Battalion, Co. H, Capt. Thomas A. Hotzclaw, two Wiard guns, 50; Palmetto Battalion, Co. I, Capt. J. R. Bowden, four 12-pounders, 50; Palmetto Battalion, Co. K, Capt. Samuel M. Richardson, 50. Total: 200.

Fort Pemberton, Lucas Battalion (Major Johnathon J. Lucas): Co. A, Capt. John H. Gary, 80; Co. B, Capt. Robert Pringle, 80; Co. C, Capt. Theodore B. Hayne, 80. Total: 240.

Fort Lamar: 2nd S.C.A., Co. B, Capt. J. W. Lancaster, 60; 2nd S.C.A., Co. K, Capt. Harry C. Culbreath, 85. Total: 145.

Fort Johnson: 2nd S.C.A., Co. I, Capt. Joseph B. Humbert, 90.

Battery Glover: 2nd S.C.A., Co. G, Capt. George W. Stallings, 110.

Batteries Haig and Palmer: 2nd S.C.A., Co. C, Capt. Medicus Rickenbacker, 90.

East James Island Lines: 2nd S.C.A., Co. A, Capt. William A. Hunter, 80; 2nd S.C.A., Co. D, Capt. William Charles, 80; 2nd S.C.A., Co. E, Capt. B. E. Dickson, 80; 2nd S.C.A., Co. H, Capt. William Kennedy, 80; 2nd S.C.A., Co. F, Capt. Thomas K. Legare, 80. Total: 400.

Cavalry: 5th S.C. Cavalry, 3 companies, Lt. Col. Robert J. Jeffords, 150.

Total First Sub-division: 2,905.

Second Sub-division: July 10, 1863: Colonel Lawrence M. Keitt.

Fort Moultrie: Four companies, 1st S.C.

Battery Bee: Two companies, 1st S.C.[1]

Battery Marshall: Three companies, 1st S.C.

Battery Beauregard: One company, 1st S.C.

Palmetto Battery: One company, 20th S.C.

Christ Church: Cavalry—Two companies, 5th S.C. Cavalry, 140; Sparks Cavalry Company, 80. Total: 220.

Mount Pleasant: Infantry—Three companies, 20th S.C., 200. Artillery—Santee Artillery, Capt. Christopher Gaillard, 75. Total: 275.

Total Second Sub-division: 1,185.

Third Sub-division,   July 10, 1863—Morris Island: Colonel Robert F. Graham.

Battery Mitchel (Oyster Point): 1st S.C.A., Co. I, Capt. John C. Mitchel, 60; 1st S.C.A., Co. E, Capt. J. Ravenel Macbeth, 70; 1st S.C.A., Detachment Co. H, Lt. H. W. Frost, 40; 1st S.C., Co. D, serving as infantry, Capt. Charles T. Haskell, 50; 21st S.C., detachment, Major George W. McIver, 400. Total: 1,021.

Battery Wagner: Gist Guard Artillery Company, Capt. Charles E. Chichester, 55; Mathewes Artillery Company, Capt. John E. Mathewes, 55; 21st S.C., detachment, Col. Robert F. Graham, 215. Total: 325.

Battery Gregg: 1st S.C.A., detachment, Co. H, Capt. Henry R. Lesesne, 50; 5th S.C. Cavalry, detachment of Couriers, 26. Total: 76.

Total Third Sub-division: 1,021.

Fourth Sub-division,   July 10, 1863—Inner Harbor: Colonel Alfred Rhett.

Fort Sumter: 1st S.C.A., Companies B, C, D, F and G, Col. Alfred Rhett, 475.

---

[1] Battery named Bee after July 10, 1863.

Castle Pinckney and Fort Ripley: Capt. William H. Peronneau, 1st S.C.A., Company K, 75.

Charleston: Charleston Battalion, Lt. Col. Peter C. Gaillard, 460; 5th S.C. Cavalry, 150; South Carolina Siege Train, Major Edward Manigault, 275. Total: 885.

Total Fourth Sub-division: 1,435.

Grand Total Charleston District: 6,546.

Table 4: UNION FORCES ON JAMES ISLAND, JULY 9–16, 1863
Estimated Effective Strength

Terry's Division: Brigadier General Alfred H. Terry.

Stevenson's Brigade (Brigadier General Thomas G. Stevenson): 10th Connecticut, 450; 97th Pennsylvania, 530; 24th Massachusetts, 590; 4th New Hampshire, 450. Total: 2,020 men.

Davis' Brigade (Colonel William W. H. Davis): 104th Pennsylvania, 600; 52nd Pennsylvania, 610; 56th New York, 600. Total: 1,810 men.

Montgomery's Brigade (Colonel James Montgomery): 2nd South Carolina, 530; 54th Massachusetts 760. Total: 1,290 men.

Artillery: Connecticut Battery, 75 men.

Cavalry: 1st Massachusetts, Co. I, 65 men.

Grand Total: 5,260 men.

Table 5: UNION FORCES FOR THE ASSAULT ON MORRIS ISLAND,
JULY 10, 1863
Estimated Effective Strength

Brigadier General Quincy A. Gillmore

North End of Folly Island: Brigadier General Truman Seymour.

Batteries: Artillery Commander, Lt. Col. Richard H. Jackson.

First Line: Four 3-inch Ordnance Rifles, Co. C, 3rd R.I. Art.; four 3.67-inch Parrotts, Co. I, 3rd R.I. Art.; four 4.2-inch Parrotts, Co. C, 1st U.S. Art.; eight 4.2-inch Parrotts, Co. D, 3rd R.I. Art.; six 3-inch Parrotts, Co. E, 3rd U.S. Art.; six 10-inch Siege Mortars, Co. B, 3rd R.I. Art.; four 10-inch Siege Mortars, Co. M, 3rd R.I. Art.

Second Line: Six 12-pound Wiard Rifles Co. F, 3rd N.Y. Art.; five 8-inch Siege Mortars Co. H, 3rd R.I. Art.

Magazines: Detachment, Co. C, 1st U.S. Artillery.

Attacking Column: Brigadier General George Strong.

First Wave: 7th Connecticut, four companies, 200; 48th New York, four companies, 210; 9th Maine, 560; 3rd New Hampshire, 550; 76th Pennsylvania, 470; 6th Connecticut, 540. Total: 2,530 men.

Second Wave: 48th New York, four companies, 210; 7th New Hampshire, 500; 100th New York, 600; 1st U.S. Artillery, Co. B, six guns, 50. Total: 1,360 men.

Reserve: 62nd Ohio, 500; 67th Ohio 470; 85th Pennsylvania, 480. Total: 1,450 men.

Grand Total: 5,340

Table 6: UNION AND CONFEDERATE CASUALTIES, JULY 10, 1863

	Estimated Strength	Killed	Wounded	Missing	Total Casualties
Union[1]	4,500	15	91	—	106
Confederate					
21st S.C.	615	14	112	56	182
1st S.C. Art. Co. I	60	*	*	*	38
1st S.C. Art. Co. E	70	*	*	*	24
1st S.C. Art. Co. H	90	*	*	*	21
1st S.C. Co. D	50	*	*	*	12
7th S.C. Batt.	400	3	—	11	14
20th S.C. four Cos.	285	—	—	—	0
Gist Guard Art.	55	—	—	—	0
Mathewes' Art.	55	—	—	—	0
Olmstead[2]	460	—	—	—	0
Couriers	26	—	—	—	0
Total	2,166	17	112	67	291

*Unreported

[1] There is no breakdown of the Union casualties by separate units.

[2] Olmstead's command consisted of Companies G, H, I, and K of the 1st Georgia Infantry, Companies A, B, D, and F of the 12th Georgia Artillery Battalion, and three companies of the 18th Georgia Infantry Battalion under the command of Colonel Charles H. Olmstead. This mixed force arrived on Morris Island after the attack on Oyster Point.

Table 7: CONFEDERATE FORCES AT BATTERY WAGNER,
JULY 11, 1863

Colonel Robert F. Graham: Four companies 20th South Carolina; 7th South
Carolina Battalion; 21st South Carolina; four companies, 1st Georgia, four
companies 12th Georgia Artillery Battalion; three companies, 18th Georgia
Battalion; detachment Company D, 1st South Carolina; Companies E and I,
1st South Carolina Artillery; Gist Guard Artillery Company; Mathewes Artillery Company. Total: 1,770 men.

Armament: Seaward, one rifled 32-pounder, one 10-inch Columbiad, one 32-
pounder; Landward, one 8-inch seacoast howitzer, one 42-pound carronade,
two 8-inch shell guns, three 32-pound carronade, one 10-inch mortar.

Table 8: UNION AND CONFEDERATE CASUALTIES, JULY 11, 1863

	Estimated Strength	Killed	Wounded	Missing	Total Casualties
Union					
7th Connecticut	200	13	29	61	103
9th Maine	560	1	32	23	56
76th Pennsylvania	470	35	123	83	241
Total	1,230	49	184	167	400
Confederate					
21st South Carolina	433	—	—	—	—
1st S.C. Art. Co. I	22	—	—	—	—
1st S.C. Art. Co. E	46	—	—	—	—
1st S.C. Art. Co. H	69	—	—	—	—
1st S.C. Art. Co. D	38	—	—	—	—
Gist Guard	55	—	—	—	—
Mathewes Artillery	55	—	—	—	—
7th S.C. Batt.	386	—	—	—	—
20th S.C.	285	—	—	—	—
Olmstead	460				
1st Georgia		1	2	3	6
12th Georgia Art. Batt.		1	—	1	2
18th Georgia Inf. Batt.		4	4	8	16
Couriers	26	—	—	—	—
Total	1,873	6	6	12	24

Table 9: CONFEDERATE REINFORCEMENTS TO THE CHARLESTON
AREA, JULY 10–18, 1863
Estimated Strengths

Unit	Strength	From	Arrival Date
7th S.C. Battalion	400	2nd District, S.C.	July 10
32 Ga.[1]	625	District of Georgia	July 10
54th Ga., six Companies[1]	350	District of Georgia	July 10
Chatham Artillery[1]	100	District of Georgia	July 10
63rd & 22nd Ga., Detach.[1]	75	District of Georgia	July 10
Olmstead's Command[1]	460	District of Georgia	July 10
11 S.C.	540	3rd District, S.C.	July 11
51 N.C.[2]	540	Wilmington, N.C.	July 11
61 N.C.[2]	550	Wilmington, N.C.	July 11
31 N.C.[2]	505	Wilmington, N.C.	July 12
Georgia Siege Train	50	District of Georgia	July 13
8th N.C.[2]	610	Wilmington, N.C.	July 14
19th Ga.[3]	380	Wilmington, N.C.	July 14
6th Ga.[3]	480	Wilmington, N.C.	July 14
Marion Artillery Company	90	2nd District, S.C.	July 14
S.C. Militia Brigade	1,010	Charleston area	July 14

Table 10: SOUTH ATLANTIC BLOCKADING SQUADRON, JULY 15, 1863

Rear Admiral John A. Dahlgren

Murrell's Inlet: *Flambeau*.

Georgetown: *Cimarron*.

Bull's Bay: *Memphis*.

Outside Charleston Bar: *New Ironsides,* Canandaigua, Housatonic, Wabash, Powhatan, Flag, Lodona, Conemaugh, Paul Jones, Ottawa, Seneca, Wissahickon, Chippewa, Norfolk Packet, G. W. Blunt*.

---

[1] Brigadier General William B. Taliaferro's command. The 63rd Georgia was made of Companies B and K while the 22nd Georgia Battalion was made up of a detachment from Company A. Olmstead's command was made up of four companies from the 1st Georgia, four companies of the 12th Georgia Artillery Battalion, and three companies of the 18th Georgia Battalion all under Colonel Charles H. Olmstead.

[2] Brigadier General Thomas L. Clingman's brigade from the District of Wilmington, N.C.

[3] Brigadier General Alfred H. Colquitt's brigade from the District of Wilmington, N.C. The brigade's other two regiments, the 27th and 28th Georgia arrived August 10, 1863.

*ironclad

Inside Charleston Bar: *Catskill,* Montauk,* Weehawken,* Nantucket,* Daffodil, O. M. Petit, Dandelion.*

Lighthouse Inlet: *Commodore McDonough.*

Stono River: *Pawnee, Huron, Marblehead.*

North Edisto River: *South Carolina.*

St. Helena Sound: *Kingfisher.*

Port Royal Sound: *Vermont, Valparaiso, Oleander, Columbine, Rescue, Patapsco,* Atlanta,* Mohawk.*

Wassaw Sound: *Nahant,* Unadilla.*

Ossabaw Sound: *Water Witch.*

St. Catherine's Sound: *Madgie.*

Sapelo Sound: *Midnight.*

Doboy Sound: *Wamsutta.*

St. Simon's Sound: *Stetin.*

Saint Andrew's Sound: *Braziliera.*

Fernandina: *Potomska.*

St. John's River: *E. B. Hale, Norwich.*

Mosquito Sound: *Para.*

Table 11: CONFEDERATE ASSAULT FORCE ON JAMES ISLAND,
JULY 16, 1863
Estimated Effective Strength

Brigadier General Alfred H. Colquitt: six companies, 25th South Carolina, Lt. Colonel J. G. Pressley, 400; 6th Georgia, Colonel T. J. Lofton, 450; 19th Georgia, Colonel A. J. Hutchins, 380; four companies, 32nd Georgia, Lt. Colonel W. Pruden, 240; Marion Artillery, (4 Napoleons), Captain E. L. Parker, 40; two companies, 5th South Carolina Cavalry, Lt. Colonel R. J. Jeffords, 80. Total: 1,590 men.

Colonel James D. Radcliffe: 61st North Carolina, Colonel J. D. Radcliffe, 550; section Chatham Artillery, (2 Napoleons), Captain J. F. Wheaton, 50; section Company A, 1st South Carolina Artillery, (2 Napoleons), Captain F. D. Blake, 50. Total: 650 men.

---

*ironclad

Colonel Charlton H. Way: six companies, 54th Georgia, Colonel C. W. Way, 350; one company, 5th South Carolina Cavalry, Captain J. C. Edwards, 40; 31st North Carolina, Colonel J. V. Jordan, 510. Total: 900 men.

Table 12: UNION AND CONFEDERATE CASUALTIES ON JAMES ISLAND, JULY 16, 1863

	Killed	Wounded	Missing	Total
Union				
1st Connecticut Battery	—	1	—	1
1st Massachusetts Cavalry	—	1	—	1
24th Massachusetts	—	1	—	1
54th Massachusetts	14	17	12	43
Total	14	20	12	46
Confederate				
Total	3	12	3	18

Table 13: UNION FORCES, JULY 18, 1863
Estimated Effective Strength

Battery Weed: Armament: Four 10-inch siege mortars.

Battery Reynolds: Armament: Five 8-inch siege mortars; two 4.2-inch Parrotts; six 3-inch Parrotts; four 3-inch ordnance rifles; two 12-pound Wiards.

Battery Hayes: Armament: Nine 4.2-inch Parrotts.

Battery O'Rourke: Armament: Five 10-inch siege mortars.

Garrison Batteries Reynolds and Weed: 3rd Rhode Island Artillery, Companies C, H, and M; 1st U.S. Artillery, Companies B and M; 3rd U.S. Artillery, Company E.

Garrison Batteries Hayes and O'Rourke: 3rd Rhode Island, Companies B, D, and I; 7th Connecticut, detachment.

Attacking Column: Brigadier General T. Seymour.

Strong's Brigade: 54th Massachusetts, 650; 6th Connecticut, 540; 48th New York, 420; 3rd New Hampshire, 550; 9th Maine, 500; 76th Pennsylvania, 290. Total: 2,950 men.

Putnam's Brigade: 7th New Hampshire, 500; 100th New York, 600; 62nd Ohio, 500; 67th Ohio, 470. Total: 2,070 men.

Stevenson's Brigade: 24th Massachusetts, 590; 10th Connecticut, 450; 97th Pennsylvania, 530; 2nd South Carolina, 530. Total: 2,110 men.

Grand Total: 7,130 men.

Table 14: CONFEDERATE FORCES ON MORRIS ISLAND, JULY 18, 1863
Estimated Effective Strength

Battery Wagner: Brigadier General W. B. Taliaferro.

Armament: Seaward, one 10-inch Columbiad, one 32 pounder. Landward, one 8-inch seacoast howitzer, three 32-pound carronades, one 42-pound carronade, two 8-inch shell guns, two 32-pound howitzers, two 12-pound howitzers, one 10-inch seacoast mortar.

Garrison: 51st North Carolina, 550; 31st North Carolina, 425; Charleston Battalion, five companies, 400; 1st South Carolina Artillery detachment, Co. A, 25; 63rd Georgia, Companies B and K and detachment of Co. D, 22nd Georgia, 75; 1st South Carolina, Co. H, 65; 1st South Carolina, Co. I, 55; Couriers, 26. Total: 1,621 men.

Battery Gregg: Captain H. Lesesne.

Armament: Two 10-inch Columbiads; one 9-inch Dahlgren, two 12-pound howitzers.

Garrison: 31st North Carolina, 80; Palmetto Battalion, detachment Co. G, 25; 1st South Carolina Artillery, Co. H. 75. Total: 180.

Table 15: UNION AND CONFEDERATE CASUALTIES, JULY 18, 1863

	Killed	Wounded	Missing	Total
Union				
Staff	—	2	—	2
54th Massachusetts	34	146	92	272
6th Connecticut	15	77	46	138
48th New York	54	112	76	242
3rd New Hampshire	2	38	6	46
9th Maine	4	94	19	117
76th Pennsylvania	2	20	2	24
7th New Hampshire	41	119	56	216
100th New York	49	97	29	175
62nd Ohio	26	87	38	151
67th Ohio	19	82	25	126
Total Union	246	890	391	1,515

	Killed	Wounded	Missing	Total
Confederate				
51st North Carolina	16	52	—	68
31st North Carolina	13	32	—	45
1st South Carolina Art., Co. A	*	*	*	5
1st South Carolina Co. H & I	9	26	3	38
63rd Georgia, Co. B & K	4	10	—	14
Charleston Battalion	6	42	2	50
Palmetto Battalion	*	*	*	2
Total Confederate				222

Table 16: DEPARTMENT OF THE SOUTH—JULY 31, 1863

Brigadier General Quincy A. Gillmore

Location	Effective Strength	Commander
Morris Island	6,900	Brig. Gen. A. Terry
Folly Island	2,500	Col. W. W. H. Davis
Hilton Head	2,220	Col. Edwin Metcalf
Port Royal Island	1,480	Brig. Gen. R. Saxton
Fort Pulaski	215	Col. H. M. Plaisted
Fernandina	250	Maj. William Ames
St. Augustine	370	Col. J. R. Hawley
Total	13,935	

Units in Charleston Area

Morris Island: Brigadier General Alfred H. Terry. *1st Brigade:* Brigadier General Israel Vogdes, 7th Conn., four companies, Capt. Sylvester Gray, 9th Maine, Lt. Col. Zina H. Robinson, 3rd N.H., Captain James F. Randlett, 4th N.H., Col. Louis Bell, 76th Pa., Capt. John S. Littell. *2nd Brigade:* Colonel Joshua B. Howell, 39th Ill., Col. Thomas O. Osborn, 62nd Ohio, Col. Francis B. Pond, 67th Ohio, Major Lewis Butler, 85th Pa., Lt. Col. Henry A. Purviance, 2nd S.C., Col. James Montgomery. *3rd Brigade:* Brigadier General Thomas G. Stevenson, 10th Conn., Major Edwin Greeley, 24th Mass., Col. Francis A. Osborn, 54th Mass., Col. Milton S. Littlefield, 7th N.H., Lt. Col. Joseph C. Abbott, 100th N.Y., Col. George B. Dandy, 97th Pa., Col. Henry R. Guss. *Artillery:* Major James E. Bailey, 3rd R.I. Heavy Artillery, Companies

---

*Unreported

A, B, C, D, H, I and M, 3rd N.Y. Artillery, section, Battery B, Lt. Edward A. Wildt, 3rd N.Y. Artillery, Battery F, Lt. Paul Birchmeyer, 48th N.Y., eight companies, Major Dudley W. Strickland,[1] 1st U.S. Artillery, Battery B, Lt. Guy V. Henry, 1st U.S. Artillery, Battery C, Lt. James E. Wilson, 3rd U.S. Artillery, Battery E, Lt. John R. Myrick, 11th Maine, detachment, Lt. Charles Sellmer. *Cavalry:* 1st Mass. Cavalry, Company I, Lt. Charles V. Holt. *Engineers:* 1st New York Engineers, nine companies, Col. Edward W. Serrell. *Marine Battalion:* Major Jacob Zeilin.

Folly Island: Colonel William W. H. Davis. *1st Brigade:* Col. William W. H. Davis, 56th N.Y., Col. Charles H. Van Wyck, 52nd N.Y., Col. John C. Dodge, 104th Pa., Lt. Col. Thompson D. Hart. *Not Brigaded:* 47th N.Y., Lt. Col. Albert B. Nicholson, Independent New York Battalion, Lt. Col. Simon Levy, *Artillery:* 1st Conn. Battery, Capt. Alfred P. Rockwell, 3rd N.Y., section, Battery B, Capt. James E. Ashcroft.

Table 17: DEPARTMENT OF SOUTH CAROLINA, GEORGIA, AND FLORIDA, AUGUST 1, 1863

General P. G. T. Beauregard

Location	Effective Strength	Commander
1st District	10,254	Brigadier General R. S. Ripley
2nd District	878	Colonel Hugh K. Aiken
3rd District	2,138	Brigadier General W. S. Walker
4th District	970	Brigadier General J. H. Trapier
Georgia	3,609	Brigadier General Hugh Mercer
East Florida	1,135	Brigadier General Joseph Finegan
Middle Florida	2,242	Brigadier General Howell Cobb
Total	21,226	

Units in Charleston Area

1st District: Brigadier General Roswell S. Ripley: 1st Sub-division, James Island: Brigadier General Johnson Hagood. *Infantry:* Olmstead's Command, Col. Charles H. Olmstead, 1st Ga., four companies, 12th Ga. Artillery Battalion, four companies, Lt. Col. Henry D. Capers, 18th Ga. Battalion, three companies, Major William S. Basinger; 19th Ga., Col. Andrew J. Hutchins; 32nd Ga., Col. George P. Harrison; 11th S.C., five companies, Lt. Col. Allen C. Izard; 21st S.C., Col. Robert F. Graham; 25th S.C., Col. Charles H. Simonton. *Cavalry:* 5th S.C. Cavalry, three companies, Capt. John C.

---

[1] Sent to St. Augustine before July 31.

Edwards. *Artillery:* 63rd Georgia, two companies, Capt. James T. Buckner; 22nd Ga. Artillery Battalion, detachment; 1st S.C. Artillery, companies A, C, F and I; 2nd S.C. Artillery, nine companies, Col. Andrew D. Frederick; Chatham Artillery Company, Capt. John F. Wheaton; 15th S.C. Heavy Artillery Battalion (Lucas Battalion), two companies, Major Johnathon J. Lucas; Palmetto Light Artillery Battalion, Companies D, E, G, H, I and K, Lt. Col. Edward B. White; Marion Artillery Company, Capt. Edward L. Parker; 18th S.C. Artillery Battalion (South Carolina Siege Train), Major Edward Manigault.

2nd Sub-division, Sullivan's Island and Mount Pleasant: *Infantry:* 31st N.C., Col. John V. Jordon; 51st N.C., Col. Hector McKethan; 7th S.C. Battalion, six companies, Lt. Col. Nelson Patrick Page; 20th S.C., Col. Lawrence M. Keitt. *Cavalry:* 5th S.C. Cavalry, Co. E, Capt. L. A. Keitt; Keitt's and Sparks's S.C. Cavalry Companies. *Artillery:* 1st S.C., Col. William Butler; Mathewes Artillery Company, Capt. John R. Butler.

3rd Sub-division, Morris Island: Brigadier General Thomas L. Clingman. *Infantry:* 6th Ga., Col. John T. Lofton; 8th N.C., Col. Henry M. Shaw; 61st N.C., Col. James Radcliffe. *Artillery:* 1st S.C. Artillery, Co. C, Capt. Charles W. Parker; Gist Guard Artillery, Capt. Charles E. Chichester; 15th S.C. Artillery Battalion (Lucas Battalion), Company B, Capt. Robert Pringle. *Cavalry:* 5th S.C. Cavalry, detachment.

4th Sub-division, harbor forts: Colonel Alfred Rhett, 1st S.C. Artillery, six companies.

5th Sub-division, Charleston: Brig. Gen. Wilmot G. De Saussure. *Infantry:* Charleston Battalion, Lt. Col. Peter C. Gaillard; 4th S.C. Militia Brigade, Brig. Gen. Wilmot G. De Saussure. *Cavalry:* 5th S.C. Cavalry, two companies, Lt. Col. Robert J. Jeffords.

Table 18: UNION BATTERIES FOR BOMBARDMENT OF FORT SUMTER, AUGUST 17, 1863

Battery Brown: Right of second parallel, 3,560 yards from Fort Sumter, 2,170 yards from Battery Gregg, 830 yards, from Battery Wagner. Two 8-inch Parrotts, one firing shot, one firing percussion shells at Sumter's gorge wall. Garrison: Company I, 3rd Rhode Island Heavy Artillery, Capt. Charles G. Strahan, 3rd R.I.H.A.

Battery Rosecrans: Left of second parallel, 3,500 yards from Fort Sumter, 2,110 yards from Battery Gregg, 830 yards from Battery Wagner. Three 6.4-inch Parrotts, one firing percussion shell, two firing shot at Sumter's gorge wall. Garrison: Company M, 3rd R.I. Heavy Artillery, detachment 178th N.Y., Captain Joseph J. Comstock, 3rd R.I.H.A.

Battery Meade: Left and front of Battery Rosecrans, 3,475 yards from Fort Sumter, 2,985 yards from Battery Gregg, 820 yards from Battery Wagner. Two 6.4-inch Parrotts, both firing percussion shells against Sumter's gorge wall. Garrison: Detachments from 3rd R.I. Heavy Artillery, 100th N.Y. and 178th N.Y., Lieutenant Henry Holbrook, 3rd R.I.H.A.

Naval Battery: Center first parallel, 3,980 yards from Fort Sumter, 2,590 yards from Battery Gregg, 1,335 yards from Battery Wagner. Two 8-inch Parrotts, two 5-inch Whitworths, firing shot and shell against Sumter's gorge. Garrison: Detachment of sailors from the *Wabash,* Captain Foxhall Parker, USN.

Battery Kearny: Extreme left of second parallel, 1,955 yards from Battery Gregg, 720 yards from Battery Wagner, three 4.2-inch Parrotts, three coehorns, Parrotts firing shot and shell on Battery Gregg, coehorns on Battery Wagner. Garrison: Detachments from companies C and K, 7th Conn., Lt. Seager S. Atwell, 7th Conn.

Battery Reynolds: First parallel, 1,135 yards from Battery Wagner, five 10-inch mortars firing on Wagner, Garrison: Company B, 3rd R.I. Heavy Artillery, detachment 178th N.Y., Capt. Albert E. Green, 3rd R.I.H.A.

Battery Weed: Rear of first parallel, 1,460 yards from Battery Wagner, five 10-inch mortars firing on Wagner. Garrison: Detachments from companies H and D, 7th Conn., Captain B. F. Skinner, 7th Conn.

Battery Hays: Left Batteries, 4,225 yards from Fort Sumter, 2,950 yards from Battery Gregg, 1,830 from Battery Wagner, seven 4.2-inch Parrotts and one 8-inch Parrott, 4.2-inch Parrotts against Wagner and Gregg, 8-inch Parrott shot and shell against Sumter's gorge wall. Garrison: Detachment Co. D, 3rd R.I. Heavy Artillery, Capt. Richard G. Shaw, 3rd R.I.H.A.

Battery Reno: Left Batteries, 4,320 yards from Fort Sumter, 2,950 yards from Battery Gregg, 1,860 yards from Battery Wagner, one 8-inch Parrott, two 6.4-inch Parrotts, 8-inch and one 6.4-inch Parrott firing shot and one 6.4-inch Parrott firing percussion shell against Sumter's gorge wall. Garrison: Company H, 3rd R.I. Heavy Artillery, detachment 178th N.Y., Capt. Augustus W. Colwell, 3rd R.I.H.A.

Battery Stevens: Left Batteries, 4,320 yards from Fort Sumter, 2,950 yards from Battery Gregg, 1,860 yards from Battery Wagner, two 6.4-inch Parrotts, one firing shot and the other percussion shell on Sumter's gorge wall. Garrison: Detachment Company C, 1st U.S. Artillery, detachment 7th Conn., Lt. James E. Wilson, 1st U.S. Artillery.

Battery Strong: Left Batteries, 4,345 yards from Fort Sumter, 2,950 yards from Battery Gregg, 1,900 yards from Battery Wagner, one 10-inch Parrott, firing shot and percussion shell on Sumter's gorge wall. Garrison: Detachment 7th Conn., Capt. Sylvester H. Gray, 7th Conn.

Battery Kirby: Left Batteries, 4,440 yards from Fort Sumter, 3,000 yards from Battery Gregg, 1,960 yards from Battery Wagner, two 10-inch mortars firing on Fort Sumter. Garrison: Detachment, 11th Maine, Lt. Charles Sellmer, 11th Maine.

Ironclads: *Montauk, Nahant, Catskill, Passaic, Patapsco, New Ironsides.*

Gunboats: *Canandaiqua, Mahaska, Ottawa, Wissahickon, Dai Ching, Lodona, Seneca.*

Table 19: DEPARTMENT OF THE SOUTH, AUGUST 31, 1863

Brigadier General Quincy A. Gillmore

Location	Effectives	Commander
Morris Island	9,145	Brig. Gen. Alfred H. Terry
Folly Island		
Vogdes Division	4,377	Brig. Gen. Israel Vodges
Gordon's Division	3,404	Brig. Gen. George H. Gordon
Hilton Head Island	1,675	Col. De Witt C. Strawbridge
Port Royal Island	1,937	Brig. Gen. Rufus Saxton
Fernandina	323	Col. Harris M. Plaisted
Fort Pulaski	189	Maj. William Ames
St. Augustine	297	Maj. Dudley W. Strickland
Headquarters	66	
Total	21,413	

Units in Charleston Area

Morris Island: *1st Brigade:* Col. Henry R. Guss, 9th Maine, Lt. Col. Zina H. Robinson; 3rd N.H., Capt. James F. Randlett; 4th N.H., Col. Louis Bell; 97th Pa., Maj. Galusha Pennypacker; *2nd Brigade:* Col. Joshua Howell, 39th Ill., Col. Thomas O. Osborn; 85th Pa., Maj. Edward Campbell; 62nd Ohio, Col. Francis Pond; 67th Ohio, Maj. Lewis Butler; *3rd Brigade:* Brig. Gen. Thomas G. Stevenson, 7th Conn., Col. Joseph R. Hawley; 10th Conn., Maj. Edwin S. Greeley; 24th Mass., Col. Francis A. Osborn; 7th N.H., Lt. Col. Joseph C. Abott; 100th N.Y., Col. George B. Dandy; *4th Brigade:* Col. James Montgomery, 54th Mass., Col. Milton S. Littlefield; 2nd S.C., Lt. Col. William W. Marple; 3rd U.S. Colored Troops, Col. Benjamin C. Tilghman; *Davis's Brigade:* Colonel William W. H. Davis, 47th N.Y., Maj. Christopher R. MacDonald; Independent N.Y. Battalion, Capt. Michael Schmitt; 52nd Pa., Lt. Col. Henry M. Hoyt; 104th Pa., Maj. Edward L. Rogers; *Artillery:* 3rd N.Y. Artillery, Battery B, Capt. James E. Ashcroft; 3rd N.Y. Artillery, Battery F,

Lt. Paul Birchmeyer; 3rd R.I. Heavy Artillery, Co. B, Capt. Albert E. Greene; 3rd R.I. Heavy Artillery, Co. C, Capt. Charles R. Brayton; 3rd R.I. Heavy Artillery, Co. D, Capt. Richard G. Shaw; 3rd R.I. Heavy Artillery, Co. H, Capt. Augustus Colwell; 3rd R.I. Heavy Artillery, Co. I, Capt. Charles G. Strahan; 3rd R.I. Heavy Artillery, Co. M, Capt. Joseph J. Comstock, Jr.; 1st U.S Artillery, Battery B, Lt. Guy V. Henry; 1st U.S. Artillery, detachment Battery C, Lt. James E. Wilson; 3rd U.S. Artillery, Battery E. Lt. John R. Myrick; 11th Maine, detachment, Lt. Charles Sellmer; *Cavalry:* 1st Mass. Cavalry, detachment Co. I, Lt. Charles V. Holt; *Marine Battalion:* Captain Edward M. Reynolds.

Folly Island: *Vogdes Division:* Brig. Gen. Israel Vogdes, *Alford's* Brigade: Col. Samuel M. Alford, 3rd N.Y., Lt. Col. Eldridge G. Floyd; 89th N.Y., Col. Harrison S. Fairchild; 103rd N.Y., Col. William Heine; 117th N.Y., Col. Alvin White; *Foster's Brigade:* Brig. Gen. Robert S. Foster; 13th Indiana, Col. Cyrus J. Dobbs; 112th N.Y., Col. Jeremiah C. Drake; 169th N.Y., Col. Clarence Buell; *African Brigade:* Brig. Gen. Edward A. Wild, 55th Mass., Col. Norwood P. Hallowell; 1st N.C., Col. James Beecher; 2nd N.C. detachment, Col. Alonzo G. Draper; 3rd N.C., one company, Capt. John Wilder; *Artillery:* 1st Conn. Battery, Capt. Alfred P. Rockwell; *Gordon's Division:* Brig. Gen. George H. Gordon, *First Brigade:* Brig. Gen. Alexander Schimmelfennig, 41st N.Y., Lt. Col. Detleo von Einsiedel; 54th N.Y., Capt. Clemens Knipschild; 127th N.Y., Col. Stewart L. Woodford; 142nd N.Y., Col. N. Martin Curtis; 74th Pa., Capt. Henry Krauseneck; 107th Ohio, Capt. William Smith; *Second Brigade:* Brig. Gen. Adelbert Ames, 17th Conn., Col. William H. Noble; 40th Mass., Lt. Col. Joseph A. Dalton; 144th N.Y., Col. David E. Gregory; 157th N.Y., Maj. James C. Carmichael; 25th Ohio, Capt. Nathaniel Haughton; 75th Ohio, Col. Andrew L. Harris.

Table 20: UNION ASSAULT COLUMN, SEPTEMBER 6, 1863
Estimated Effective Strength

Brigadier General Alfred Terry

Spearhead: Colonel R. H. Guss, 3rd New Hampshire, 500; 97th Pennsylvania, 480. Total: 980 men.

Stevenson's Brigade: Brigadier General T. G. Stevenson, 4th New Hampshire 400; 9th Maine, 450; 7th Connecticut, 450; 10th Connecticut, 400; 24th Massachusetts, 530; 7th New Hampshire, 400; 100th New York, 400. Total: 3,030 men.

Davis' Brigade: Colonel W. W. H. Davis, 47th New York, 380; 52nd Pennsylvania, 450; 104th Pennsylvania, 500, Independent New York Battalion, 250. Total: 1,580 men.

Howell's Brigade: Colonel J. B. Howell, 39th Illinois, 450; 85th Pennsylvania, 400; 62nd Ohio, 400; 67th Ohio, 400. Total: 1,650 men.

Reserve Brigade: Colonel J. Montgomery, 54th Massachusetts, 400; 2nd South Carolina, 480; 3rd U.S. Colored Troops, 500. Total: 1,380 men.

Grand Total: 8,620 men.

Table 21: DAMAGE TO MONITORS, JULY 10–SEPTEMBER 7, 1863

Name	Hits	Damage
Catskill	86	Pilothouse buckled; five holes in deck.
Montauk	154	Turret jammed; two holes in deck; leaking; 11-inch Dahlgren disabled.
Lehigh	36	Two holes in deck; five holes in side.
Passaic	90	Pilothouse and turret revolving together.
Nahant	69	Smoke box loose; good condition.
Patapsco	96	Turret beams broken; three holes in deck; 8-inch Parrott damaged but serviceable.
Weehawken	134	Six holes in deck.
Nantucket	82	Two holes in deck.

Table 22: UNION CASUALTIES, JULY–SEPTEMBER, 1863

Unit	Killed	Wounded	Missing	Total
6th Conn.	15	77	46	138
7th Conn.	15	36	61	112
10th Conn.	—	2	2	4
17th Conn.	1	1	—	2
39th Ill.	1	9	—	10
9th Maine	9	138	42	189
11th Maine	—	2	—	2
24th Mass.	4	8	1	13
40th Mass.	—	6	—	6
54th Mass.	51	171	104	326
3rd N.H.	6	65	6	77
4th N.H.	3	10	—	13
7th N.H.	42	125	56	223
1st N.Y. Engineers	4	17	—	21
3rd N.Y. Artillery	—	5	—	5
47th N.Y.	—	2	—	2

Unit	Killed	Wounded	Missing	Total
48th N.Y.	54	112	76	242
100th N.Y.	60	128	35	223
144th N.Y.	1	1	—	2
157th N.Y.	1	—	—	1
N.Y. Independent Battalion	2	1	—	3
62nd Ohio	27	89	38	154
67th Ohio	21	93	25	139
75th Ohio	1	3	—	4
52nd Pa.	—	3	—	3
76th Pa.	37	82	85	204
85th Pa.	10	58	—	68
97th Pa.	3	6	—	9
104th Pa.	2	15	—	17
3rd R.I. Artillery	3	13	—	16
3rd U.S. Colored Troops	6	12	—	18
1st U.S. Art., Co. B	—	3	—	3
1st U.S. Art., Co. C	—	2	—	2
3rd U.S. Art., Co. E	1	5	—	6
1st Conn. Battery	—	2	—	2
1st Mass. Cavalry	—	2	—	2
July 10 Assault	15	91	—	106
Total	381	1372	565	2,318

Table 23: CONFEDERATE CASUALTIES, JULY–SEPTEMBER, 1863
(based on conflicting reports)

Unit	Killed	Wounded	Missing	Total
Staff	1	3	—	4
1st Ga.	3	7	3	10
12th Ga. Art. Battalion	2	8	3	13
18th Ga. Battalion	7	7	—	14
23rd Ga.	2	9	—	11
27th Ga.	2	4	—	6
28th Ga.	3	22	—	25
32nd Ga.	2	22	—	24
54th Ga.	6	9	—	15
63rd Ga.	5	7	—	12
8th N.C.	4	43	—	47
31st N.C.	13	32	—	45
51st N.C.	17	60	—	77

Unit	Killed	Wounded	Missing	Total
61st N.C.	6	35	76	117
1st S.C.A.	18	50	52	120
2nd S.C.A.	2	15	1	18
1st S.C.	10	32	22	64
20th S.C.	9	24	—	33
21st S.C.	4	11	—	15
25th S.C.	16	124	3	143
Charleston Battalion	13	70	2	85
7th S.C. Battalion	3	—	11	14
Gist Guard Artillery	3	7	—	10
Lucas Battalion	5	33	—	38
Marion Artillery	—	1	—	1
Mathewes Artillery	—	8	—	8
Palmetto Battalion	3	18	—	21
Siege Train	1	12	—	13
Navy	—	1	—	1
James Island, July 16	3	12	3	18
Total	163	686	173	1,022

Table 24:   DEPARTMENT OF THE SOUTH,
SEPTEMBER–OCTOBER, 1863

Brigadier General Q. A. Gillmore

	Effectives	Present Sick
Headquarters	71	—
Morris Island	8,734	2,246
Folly Island		
North end	3,648	1,175
South end	3,119	771
Hilton Head	1,728	351
Port Royal Island	1,798	798
Fernandina	359	70
Fort Pulaski	205	7
Saint Augustine	327	20
Total	19,989	5,438

Table 25: DEPARTMENT OF SOUTH CAROLINA, GEORGIA, AND
FLORIDA, SEPTEMBER–OCTOBER 1863

General Pierre G. T. Beauregard

Effectives

1st District	15,643	Brig. Gen. R. S. Ripley
Reserve	2,069	Brig. Gen. Henry A. Wise
2nd District	962	Col. H. K. Aiken to Oct. 15, then Brig. Gen. B. H. Robertson
3rd District	2,240	Brig. Gen. W. S. Walker
4th District	1,051	Brig. Gen. J. H. Trapier
Georgia	3,804	Brig. Gen. H. W. Mercer
Middle Florida	1,853	Brig. Gen. H. Cobb to October 6, then Brig. Gen. William M. Gardner
East Florida	1,770	Brig. Gen. J. Finegan
Total	28,898	

Units near Charleston

1st District: Brigadier General Roswell S. Ripley. 1st Sub-division: Brigadier General William B. Taliaferro, *Infantry:* Olmstead's Command, Col. Charles H. Olmstead, four companies, 1st Ga.; four companies, 12th Ga. Artillery Battalion, Lt. Col. Henry D. Capers; 6th Ga., Col. John T. Lofton; 19th Ga., Col. A. J. Hutchins; 23rd Ga., Major M. R. Ballenger; 27th Ga., Maj. James Gardner; 28th Ga., Col. Tully Graybill; 32nd Ga., Col. George B. Harrison, Jr.; 54th Ga., Col. Charleton H. Way; 8th N.C., Col. Henry M. Shaw; 31st N.C., Col. John V. Jordon; *Anderson's Brigade:* Brig. General George T. Anderson, (arrived September 9), 7th Ga., Col. William W. White; 8th Ga., Col. John R. Towers; 9th Ga., Col. Benjamin Beck; 11th Ga., Col. Francis H. Little; 59th Ga., Col. Jack Brown; *Hagood's Brigade:* Brig. General Johnson Hagood, 11th S.C., Colonel Frederick H. Gantt; 21st S.C., Col. Robert F. Graham; 25th S.C., Col. Charles H. Simonton; *Cavalry:* 5th S.C. Cavalry, five companies, Col. John Dunovant; *Artillery:* 1st S.C.A., five companies, Maj. Ormsby Blanding; 2nd S.C.A., nine companies, Col. Andrew D. Frederick; 3rd S.C. Artillery Battalion (Palmetto Battalion), five companies, D, E, H, I, and K, Lt. Col. Edward B. White; Chatham Artillery Company, Capt. John F. Wheaton; 18th S.C. Artillery Battalion (South Carolina Siege Train), Major Edward Manigault; 12th Ga. Artillery Battalion, Company C, Capt. W. W. Billopp; 15th S.C. Artillery Battalion (Lucas Battalion), Maj. Johnathon J. Lucas; Marion Artillery Company, Capt. E. L. Parker; Mathewes Artillery Company, Capt. John R. Mathewes.

2nd Sub-division: Brig. General Thomas L. Clingman, *Infantry:* 18th Ga. Battalion, three companies, Maj. William S. Basinger; 51st N.C., Col. Hector

McKethan; 61st N.C., Col. James D. Radcliffe; 7th S.C. Battalion, Lt. Col. Patrick H. Nelson; 20th S.C., Lt. Col. Olin M. Dantzler; *Evans' Brigade:* Brig. General Nathan G. Evans, 17th S.C., Col. Fritz W. McMaster; 18th S.C., Col. William H. Wallace; 22nd S.C., Lt. Col. James O'Connell; 23rd S.C., Col. Henry L. Benbow; 26th S.C., Col. Alexander D. Smith; Holcombe Legion, Lt. Col. William J. Crawley; *Cavalry:* 5th S.C. Company, Company E, Capt. Louis A. Whilden; Peterkin's Cavalry Company, Capt. J. A. Peterkin; Spark's Cavalry Company, Capt. A. D. Sparks; *Artillery:* 1st S.C.A., Co. K, Capt. Alfred S. Gaillard; 1st S.C., Col. William Butler; German Artillery, Capt. Frederick W. Wagener; Macbeth Artillery Company, Capt. B. A. Jeter.

Harbor Forts: *Fort Sumter:* Major Stephen Elliott, Jr., Charleston Battalion, Maj. Julius A. Blake; *Castle Pinckney and Fort Ripley,* 1st S.C.A., Co. G, Capt. William H. Peronneau.

Charleston: Brig. Gen. Wilmot De Saussure, *Infantry:* 1st S.C. Militia, Col. Edward Magrath; 18th S.C. Militia, Col. John E. Carew; Cadet Battalion, Maj. John B. White; 5th S.C. State Troops, Col. James H. Williams; *Cavalry:* 4th S.C. Cavalry, Company K, Capt. Robert H. Colcock; 5th S.C. Cavalry, Companies D and H, Lt. Col. Robert J. Jeffords. *Artillery:* 1st S.C. Artillery Militia, Col. John A. Wagener; Palmetto Battalion, Company A, Capt. William E. Earle (Furman Artillery), Gist Guard Artillery Company, Capt. Charles E. Chichester; 1st S.C.A., Companies D and H. *Sailors:* boat details, three companies, Capt. Thomas J. China.

Reserve—Saint Andrews Parish: Brigadier General Henry A. Wise, (arrived September 19) 4th Va. Heavy Artillery, serving as infantry, Col. J. Thomas Goode; 26th Va., Col. Powhatan R. Page; 46th Va., Col. Richard T. W. Duke; 59th Va., Col. William B. Tabb.

Table 26: CONFEDERATE COMMANDERS OF MORRIS ISLAND, JULY 9–SEPTEMBER 7, 1863

Commanders of Morris Island: Col. Robert F. Graham, July 9–12; Brig. Gen. William B. Taliaferro, July 13–18; Brig. Gen. Johnson Hagood, July 19–22; Taliaferro, July 23–25; Brig. Gen. Alfred Colquitt, July 26–27; Brig. Gen. Thomas Clingman, July 28–August 1; Col. Lawrence Keitt, August 2–5; Hagood, August 6–10; Col. George P. Harrison, August 11–15; Keitt, August 16–21; Hagood, August 22–27; Colquitt, August 28–September 3; Keitt, September 4–7.

Artillery Commanders of Morris Island: Lt. Col. Joseph A. Yates, July 9–14; Lt. Col. John C. Simkins (KIA), July 15–18; Lt. Col. Delaware Kemper, July 19–24[1]; Capt. Charles E. Chichester, July 25–29; Major Frederick F. Warley,

---

[1] Kemper was relieved by Lt. Col. Yates after Kemper became ill.

July 30–August 5; Lt. Col. J. Welsman Brown, August 6–9; Chichester, August 10–16; Capt. Robert Pringle (KIA), August 17–18; Warley, August 19–24; Brown, August 25–29; Warley (wounded and captured), August 30–September 3; Capt. Julius D. Huguenin, September 4–7.

Chief Engineers: Capt. Langdon Cheves (KIA), July 9–10; Capt. William M. Ramsey, July 11–26; Capt. John Gregorie, July 27–August 1; Capt. Robert A. Stiles, August 2–10; Capt. James Wampler (KIA), August 11–17; Gregorie, August 18–23; Capt. John T. Champneys, August 24–30; Capt. Thomas B. Lee, August 31–September 7.

Commanders of Battery Gregg: Capt. Henry Lesesne, July 9–26; Capt. Charles W. Parker, July 27–August 6; Lesesne, August 7–18; Capt. Robert C. Gilchrist, August 19–29; Capt. Julius Huguenin, August 30–September 3; Lesesne, September 4–7.

Table 27: CONFEDERATE GARRISON OF MORRIS ISLAND,
JULY 9–SEPTEMBER 7, 1863[1]

July 9: 1,021 men; *Infantry:* 21st S.C., Co. D, 1st S.C. *Artillery:* Companies E and I, 1st S.C.A., Gist Guard Art., Mathewes Art., Co. H, 1st S.C.A. (Gregg), Couriers.

July 10: Same as July 9.

July 11: 1,845 men; *Infantry:* 21st S.C., Co. D, 1st S.C., 7th S.C. Battalion, four companies, 20th S.C., Olmstead's Command: four companies, 1st Ga., four companies, 12th Ga. Art. Battalion, three companies, 18th Ga. Battalion. *Artillery:* companies E and I, 1st S.C.A., Mathewes Art. Co., Gist Guard Art. Co., Co. H, 1st S.C.A. (Gregg), Couriers.

July 12; same as July 11.

July 13: 2,000 men; *Infantry:* 51st N.C., 7th S.C. Battalion, four companies, 20th S.C., Olmstead's Command: four companies, 1st Ga., four companies, 12th Ga. Art. Battalion, three companies, 18th Ga. Battalion. *Artillery:* det.,

---

[1]Exchanges of units occurred at night and were often delayed by weather, lack of transportation, and enemy activity. The garrison listed is the reported garrison, but sometimes units would be forced to remain on the island past their designated withdrawal while awaiting transportation. Gregg indicates garrison of Battery Gregg, The Palmetto Artillery Battalion was the 3rd S.C. (Light) Artillery Battalion. The Lucas Artillery Battalion was the 15th S.C. Heavy Artillery Battalion. The S.C. Siege Train was the 18th S.C. Heavy Artillery Battalion. The 12th Ga. Heavy Artillery Battalion was serving as infantry. The 1st S.C. usually served as artillery and was later designated the 3rd South Carolina Artillery Regiment.

Co. A, 22nd Ga. Art. Battalion, det., Co. A, 1st S.C.A., Gist Guard Art., Mathewes Art., Co. H, 1st S.C.A. (Gregg), Couriers.

July 14: 2,400 men; *Infantry:* 51st N.C., 7th S.C. Battalion, four companies, 20th S.C., five companies, Charleston Battalion; Olmstead's Command, four companies, 1st Ga., four companies, 12th Ga. Art. Battalion, three companies, 18th Ga. Battalion. *Artillery:* Companies B & K, 63rd Ga. det., Co. A, 22nd Ga. Art. Battalion; det., Co. A, 1st S.C.A.; Gist Guard Art. Co.; Mathewes Art. Co.; det. Co. G, Palmetto Art. Battalion; Co. H, 1st S.C.A. (Gregg); couriers.

July 15: 1,784 men; *Infantry:* 51st N.C.; one company, 20th S.C.; five companies, Charleston Battalion; Olmstead's Command, four companies, 1st Ga., four companies, 12th Ga. Art. Battalion, three companies, 18th Ga. Battalion. *Artillery:* Gist Guard Art. Co.; Mathewes Art. Co.; det., Co. A, 1st S.C.A.; companies B and K, 63rd Ga.; det., Co. A, 22nd Ga. Art. Battalion; det. Co. G, Palmetto Art. Battalion; Co. H, 1st S.C.A., Co. H (Gregg); couriers.

July 16: 1,784 men; *Infantry:* 51st N.C.; one company, 20th S.C.; five companies, Charleston Battalion; Olmstead's Command, four companies, 1st Ga., four companies, 12th Ga. Art. Battalion, three companies, 18th Ga. Battalion. *Artillery:* Companies B and K, 63rd Ga.; det., Co. A, 22nd Ga. Art. Battalion; Companies H and I, 1st S.C.; det., Co. A, 1st S.C.A., det. Co. G, Palmetto Art. Battalion; Co. H, 1st S.C.A. (Gregg); couriers.

July 17: 1,784 men; *Infantry:* 51st N.C.; 31st N.C.; five companies, Charleston Battalion. *Artillery:* Companies B and K, 63rd Ga.; det. Co. A, 22nd Ga. Art. Battalion; Companies H and I, 1st S.C.; det., Co. A, 1st S.C.A.; det., Co. G, Palmetto Art. Battalion; Co. H, 1st S.C.A. (Gregg); couriers.

July 18: 1,781 men; *Infantry:* 51st N.C.; 31st N.C.; five companies, Charleston Battalion. *Artillery:* Companies B and K, 63rd Ga.; det., Co. A, 22nd Ga. Art. Battalion; Companies H and I, 1st S.C.; det., Co. A, 1st S.C.A.; Det. Co. G, Palmetto Art. Battalion; Co. H, 1st S.C.A. (Gregg); couriers.

July 19: *Infantry:* 20th S.C.; 32nd Ga. *Artillery:* Co. G, 1st S.C.A.; Gist Guard Art. Co.; Co. A, Lucas Art. Battalion; det., Co. G, Palmetto Art. Battalion; Co. H, 1st S.C.A. (Gregg); couriers.

July 20: *Infantry:* 20th S.C.; 21st S.C.; 32nd Ga. *Artillery:* Co. G, 1st S.C.A.; det., Co. C, S.C. Siege Train; Co. A, Lucas Art. Battalion; det., Co. G, Palmetto Art. Battalion; Gist Guard Art. Co.; Co. H, 1st S.C.A. (Gregg); couriers.

July 21: *Infantry:* 20th S.C.; 21st S.C. *Artillery:* Co. G, 1st S.C.A. det. Co. C, S.C. Siege Train; Co. A, Lucas Art. Battalion; det., Co. G, Palmetto Art. Battalion; Gist Guard Art. Co.; Co. H, 1st S.C.A. (Gregg); couriers.

July 22: 1,444 men; *Infantry:* 8th N.C.; 21st S.C.; 20th S.C.; Olmstead's command, four companies, 1st Ga.; four companies, 12th Ga. Art. Battalion, three companies, 18th Ga. Battalion. *Artillery:* Co. G, 1st S.C.A.; det., Co. C, S.C. Siege Train; Co. B, Lucas Art. Battalion; det., Co. G, Palmetto Art. Battalion; Gist Guard Art. Co.; Co. H, 1st S.C.A. (Gregg); couriers.

July 23: *Infantry:* 8th N.C.; 21st S.C.; 20th S.C.; Olmstead's command, four companies, 1st Ga., four companies, 12th Ga. Art. Battalion, three companies, 18th Ga. Battalion. *Artillery:* Mathewes Art. Co.; det. Co. C, S.C. Siege Train; Co. B, Lucas Art. Battalion; det., Co. G, Palmetto Art. Battalion; Gist Guard Art. Co.; Co. H, 1st S.C.A. (Gregg); couriers.

July 24: same as July 23.

July 25: *Infantry:* 6th Ga.; 8th N.C.; 61st N.C. *Artillery:* Mathewes Art. Co.; det., Co. C, S.C. Siege Train; Co. B, Lucas Art. Battalion; det., Co. G, Palmetto Art. Battalion; Co. H, 1st S.C.A. (Gregg); couriers.

July 26: *Infantry:* 61st N.C.; 8th N.C.; 6th Ga. *Artillery:* Mathewes Art. Co.; det. Co. C, S.C. Siege Train; Companies B and C, Lucas Art. Battalion; Co. H, 1st S.C.A. (Gregg); couriers and sharpshooters.

July 27: *Infantry:* 61st N.C.; 8th N.C.; 6th Ga. *Artillery:* Co. G, 2nd S.C.A.; Companies B and C, Lucas Art. Battalion; S.C. det., Co. C, Siege Train; 1st S.C.A. (Gregg); couriers and sharpshooters.

July 28: Same as July 27.

July 29: Same as July 27.

July 30: *Infantry:* 61st N.C.; 51st N.C.; 20th S.C.; six companies, 54th Ga. *Artillery:* Co. G, 2nd S.C.A.; Companies B and C, Lucas Art. Battalion; new det., Co. C, S.C. Siege Train; det., Chatham Art. Co.; Co. C, 1st S.C.A. (Gregg); couriers and sharpshooters.

July 31: Same as July 30.

August 1: *Infantry:* 1,753 men; 19th Ga.; 51st N.C.; 20th S.C.; six companies, 54th Ga. *Artillery:* Co. A, 2nd S.C.A.; det., Co. C, S.C. Siege Train; det., Chatham Art Co.; Company E, Charleston Battalion; Co. C, 1st S.C.A. (Gregg); couriers and sharpshooters.

August 2: Same as August 1.

August 3: Same as August 1.

August 4: *Infantry:* 19th Ga.; 20th S.C.; 21st S.C.; five companies, Charleston Battalion, *Artillery:* Co. A, 2nd S.C.A.; det., Co. C, S.C. Siege Train; det., Chatham Art. Co.; Co. E, Charleston Battalion; Co. C, 1st S.C.A. (Gregg); couriers and sharpshooters.

August 5: Same as August 4.

August 6: *Infantry:* 8th N.C.; 20th S.C.; 21st S.C.; five companies, Charleston Battalion. *Artillery:* Gist Guard Art. Co.; Mathewes Art. Co.; det., Marion

Art. det., Co. B, S.C. Siege Train; Co. C, 1st S.C.A. (Gregg); couriers and sharpshooters.

August 7: 1,276 men; *Infantry:* 8th N.C.; 61st N.C.; 21st S.C.; five companies, Charleston Battalion. *Artillery:* det., Co. E, 1st S.C.A.; Gist Guard Art. Co.; Mathewes Art. Co.; det., Marion Art. Co.; det. Co. B, S.C. Siege Train; Co. H, 1st S.C.A. (Gregg); couriers and sharpshooters.

August 8: *Infantry:* 8th N.C.; 61st N.C.; 21st S.C. *Artillery:* det., Co. E, 1st S.C.A.; Gist Guard Art. Co.; Mathewes Art. Co.; det., Marion Art. Co.; det., Co. B, S.C. Siege Train; Co. H, 1st S.C.A. (Gregg); couriers and sharpshooters.

August 9: 1,281 men; *Infantry:* 8th N.C.; 61st N.C.; 21st S.C. *Artillery:* det., Co. E, 1st S.C.A.; Gist Guard Art. Co.; Mathewes Art. Co.; det., Marion Art. Co.; det. Co. B, S.C. Siege Train; Co. H, 1st S.C.A. (Gregg); couriers and sharpshooters.

August 10: *Infantry:* 8th N.C.; 61st N.C. *Artillery:* det., Co. B, 1st S.C.A.; Gist Guard Art. Co.; Mathewes Art. Co.; det. Marion Art. Co.; det. Co. B, S.C. Siege Train; Co. H, 1st S.C.A. (Gregg); couriers and sharpshooters.

August 11: 1,007 men; *Infantry:* 8th N.C.; 61st N.C. *Artillery:* det., Co. E, 1st S.C.A.; Gist Guard Art. Co.; Mathewes Art. Co.; det. Marion Art. Co.; det., Co. B, S.C. Siege Train; Co. H, 1st S.C.A., Co. H (Gregg); couriers and sharpshooters.

August 12: 1,245 men; *Infantry:* 51st N.C.; Olmstead's command, four companies, 1st Ga., four companies, 12th Ga. Art. Battalion, three companies, 18th Ga. Battalion. *Artillery:* det., Co. E, 1st S.C.A.; Co. G, 2nd S.C.A., Co. A, Lucas Art. Battalion; det. Co. S.C. Siege Train; det., Chatham Art. Co.; Co. H, 1st S.C.A. (Gregg); couriers and sharpshooters.

August 13: 1,137 men; *Infantry:* 51st N.C.; Olmstead's command, four companies, 1st Ga., four companies, 12th Ga. Art. Battalion, three companies, 18th Ga. Battalion. *Artillery:* det., Co. E, 1st S.C.A.; Co. G, 2nd S.C.A.; Co. A, Lucas Art. Battalion; det. Co. C, S.C. Siege Train; det., Chatham Art. Co.; Co. H, 1st S.C.A. (Gregg); couriers and sharpshooters.

August 14: same as August 13.

August 15; 1,158 men, same as August 13.

August 16: *Infantry:* 21st S.C.; 20th S.C.; four companies, 1st Ga. *Artillery:* det., Co., E, 1st S.C.A.; Co. E, Lucas Art. Battalion; Co. E, Charleston Battalion; det., Co. C, S.C. Siege Train; Co. H, 1st S.C.A. (Gregg); couriers and sharpshooters.

August 17: same as August 16.

August 18: *Infantry:* 21st S.C.; 20th S.C.; four companies, 1st Ga. *Artillery:* det. Co. K, 1st S.C.A.; Co. B, Lucas Art. Battalion; Co. E, Charleston

Battalion; det., Co. C, S.C. Siege Train; Co. H, 1st S.C.A. (Gregg); couriers and sharpshooters.

August 19: same as August 18.

August 20: *Infantry:* 20th S.C.; 21st S.C.; five companies, Charleston Battalion. *Artillery:* det., Co. K, 1st S.C.A.; Co. E, Charleston Battalion; Co. B, Lucas Art. Battalion; det., Co. C, S.C. Siege Train; Co. H, 1st S.C.A. (Gregg); couriers and sharpshooters.

August 21: 1,058 men; *Infantry:* 20th S.C.; 21st S.C.; five companies, Charleston Battalion. *Artillery:* Co. H, 2nd S.C.A.; Co. B, Lucas Art. Battalion; Co. E, Charleston Battalion; det., Co. C, S.C. Siege Train; det., Co. A, Palmetto Art. Battalion; det., Co K, 1st S.C.A.; Gist Guard Art. Co. (Gregg); couriers and sharpshooters.

August 22: 1,093 men; *Infantry:* 20th S.C.; 21st S.C.; five companies, Charleston Battalion. *Artillery:* det., Co. K. 1st S.C.A.; Co. H, 2nd S.C.A; Co. C, Lucas Art. Battalion; det. Co. A, Palmetto Art. Battalion; Marion Art. Co.; det., Co. C, S.C. Siege Train; Gist Guard Art. Co. (Gregg); couriers and sharpshooters.

August 23: *Infantry:* six companies, 54th Ga.; 61st N.C.; five companies, Charleston Battalion. *Artillery:* det., Co. K, 1st S.C.A.; Co. H, 2nd S.C.A.; Co. C, Lucas Art. Battalion; Marion Art. Co.; det., Co. C, S.C. Siege Train; det., Co. A, Palmetto Art. Battalion; Gist Guard Art. Co. (Gregg); couriers and sharpshooters.

August 24: same as August 23.

August 25: same as August 23.

August 26: *Infantry:* 61st N.C.; six companies, 54th Ga.; five companies, Charleston Battalion. *Artillery:* det., Co. K, 1st S.C.A.; Co. C, Lucas Art. Battalion; Co. B, S.C. Siege Train; Marion Art. Co.; Gist Guard Art. Co. (Gregg); couriers and sharpshooters.

August 27: 1,546 men; *Infantry:* 61st N.C.; six companies, 54th Ga.; five companies, Charleston Battalion. *Artillery:* Co. F, 2nd S.C.A.; det., Chatham Art. Co.; det., Mathewes Art.; Co. B, S.C. Siege Train; Gist Guard Art. Co. (Gregg); couriers and sharpshooters.

August 28: *Infantry:* six companies, 54th Ga.; 23rd Ga.; 20th S.C.; 8th N.C. *Artillery:* Co. F, 2nd S.C.; det., Chatham Art. Co.; det., Mathewes Art. Co.; Co. B, S.C. Siege Train; Gist Guard Art. Co. (Gregg); couriers and sharpshooters.

August 29: 1,328 men; *Infantry:* six companies, 54th Ga.; 23rd Ga.; 20th S.C.; 8th N.C. *Artillery:* Co. F, 2nd S.C.A.; det., Chatham Art. Co.; det., Mathewes Art. Co.; Co. B, S.C. Siege Train; Gist Guard Art. Co. (Gregg); couriers and sharpshooters.

August 30: 1,509 men; *Infantry:* 32nd Ga.; 23rd Ga.; 20th S.C.; 8th N.C. *Artillery:* Co. F, 2nd S.C.A.; det., Chatham Art. Co.; det., Mathewes Art. Co.; Co. B, S.C. Siege Train; Co. A, 1st S.C. (Gregg); couriers and sharpshooters.

August 31: 1,404 men; *Infantry:* 32nd Ga.; 8th N.C.; 28th Ga.; 27th Ga. *Artillery:* Co. F, 2nd S.C.A.; det., Chatham Art. Co.; Co. E, Palmetto Battalion; det., Mathewes Art. Co.; Co. A, 1st S.C. (Gregg); couriers and sharpshooters.

September 1: 1,496 men, units same as August 31.

September 2: 1,566 men; *Infantry:* 32nd Ga.; 8th N.C.; 28th Ga.; 27th Ga.; 25th S.C. *Artillery:* Co. F, 2nd S.C.A.; det., Chatham Art. Co.; det., Mathewes Art. Co.; Co. E, Palmetto Battalion; Co. A, 1st S.C. (Gregg); couriers and sharpshooters.

September 3: 1,542 men; *Infantry:* 32nd Ga.; 8th N.C.; 28th Ga.; 27th Ga.; 25th S.C. *Artillery:* Co. A, 2nd S.C.A.; Co. D, Palmetto Battalion; Co. E, Palmetto Battalion; Co. A, 1st S.C. (Gregg); couriers and sharpshooters.

September 4: *Infantry:* 32nd Ga.; 8th N.C.; 28th Ga.; 27th Ga.; 25th S.C. *Artillery:* Co. A, 2nd S.C.A.; Companies D and E, Palmetto Battalion; Co. A, 1st S.C. (Gregg); couriers and sharpshooters.

September 5; *Infantry:* 28th Ga.; 27th Ga.; 25th S.C. *Artillery:* Co. A, 2nd S.C.A.; Companies D and E, Palmetto Battalion; Co. A, 1st S.C. (Gregg); couriers and sharpshooters.

September 6: same as September 5.

September 7: same as September 5.

Table 28: STATIONS OF U.S. IRONCLADS JULY 9–SEPTEMBER 7, 1863

New Ironsides: July 9–September 7, off Charleston.

Catskill: July 9–August 19, off Charleston; August 20 at sea; August 21–September 7 at Port Royal.

Lehigh: July 9–July 22, at Hampton Roads, July 23–24 at sea; July 25–August 22 at New York; August 23–29 at sea; August 30–September 7, off Charleston.

Nahant: July 9–at sea from Port Royal; July 10–12, off Charleston; July 13, at sea; July 14, at Port Royal; July 15, at sea; July 16–August 1, at Wassaw Sound, Georgia; August 2, at sea; August 3–11, at Port Royal; August 12, at sea; August 13–September 7, off Charleston.

Nantucket: July 9–10; Stono River; July 11–25, off Charleston; July 26, at sea; July 27–31, at Port Royal; August 1, at sea; August 2–September 7, at Wassaw Sound, Georgia.

Montauk: July 9–August 4, off Charleston; August 5, at sea; August 6–11, at Port Royal; August 12, at sea; August 13–September 7, off Charleston.

Passaic: July 9–20, New York; July 21–24, at sea; July 25–September 7, off Charleston.

Patapsco: July 9, at sea; July 10–15, at Port Royal, July 16, at sea; July 17–September 7, off Charleston.

Weehawken: July 9–28, off Charleston; July 29, at sea; July 30–August 9, at Wassaw Sound, Georgia, August 10, at sea; August 11–September 7, off Charleston.

Table 29: VESSELS OF THE SOUTH ATLANTIC BLOCKADING
SQUADRON, JULY 15–SEPTEMBER 7, 1863

Rear Admiral John A. Dahlgren

Name	Type	Guns	Tonnage	Crew
Atlanta	ironclad steamer	4	1,006	100*
Augusta	sidewheel steamer	10	1,310	157
Augusta Dinsmore	screw steamer	2	834	70
Bainbridge	brig	12	259	100
Braziliera	bark	6	540	68
C. P. Williams	mortar schooner	4	210	45
Canandaigua	screw steamer	10	2,030	163
Catskill	monitor	2	1,875	74
Chippewa	screw steamer	4	507	85
Cimarron	sidewheel steamer	6	933	122
Columbine	screw steamer, tug	2	133	24
Commodore McDonough	sidewheel steamer	6	532	75
Conemaugh	sidewheel steamer	8	1,105	125
Daffodil	steam tug	2	160	28
Dai Ching	screw steamer	7	520	83
Dandelion	screw steamer, tug	2	111	22
E. B. Hale	screw steamer	5	192	50
Flag	screw steamer	7	938	140
Flambeau	screw steamer	5	900	92
G. W. Blunt	schooner	2	121	16
Home	screw steamer	3	713	88
Housatonic	screw steamer	13	1,934	160
Huron	screw steamer	4	507	76
Ironsides Jr.	bark	6*	540*	68*

*Estimated

Name	Type	Guns	Tonnage	Crew
John Adams	sloop	8	700	118
Kingfisher	bark	6	451	95
Lehigh	monitor	2	1,875	80
Lodona	screw steamer	7	860	97
Madgie	screw steamer	3	218	45
Mahaska	sidewheel steamer	6	1,060	145
Marblehead	screw steamer	6	507	81
Memphis	screw steamer	7	791	100
Midnight	bark	7	386	70
Mohawk	screw steamer	5	464	65
Montauk	monitor	2	1,875	67
Nahant	monitor	2	1,875	76
Nantucket	monitor	2	1,875	85
New Ironsides	ironclad frigate	18	4,120	449
Norfolk Packet	mortar schooner	5	349	40
Norwich	screw steamer	5	349	40
O. M. Petit	sidewheel steamer	2	165	30
Oleander	sidewheel tug	2	246	35
Ottawa	screw steamer	5	507	90
Para	mortar schooner	3	200	34
Passaic	monitor	2	1,875	70
Patapsco	monitor	2	1,875	72
Paul Jones	sidewheel steamer	8	1,210	148
Pawnee	screw steamer	10	1,289	151
Philadelphia	sidewheel steamer	1	500	24
Potomska	screw steamer	6	287	77
Powhatan	sidewheel frigate	9	3,765	273
Racer	mortar schooner	3	252	36
Rescue	screw tug	2	111	20
Seneca	screw steamer	4	507	84
South Carolina	screw steamer	8	1,165	105
Stettin	screw steamer	5	600	72
Unadilla	screw steamer	6	507	90
Valapariso	bark	6*	402	36
Vermont	Ship-of-the-Line	18	2,633	153
Wabash	screw frigate	45	3,274	568
Wamsutta	screw steamer	6	270	75
Water Witch	sidewheel steamer	4	378	73
Weehawken	monitor	2	1,875	72
Wissahickon	screw steamer	5	507	80
Total		388	58,348	6,188

---

*Estimated

Table 30:   COMMANDERS OF UNION IRONCLADS, JULY 10–
SEPTEMBER 7, 1863

Catskill: July 9–19, Commander George W. Rodgers. July 20 on, Lt. Commander Charles C. Carpender.

Lehigh: July 9–August 7, Commander John C. Howell. August 8 on, Commander Andrew Bryson.

Montauk: July 9–August 22, Commander Donald Fairfax. August 23, Lt. Commander Oscar C. Badger. August 23 on, Lt. Commander John L. Davis.

Nahant: July 9–August 29, Commander John Downes. August 29 on, Lt. Commander John Cornwell.

Nantucket: July 9 on, Commander John C. Beaumont.

New Ironsides: July 9 on, Captain Stephen C. Rowan.

Passaic: July 9 on, Lt. Commander Edward Simpson.

Patapsco: July 9–July 15, Lt. Commander Henry Erben. July 15–July 18, Acting Master William Hamilton. July 18–August 21, Lt. Commander Oscar C. Badger.[1] August 21 on, Commander Thomas Stevens.

Weehawken: July 9 on, Commander Edmund R. Colhoun.

Fleet Captains: July 9–19, Captain William Rogers Taylor. July 20–August 17, Commander George W. Rodgers. August 17–September 1, Lt. Commander Oscar Badger. September 2 on, Captain George F. Emmons.

Table 31:   CONFEDERATE NAVAL FORCES AT CHARLESTON

Station Commander: Captain Duncan Ingraham

Squadron Commander: Commander John R. Tucker

Vessels

Chicora: ironclad ram, four guns, Commander Thomas T. Hunter.

Palmetto State: ironclad ram, four guns, 1st Lieutenant John Rutledge.

Charleston: ironclad ram, six guns, Commander Isaac N. Brown.

---

[1] During this period Lt. Commander Francis M. Bunce would command the *Patapsco* whenever Lt. Commander Badger left the vessel, but Badger commanded the ship during all engagements.

Juno:[1] picket boat, armed with a spar torpedo, 1st Lieutenant Philip Porcher, though in early September she was on at least one occasion commanded by 1st Lieutenant Alexander F. Warley.

Indian Chief: receiving ship, First Lieutenant William G. Dozier.

---

[1] Impressed into service, the *Juno* was not officially purchased by the Confederacy until December 1863.

Notes

Introduction

1. Stephen Walkley, *History of the Seventh Connecticut Volunteer Infantry* (Southington, 1905), 69–70.
2. Although contemporary usage prefers "it" when referring to ships, the author has used the sentimental "she" throughout this work with deliberate intent, in an effort to more fully draw the reader into the scene of *Gate of Hell*.
3. For information on the fortifications on Morris Island and around Charleston Harbor after South Carolina seceeded, see the David F. Jamison Papers, Washington and Lee University, Lexington, Virginia. *War of the Rebellion: A Compilation of the Union and Confederate Armies*. 128 vols., (Washington: Government Printing Office, 1902), Ser. 1, Vol. 1:21–24, 132–36, 240–50; vol. 4:228–35. Hereafter listed as *O.R.A.*, all citations will be Series 1 unless otherwise noted. Alexander A. Holley, *A Treatise on Ordnance and Armour* (New York: D. Van Nostrand, 1865), 50; E. Milby Burton, *The Siege of Charleston: 1861–1865* (Columbia: University of South Carolina Press, 1970), 16–17.

Chapter 1. The Prize and Its Defenses

1. Robert C. Gilchrist, "Confederate Defense of Morris Island," *Charleston Yearbook, 1884* (Charleston: News and Courier Press, 1884): 352; Abner Doubleday, *Reminiscences of Forts Sumter and Moultrie in 1860–1861* (New York: Harper and Brothers, Publishers, 1876), 143–47; *O.R.A.*, 1:21–24; Holley, *Ordnance and Armour*, 36–50; P. T. G. Beauregard, "Torpedo Service in Harbor and Water Defences of Charleston," *Southern Historical Society Papers*, 5 (April 1878): 146–61.
2. The Blakely was batteried with two 42-pounders. The three 8-inch Columbiads were mounted in the Stevens Battery which was shielded in an iron casemate from Fort Sumter's fire. The two batteries were separated by a mortar battery. *O.R.A.*, 1:240–50; Doubleday, *Reminiscences of Forts Sumter and Moultrie*, 145–46; Holley, *Treatise on Ordnance and Armor*, 50.
3. Joseph G. Totten, *Report of the Chief Engineers on the Subject of National Defenses* (Washington: A. Boyd Hamilton, 1851); Holley, *Treatise on Ordnance and Armor.*
4. Stephen R. Wise, *Lifeline of the Confederacy: Blockade Running During*

the Civil War (Columbia: University of South Carolina Press, 1988), 17, 122–25, 251–54; *O.R.A.,* 1:314–17.

5. George W. Cullum, *Biographical Register of the Officers and Graduates of West Point,* 2 vols. (Boston: Houghton, Mifflin and Company, 1891), 2:76–77; Doubleday, *Reminiscences,* 153–54; *O.R.A.,* 4:1, 336; Ezra J. Warner, *Generals in Gray: Lives of the Confederate High Commanders* (Baton Rouge: Louisiana State University Press, 1959), 257.

6. *O.R.A.,* 6:151, 153, 160; E. Milby Burton, *The Siege of Charleston: 1861–1865* (Columbia: University of South Carolina Press, 1970), 61–64; Cullum, *Biographical Register,* 2:76–77; Johnson Hagood, *Memoirs of the War of Secession* (Columbia: The State Company, 1910), 51–57.

7. *O.R.A.,* 6:309; Hagood, *Memoirs,* 51–57.

8. Lee established his headquarters at Coosawhatchie, South Carolina, midway between Charleston and Savannah. Among the positions abandoned were Saint Simon's Island, Jekyll Island, and Brunswick, Georgia, and Amelia Island, Florida. *O.R.A.,* 6:327, 367, 379, 391.

9. *O.R.A.,* 6:356–57; A. A. Long, "Seacoast Defenses of South Carolina and Georgia, "*Southern Historical Society Papers,* 1 (February 1873): 106; *O.R.A.,* 6:366; Totten, *Report on National Defenses;* Douglas Southall Freeman, 4 vols., *R. E. Lee: A Biography* (New York: Charles Scribner's Sons, 1962), 1:613–14.

10. Gilchrist, "Confederate Defense of Morris Island," 353; *O.R.A.,* 14:538; John C. Pemberton, *Pemberton: Defender of Vicksburg* (Chapel Hill: University of North Carolina Press, 1942), 10–15; *O.R.A.,* 6:420, 423; 14:495, 499–500, 521; Hagood, *Memoirs,* 39–62; Michael B. Ballard, *Pemberton: A Biography* (Jackson: University of Mississippi Press, 1991), 91–113.

11. *O.R.A.,* 14:51–53, 86–88, 347–48, 353–54.

12. *O.R.A.* 14:665; Gilchrist, "Confederate Defense of Morris Island," 353; H. D. D. Twiggs, "The Defense of Battery Wagner," *Southern Historical Society Papers,* 20, (January–December, 1882), 168–70.

13. Langdon Cheves Papers, South Carolina Historical Society, Charleston, South Carolina; *O.R.A.,* 7:13, 16, 17, 18.

14. *O.R.A.,* 14:653; Quincy Adams Gillmore, *Engineer and Artillery Operations Against the Defenses of Charleston Harbor in 1863* (New York: Nostrand, 1865), 28.

15. *O.R.A.,* 7:320; 14:665; *Charleston Courier,* July 18, 1862.

16. Gilchrist, "Confederate Defense of Morris Island," 353; S. R. Ashe, "Life at Fort Wagner," *Confederate Veteran,* 25 (1927), 254.

17. *O.R.A.,* 28 (pt. 1):96.

18. *O.R.A.,* 14:503–6, 514–16, 521, 560, 563–65, 567, 569–70, 603–4.

19. *O.R.A.,* 14:582, 588, 597–98, 601, 608, 609, 820–32, 926; Alfred Roman, *The Military Operations of General Beauregard* (New York: Harper and Brothers, 1884), 2:26.

20. *O.R.A.,* 11 (pt. 2): 626, 19 (pt. 1): 1021, 1026, 1033; Roman, *Operations of*

General Beauregard, 2:25–27; *O.R.A.*, 17:635, 641, 642, 668; Cullum, *Biographical Register*, 1:542, 2:76–77.

21. Holley, *A Treatise on Ordnance and Armor*, 50–56, 127–39; *O.R.A.*, 14:820–32; Warren Ripley, *Artillery and Ammunition of the Civil War* (New York: Van Nostrand Reinhold Company, 1970) 13–69; 109–36; C. Jacobi, *Gesogenen Geschuetze der Amerikaner bei der Belagerung von Charleston . . .* ("The Rifled Guns of the Americans at the Siege of Charleston"), Translated by Anne Beehler (Berlin: Striker, 1866), 32–33.

22. *O.R.A.*, 7:133–67; Quincy A. Gillmore, "Siege and Capture of Fort Pulaski," *Battles and Leaders of the Civil War*, 4 vols. (New York: Thomas Yoseloff, 1956), 2:1–12.

23. Madeleine V. Dahlgren, *Memoirs of John H. Dahlgren* (Boston: Osgood, 1882), 391–95; Oscar W. Farenholt, *The Monitor Catskill: A Year's Reminiscences* (San Francisco: Shannon, 1912), 16; Holley, *A Treatise on Ordnance and Armor*, 106–21; Ripley, *Artillery and Ammunition*, 87–107; William T. Adams, "Guns for the Navy," *Ordnance* (January–February, 1961): 508–11; *Civil War Naval Ordnance* (Washington, D.C.: Naval History Division, 1969), 1–25.

24. Holley, *A Treatise on Ordnance and Armor*, 127–39: *O.R.A.*, 16:820–32.

25. R. O. Crowley, "The Torpedo Service," *Century Illustrated Magazine*, 56 (June 1898): 296–98; Milton E. Perry, *Infernal Machines* (Baton Rouge: Louisiana State University Press, 1965), 50–51.

26. The *Chicora* was built by the state of South Carolina and was launched in August 1862, followed by the *Palmetto State* in October. The *Palmetto State* was built by the Confederate government. The two vessels were 150 feet long and had a beam of 35 feet. Both mounted four guns and had very poor engines. Under construction at Charleston was the ironclad ram *Charleston*, which was about 180 feet long and mounted six guns. The *Charleston* had better engines, but her construction was delayed due to a shortage of iron. Robert Holcombe, *Notes on the Construction of Confederate Ironclads* (Savannah: U.S. Army Corps of Engineers, 1980), 1–23; William N. Still, Jr. *Confederate Shipbuilding* (Athens: University of Georgia Press, 1969), 112–20; William N. Still, Jr. *Iron Afloat* (Nashville: Vanderbilt University Press, 1979), 112–16.

27. Thomas Jordan, "Seacoast Defenses of South Carolina and Georgia," *Southern Historical Society Papers*, 1 (June 1876): 405; *O.R.A.*, 14:877–78, 880–81.

28. Robert Erwin Johnson, *Rear Admiral John Rodgers* (Annapolis: United States Naval Institute, 1967), 238; Gustavus Vasa Fox, *Confidential Correspondence of Gustavus Fox: Assistant Secretary of the Navy, 1861–1865*, edited by Robert Means Thompson and Richard Wainwright, 2 vols. (New York: De Vinne Press, 1918), 1:173; Richard S. West, Jr., *Gideon Welles: Lincoln's Navy Department* (Indianapolis: Bobbs-Merrill Company, 1943), 223–24; Percival Drayton, *Naval Letters from Captain Percival Drayton: 1861–1865* (Presented to the New York Public Library

in 1906 by Gertrude L. Hoyte), 29; Theodore D. Jervey, "Charleston During the Civil War," *Annual Report of the American Historical Association for the Year 1913*, (Washington: Government Printing Office, 1915), 1:172–73; Marcus W. Price, "Ships that Tested the Blockade of the Carolina Ports," *American Neptune*, 8 (April 1948): 197; Alfred P. Rockwell, "The Operations Against Charleston," *Military Historical Society of Massachusetts Papers*, 9:161–62, 186; Wise, *Lifeline of the Confederacy*, 122–24.

29. Samuel Francis Du Pont, *Samuel Francis Du Pont: A Selection from His Civil War Letters*, edited by John D. Hayes, 3 vols. (Ithaca: Cornell University Press, 1969), 2:236, 237, 241–49.

30. *O.R.A.*, 6:228–35, 14:124, 144, 376, 380–82, 384, 388, 391, 464; F. A. Mitchel, *Ormsby MacKnight Mitchel: Astronomer and General* (Boston: Houghton, Mifflin and Company, 1887), 358–81.

31. *O.R.A.*, 14:389, 392, 451; Du Pont, *Civil War Letters*, 2:321–22, 347, 373; *War of the Rebellion: Official Records of the Union and Confederate Navies*, 31 vols., (Washington: Government Printing Office, 1902), Ser. 1, 13:510–11. Hereafter this will be cited as *O.R.N.*, the series will always be 1, unless noted otherwise.

32. *O.R.A.*, 6:228–35, 14:396–428, 28:2; Du Pont, *Civil War Letters*, 2:443–44.

33. The monitors were to have 11-inch and 15-inch Dahlgrens, but production of the monster cannons was slow, so the Parrotts were substituted on certain vessels. The navy termed the 8-inch guns 150-pounders, the army used the same gun with 200-pound shot. To save confusion the Parrotts will hereafter be referred to by the size of the bore. While the monitors were being sent to Port Royal, a study was undertaken by Rear Admiral Stephen P. Lee to check the feasibility of using the *Monitor* and some of the *Passaic* class monitors against Wilmington, North Carolina. The project was eventually dropped and the ironclads continued on to Port Royal. *O.R.A.*, 14:394–400; Committee of the Regimental Association, *Maine Regiment: The Story of the Eleventh* (New York: Little, 1896), 113–14; Fox, *Correspondence*, 1:119, 122–23, 173, 160–61; West, *Gideon Welles*, 219–22; Du Pont, *Civil War Letters*, 2: 91–146; Johnson, *John Rodgers*, 225–26, 238; U.S. Congress, *Report on the Conduct of the War*, Rep. Comm. No. 108, 4 (Pt. 3, 37th Cong., 3rd Sess.): 415–21; *O.R.N.*, 8:298; *Armored Vessels*, 51.

34. *Armored Vessels*, 16, 33, 53–55; Johnson, *John Rodgers*, 238; Du Pont, *Civil War Letters*, 3:128; Drayton, *Naval Letters*, 29.

35. *O.R.N.*, 14:3–73; Du Pont, *Civil War Letters*, 3:538–52.

36. Eldridge J. Copp, *Reminiscences of the War of Rebellion* (Nashua: Telegraph Publishing Company, 1911), 200; Smith B. Stowits, *History of the One-hundredth New York Volunteers* (Buffalo: Matthewes and Warren, 1870), 143–44; *O.R.A.* 14:432, 439–42; Du Pont, *Civil War Letters*, 2:521.

37. Du Pont, *Civil War Letters*, 2:551; C. R. P. Rodgers "Du Pont's Attack at Charleston," *Battles and Leaders of the Civil War,* 4 vols. (New York: Thomas Yoseloff, 1956), 4:32–47.
38. Frank Vizetelly, "Charleston Under Fire," *Cornhill Magazine*, (July 1864): 99–100; Farenholt, *The Monitor Catskill*, 12; C. R. P. Rodgers, "Du Pont's Attack at Charleston," 4:32–47; *O.R.N.,* 14:135–36, 146.
39. *John Rodgers*, 243–46; C. R. P. Rodgers, "Du Pont's Attack on Charleston," 4:32–47; *O.R.N.,* 14:3–36.
40. W. W. H. Davis, *History of the 104th Pennsylvania* (Philadelphia: Rodgers, 1866), 57–58; Stowits, *One-hundredth New York*, 160–65; *O.R.A.,* 14:437–38; Copp, *Reminiscences of the War*, 208; Du Pont, *Civil War Letters,* 3:41, 111; Richard P. Galloway, compiler and editor, *One Battle Too Many: The Writings of Simon's Bolivar Hulbert, Private, Company E, 100th Regiment, New York State Volunteers 1861–1864* (Privately Published, 1987), 179.
41. Johnson, *John Rodgers*, 250; Du Pont, *Letters*, 3:40.
42. Johnson, *John Rodgers*, 250; Du Pont, *Letters*, 3:40, 50–88; *Armored Vessels*, 110; Gideon Welles, *Diary of Gideon Welles*, 3 vols. (Boston: Houghton, Mifflin Company, 1911), 1:288.
43. *O.R.A.,* 14:455–70.

Chapter 2: The Plan for Morris Island

1. Gillmore outlined plans to take Charleston in December 1861 while the chief engineer for the Port Royal Expedition. Gillmore, *Engineer and Artillery Operations*, 12–14; Cullum, *Biographical Register*, 2:368–70; William S. Stryker, "Three Days in the Civil War," n.d., William R. Perkins Library, Duke University; *O.R.A.,* 6:212–13; 28 (Pt. 1): 3, 14:459; Gillmore "Fort Pulaski," 1–12.
2. Du Pont, *Letters*, 3:41–42, 74, 111, 173; *O.R.A.,* 14:451.
3. Du Pont, *Letters*, 3:41–42.
4. Welles, *Diary*, 1:312–314; John A. Foote, "Notes on the Life of Admiral Foote," in *Battles and Leaders of the Civil War* 4 vols. (New York: Thomas Yoseloff, 1956), 1:347.
5. Welles, *Diary*, 1:317.
6. *Armored Vessels*, 112; Du Pont, *Letters*, 3:180; Farenholt, *The Monitor Catskill*, 12–13; Albert Gleaves, *Life and Letters of Rear Admiral Stephen B. Luce* (New York: Putnam, 1925), 91. Fox, *Correspondence*, 1:160–61.
7. Dahlgren, *Memoirs*, 525–26; Gillmore, *Engineer and Artillery Operations*, 22.
8. The vessels from the second class of monitors, the *Canonicus* class, were still under construction. Only the *Lehigh, Sangamon*, of the *Passaic* class, and the double-turreted monitor *Onondaga* were available, and they were required to watch the Confederate ironclads at Richmond. Dahlgren, *Memoirs*, 392–93.
9. Welles, *Diary*, 1:325–26, 335, 337; Dahlgren, *Memoirs*, 395; *O.R.A.*

14:465; Frederic Denison, *Shot and Shell: The Third Rhode Island Heavy Artillery Regiment* (Providence: J. A. & R. A. Reid, 1879), 163.

10. *O.R.A.*, 28 (Pt. 2):4; Daniel Eldridge, *The Third New Hampshire Regiment* (Boston: E. B. Stillings, 1893), 289; Smith B. Mott, *The Campaigns of the Fifty-second Pennsylvania Volunteer Infantry* (Philadelphia: Lippincott, 1911), 125; Du Pont, *Letters*, 3:173–74.

11. Elias A. Bryant, *The Diary of Elias A. Bryant* (Concord: Rumford Press, n.d.), 101; Luther S. Dickey, *History of the Eighty-fifth Regiment Pennsylvania Volunteer Infantry* (New York: J. C. Powers, 1915), 256–58; Albert H. C. Jewett, *A Boy Goes to War* (Bloomington: privately printed, 1944), 35–37; George Stoddard, "The 100th Regiment on Folly Island," *Niagara Frontier*, 1 (1954):78–80; Charles K. Caldwell, *The Old Sixth Regiment: Its War Record* (New Haven: Tuttle, Morehouse and Taylor, 1875), 64; *O.R.A.*, 14:446, and 28 (Pt. 1):350–51; D. L. Thompson Papers, D. Thompson to mother, August 1863, Fort Sumter National Monument, Sullivan's Island, South Carolina; Galloway, *One Battle Too Many*, 206.

12. Ibid.

13. Ibid.

14. Stryker, "Three Days in the Civil War;" Alfred Marple Letters and Diary, June 18, 1863, South Caroliniana Library, University of South Carolina, Columbia, South Carolina.

15. *O.R.A.*, 14:446; Henry Little, *The Seventh Regiment* (Concord: J. Evan, 1896), 102; Alvin C. Voris, "Charleston in the Rebellion," *Sketches of War History* (Cincinnati: Robert Clarke, 1888), 321; Stryker, "Three Days in the Civil War."

16. *O.R.A.*, 28 (Pt. 1):535; Eldridge, *The Third New Hampshire Regiment*, 297; Denison, *Shot and Shell*, 162–63; Stryker, "Three Days in the Civil War;" Caldwell, *Sixth Regiment*, 64; Stowits, *One-Hundreth New York*, 183; Little, *Seventh Regiment*, 103–6; *O.R.A.*, 28 (Pt. 1):350–51; Marple Diary, June 18, 1863.

17. Charles M. Clark, *The History of the Thirty-ninth Regiment Illinois Volunteer Veteran Infantry (Yates Phalanx) in the War of the Rebellion 1861–1865* (Chicago: Veteran Association of the Regiment, 1889), 126–28.

18. Eldridge, *Third New Hampshire*, 290–92; Cullum, *Biographical Register*, 2:151–53, 449; Ezra J. Warner, *Generals in Blue: Lives of Union Commanders* (Baton Rouge: Louisiana State University Press, 1964), 442–43, 483–84, 497–98.

19. *O.R.A.*, 28 (Pt. 1):8; Denison, *Shot and Shell*, 1–159; Herbert W. Beecher, *History of the First Light Battery Connecticut Volunteers, 1861–1865* 2 vols. (New York: A. T. De la Mare Ptgard Publishing Company, 1901), 1:1–250; Walkley, *Seventh Connecticut*, 66–70.

20. Holley, *Ordnance and Armor*, 50–56; Ripley, *Artillery and Ammunition*, 57–58, 109; Jacobi, *Gesogenen Geschuetze der Amerikaner*, 32–33.

21. The regiments that had seen action at the Seven Days were 10th Connecticut, 24th Massachusetts, 52nd Pennsylvania, 104th Pennsylvania,

11th Maine, 100th New York, N.Y. Independent Battalion, 56th New York, 85th Pennsylvania, 39th Illinois, 62nd Ohio, 67th Ohio, and Batteries B and F, 3rd New York Artillery. *O.R.A.*, 28:7–9.

22. The initial regiment raised by Hunter was sometimes called the 1st South Carolina, though it was never officially mustered in and should be termed Hunter's Regiment. Thomas Wentworth Higginson, *Army Life in a Black Regiment* (Williamstown, Massachusetts: Corner House Publishers, 1984), 1–6, 272–77; *O.R.A.*, 14:333, 341, 377, 378, Ser. 3, 2:29–31, 43, 50–60, 152–53; Dudley Taylor Cornish, *The Sable Arm* (New York: W. W. Norton, 1966), 35–55, 132.

23. Higginson, *Army Life*, 1–36; Cornish, *Sable Arm*, 132; Willie Lee Rose, *Rehearsal for Reconstruction: The Port Royal Experiment* (New York: Oxford University Press, 1964), 193–198.

24. Marple Letters, A. Marple to wife, June 6, 1863; Davis, *104th Pennsylvania*, 181–217; *Eleventh Maine* 108; Alfred S. Roe, *The Twenty-fourth Regiment Massachusetts Volunteers 1861–1866* (Worcester: Twenty-fourth Veteran Association, 1907), 179; John W. M. Appleton Letter Journal, July 10, 1863, University of West Virginia Library, University of West Virginia, Morgantown, West Virginia.

25. The men from Foster's command caused a great deal of trouble among the African-American communities on St. Helena Island. They robbed the former slaves of food, disrupted their homes, and reportedly burned some quarters. In the midst of this was a problem of command between Foster and Hunter which resulted in Foster leaving the department. Many of Foster's officers, including General Thomas Stevenson, tried to resist Hunter's authority. Stevenson was briefly detained by Hunter, who claimed that Stevenson had refused to serve with black troops. Stevenson denied the story, and there is no proof that he ever made the statement, but it was reported in Northern newspapers. Roe, *Twenty-fourth Regiment*, 178–81; Elizabeth Ware Pearson, editor, *Letters from Port Royal* (New York: Arno Press and the New York Times, 1969), 162–64; Rupert Sargent Holland, editor, *Letters and Diary of Laura Towne* (New York: Negro University Press, 1969), 100–2; *New York Tribune*, February 27, 1863.

26. Luis F. Emilio, *A Brave Black Regiment: History of the Fifty-fourth Regiment of Massachusetts Volunteer Infantry 1863–1865* (New York: Arno Press, 1969), 1–25; Cornish, *The Sable Arm*, 105–6; Benjamin Quarles, *The Negro in the Civil War* (Boston: Little, Brown, 1953), 8–10; *Xenia Torchlight*, June 6, 1863.

27. Quarles, *The Negro in the Civil War*, 11–13; Cornish, *The Sable Arm*, 148; Emilio, *Brave Black Regiment*, 24–35.

28. Emilio, *Brave Black Regiment*, 1–25, 339–44.

29. George S. Stearns Collection, J. Montgomery to Mrs. Stearns, April 12, 1863, Kansas State Historical Society, Topeka, Kansas.

30. Rose, *Rehearsal for Reconstruction*, 244–55; Higginson, *Army Life*, 6–

47; W. E. Burghardt DuBois, *John Brown*, (New York: International Publishers, 1962), 188–91; Cornish, *The Sable Arm*, 88–90, 138–40.

31. Marple Letters, A. Marple to wife, June 6, 1863; Rose, *Rehearsal for Reconstruction*, 244–48; *O.R.A.*, 14:290–308, 462; *Beaufort Free South*, June 6, 1863.

32. *Beaufort Free South*, June 6, 1863; Marple Letters, A. Marple to wife, June 6, 1863; Higginson, *Army Life*, 225–26.

33. *Beaufort Free South*, June 6, 1863; Rose, *Rehearsal for Reconstruction*, 251–55; Marple Letters, A. Marple to wife, June 6, 1863; Emilio, *Brave Black Regiment*, 38–41.

34. *O.R.A.*, 14:463–64, 599, Ser. 2, 5:797, 807–8, 867, 940–41; Cornish, *The Sable Arm*, 158–63; Appleton Journal, June 9, 1863; B. G. Wilder Collection, clipping from the *Boston Evening Post*, May 3, 1916, Cornell University Library, Cornell University, Ithaca, New York; Marple Letters, A. Marple to wife, June 18, 1863; Howard C. Westwood, "Captive Black Soldiers in Charleston—What to do?" *Civil War History* 28 (March 1982), 29–31.

35. Though Shaw protested the plundering of Darien, some of the loot from the raid eventually found its way into the tents of officers from the 54th Massachusetts in their camps on Folly Island. Charles P. Bowditch, "War Letters of Charles P. Bowditch," *Massachusetts Historical Society Proceedings* 57 (February–April 1924):436; *Beaufort Free South*, June 20, 1863; Emilio, *Brave Black Regiment*, 39–44; Robert G. Shaw Papers, R. Shaw to wife, June 9, 1863, R. Shaw to Governor Andrew, June 14, 1863; Boston Public Library, Boston, Massachusetts; *O.R.A.*, 14:426, 463–64, 465–67.

36. Emilio, *Brave Black Regiment*, 49; Shaw Letters, R. Shaw to G. Strong, July 6, 1863; Cornish, *The Sable Arm*, 150; Brenda Stevenson, editor, *The Journals of Charlotte Forten Grimke* (New York: Oxford University Press, 1988), 493–94; *Boston Evening Post*, May 3, 1916; Robert G. Shaw, *Memorial* (Cambridge: Cambridge University Press, 1864), 35.

37. Stowits, *One-Hundreth New York*, 184, 191; Stoddard, "Folly Island," 103.

38. Du Pont, *Letters*, 3:182, 194; *O.R.N.*, 14:230.

39. Secretary of the Navy, *Report of the Secretary of the Navy in Relation to Armored Vessels* (Washington, D.C.: Government Printing Office, 1864), 113; Du Pont, *Letters*, 3:207.

40. Du Pont, *Letters*, 3:182, 194.

41. Dahlgren, *Memoirs*, 391–95; Farenholt, *Monitor Catskill*, 16.

42. Dahlgren, *Memoirs*, 396–97.

43. Dahlgren, *Memoirs*, 397–400; Emilio, *A Brave Black Regiment*, 52; *O.R.A.*, 28 (pt. 1):10; James Toutelloutte, *A History of Company K of the Seventh Connecticut Volunteer Infantry in the Civil War* (n.p., 1910), 107–8.

44. Though Beauregard was quite concerned over the shortage of personnel

in his own departments, he did take time in mid-May to write to General Joseph Johnston suggesting a plan to relieve Vicksburg. Beauregard called for the reinforcement of the Confederate army in Tennessee, which would then attack northward into Kentucky. He concluded that such a strike would pull Grant away from Vicksburg and lead to a climatic Confederate victory. *O.R.A.*, 14:901, 924, 926, 940, 941, 964, 28: (Pt. 2):140, 149, 161–62, 176; Alfred Roman, *The Military Operations of General Beauregard*, 2 vols. (New York: Harper and Brothers, 1884), 2:80–90.

45. *O.R.A.*, 14:893.
46. *O.R.A.*, 14:881.
47. *O.R.A.*, 28 (Pt. 1):65.
48. *O.R.A.*, 28 (Pt. 2):184, 14:956.
49. Roswell S. Ripley, *Correspondence Relating to Fortifications of Morris Island* (New York: J. J. Coulon, 1878), 1–25.
50. *O.R.A.*, 14:948, 958–59, 972, 1021–22; *Ripley Correspondence*, 1–25.
51. The batteries on the southern end of Morris Island were sometimes referred to as Battery Mitchel. *Charleston Courier*, July 10, 1863; *O.R.A.*, 14:964–65, 28 (Pt. 1):414; John Johnson, *The Defense of Charleston Harbor* (Charleston: Walker Evans, Cogswell, 1890), 87; Charles Inglesby, Historic Sketch of the First Regiment of *South Carolina Artillery (Regulars)* (Charleston: Walker, Evans and Cogswell, 1890), 10; Roman, *Military Operations*, 2:iii.
52. Gilchrist, "Confederate Defense of Morris Island," 386; Gillmore, *Engineer and Artillery Operations*, 44; Johnson, *Defense of Charleston Harbor*, 87; *O.R.A.*, 28 (Pt. 1):370; Charles H. Olmstead, *Reminiscences of Service with the First Volunteer Regiment of Georgia* (Savannah: J. H. Estrill, 1879), 5; Twiggs, "Defense of Battery Wagner," 170.
53. Ibid.
54. Initial reports on the Battle of Gettysburg gave a victory to Lee's army, so some speculations had the transports hurrying reinforcements north to protect Baltimore and Washington. Roman, *Military Operations*, 2:iii; *O.R.A.*, 14:964–65; Voris, *Sketches of War History*, 307; *Charleston Courier*, July 8, 1863; Department of South Carolina, Georgia and Florida, "Letters Sent by the Department of South Carolina, Georgia and Florida, 1863–1864," Old Military Records Division, Beauregard to C. Macbeth, July 9, 1863; C. F. Girard, "Visit to the Confederate States of America in 1863," *Confederate Centennial Studies*, No. 21 (Tuscaloosa: Confederate Publishing Company, 1956), 43.

Chapter 3: The Initial Assault

1. Little, *Seventh Regiment*, 105; Walter D. Briggs, *Civil War Surgeon in a Colored Regiment*, (Berkeley: University Press, 1960), 104.
2. *O.R.N.*, 14:220, 314, 327; George E. Belknap, "Reminiscences of the

Siege of Charleston," *Military Historical Society of Massachusetts Papers*, 12:175–76.

3. Toutelloutte, *History of Company K*, 107–8.

4. Clara Barton Papers, Diary, April 2–6, 1863, and C. Barton to Cousin Vira, June 26, 1863, Library of Congress, Washington, D.C.; Voris, "Charleston in the Rebellion," 334–35; J. J. Craven, "Report Extract," in *Medical and Surgical History of the War of the Rebellion*, 3 vols. (Washington, D.C.: Government Printing Office, 1870), 1 (Pt. 1):241; Isabel Ross, *Angel of the Battlefield* (New York: Harper and Brothers, 1956), 61; Percy H. Epler, *The Life of Clara Barton* (New York: Macmillan Company, 1927), 76–77.

5. Clara Barton Papers, C. Barton to Cousin Vira, July 11, 1863; Voris, "Charleston in the Rebellion," 334–35; J. J. Craven, "Report Extract," 1 (Pt. 1): 241; Ross, *Angel of the Battlefield*, 61; Epler, *Clara Barton*, 76–77.

6. The Confederate obstructions were placed in the Folly River in two rows alternating with each other, four feet apart in each row. The two rows were three feet apart. Though an effective barrier, they were not guarded by any fixed work so the Union engineers were able to clear them without any enemy interference. *O.R.A.*, 28 (Pt. 1):226–27; Toutelloutte, *History of Company K*, 107.

7. Toutelloutte, *History of Company K*, 107; *O.R.N.*, 14:327.

8. *O.R.N.*, 14:337–38, 347; *O.R.A.*, 28 (Pt. 2):183; Peter Burchard, *One Gallant Rush* (New York: St. Martin Press, 1965), 121; John W. Appleton, "That Night at Fort Wagner, by One Who Was There," *Putnam's Magazine*, 4 (1869):9; Beecher, *Connecticut Battery*, 1:251.

9. Eldridge, *Third Company New Hampshire*, 300; Toutelloutte, *The History of Company K*, 108; Jacobi, *The Rifled Batteries*, 7–10; Denison, *Shot and Shell*, 163.

10. *Armored Vessels*, 220; Copp, *Reminiscences of the War*, 225–27; Caldwell, *The Old Sixth Regiment*, 66; Little, *Seventh Regiment*, 107; Toutelloutte, *History of Company K*, 108; Gillmore, *Engineer and Artillery Operations*, 28.

11. *O.R.N.*, 14:317, 320, 325–26, 329–30; *Armored Vessels*, 579–80; Dahlgren, *Memoirs*, 398, 527.

12. Samuel Jones, *Siege of Charleston* (Charleston: Walker, Evans, Cogswell, 1890), 212–13; Stryker, "Three Days in the Civil War," Little, *Seventh Regiment*, 109.

13. Eldridge, *Third New Hampshire*, 300–302; *O.R.A.*, 28 (Pt. 1):354; Orville Repton Papers, O. Repton to sister, July 12, 1863, South Caroliniana Library, University of South Carolina, Columbia, South Carolina.

14. *Charleston Courier*, July 16, 1863; *Richmond Dispatch*, July 14, 1863; Johnson, *Defense of Charleston Harbor*, 90; William Lawrence Haskins, *The History of the First Regiment of Artillery* (Portland: Thurston, 1879), 178; Repton Papers, O. Repton to sister July 12, 1863; Orlando Soutelle

Papers, O. Soutelle to parents, July 11, 1863, U.S. Army Military History Institute, Carlise, Pennsylvania.

15. *O.R.N.*, 14:317, 320, 325–26, 329–30; *Armored Vessels*, 579–80; Dahlgren, *Memoirs*, 398, 527.

16. Elizabeth Ware Pearson, *Letters from Port Royal*, (New York: Arno Press, 1969), 194; *O.R.N.*, 14:329.

17. Caldwell, *Sixth Regiment*, 111; Little, *Seventh Regiment*, 108; Copp, *Reminiscences of the War*, 227–28; Johnson, *The Defense of Charleston Harbor*, 90; Eldridge, *Third New Hampshire*, 301–2; *O.R.A.*, 28 (Pt. 1):357–61; *Charleston Mercury*, July 17, 1863; Soutelle Papers, O. Soutelle to parents, July 11, 1863; *Charleston Mercury*, July 17, 1863.

18. Caldwell, *Sixth Regiment*, 111; Little, *Seventh Regiment*, 108; Copp, *Reminiscences of the War*, 227–228; Eldridge, *Third New Hampshire*, 301–2; Soutelle Papers, O. Soutelle to parents, July 11, 1863; James A. Porter, "Personal Recollections of the Attack on Fort Wagner," Edited by James A. Chisman, *South Carolina Historical Magazine*, 81 (July 1980):247–49. Walkley, *Seventh Connecticut*, 73–74; *Charleston Daily Courier*, July 23, 1863.

19. *O.R.A.*, 28 (Pt. 1):354–55, 413–14; Toutelloutte, *History of Company K*, 111–13, 154; Copp, *Reminiscences of the War*, 229; Belknap, "The Siege of Charleston," 176; Caldwell, Sixth Regiment, 67; Davis, *History of the 104th Pennsylvania*, 245–46; Eldridge, *Third New Hampshire*, 302; Johnson, *Defense of Charleston Harbor*, 90; *O.R.A.*, 28 (Pt. 1):413–14.

20. Gilchrist, "Confederate Defense of Morris Island," 361; Hagood, *Memoirs*, 136; Jones, *Siege of Charleston*, 214; Johnson, *Defense of Charleston*, 90; *O.R.A.*, 28 (Pt. 1):414; *Charleston Mercury*, July 13, 1863; William A. Gyles Papers, W. Gyles letter, July 10, 1863, South Caroliniana Library, University of South Carolina, Columbia, South Carolina.

21. Caldwell, *Old Sixth Regiment*, 68; Copp, *Reminiscences of the War*, 230–34; Little, *Seventh Regiment*, 109–13; Toutelloutte, *History of Company K*, 112, 163, 173; Eldridge, *Third New Hampshire*, 303–4; Stryker, "Three Days in the Civil War."

22. Alvah Folsom Hunter, *A Year on a Monitor and the Destruction of Fort Sumter*, edited by Craig L. Symonds (Columbia: University of South Carolina Press, 1987), 98–101; *O.R.N.*, 14:319–21; Frederick Stow Papers, F. Stow to sister, August 20, 1863, United States Army Military History Institute, Carlise Barracks, Carlise, Pennsylvania.

23. Stryker, "Three days in the Civil War."

24. *O.R.A.*, 28 (Pt. 2):414; Repton Papers, O. Repton to sister, July 12, 1863; Porter, "Personal Recollections," 247–49.

25. Stryker, "Three Days in the Civil War."

26. Little, *Seventh Regiment*, 109–10; Johnson, *Defense of Charleston*, 90; Davis, *History of the 104th Pennsylvania*, 246; *O.R.A.*, 28 (Pt. 1):414.

27. *Armored Vessels*, 217; Paul H. Kendricken, *Memoirs of Paul Henry Kendricken* (Boston, 1910) 215–20.

28. Caldwell, *Sixth Regiment*, 81–82; *O.R.A.*, 28 (Pt. 1):526–27.
29. William T. Haskell, brother to Charles Haskell, was killed at Gettysburg. *Charleston Mercury*, July 17, 1863; Gilchrist, *Charleston Yearbook, 1884*, 361.
30. *O.R.A.*, 28 (Pt. 2):183–90; Department of South Carolina, Georgia and Florida, Letters Sent, 285–86; Theodore Honour Papers, T. Honour to wife, July 12 and 16, 1863, South Caroliniana Library, University of South Carolina, Columbia, South Carolina.
31. *Charleston Courier*, July 18, 1863; Little, *Seventh Regiment*, 107; Beecher, *Connecticut Volunteers*, 1:236–50; Higginson, *Army Life*, 169–84.
32. *O.R.A.*, 28 (Pt. 1):128; Ripley, *Correspondence*, 35; Olmstead, *Reminiscences of Service*, 1–4; Hagood, *Memoirs of the War*, 121.
33. Olmstead, *Reminiscences of Service*, 1–4; Roman, *Military Operations*, 2:114.
34. Though grape shot was no longer standard ammunition for field and siege guns, the Confederates at Charleston supplied their artillery with a large quantities of stands of grape for their guns located in fixed positions. *O.R.A.*, 28 (Pt. 1):523; Olmstead, *Reminiscences of Service*, 5; Johnson, *Defense of Charleston*, 94; *O.R.A.*, 28 (Pt. 1):114.
35. Little, *Seventh Regiment*, 109–10; Johnson, *Defense of Charleston*, 90; Davis, *History of the 104th Pennsylvania*, 246; *O.R.A.*, 28 (Pt. 1):414.
36. *Charleston Courier*, July 25, 1863; Toutelloutte, *History of Company K*, 114–15; *O.R.A.*, 28 (Pt. 1):356–60; Charles M. Clark, *Thirty-ninth Regiment Illinois*, 136; Savannah Morning News, *Historic Sketch of the Savannah Volunteer Infantry* (Savannah: Savannah Morning News Steam Print, 1886) 16; Walkley, *Seventh Connecticut*, 75–78.
37. *O.R.A.*, 28 (Pt. 1):414; Jones, *Siege of Charleston*, 218; Johnson, *Defense of Charleston*, 94.
38. Toutelloutte, *History of Company K*, 116–80; Olmstead, *Reminiscences of Service*, 5–6; *O.R.A.*, 28 (Pt. 1):356.
39. Toutelloutte, *History of Company K*, 118, 155, 175, 178–80; Johnson, *Defense of Charleston*, 95; *O.R.A.*, 28 (Pt. 1):360–61; Walkley, *Seventh Connecticut*, 75–78; Porter, "Personal Recollections," 250.
40. *O.R.A.*, 28 (Pt. 1):210–12, 361; Jones, *Siege of Charleston*, 219–20; Johnson, *Defense of Charleston*, 95.
41. Gillmore appointed himself the department's chief engineer while Captain Brooks was placed on Gillmore's staff and later promoted to Major, U.S. Volunteers. *O.R.A.*, 28 (Pt. 1):13, 356, 364, (Pt. 2):19–20; Jones, *Siege of Charleston*, 222. Cullum, *Biographical Register*, 2:573, 587–88.
42. *O.R.A.*, 28 (Pt. 1):13–15, (Pt. 2):20–21; Jones, *Siege of Charleston*, 224.
43. Voris, "Charleston in the Rebellion," 326–27; Stowits, *One-Hundreth New York*, 190; H. D. D. Twiggs, "Perilous Adventure at Battery Wagner," *Confederate Veteran* 12 (March 1904):104–6; *Charleston Mercury*, July 16, and 27, 1863.

44. Kendrick, *Memoirs*, 216–17; *Armored Vessels*, 581; Stow Papers, F. Stow to sister, August 20, 1863.
45. *O.R.A.*, 14:337, 343, 344.
46. Girard, "Visit to the Confederate States," 49; *Charleston Daily Courier*, July 10, 14, and 16, 1863; *Charleston Mercury*, July 10 and 13, 1863.
47. Roman, *Military Operations*, 2:95–97; Hagood, *Memoirs of the War*, 121; Daniel E. W. Smith, ed. *Mason Smith Family Letters* (Columbia: University of South Carolina Press, 1950), 123; *O.R.A.*, 28 (Pt. 2):194.
48. *O.R.A.*, 28 (Pt. 1):368–69, 523, (Pt. 2):191; Warren Ripley, editor, *Siege Train: The Journal of a Confederate Artilleryman in the Defense of Charleston* (Columbia: University of South Carolina Press, 1986), 1–4.
49. Roman, *Military Operations*, 2, 90–115; *O.R.A.*, 28 (Pt. 1):61–75, (Pt. 2):196–97, 200–201; Jones, *Siege of Charleston*, 224.
50. *O.R.A.*, 28 (Pt. 2):195–98, 200–201.
51. *O.R.A.*, 28 (Pt. 1):74, 370; Roman, *Military Operations*, 2:115.
52. *O.R.A.*, 28 (Pt. 2):195, 305; Ser. 4, 2:662–64; Still, *Confederate Shipbuilding*, 112–20; *O.R.N.*, 14:728; James Harvey Toomb, "Submarines and Torpedo Boats," *Confederate Veteran* 34 (April 1914):168–69; David P. Werlich, *Admiral of the Amazon: John Randolph Tucker* (Charlottesville, Virginia: University Press of Virginia, 1990), 53; Eldridge, *Third New Hampshire*, 334.
53. Olmstead, Charles F. "The Memoirs of Charles F. Olmstead," *Georgia Historical Quarterly*, 49 (1960):7–8; Twiggs, "The Defence of Battery Wagner," 171; *O.R.A.*, 28 (Pt. 1):416–17; Warner, *Generals in Gray*, 297–98; Records of W. B. Taliaferro, Compiled Service Records of Confederate Soldiers, Record Group 109, National Archives, Washington, D.C.
54. Johnson, *Defense of Charleston*, 100–101; *O.R.A.*, 28 (Pt. 1):371–72, 416–17, 541–43.
55. Beecher, *Connecticut Volunteers*, 1:255; Burchard, *One Gallant Rush*, 122; Emilio, *Brave Black Regiment*, 52–64; Appleton Journal, July 13, 1863.
56. Beecher, *Connecticut Volunteers*, 1:255; Mott, *Fifty-second Pennsylvania*, 128; Alfred S. Roe, *Twenty-fourth Massachusetts* 202.
57. *O.R.A.*, 28 (Pt. 1):586–88, 591; John C. Wheaton, *Reminiscences of the Chatham Artillery During the War* (Savannah: Press of the Morning News, 1887), 9–10; Hagood, *Memoirs of the War*, 137; Baron William Henry Von Eberstein Papers, Manuscript, 134–35, East Carolina University, Greenville, North Carolina.
58. *O.R.A.*, 14:345; Davis, *104th Pennsylvania*, 234–35; Mott, *Fifty-second Pennsylvania*, 128–29.
59. Emilio, *Brave Black Regiment*, 57–66; Davis, *104th Pennsylvania*, 234–36; Appleton, "That Night at Fort Wagner," 10; Burchard, *One Gallant Rush*, 122–24; Beecher, *Connecticut Volunteers*, 1:256–61; H. Clay Trumball, *The Knightly Soldier*, (Philadelphia: John D. Wattles, 1892),

134–36; "Poetry and Incidents," *Rebellion Record*, (New York: D. Van Nostrand, 1864), 8:5; Honour Papers, T. Honour to wife, July 16, 1863.

60. *O.R.A.*, 28 (Pt. 1):586–88; Appleton Journal, July 16 and 17, 1863; *Xenia Torchlight*, December 23, 1863.

61. Davis, *104th Pennsylvania*, 236; *O.R.A.*, 28 (Pt. 1):583.

62. Emilio, *Brave Black Regiment*, 62; *Charleston Courier*, July 17, 1863; Marple Letters, A. Marple to wife, July 12, 1863.

63. Emilio, *Brave Black Regiment*, 62; Robert Gould Shaw, "Letters," *Magazine of History*, 19 (1914):229.

64. Marple Letters, A. Marple to wife, July 12, 1863; Shaw Letters, Boston Library, G. Shaw to wife, 17 July 1863; Emilio, *Brave Black Regiment*, 66–69.

Chapter 4: The Grand Assault

1. *O.R.A.*, 28 (Pt. 1):207–8, (Pt. 2):205.

2. *Charleston Courier*, July 25, 1863; *O.R.A.*, 28 (Pt.2):202, (Pt.1):404; Walter Clark, *Histories of Several Regiments from North Carolina* (Raleigh: E. M. Uzzell, 1901), 3:207.

3. Gillmore, *Engineering and Artillery Operations*, 39–40; Dahlgren, *Memoirs*, 401.

4. Dahlgren, *Memoirs*, 402, *Armored Vessels*, 211; *O.R.N.*, 14:348–54; David D. Porter, *The Naval History of the Civil War* (New York: Sherman Publishing Company, 1886) 436–37: Johnson, *Defense of Charleston*, 102.

5. Little, *Seventh Regiment*, 117–19; Copp. *Reminiscences of the War*, 239–40; Jones, *Siege of Charleston*, 223.

6. *O.R.A.*, 28 (Pt. 1):417–18; Porter, *Naval History*, 437.

7. Denison, *Shot and Shell*, 169; Ripley, *Siege Train*, 5.

8. *Charleston Courier*, July 21, 1863; *O.R.A.*, 28 (Pt. 2):417–18; Gyles Papers, W. Gyles, letters of July 15 and 18.

9. A search of Confederate rolls reveals no Provost Flinn. In the Charleston Battalion are Private James Flynn and a Private John Flynn. Twiggs, "Defense of Battery Wagner," 175–76; Jones, *Siege of Charleston*, 235; Eldridge, *Third New Hampshire*, 312–14; *O.R.A.*, 28 (Pt. 1):417–18. For a different version of the Flag falling see "Coastal Current Insight: Confederate and Union Military," Coastal Heritage Society, Savannah, Georgia.

10. Henry Kershaw DuBose, *The History of Company B, Twenty-first Regiment South Carolina Volunteers Confederate States Provisonal Army* (Columbia: R. L. Bryan, 1909), 25; Twiggs, "Defence of Battery Wagner," 177; David B. Harris Papers, D. Harris to wife, 29 July 1863, Perkins Library, Duke University, Durham, North Carolina; Department of South Carolina, Georgia and Florida, Letters Sent, W. Taliaferro to R. Ripley, July 18, 1863.

11. *O.R.N.*, 14:359–66; Dahlgren, *Memoirs*, 405.

12. *O.R.A.*, 28 (Pt. 1):76–77, (Pt. 2):207–8; Olmstead, *Reminiscences of*

Service, 9; Edward H. Cummins, "The Signal Corps in the Confederate Army," *Southern Historical Society Papers*, 16 (January–December 1918):104; Frank Vizetelly, "When Charleston was Under Fire," *New Age Magazine*, (September, 1911):227; Twiggs, "Defence of Battery Wagner," 178; Gilchrist, "Confederate Defence of Morris Island," 367, 382–83; Jones, *Siege of Charleston*, 235; Johnson, *Defense of Charleston Harbor*, 103.

13. *O.R.A.*, 28, (Pt. 1):417–18, 525, 543–44; *Charleston Daily Courier*, July 22 and 24, 1863.
14. Emilio, *Brave Black Regiment*, 68–73; Shaw, "Letters," 230; *New York National Anti-Slavery Standard*, August 8, 1863.
15. Emilio, *Brave Black Regiment*, 75; *O.R.A.*, 28, (Pt. 1):348; *New York National Anti-Slavery Standard*, August 8, 1863; Testimony by a special correspondent of the *New York Tribune* before the American Freedman's Inquiry Commission, New Orleans, (February 1864). Testimony of Nathaniel Page, Record Group 94, National Archives, Washington, D.C.; Iva Berlin, *The Black Military Experience* (Cambridge: University Press, 1982), 534–35; Joseph T. Glatthaar, *Forged in Battle: The Civil War Alliance of Black Soldiers and White Officers* (New York: The Free Press, 1990), 137.
16. *O.R.A.*, 28, (Pt. 1):346; Eldridge, *Third New Hampshire*, 320; Little, *Seventh Regiment*, 119; Voris, "Charleston in the Rebellion," 327.
17. For the attack, some regiments were drawn up by wing, which is a formation where the regiment is split in half, five companies to a wing and formed one behind the other. Each wing is made up of a line two men deep with twenty-five yards between the wings. It can also be referred to as being formed by battalion, with one battalion being the equivalent of a wing. It is sometimes called a column by battalions. Isaiah Price, *History of the Ninety-seventh Regiment Pennsylvania Volunteer Infantry* (Philadelphia: Published by the Author, 1875), 168–69; Little, *Seventh Regiment*, 119–20; Copp, *Reminiscences of the War*, 239; Trumbull *Knightly Soldier*, 140; Porter, *Naval History*, 437; Appleton Journal 18 July 1863; Holland, *Letters and Diary of Laura Towne*, 100.
18. Emilio, *Brave Black Regiment*, 72–78; Appleton Journal, July 18, 1863.
19. James McPherson, *Marching Towards Freedom* (New York: Alfred A. Knopf, 1967), 98; Emilio, *Brave Black Regiment*, 78–79; Appleton Journal, July 18, 1863.
20. Though versions of Strong's speech vary, he did ask who would pick up the flag should it fall, stating that both the rebels and the attackers were tired and hungry, and that they were to go in with the bayonet. Emilio, *Brave Black Regiment*, 77; *Boston Liberator*, 31 July 1863; *Xenia Torchlight*, December 23, 1863; Wilder Papers, G. Pope to B. Wilder, February 23, 1916; Appleton Journal, July 18, 1863; *New York Anti-Slavery Standard*, August 1, 1863; Richard H. L. Jewett Papers, letter of July 19, 1863. Boston Anthenaeum, Boston, Massachusetts.

21. Eldridge, *Third New Hampshire*, 386; 136; Emilio, *Brave Black Regiment*, 77–80; Martha Nicholson McKay, *When the Tide Turned in the Civil War* (Indianapolis: Hollenbeck Press, 1929), 51; Beecher, *Connecticut Volunteers*, 1:264; Caldwell, *Sixth Regiment*, 71.
22. Emilio, *Brave Black Regiment*, 78–82; O.R.A., 28 (Pt. 1):347–48; Appleton, "That Night at Wagner," 13–15; *Charleston Courier*, July 20, August 10, 1863; George Washington Williams, *A History of the Negro Troops in the War of Rebellion, 1861–1865* (New York: Bergman Publishers, 1888), 197; McKay, *When the Tide Turned*, 59; Jones, *Siege of Charleston*, 138; Davis, *104th Pennsylvania*, 239; Appleton Journal, July 18, 1863; Wilder Papers, undated letter of E. Hallowell; Jewett Papers, letter of 19 July; *Boston Evening Post*, May 3, 1916; Letter of William C. Carney from a private collection; *Boston Journal*, August 4, 1863; Cabot J. Russell Papers, Statement of S. A. Swailes, August 12 , 1863, New York Public Library, New York.
23. Some accounts have Shaw falling into a gun pit, and one report has him being bayoneted. Emilio, *Brave Black Regiment*, 82–85; *Charleston Courier*, August 10, 1863; Williams, *History of the Negro Troops*, 199; Stryker, "Three Days in the Civil War,"; "Poetry and Incidents," in *Rebellion Record*, 8: 16; For another version of Shaw's death see *Charleston News and Courier*, June 14, 1927; Appleton Journal, July 18, 1863.
24. Emilio, *Brave Black Regiment*, 82–85; Appleton, "That Night at Wagner," 14–15.
25. Emilio, *Brave Black Regiment*, 82–85; Gilchrist, "Confederate Defense of Morris Island," 368; Stryker, "Three Days in the Civil War"; "Poetry and Incidents," in *Rebellion Record*, 8:16; Appleton Journal, July 18, 1863.
26. Caldwell, *Sixth Regiment*, 70–78.
27. James Moses Nichols, *Perry's Saints* (Boston: D. Lothrop, 1886), 169–74; William J. Carleton, *Company D: The Die No Mores of the 48th Regiment New York State Volunteers 1861–1865*, (Privately Printed, 1892), 2–6, 17.
28. O.R.A., 28 (Pt. 1):347–48; Copp. *Reminiscences of the War*, 241.
29. Eldridge, *Third New Hampshire*, 315–21; John Bedel "History Sketch of the Third New Hampshire Volunteers," *The Granite Monthly*, 3 (September 1880):527–28.
30. O.R.A., 28 (Pt. 1):347–48; Eldridge, *Third New Hampshire*, 320–21; *Charleston Courier*, July 20, 1863; Charles Carleton Coffin, *Four Years of Fighting* (Boston: Tichnor and Fields, 1886) 119–20; Little, *Seventh New Hampshire*, 120–21.
31. O.R.A., 28 (Pt. 1):416–21, 524–25; Eldridge, *Third New Hampshire*, 320–23; Johnson, *Defense of Charleston*, 105–6; Jones, *Siege of Charleston*, 243; Little, *Seventh Regiment*, 121–26; Voris, "Charleston in the Rebellion," 329; *Charleston Courier*, July 20, 21, and 22, 1863; Inglesby, *First Regiment South Carolina Artillery*, 123; Appleton, "That Night at

Wagner," 16; *Charleston Mercury*, August 7, 1863; *Charleston Courier* July 25, 1863; Johnson, *Defense of Charleston*, lxxxix.

32. Price, *Ninety-seventh Regiment*, 172–74; Roe, *Twenty-fourth Regiment*, 205–6; Trumbull, *Knightly Soldier*, 144–45.

33. Emilio, *Brave Black Regiment*, 89; S.J. Cobb, "Service of Tar Heels," *Confederate Veteran* (May 1900):215–16.

34. Trumbull, *Knightly Soldier*, 145; Price, *Ninety-seventh Regiment*, 174.

35. Clara Barton Papers, Diary, July 11, 1863; Craven, "Report of Surgeon Craven," 241; Voris, "Sketches of War History," 330–34; Appleton Journal, July 18, and 19, 1863.

36. *O.R.A.*, 28, (Pt. 2):208–9.

37. Gilchrist, "Confederate Defense of Morris Island," 370.

38. Gilchrist, "Confederate Defense of Morris Island," 371; Coffin, *Four Years of Fighting*, 349; *Charleston Courier*, July 21, 1863; Eldridge, *Third New Hampshire*, 387; William Stanley Poole, *Vizetelly Covers the Confederacy*, (Tuscaloosa: Confederate Centennial Studies, 1957), 90; Harris Papers, D. Harris to wife, July 29, 1863; Cobb. "Service of Tar Heels," 216.

39. Carleton, *Die No Mores*, 2; Nichols, *Perry's Saints*, 170; *O.R.A.*, 28, (Pt.1):210–12, 406; *Charleston Courier*, July 25, 1863; Johnson, *Defense of Charleston*, p. lxxxix.

40. *O.R.N.*, 14:363; Gilchrist, "Confederate Defense of Morris Island," 371; Hagood, *Memoirs of the War*, 142–44; Pearson, *Letters from Port Royal*, 198; Eldridge, *Third New Hampshire*, 387; Denison, *Shot and Shell*, 120, Emilio, *Brave Black Regiment*, 99–102; Jones, "Letters," 139.

41. Appleton, "That Night at Wagner," 15–16; Toutelloutte, *History of Company K*, 182; W. F. C. Peck, "Four Years Under Fire at Charleston," *Harpers New Monthly Magazine*, 31 (August 1865):362; Department of South Carolina, Georgia and Florida, Letters Sent, 1863–1864, T. Jordon to G. Ripley, July 20, 1863; *Charleston Daily Courier*, July 20, 1863; *O.R.A.*, Ser. 2, 5:797, Series 3, 3:153–55; *O.R.N.*, 14:363; Gilchrist, "Confederate Defense of Morris Island," 371; Hagood, *Memoirs of the War*, 142–44; Pearson, *Letters from Port Royal*, 198; Eldridge, *Third New Hampshire*, 387; Denison, *Shot and Shell*, 120, Emilio, *Brave Black Regiment*, 99–102; Jones, "Letters," 139; Wilder Papers, G. Harrison to B. Wilder, March 19, and 25, 1915.

42. Carleton, *Die No Mores*, 2; Nichols, *Perry's Saints*, 170; *O.R.A.*, 28, (Pt. 1):210–12; McKay, "When the Tide Turned," 60; Emilio, *Brave Black Regiment*, 89–92.

43. *O.R.A.*, 28, (Pt. 2):21–22; Roman, *Military Operations*, 2:120; Du Pont, *Letters*, 3:205; Burton, *Siege of Charleston*, 169.

Chapter 5: The Siege Begins

1. Gillmore, *Engineering and Artillery Operations*, 46–56; *O.R.A.*, 28 (Pt. 2):21–24; Roman, *Military Operations*, 2:120; Du Pont, *Letters*, 3:205; Burton, *Siege of Charleston*, 169.

2. Ibid.
3. *O.R.A.*, 28 (Pt. 1):273–79, 303–8.
4. *O.R.A.*, 28 (Pt. 2):26–27; *O.R.N.*, 14:374–91, 409.
5. Olmstead, *Reminiscences of Service*, 10–11; Hagood, *Memoirs of the War*, 187; Ripley, *Siege Train*, 125–26.
6. *O.R.A.*, 28 (Pt. 1):374; Hagood, *Memoirs of the War*, 183.
7. *O.R.A.*, 28 (Pt. 2):39, 45, 47, 205, 376; Department of South Carolina, Letters Sent, T. Jordan to R. Riply, 20 July 1863; Pearson, *Letters from Port Royal*, 198; James H. Clark, *The Iron Hearted Regiment* (Albany: J. Munsell, 1865), 65. There has always been some speculation as to whether the body returned was Putnam's or Shaw's. Colonel Robert H. Anderson, a classmate of Putnam at West Point, was present at Wagner when the body was disinterred and reported that he identified the body as Putnam's, but he had not seen Putnam since 1857. Anderson said the uniform on the body had shoulder straps showing the rank of colonel, but Putnam had not worn any rank insignia on the day of the battle. The only other colonel buried in front of Wagner was Shaw. Both Shaw and Putnam had similar features and build.
8. *O.R.A.*, 28 (Pt. 2):227; Clark, *North Carolina Regiments*, 1:393; Olmstead, *Reminiscences of Service*, 10–11; Gilchrist, "Confederate Defense of Morris Island," 372; Caldwell, Sixth Regiment, 76, *Charleston Mercury*, August 12, 1863; Girard, "Visit to Confederate States," 51; *Charleston Courier*, July 25, 1863; *O.R.N.*, 4: 390–94; *Hilton Head New South*, August 1, 1863; Stryker, "Three Days in the Civil War;" Department of South Carolina, Georgia and Florida, Letters Sent, W. Taliaferro to R. Ripley, July 24, 1863.
9. *O.R.A.*, 28 (Pt. 2):39, 45, 47, 205, 376; Department of South Carolina, Letters Sent, T. Jordon to R. Ripley, 20 July 1863, W. Peronneau to A. Nance, July 19, 1863; Pearson, *Letters From Port Royal*, 198; James H. Clark, *The Iron Hearted Regiment* (Albany: J. Munsell, 1865), 65; Emilio, *Brave Black Regiment*, 396–425; Woodward, "Captive Black Union Soldiers," 28–44; Confederate States of America, *Journal of the Congress of the Confederate States of America*, 7 vols. (Washington, D.C.: Government Printing Office, 1889), Ser. 1, 3:386–87, Ser. 2, 4:245–46; *Charleston Courier*, July 18 and 23, 1863, August 12, 1863; *Harper's Weekly*, April 8, 1865; Pickens-Bonham Papers, J. Seddon to M. Bonham, 1 September 1863, Library of Congress, Washington, D.C.; Governor M. L. Bonham Papers, M. Bonham to J. Carew, 8 December 1864, South Carolina Archives, Columbia, South Carolina; Account of John E. Carew on maintenance of Negro prisoners of war, 1863–1864, General Assembly Papers, Penal System Accounts, 1864, South Carolina Archives, Columbia, S.C.; Honour Papers, T. Honour to his wife, 18 July 1863; Russell Papers, statement of J. Baird, 1 June 1865; Muster Roles of the 54th Massachusetts, Massachusetts National Guard Supply Depot, Natick, Massachusetts. *Charleston Mercury*, August 12, 13, 14, and 15,

1863. Additional, though romanticized, information can also be found in
Willard Glazier, *The Capture, the Prison Pen and the Escape*. (New
York: United States Publishing Company, 1868); an interesting
fictionalized account of the trial can be found in Mary Hall Leonard, *The
Days of the Swamp Angel* (New York: Neale Publishing Company, 1914).
In her novel, the lawyer for the black troops suffers at the hands of his
fellow citizens for his role in the trial.

10. William H. Echols, "Press Copies of Letters Sent by Major William H.
Echols, Chief Engineer, July 1863–February 1864, letter of 30 July 1863,
Record Group 109, National Archives, Washington, D.C.; Iredell Jones,
"Letters from Fort Sumter in 1862 and 1863," *Southern Historical
Society Papers*, 12 (January–June 1884): 162; *O.R.A.*, 28 (Pt. 1):575–78,
(Pt. 2):151, 159, 224, 226, 230, 257, 268, 286, 289, 315, 323; Sallie
Lightfoot Tarleton Papers, R. Tarleton to S. Lightfoot, March 2, 1864,
East Carolina University Library, East Carolina University, Greenville,
North Carolina.

11. Pressley, "Wee Nee Volunteers," 157; Burton, *Siege of Charleston*, 172;
O.R.A., 28 (Pt. 1):75, 376, 409, 412.

12. Echols Letterbook, August 22, 1863; Burton, *Siege of Charleston*, 252;
William N. Still, Jr. *Iron Afloat: The Story of the Confederate Amorclads*
(Nashville: Vanderbilt University Press, 1971), 114; Williams Middleton
Papers, W. Middleton to wife, August 20 and 23, 1863, South Caroliniana
Library, University of South Carolina, Columbia, South Carolina.

13. *O.R.A.*, 28 (Pt. 1):371, (Pt. 2):220; *O.R.N.*, 14:724; T. W. Glassel,
"Reminiscences of Torpedo Service in Charleston Harbor," *Southern
Historical Society Papers*, 4 (November 1877):225–35.

14. *O.R.A.*, 28 (Pt. 1):257, 482; Ashe, "Life at Fort Wagner," 256; *Military
Operations*, 2:122–25.

15. Roman, *Military Operations*, 2:154–55; *O.R.A.*, 28 (Pt. 1):410–12;
Hagood, *Memoirs of the War*, 181.

16. Hagood, *Memoirs of the War*, 184; Roman, *Military Operations*, 1:123;
Clark, *North Carolina Regiments*, 1:393–94; Ashe, "Life at Fort
Wagner," 255; Department of South Carolina, Georgia and Florida,
Letters Sent, T. Jordon to R. Ripley, July 19, 1863.

17. *O.R.A.*, 28 (Pt. 1):410–12.

18. Gilchrist, "Confederate Defense of Morris Island," *South Carolina
Historical Magazine*, 57 (January 1956):4; Albert Rhett Elmore,
"Incidents of Service with the Confederate Light Dragoons,"
Confederate Veteran, (December 1916):538–40.

19. John Harleston, "Battery Wagner on Morris Island," *South Carolina
Historical Magazine*, 57 (January 1956):4; Elmore, "Incidents of
Service," 538–40.

20. Hagood, *Memoirs of the War*, 181.

21. Hagood, *Memoirs of the War*, 185; Echols, Letterbook, July 30 and 31,
August 1, 1863.

22. *O.R.A.*, 28 (Pt. 1):351, (Pt. 2):232; Echols, Letterbook, July 30 and 31, 1863; Denison, *Shot and Shell*, 186; Burton, *Siege of Charleston*, 173; Mott, *Fifty-second Pennsylvania*, 263; Lewis Pinckney Jones, "Ambrosio José Gonzales, A Cuban Patriot in Carolina," *South Carolina Historical Magazine* 56 (April 1955):67–76.

23. Price, *Ninety-seventh Regiment*, 184; Stowits, *One-hundredth New York*, 209; *Maine Regiment*, 149; Roman, *Military Operations*, 1:123; *Charleston Mercury*, August 6, 1863; O.R.A., 28 (Pt. 1):593–95.

24. After the capture of Haines's launch, Admiral Dahlgren received word that some of the crew had been fired on while in the water. Dahlgren sent a dispatch to the Confederate high command demanding an explanation. The reply came from Flag Officer Tucker who denied the allegation. Two sailors from the launch were later found on the beach of Sullivan's Island and placed in prison with the rest of the Federal sailors. It seems that two or three Union sailors did drown trying to escape, while another eight reached safety. *O.R.N.*, 14:421–27, 725, 726; *O.R.A.*, 28 (Pt. 2):251–52.

25. Denison, *Shot and Shell*, 145; *O.R.A.*, 28 (Pt. 1):273.

Chapter 6: The Siege Continues

1. The regiments from the Army of the Potomac were the 41st New York, 54th New York, 157th New York, 74th Pennsylvania, 107th Ohio, 25th Ohio, 75th Ohio, and the 17th Connecticut. The regiments from the Department of the Virginia were the 142nd New York, 40th Massachusetts, and the 144th New York. George Henry Gordon, *A Diary of Events in the War of the Great Rebellion: 1863–1865* (Boston: Osgood, 1882), 168–78: Toutelloutte, *History of Company K*, 121–22; Welles, *Diary*, 1:382–85; *O.R.A.*, 28 (Pt. 2):29–30; *O.R.N.*, 14:380, 401.

2. Bowditch, "Letters," 425–27.

3. Walkley, *Seventh Connecticut*, 91; Toutelloutte, *History of Company K*, 121; Charles Fox, Letterbooks of the 55th Massachusetts, August 9–14, 1863, Massachusetts Historical Society, Boston Massachusetts; Bowditch, "Letters," 425–27; Robert Dysart Diary, August 12–16, 1863, U.S. Army Military History Institute, Carlise, Pennsylvania; David G. Martin, *Carl Bornemann's Regiment: The Firty-first New York Infantry (DeKalb Regt.) in the Civil War* (Highstown, New Jersey: Longstreet House, 1987), 256–58.

4. Gillmore, *Engineer and Artillery Operations*, 45; Mott, *Fifty-second Pennsylvania*, 136; Kimball, *Company I*, 34–35; Little, *Seventh Regiment*, 130–31; Davis, *104th Pennsylvania*, 251.

5. Fox, Letterbooks, August 9–14, 1863; Bowditch, "Letters," 430, 432, 437, 438; Clark, *The Thirty-ninth Regiment*, 130; M.L.S. Jackson Diary, August 2–15, 1863, U.S. Army Military History Institute, Carlise Army Barracks, Carlise, Pennsylvania.

6. *O.R.A.*, 28 (Pt. 1):281–82, 327, Ser. 3, 2:250–52; 404–5, 420; Orville Samuel Kimball, *History and Personal Sketches of Company I, 103rd*

New York State Volunteers 1862–1864 (Elmira: Facts Printing Company, 1900), 34; Charles B. Fox, *Record of the Service of the Fifty-fifth Regiment of Massachusetts Volunteer Infantry* (Cambridge: John Wilson and Son, 1868), 11–12; Emilio, *Brave Black Regiment*, 47–48, 105–9, 130, 155; Cornish, *The Sable Arm*, 184–85; Higginson, *Army Life in a Black Regiment*, 280–92; Howard C. Westwood, "The Cause and Consequence of a Union Black Soldier's Mutiny and Execution," *Civil War History* 31 (September, 1985):224–26.

7. *O.R.A.*, 28 (Pt. 1):276–79; Eldridge, *Third New Hampshire*, 376–77.

8. *O.R.A.*, 28 (Pt. 1):307–8.

9. Davis, *104th Pennsylvania*, 251; Fox, *Fifty-fifth Regiment*, 11–12; *O.R.A.*, 28 (Pt. 1):279, 313, 316–17.

10. *O.R.A.*, 28 (Pt. 1):303–23.

11. *O.R.A.*, 28 (Pt. 1):312, 318–23; Gillmore, *Engineer and Artillery Operations*, 47–53; Denison, *Shot and Shell*, 168; Copp, *Reminiscences of the War*, 287.

12. *O.R.A.*, 28 (Pt. 1):18–26, 278, 342–48; Beecher, *Connecticut Volunteers*, 1:274; Little, *Seventh Regiment*, 134; Denison, *Shot and Shell*, 172; Nichols, *Perry's Saints*, 177; Ripley, *Siege Train*, 5–33.

13. Jewett, *A Boy Goes to War*, 40–41.

14. There is evidence that men from the 54th Massachusetts served with Ela's unit. If so, it would have been one of the first integrated units in the army. *O.R.A.*, 28 (Pt. 1):323–24; Little, *Seventh Regiment*, 163; Toutelloutte, *A History of Company K*, 166, 174.

15. Davis, *104th Pennsylvania*, 251; *O.R.A.*, 28 (Pt. 1):279, 313, 316–17, 327, 335–40; Bowditch, Letters," 432; Fox, *Fifty-fifth Regiment*, 11–12; Emilio, *Brave Black Regiment*, 105–7.

16. Davis, *104th Pennsylvania*, 262–64; Repton Papers, O. Repton to sister, August 15, 1863; Dickey, *Eighty-fifth Pennsylvania*, 274.

17. Fox, *Fifty-fifth Regiment*, 11–12; Emilio, *Brave Black Regiment*, 105–7.

18. Davis, *104th Pennsylvania*, 251; Franklin McGrath, *The History of the 127th New York Volunteers, "Monitors"* (n.p., 1898), 74; J. A. Mowris, *A History of the One hundred and seventeenth Regiment New York Volunteers* (Hartford: Case, Lockwood and Company, 1866), 83–84.

19. *O.R.A.*, 28 (Pt. 1):36–38; Little, *Seventh Regiment*, 153.

20. Denison, *Shot and Shell*, 179; William S. Stryker, "The Swamp Angel: The Gun Used in Firing on Charleston in 1863." *Magazine of American History*, 14 (December, 1886):553–60; William S. Stryker, "The Swamp Angel," *Battles and Leaders of the Civil War*, (New York: Thomas Yoseloff, 1956), 4:72–74.

21. *O.R.A.*, 28 (Pt. 1):230–39; Price, *Ninety-Seventh Regiment*, 134–47; *Maine Regiment*, 142; Stryker, "The Swamp Angel: The Gun," 553–60; Stryker, "The Swamp Angel," 72–74.

22. *O.R.A.*, 28 (Pt. 1):230–39; Price, *Ninety-Seventh Regiment*, 134–47; *Maine Regiment*, 142; Stryker, "The Swamp Angel: The Gun," 553–60;

Stryker, "The Swamp Angel," 72–74; Denison, *Shot and Shell*, 179–80; Bowditch, "Letters," 434–36.

23. *O.R.N.*, 14:376–80, 388, 402–3, 437–38.
24. *O.R.A.*, 14:386, 395, 401, 414, 418, 432–33.
25. *O.R.A.*, 14:376–77, 382, 388–90, 398, 402, 419; Kendricken, *Memoirs*, 123.
26. *O.R.N.*, 14:386, 395, 401, 414, 418, 432–33, 429–40.
27. The gunboats were the *Canandaigua, Cimarron, Ottawa, Wissahickon, Seneca, Dai Ching, Lodona, Mahaska. O.R.N.*, 14:452; Dahlgren, *Memoirs*, 400–408.
28. *O.R.A.*, 28 (Pt. 2):38, 41, 71; Eldridge, *Third New Hampshire*, 346.

Chapter 7: The Bombardment of Fort Sumter

1. Gordon, *War Diary*, 179; Denison, *Shot and Shell*, 174; William Lawrence Haskins, *The History of the First Regiment of Artillery from its Organization in 1821 to January 1st 1876* (Portland: B. Thurston and Company, 1879), 534.
2. Eldridge, *Third New Hampshire*, 350; *O.R.A.*, 28 (Pt. 1):21–22, 212–16; Denison, *Shot and Shell*, 173.
3. *O.R.A.*, 28 (Pt. 2):43; *O.R.N.*, 14:472–83.
4. John Caldwell Tidball, *Manual of Heavy Artillery Service* (Washington: J. J. Chapman, 1880), 79–83; *Maine Regiment*, 154–55; *O.R.A.*, 28 (Pt. 1):219–24, 608–22.
5. Tidball, *Heavy Artillery*, 79–83; *Maine Regiment*, 154–55; *O.R.A.*, 28 (Pt. 1):219–24, 608–22; Denison, *Shot and Shell*, 173.
6. *O.R.A.*, 28 (Pt. 1):219–24, 608–22; Jacobi, *Rifled Batteries*, 37; Warner, *Generals in Blue*, 512–13.
7. Dickey, *Eighty-fifth Regiment*, 275; *O.R.A.*, 28 (Pt. 1):217, 222, 608–22; Gordon, *War Diary*, 183–84.
8. Gordon, *War Diary*, 189; *O.R.A.*, 28 (Pt. 1):222–27; Walkley, *Seventh Connecticut*, 94–95; Bowditch, "Letters," 438.
9. *O.R.A.*, 28 (Pt. 1):224; Fox Letterbooks, August 18–21, 1863; Denison, *Shot and Shell*, 175; Alexander Vance Diary, August 12, 1863, Fort Sumter National Monument, Charleston, South Carolina.
10. *O.R.A.*, 28 (Pt. 1):608–16; James Harvey McKee, *Back in War Times* (New York: Horace E. Bailey, 1903), 128; Jones, "Letters from Fort Sumter," 212–13, 254; W. Gordon McCabe's Impression of the Bombardment of Charleston," *South Carolina Historical Magazine* 71 (October, 1970):266–69; Smith, *Mason-Smith*, 62; Ashe, "Life at Fort Wagner," 256; Roman, *Military Operations*, 2:126–27.
11. Gordon, *War Diary*, 191; *O.R.A.*, 28 (Pt. 1):216–17; Burn Family Papers, W. Burn to master, August 25, 1863, South Caroliniana Library, Columbia, South Carolina.
12. Denison, *Shot and Shell*, 175–78; Honour Papers, T. Honour to wife, August 17 and 18, 1863; Dickey, *Eighty-fifth Regiment*, 274.

13. *O.R.A.*, 28 (Pt. 1):608–16, (Pt. 2):300, 309; Roman, *Military Operations*, 1:144; Jones, "Letters From Fort Sumter," 254–55; Ashe, "Life at Fort Wagner," 256; Roman, *Military Operations*, 1:126–27.

14. *O.R.N.*, 14:452–54, 457, 472–73; *O.R.A.*, 28 (Pt. 2):44; Farenholt, *Monitor Catskill*, 9; Kendricken, *Memoirs*, 219; Gordon, *War Diary*, 183–84.

15. *O.R.A.*, 14:719, 28 (Pt. 2):44, 49, 191, 229, 249, 251; George E. Belknap, "Reminiscences of the New Ironsides off Charleston," *United Service*, 1 (January, 1879):77–78; Burton, *Siege of Charleston*, 216–19; *O.R.N.*, 14:498–500; Middleton Papers, W. Middleton to wife, August 21, 1863.

16. *O.R.N.*, 14:470, 478; Dahlgren, *Memoirs*, 554–55, 560.

17. Ibid.

18. Jim Dan Hill, *The Civil War Sketchbook of Charles Ellery Stedman* (San Rafeal: Presidio Press, 1976), 171.

19. Roman, *Military Operations*, 1:126; *O.R.A.*, 28 (Pt. 1):470–71.

20. Wampler was killed on August 17, after taking a chair vacated by Surgeon Henry B. Horlbeck. *O.R.A.*, 28 (Pt. 1):466–79; *Charleston Yearbook, 1884*, 381; *Charleston Mercury*, August 18, 1863.

21. *O.R.A.*, 28 (Pt. 1):437–44; Hagood, *Memoirs of the War*, 182–88.

22. *O.R.A.*, 28 (Pt. 1):235–36; Stryker, "Swamp Angel," 558–59; Peck, "Four Years," 363; *Maine Regiment*, 139–44.

23. W. Stanley Hoole, *Vizetelly Covers the Confederacy* (Tuscaloosa: Confederate Publishing Company, 1957), 93–99; Middleton Papers, W. Middleton to wife, August 24 and 25, 1863.

24. *O.R.A.*, 28 (Pt. 2):57–62; Jones, "Letters From Fort Sumter," 257.

25. *O.R.A.*, 28 (Pt. 1):235–36; *Maine Regiment*, 144–46; Jacobi, *Rifled Batteries*, 42.

26. Gordon, *War Diary*, 195–96.

27. *O.R.A.*, 28 (Pt. 1):294–96, 504–6; Eldridge, *Third New Hampshire*, 354.

28. Hagood, *Memoirs of the War*, 187; Rockwell, "Operations Against Charleston," 190; Roe, *Twenty-fourth Regiment*, 213–17; Eldridge, *Third New Hampshire*, 354–55; *O.R.A.*, 28 (Pt. 1):294–96, 499–500, 504–6.

29. Harleston, "Battery Wagner," 2; *O.R.A.*, 28 (Pt. 2):309–10, 312; Roe, *The Twenty-fourth Massachusetts*, 212–14.

30. Captain Francis D. Lee spent most of his time working on torpedo boats and spar torpedoes. Captain M. Gray was in charge of the Torpedo Bureau while a Colonel Lewis M. Hatch briefly worked with torpedoes in the Stono River in early August. Hatch was replaced by Major Elliott on August 10. Up to this time, Elliott had been the ordnance officer in the department's third district. Beauregard, "Torpedo Service," 147–50; *O.R.A.*, 28 (Pt. 2):228, 230, 271–72, 285, 289, 300, 311–12; Tarleton Papers, R. Tarleton to S. Lightfoot, 2 March 1864; Elliott Papers, S. Elliott to Wife, August 20, 22, 30, and 31, 1863, South Caroliniana Library, Columbia, South Carolina; Department of South Carolina, Letters Sent, A. Gonzales to T. Jordon, 16 July 1863; *Charleston Mercury*, September 2, 1863.

31. "Running the Blockade," *Southern Historical Society Papers* 24 (January–December 1896):225–29; Beauregard, "Torpedo Service," 158–60; Pressley, "Wee Nee Volunteers," 172; Jones, "Letters From Fort Sumter," 546; *O.R.A.*, 28 (Pt. 2):291, 296, 302, 313, 329, 337, 343, 387–88.
32. *O.R.A.*, 28 (Pt. 1):687–712.
33. Hagood, *Memoirs of the War*, 184; Harleston, "Battery Wagner," 8; Elmore, "Incidents of Service," 541; Jones, "Letters From Fort Sumter," 161.
34. Claudine Rhett, "Frank H. Harleston," *Southern Historical Society Papers* 10 (July 1882):315–16; Izlar, "Edisto Rifles," 43; Elmore, "Incidents of Service," 539; Ashe, "Life at Fort Wagner," 254; *O.R.A.*, 28 (Pt. 1):504–5.
35. Jones, "Letters From Fort Sumter," 161; T. Harry Williams, *P. T. G. Beauregard: Napoleon in Grey* (Baton Rouge: Louisiana State University, 1955), 196.
36. Ibid.

Chapter 8: The Campaign Ends

1. *O.R.A.*, 28 (Pt. 2):323.
2. *O.R.A.*, 28 (Pt. 1):295–96; Dickey, *Eighty-fifth Regiment*, 277; Jewett, *A Boy Goes to War*, 45; Eldridge, *Third New Hampshire*, 356; Denison, *Shot and Shell*, 184; *Harper's Weekly*, 19 September 1863.
3. *O.R.A.*, 28 (Pt. 1):310.
4. Little, *Seventh Regiment*, 167–68; Jewett, *A Boy Goes to War*, 38–39; *Maine Regiment*, 153; Bryant, *Diary*, 114; Denison, *Shot and Shell*, 171; Copp, *Reminiscences of the War*, 258–59.
5. Price, *Ninety-seventh Regiment*, 190–93; Jewett, *A Boy Goes to War*, 43; Dickey, *Eighty-fifth Regiment*, 277–79.
6. Clara Barton Papers, C. Barton to Cousin Vira, August 30, 1863; Bryant, *Diary*, 117–19.
7. McKee, *Back in War Times*, 121; Briggs, *Civil War Surgeon*, 102, 108; Copp, *Reminiscences of the War*, 257; Emilio, *Brave Black Regiment*, 107.
8. McKee, *Back in War Times*, 121; Briggs, *Civil War Surgeon*, 108; Dickey, *Eighty-fifth Regiment*, 270, 274; Beecher, *Connecticut Volunteers*, 1:283–84; Fox Letterbooks, August 18–21, 1863.
9. Kimball, *Company I*, 35; McGarth, *127th New York*, 71–73; Toutelloutte, *History of Company K*, 120; Briggs, *Civil War Surgeon*, 102; Little, *Seventh Regiment*, 131–32; Beecher, *Connecticut Volunteers*, 1:271; Frances Perkins, "Two Years with a Colored Regiment," *New England Magazine*, 17 (1897–1898):535; Bowditch, "Letters," 429; Marple Letters, A. Marple to wife, July 22, 1863; Thompson Papers, letter of September 9, 1863; Roe, *Twenty-fourth Massachusetts*, 207; Fox Letterbooks, August 21–September 5, 1863; *O.R.A.*, 28 (Pt. 2):27–28.

10. Mowris, *One Hundred and Seventeenth Regiment*, 80–83; McKee, *Back in War Times*, 132–34; Briggs, *Civil War Surgeon*, 112.

11. *O.R.A.*, 28 (Pt. 1):237.

12. *O.R.A.*, 28 (Pt. 2):27–28; Roe, *Twenty-fourth Regiment*, 207; McKee, *Back in War Times*, 134; Galloway, *One Battle Too Many*, 239–40; Eldridge, *Third New Hampshire*, 364.

13. Mary F. Gage briefly assisted Clara Barton, but Barton did not allow her to stay very long. Barton Papers, undated letter; Stowits, *One-hundredth New York*, 211; Ross, *Angel of the Battlefield*, 57–58; Epler, *Clara Barton*, 78–79.

14. Ibid.

15. Stowits, *One-hundredth New York*, 218; Price, *Ninety-seventh Regiment*, 95.

16. Different sources list different cannon as still being servicable in Fort Sumter at this time. The cannon were often dismounted during the day and remounted at night. One source lists, instead of the Dahlgren gun, a rifled-banded 42-pounder as still being mounted at this time. Johnson, *Defense of Charleston*, 120–32; *O.R.A.*, 28 (Pt. 1):616–22; Gordon, *War Diary*, 197–203; Gillmore, *Military and Engineer Operations*, 63–65; Dahlgren, *Memoirs*, 313; Farenholt, *Monitor Catskill*, 8–11; *O.R.N.*, 14:514–17, 521, 524; Oscar Charles Badger Paper, August 26, 1863, South Caroliniana Library, University of South Carolina, Columbia, South Carolina.

17. *O.R.N.*, 14:530–32, 566–67.

18. Gordon, *War Diary*, 206–10; Fox Letterbooks, August 27, 1863; Dickey, *Eighty-fifth Regiment*, 279; Bowditch, "Letters," 440–41; Emilio, *Brave Black Regiment*, 118–20; Alexander Vance Diary, September 1, 1863, Fort Sumter National Monument, Sullivan's Island, South Carolina.

19. Izlar, *Edisto Rifles*, 40–41; Pressley, "Wee Nee Volunteers," 155–68; Roman, *Military Operations*, 2:127–30; Burton, *Siege of Charleston*, 178; *O.R.A.*, 28 (Pt. 1):445–52; Harleston, "Battery Wagner," 8; Harris Papers, D. Harris to wife, September 9, 1863.

20. Smith, *Mason Smith*, 64; Harleston, "Battery Wagner," 5; Cummins, "Signal Corps," 104.

21. Harleston, "Battery Wagner," 3–7.

22. Ibid.

23. Roman, *Military Operations*, 2:131, 152; Elliott Papers, S. Elliott to wife, 20, 28, and 31 August, 6 September, 1863; *Charleston Mercury*, September 2, 1863; *O.R.A.*, 28 (Pt. 2):322.

24. *O.R.N.*, 14:530–32; Gordon *War Diary*, 206–10.

25. Alexander F. Warley, CSN, took the picket vessel *Juno* in search of his brother. He braved the bombardment on September 6, to approach Morris Island, but was unable to gain any information. *O.R.N.*, 14:536–37; Stowits, *One-Hundredth New York*, 219–20; Pressley, "Wee Nee Volunteers," 158–59; Gilchrist, "Defense of Morris Island," 385;

Eldridge, *Third New Hampshire,* 392; Stowits, *One Hundredth New York,* 219–20; Roe, *Twenty-fourth Massachusetts,* 222.

26. *O.R.A.,* 28 (Pt. 1):218.
27. *O.R.A.,* 28 (Pt. 1):26, 299–303; *O.R.N.,* 14:558–67.
28. *O.R.A.,* 28 (Pt. 1):27, 208–9, 299–303; Little, *Seventh Regiment,* 176–80.
29. *O.R.A.,* 28 (Pt. 1):100–103.
30. *O.R.A.,* 28 (Pt. 1):480–82; Pressley, "Wee Nee Volunteers," 160–62; Frank Moore, *The Civil War in Song and Story* (New York: P. F. Collier, 1889), 137; Harleston, "Battery Wagner," 6.
31. Norris, "Signal Corps," 105; Gilchrist, "Defense of Morris Island," 385; Harleston, "Battery Wagner," 9; *O.R.A.,* 28 (Pt. 1):490, 531–32.
32. Olmstead, *Reminiscences of Service,* 14; Harleston, "Battery Wagner," 9.
33. Roman, *Military Operations,* 2:132; *O.R.A.,* 28 (Pt. 1):100–103, 479–92; Honour Papers, T. Honour to wife, September 7, 1863.
34. *O.R.A.,* 28 (Pt. 1):106–10, 400–405.
35. *O.R.A.,* 28 (Pt. 1):479–92, 520–21, 522–23, 540–41; Pressley, "Wee Nee Volunteers," 166–70; Elmore, "Incidents of Service," 540; Gilchrist, "Confederate Defenses of Morris Island," 394; Harleston, "Battery Wagner," 11–13; Cummins, "Signal Corps," 104; Thomas A. Huguenin Papers, Autobiography, Duke University Library, Durham, North Carolina.
36. Eldridge, *Third New Hampshire,* 364, Dickey, *Eighty-fifth Regiment,* 280; Robert Meade to Richard Meade, September 8, 1863, Robert L. Meade Papers, Marine Corps Research Center, Quantico, Virginia.
37. Gillmore, *Military and Engineer Operations,* 75; Copp; *Reminiscences of the War,* 269–74; William L. Hyde, *History of the One hundred and twelfth Regiment New York Volunteers* (Freedonia: McKinstry and Company, 1866), 54–55; Price, *Ninety-seventh Regiment,* 198; Clark, *Thirty-ninth Regiment,* 145; Toutelloutte, *History of Company K,* 174; Little, *Seventh Regiment,* 159–61; Eldridge, *Third New Hampshire,* 365–66; Dickey, *Eighty-fifth regiment,* 280; *O.R.N.,* 14:456–550; Wilder Papers, undated letter of W. Pratt to wife, F. Peet to B. Wilder, September 7, 1914; *Washington National Tribune,* 12 and 20 August 1914; Copp, *Reminiscences of the War,* 272–74; Frederick T. Peet, *Civil War Letters and Documents of Frederick Towlinson Peet* (Newport, R.I., 1917), 239–41; Meade Papers, Robert Meade to Richard Meade, September 8, 1863.
38. Harleston, "Battery Wagner," 13; *O.R.A.,* 28 (Pt. 1):27, 108–9, 401–2; Harris Papers, Harris to his wife, September 9, 1863; Lopp, *Reminiscences of the War,* 272–74; Wilder Papers, undated *Washington National Tribune* article by James Rondlett.

Conclusion

1. *O.R.N.,* 14:549–79; Frederick Stow Papers, F. Stow to father, 6–7 September 1863.

2. *O.R.N.*, 14:608–09.

3. *O.R.N.*, 14:606–40; Roe, *Twenty-Fourth Massachusetts*, 222–33.

4. *O.R.N.*, 14:566–79, 606–40; Gordon, *War Diary*, 202, 216.

5. Letter of Stephen Elliott to his sister, September 9, 1863, Francis Williamson Collection, Parris Island Museum, Parris Island, South Carolina; Elliott Papers, S. Elliott to wife, September 6, 1863; *O.R.A.*, 28 (Pt. 2):119.

6. Stryker, "Three Days in the Civil War."

7. Mowris, *One hundred and seventeenth Regiment*, 84; Gordon, *War Diary*, 211; Little, *Seventh Regiment*, 160–67, 184–89; *Maine Regiment*, 151; *O.R.A.*, 28 (Pt. 1):37–38; Fox, "Letterbooks," August 27, September 7–October 1, 1863.

8. *O.R.N.*, 14:675–84, 15:60–97; Gordon, *War Diary*, 222, 244–46; Dahlgren, *Memoirs*, 415–16, 507, 575–89.

9. *O.R.A.*, 28 (Pt. 1):31–38; *O.R.N.*, 16:429–55; Gordon, *War Diary*, 244–46; Dahlgren, *Memoirs*, 415, 507, 575–80; Welles, *Diary*, 1:466–67, 475, 520–21; Eldridge, *Third New Hampshire*, 393; Bowditch, "Letters," 440; Vance Diary, September 1–8, 1863.

10. The "New Lines" along the Stono River were built at the request of Colonel C. H. Simonton. They were started on August 9, 1863, and completed in November 1863. They were sometimes referred to as the "Simonton Lines." *O.R.A.*, 28 (Pt. 2):7–9, 31–34, 73–76, 140, 151, 159, 230, 249, 268, 272, 315, 324–28, 385; *Charleston Mercury*, August 18, 1863.

11. Colonel David B. Harris died of yellow fever in Charleston on October 10, 1864. Wise, *Lifeline of the Confederacy*, 122–28; Peck, "Four Years under Fire at Charleston," 364; Horatio L. West, "The Blockading Service," *Military Order of the Loyal Legion of the United States. The Commandery of the State of Illinois*, 4 vols. (Chicago: A. C. McClurg, 1891–1912), 2:241–43.

12. *Charleston Courier*, August 10, 1863; *Maine Regiment*, 108–9; Stowits, *One Hundredth New York*, 193; *O.R.A.*, 28 (Pt. 1):328–31; A. R. Barlow, *Company G* (Syracuse: A. H. Hull, 1899), 195–96; Bowditch, "Letters," 441, 446; George H. Gordon Papers, G. Gordon to G. Stearns, June 13, 1864, Lincoln Memorial Shrine, Redlands, California.

13. *Armored Vessels*, 585–96; Dahlgren, *Memoirs*, 545, 560; *O.R.N.*, 14:590–605; Stephen R. Wise, "United States Monitors of 1863," *United States Navy*, vol. 1, (September 1976): 35–40.

14. *O.R.A.*, 28 (Pt. 1):39–40, 90–92, 116; Eldridge, *Third New Hampshire*, 1013–1014.

15. Ross, *Angel of the Battlefield*, 66; Clara Barton Papers, C. Barton to Soldiers Relief Committee, October 10, 1863, C. Barton to I. Barton, October 11, 1863.

Bibliography

Manuscripts

Boston Anthenaeum, Boston, Massachusetts
  Richard H. L. Jewett Papers
Boston Public Library, Boston, Massachusetts
  Thomas W. Higginson Papers
  Robert Gould Shaw Papers
Buffalo Historical Society, Buffalo, New York
  One-hundreth Regiment Veterans Association Papers
  Edward Leigh Cook Papers
College of William and Mary, Williamsburg, Virginia
  William B. Taliaferro Papers
Cornell University Library, Department of Manuscripts and University
Archives, Ithaca, New York
  C. B. Parsons Papers
  B. G. Wilder Collection
Duke University Library, Durham, North Carolina
  John L. Clifton Papers
  David B. Harris Papers
  Thomas A. Huguenin Papers
  Thomas Jordon Papers
  Charles Phineas Lord Papers
  Benjamin M. Stevens Papers
  William S. Stryker Papers
  Artha Brailsford Wescoat Diary
  United States Department of War Ordnance Papers
East Carolina University Library, Greenville, North Carolina
  Sallie Lightfoot Tarleton Papers
  Baron William Henry von Eberstein Papers
Eleutherian Mills Historical Library, Greenville, Delaware
  Samuel F. Du Pont Papers, microfilm edition
Fort Sumter/Moultrie National Monument, Sullivan's Island, South Carolina
  J. T. Chompneys Papers
  Alexander Vance Diary
  D. L. Thompson Papers
  Wilson Letter
Harvard University, Houghton Library, Cambridge, Massachusetts
  Robert Gould Shaw Collection

Kansas State Historical Society, Topeka, Kansas
    George S. Stearns Papers
Library of Congress, Washington, D.C.
    American Freedmen's Inquiry Commission
    Clara Barton Collection
    P. G. T. Beauregard Papers
    John Dahlgren Papers
    Pickens-Bonham Papers
    John Rodgers Papers
    Alfred Roman Papers
    Gideon Welles Papers
    Edward Willis Papers
Lincoln Memorial Shrine, Redlands, California
    George H. Gordon Papers
Marine Corps Historical Division, Washington Navy Yard, Washington, D.C.
    Personal Papers Collection
    Frederick T. Peet Collection
Marine Corps Research Center, Quantico, Virginia
    Robert L. Meade Papers
Massachusetts Historical Society, Boston, Massachusetts
    Luis Emilio Scrapbooks
    Fifty-fourth Massachusetts Infantry Regimental Papers
    Charles Fox Letterbooks
    Photograph Collection
    Robert Gould Shaw Collection and Manuscripts
Massachusetts National Guard Supply Depot, Natick, Massachusetts
    Letters from Officers
    Muster Roles of the 54th Massachusetts
National Archives, Washington, D.C.
    Record Group 24
        Bureau of Naval Personnel, Deck Logs
    Record Group 94
        American Freedmen's Inquiry Commission
    Record Group 109
        Charleston Engineer Department Records
        Compiled Service Records of Confederate Soldiers
        Department of South Carolina, Georgia and Florida Records,
            Letters Sent
        Regimental Day Books
        William H. Echols, Letters Sent
    Record Group 127
        Records of the United States Marine Corps
New York Public Library, New York, New York
    Cabot J. Russell Papers

Parris Island Museum, Marine Corps Recruit Depot, Parris Island, South Carolina
    Francis Williamson Collection
South Carolina Department of Archives and History, Columbia, South Carolina
    Governor M. L. Bonham Papers
    Account of Negro Prisoners of War, 1863–1864, General Assembly Papers
South Carolina Historical Society, Charleston, South Carolina
    William C. Bee and Company Papers
    Cheves Papers
    Confederate States of America Papers
    John Johnson Papers
    H. Lee Papers
    Records of the 1st Military District
    A. T. Smythe Papers
South Caroliniana Library, University of South Carolina, Columbia, South Carolina
    Oscar Charles Badger Papers
    Milledge Luke Bonham Papers
    Burn Family Papers
    William A. Gyles Papers
    Theodore Honour Papers
    Alfred Marple Diary and Letters
    Williams Middleton Papers
    Orville Repton Papers
Southern Historical Collection, University of North Carolina, Chapel Hill, North Carolina
    Thomas Lanier Clingman Papers
    Confederate Engineer Records
    Jeremy Francis Gilmer Papers
    Grimball Family Papers
    Elliott and Gonzales Family Papers
    Habersham, Elliott Papers
    Hatch Family Papers
    Hughes Family Papers
    Charles Hart Olmstead Papers
United States Military History Institute, Carlise Army Barracks, Carlise, Pennsylvania
    J. Henry Beatty Papers
    John C. Burce Papers
    James Clegg Papers
    Robert Dysart Diary
    Quincy Adams Gillmore Papers
    John Guest Papers
    Carroll E. Kingsley Papers

Perry Mitchel Papers
M. L. S. Jackson Diary
George C. Remey Papers
John W. Sanborn Papers
A. J. Sargent Papers
Theodore W. Skinner Papers
Andre J. Smith Papers
Orlando Soutelle Papers
James Sheppard Papers
Frederick Stow Papers
Edward Shuey Papers
John W. Turner Papers
Washington and Lee University, Lexington, Virginia
    David F. Jamison Papers
West Virginia University Library, Morgantown, West Virginia
    John W. M. Appleton Letterbook and Journal

Newspapers

Beaufort Free South
Boston Daily Journal
Boston Globe
Boston Herald
(Boston) The Liberator
Buffalo Morning Express
Charleston Daily Courier
Charleston Mercury
Harpers Weekly
New York National Anti-Slavery Standard
New York Times
Port Royal (Hilton Head) New South
Richmond Dispatch
Washington National Tribune
Xenia (Ohio) Torchlight

Printed Primary Sources, Public Documents, and Reminiscences

Allen, W. "The Defenses of Charleston Harbor in the Civil War." *New England and Yale Review* 53 (November 1890): 406–10.
Appleton, John W. "That Night at Fort Wagner by One Who Was There." *Putnam's Magazine* 4 (1896): 9–16.
Ashe, S. R. "Life at Fort Wagner." *Confederate Veteran* 35 (July 1927): 254–56.
Barlow, A. R. *Company G.* Syracuse: A. W. Hall, 1899.
Beauregard, Pierre G. T. "The Defense of Charleston." In *Battles and*

Leaders of the Civil War. 4 vols, 4:1–23. New York: Thomas Yoseloff, 1966.

————. "Torpedo Service in Harbor and Water Defences of Charleston." *Southern Historical Society Papers* 5 (April 1878): 146–61.

Bedel, John. "Historical Sketch of the Third New Hampshire Volunteers." *The Granite Monthly* 3 (September 1880): 516–34.

Beecher, Herbert W. *History of the First Light Battery Connecticut Volunteers, 1861–1865.* 2 vols. New York: A. T. Dela Mare Ptgard Publishing Company, 1901.

Belknap, George E. "Reminiscence of the New Ironsides Off Charleston." *United Service* 1 (January 1879): 63–82.

————. "Reminiscences of the Siege of Charleston." *Military Historical Society of Massachusetts Papers* 7:155–208.

Boggs, William R. *Military Reminiscences of General Wm. R. Boggs.* Durham: Seeman Printing, 1913.

Bowditch, Charles P. "War Letters of Charles P. Bowditch." *Massachusetts Historical Society Proceedings* 57 (February–April 1924): 412–73.

Briggs, Walter D. *Civil War Surgeon in a Colored Regiment.* Berkeley and Los Angeles: University of California Press, 1960.

Bryant, Elias A. *The Diary of Elias Bryant.* Concord: Rumford Press, n.d.

Caldwell, Charles K. *The Old Sixth Regiment: Its War Record.* New Haven: Tuttle, Morehouse and Taylor, 1875.

Carleton, William J. *Company D: The Die No Mores of the 48th N.Y.S.V.* n.p., 1912.

Clark, Charles M. *The History of the Thirty-ninth Regiment Illinois Volunteer Veteran Infantry (Yates Phalanx).* Chicago: Veteran Association of the Regiment, 1889.

Clark, James H. *The Iron Hearted Regiment, An Account of the Battles, Marches and Gallant Deeds Performed by the 115th Regiment New York Volunteers.* Albany: J. Munsell, 1865.

Coastal Heritage Society. "Coastal Current Insight: Confederate and Union Military." Savannah, Ga.: Coastal Heritage Society, n.d.

Cobb, S. J. "Service of Tar Heels." *Confederate Veteran* 8 (May 1900): 215–16.

Coffin, Charles Carleton. *Four Years of Fighting.* Boston: Tichnor and Fields, 1886.

Committee of the Regimental Association. *Maine Regiment: The Story of the Eleventh.* New York: Little, 1896.

Confederate States of America. *Journal of the Congress of the Confederate States of America 1861–1865.* 7 vols. Washington: Government Printing Office, 1904–05.

Copp, Eldridge J. *Reminiscences of the War of the Rebellion.* Nashua: Telegraph Publishing Company, 1911.

Croom, Wendell D. *The War: History of Company C, Sixth Georgia.* Fort Valley: Georgia Advertiser Office, 1879.

Crowley, R. O. "The Torpedo Service." *Century Illustrated Magazine* 56 (June 1898): 290–300.

Culp, Edward C. *25th Ohio Veteran Volunteer Infantry.* Topeka: George W. Crane and Company, 1885.

Cummins, Edward H. "The Signal Corps in the Confederate Army." *Southern Historical Society Papers* 16 (January–December 1888): 91–107.

Dahlgren, Madeleine V. *Memoirs of John H. Dahlgren.* Boston: Osgood, 1882.

Davis, W. W. H. *History of the 104th Pennsylvania.* Philadelphia: Rogers, 1886.

Denison, Frederick *Shot and Shell.* Providence: J. A. and R. A. Reid, 1879.

Dickey, Luther S. *History of the Eighty-fifth Regiment Pennsylvania Volunteer Infantry 1861–1865.* New York: J. C. and W. E. Powers, 1915.

Doubleday, Abner. *Reminiscences of Forts Sumter and Moultrie in 1860–1861.* New York: Harper Brothers, 1876.

Douglass, Frederick. *Life and Times of Frederick Douglass.* Hartford: Park Publishing Company, 1881.

Douglass, Lewis. "From Charleston." *Douglass Monthly Magazine*, August, 1863.

Drayton, Percival. *Naval Letters from Captain Percival Drayton, 1861–1865.* N.p., n.d.

DuBose, Henry Kershaw. *The History of Company B, Twenty-first Regiment South Carolina Volunteers Confederate States Provisional Army.* Columbia: R. L. Bryan, 1909.

Duncan, Russell, ed. *Blue Eyed Child of Fortune: Civil War Letters of Robert Gould Shaw.* Athens: University of Georgia Press, 1992.

Dyer, Elisha. *Annual Report of the Adjutant General of the State of Rhode Island and Providence Plantations for the Year 1865.* Providence: E. L. Freeman and Son, 1895.

Edwards, W. H. *A Condensed History of the Seventeenth Regiment S.C.V., C.S.A.* Columbia: R. L. Bryan, 1908.

Eldridge, Daniel. *The Third New Hampshire Regiment.* Boston: E. B. Stillings, 1893.

Elmore, Albert Rhett. "Incidents of Service with the Confederate Light Dragoons." *Confederate Veteran* 24 (December 1916), 538–43.

Emilio, Luis F. *A Brave Black Regiment.* New York: Arno Press, 1969.

Ericsson, John. "The Early Monitors." In *Battles and Leaders in the Civil War.* 4 vols, 1:30–31. New York: Thomas Yoseloff, 1956.

Farenholt, Oscar W. *The Monitor Catskill: A Year's Reminiscences.* San Francisco: Shannon, 1912.

Fisk, Joel C., and William H. D. Blake. *A Condensed History of the 56th Regiment New York Veteran Volunteer Infantry.* Newburgh: Journal Printing House, 1906.

Foote, John A. "Notes on the Life of Admiral Foote." In *Battles and Leaders of the Civil War.* 4 vols, 1:347. New York: Thomas Yoseloff, 1956.

Fox, Charles Bernard. *Record of the Service of the Fifty-fifth Regiment of Massachusetts Volunteer Infantry*. Cambridge: John Wilson and Son, 1868.

Galloway, Richard P. *One Battle Too Many: The Writings of Simon Bolivar Hulbert, Private, Company E, 100th Regiment, New York State Volunteers 1861–1864*. Privately Published, 1987.

Gilchrist, Robert C. "Confederate Defense of Morris Island." In *Charleston Yearbook, 1884*. Charleston: News and Courier Press, 1884.

Gillmore, Quincy Adams. *Engineer and Artillery Operations Against the Defenses of Charleston Harbor in 1863*. New York: Norstrand, 1865.

––––––. "Siege and Capture of Fort Pulaski." In *Battles and Leaders of the Civil War*. 4 vols, 2:1–12. New York: Thomas Yoseloff, 1956.

Girard, C. F. "Visit to the Confederate States of America in 1863." *Confederate Centennial Studies*. Tuscaloosa: Confederate Publishing Company, 1956.

Glassell, T. W. "Reminiscences of Torpedo Service in Charleston Harbor." *Southern Historical Society Papers* 4 (November 1877): 225–35.

Glazier, Willard. *The Capture, the Prison Pen, and the Escape*. New York: United States Publishing Company, 1868.

Gleaves, Albert. *Life and Letters of Rear Admiral Stephen B. Luce*. New York: Putnam, 1925.

Gordon, George Henry. *A War Diary of Events in the War of the Great Rebellion: 1863–1865*. Boston: Osgood, 1882.

Hagood, Johnson. *Memoirs of the War of Secession*. Columbia: The State Company, 1910.

Hall, Henry, and James Hall. *Cayuga in the Field*. Syracuse: Truair, Smith and Company, 1873.

Hamilton, Henry S. *Reminiscences of a Veteran*. Concord: Republican Press Association, 1897.

Hamilton, John A. "General Stephen Elliott, Lieutenant James A. Hamilton and Elliott's Torpedoes." *Southern Historical Society Papers* 10 (April 1882): 183–86.

Harleston, John. "Battery Wagner on Morris Island." *South Carolina Historical Magazine* 57 (January 1956): 1–13.

Hawkes, Esther Hill. *A Woman Doctor's Civil War: Esther Hill Hawks Diary*. Edited by Gerald Schwartz. Columbia: University of South Carolina Press, 1984.

Hayes, John D., ed. *Samuel Francis Du Pont: A Selection From his Civil War Letters*. 3 vols. Ithaca: Cornell University Press, 1969.

Higginson, Thomas W. *Army Life in a Black Regiment*. Williamstown, Mass.: Corner House Publishers, 1984.

Hill, Jim Dan. *The Civil War Sketchbook of Charles Ellery Stedman*. San Rafael: Presidio Press, 1976.

Holland, Rupert Sargent, ed. *Letters and Diary of Laura M. Towne*. New York: Negro Universities Press, 1969.

Hudson, Joshua Hilary. *Sketches and Reminiscences*. Columbia: The State Company, 1903.

Hunter, Alvah Folsom. *A Year on a Monitor and the Destruction of Fort Sumter.* Edited by Craig L. Symonds. Columbia: University of South Carolina Press, 1987.

Hyde, William L. *History of the One Hundred and Twelfth Regiment New York Volunteers.* Fredonia: McKinstry and Company, 1866.

Inglesby, Charles. *Historic Sketch of the First Regiment of South Carolina Artillery (Regulars).* Charleston: Walker, Evans, Cogswell, 1890.

Izlar, William Volmore. *A Sketch of the War Record of the Edisto Rifles: 1861–1865.* Columbia: State Printer, 1914.

Jacobi, C. *Gerzogenen Geschuetzo der Amerikaner bei der Belagerung Von Charleston.* Translated by Anne Beehler. Berlin: Strokker, 1886.

James, Martin S. "War Reminiscences." In *Personal Narratives of the Events in the War of the Rebellion.* Providence: Snow and Farnham Company, 1911.

Jervey, Theodore D. "Charleston During the Civil War." In *Annual Report of the American Historical Association for the Year 1913.* Vol. 1. Washington: Government Printing Office, 1915.

Jewett, Albert Henry Clay. *A Boy Goes to War.* Bloomington, 1944.

Johnson, John. *The Defense of Charleston Harbor.* Charleston: Walker, Evans, Cogswell, 1890.

Jones, Garth W. "The Assault on Fort Wagner." In *Military Order of the Loyal Legion of the United States, Wisconsin Commandery,* 1:9–30. Milwaukee: Buddick, Armitage and Allen, 1891.

Jones, Iredell. "Letters from Fort Sumter in 1862 and 1863." *Southern Historical Society Papers,* 12 (January–June, 1884): 5–7, 137–39, 160–62, 212–15, 253–58, 543–46.

Jones, Samuel. *The Siege of Charleston.* Charleston: Walker, Evans, Cogswell, 1890.

Jordon, Thomas. "Seacoast Defences of South Carolina and Georgia." *Southern Historical Society Papers* 1 (June 1876):403–7.

Kendricken, Paul Henry. *Memoirs of Paul Henry Kendricken.* Boston, 1910.

Kimball, Orville Samuel. *History and Personal Sketches of Company I, 103 NYSV 1862–1864.* Elmira: The Facts and Printing Company, 1900.

Linehan, John C. "War Pictures." *The Granite Monthly* 18 (June 1895): 83–88, 143–51, 208–15, 307–14, 356–60, 456–57.

Little, Henry F. *The Seventh Regiment.* Concord: J. Evan, 1896.

Long, A. L. "Letter." *Southern Historical Society Papers* 2 (November, 1876): 239–40.

———. "Seacoast Defences of South Carolina and Georgia." *Southern Historical Society Papers* 1 (February, 1876): 103–7.

McCabe, W. Gordon. "McCabe's Impression of the Bombardment of Charleston." *South Carolina Historical Magazine* 71 (October, 1970): 266–69.

McGarth, Franklin. *The History of the 127th New York Volunteer Monitors."* N.p., 1898.

McKee, James Harvey, *Back in War Times*. New York: E. Bailey, 1903.

Martin, David G. *Carl Bornemann's Regiment: The Forty-first New York Infantry (DeKalb Regt.) in the Civil War*. Highstown, New Jersey: Longstreet House, 1987.

Metcalf, Edwin. "Personal Incidents in the Early Campaigns of the Third Regiment Rhode Island Volunteers and the Tenth Corps. In *Personal Narratives of the Battles of the Rebellion*. Providence: Sidney S. Rider, 1879.

Moore, Francis. *Ghosts or Devils I'm Done*. Deadwood, S. D.: Cole and Son, 1908.

Moore, Frank, comp. *The Civil War in Song and Story*. New York: P. F. Collier, 1889.

Mott, Smith B. *The Campaigns of the Fifty-second Pennsylvania Volunteer Infantry*. Philadelphia: Lippincott, 1911.

Mowris, J. A. *A History of the One Hundred and Seventeenth Regiment New York Volunteers*. Hartford: Case, Lockwood and Company. 1866.

Nichols, James Moses. *Perry's Saints*. Boston: D. Lothrop, 1886.

Official Atlas of the Civil War. New York: Thomas Yoseloff, 1956.

Olmstead, Charles H. "The Memoirs of Charles F. Olmstead." *Georgia Historical Quarterly* 44 (1960): 56–73, 186–201, 306–20, 419–34.

———. *Reminiscences of Service with the First Volunteer Regiment of Georgia*. Savannah: J. H. Estrill, 1879.

Owen, Dock. *Camp Fire and Reminiscences*. N.p., n.d.

Palmer, Abraham John. *The History of the Forty-eighth Regiment New York State Volunteers*. Brooklyn: Veteran Association of the Regiment, 1885.

Pearson, Elizabeth Ware. *Letters from Port Royal*. New York: Arno Press, 1969.

Peet, Frederick T. *Civil War Letters and Documents of Frederick Tomlinson Peet*. Newport, R.I., 1917.

———. *Personal Experiences in the Civil War*. New York: privately printed, 1905.

Peck, W. F. G. "Four Years Under Fire at Charleston." *Harpers New Monthly Magazine* 31 (August 1865): 358–66.

Perkins, Francis Beecher. "Two Years With a Colored Regiment." *New England Magazine* 17 (1892–98): 533–43.

"Poetry and Incidents." In *Rebellion Record: A Diary of American Events, 1860–1864*. Vol. 8. New York: D. Van Nostrand, 1864.

Porter, David D. *The Naval History of the Civil War*. New York: Sherman Publishing Company, 1886.

Porter, John A. "Personal Recollections of the Attack on Fort Wagner." Edited by James A. Chisman. *South Carolina Historical Magazine* 81 (July 1980): 245–57.

Powe, James Harrington. *Reminiscences and Sketches of Confederate Times by One Who Lived Through Them*. Columbia, R. L. Bryan, 1909.

Pressley, John G. "The Wee Nee Volunteers of Williamsburg District South

Carolina in the First (Hagood's) Regiment." *Southern Historical Society Papers* 16 (January–December, 1888): 116–94.

Price, Isaiah. *History of the Ninety-Seventh Regiment Pennsylvania Volunteer Infantry*. Philadelphia, 1875.

Punch Magazine. "The Great Cannon Game." (May 9, 1863): 190–91.

Raines, G. J. "Torpedoes." *Southern Historical Society Papers*, 3 (May–June 1877): 255–60.

Redkey, Edwin S., ed. *A Grand Army of Black Men: Letters from African American Soldiers in the Union Army, 1861–1865*. Cambridge: University Press, 1992.

Ripley, Roswell S. *Correspondence Relating to Fortification of Morris Island*. New York: J. J. Coulon, 1878.

Ripley, Warren, ed. *Siege Train: The Journal of a Confederate Artilleryman in the Defense of Charleston*. Columbia: University of South Carolina Press, 1986.

Rockwell, Alfred P. "The Operations Against Charleston." *Military Historical Society of Massachusetts Papers* 9:159–93.

Roe, Alfred S. *The Twenty-Fourth Massachusetts Volunteers, 1861–1866*. Worcester: Twenty-fourth Veteran Association, 1907.

Rodgers, C. R. P. "Du Pont's Attack at Charleston." In *Battles and Leaders in the Civil War*. 4 vols., 1:32–47. New York: Thomas Yoseloff, 1956.

Rogers, Seth. "Letters of Dr. Seth Rogers, 1862, 1863." *Massachusetts Historical Society Proceedings* 43 (October, 1909–June 1910): 337–98.

Roman, Alfred. *The Military Operations of General Beauregard*. 2 vols. New York: Harper and Brothers, 1884.

"Running the Blockade: Daring Exploits at Charleston in War Times." *Southern Historical Society Papers* 24 (January–December 1896).

Savannah Morning News. *Historical Sketch of the Savannah Volunteer Battalion*. Savannah: Morning News Steam Printers, 1886.

Scheibert, Justus. *Seven Months in the Rebel States During the North American War, 1863*. Translated by Joseph C. Hayes. Tuscaloosa: Confederate Publishing Company, 1858.

Scheliha, Victor Ernst Karl Rudolph Von. *A Treatise on Coast Defence*. London: E. and F. N. Spon, 1868.

Secretary of the Navy. *Report of the Secretary of the Navy in Relation to Armored Vessels*. Washington: Government Printing Office, 1864.

Seymour, Thomas. "Notes and Queries." *Southern Historical Society Papers* 10 (January–February 1882):238–39.

Shaw, Robert G. *Memorial*. Cambridge: Cambridge University Press, 1864.

Shaw, Robert Gould. "Letters." *Magazine of History* 18 (1914): 226–31.

Sixty-Seventh Ohio Veteran Volunteer Infantry. Massillon: Ohio Printers and Publishers Company, 1922.

Smith, Daniel Elliott Huger. *Mason Smith Family Letters, 1860–1868*. Columbia: University of South Carolina Press, 1950.

Smith, Jacob. *Camps and Campaigns of the 107th Regiment Ohio Volunteer Infantry*. N.p., 1910.

Soley, James Russell. "Minor Operations of the South Atlantic Squadron under Du Pont." In *Battles and Leaders of the Civil War*. 4 vols. 1:23–27. New York: Thomas Yoseloff, 1956.

Stevens, Hazard. "Military Operations in South Carolina in 1862, Against Charleston, Port Royal Ferry, James Island, Secessionville." *Military Historical Society of Massachusetts Papers* 9:111–58.

Stevens, Thomas H. "The Boat Attack On Sumter." *Battles and Leaders in the Civil War*. 4 vols. 1:47–51. New York: Thomas Yoseloff, 1956.

Stevenson, Brenda, ed. *The Journals of Charlotte Forten Grimke*. New York: Oxford University Press, 1988.

Stoddard, George. "The 100th Regiment of Folly Island." *Niagara Frontier* 1 (1954): 77–81, 113–16.

Stories of Our Soldiers. Collected by the *Boston Journal*. Boston: Journal Newspaper Company, 1893.

Stowits, Smith B. *History of the One-Hundredth New York Volunteers*. Buffalo: Matthewes and Warren, 1870.

Stryker, William S. "The Swamp Angel." In *Battles and Leaders of the Civil War*. 4 vols. 4:72–74. New York: Thomas Yoseloff, 1956.

———. "The Swamp Angel: The Gun Used in Firing on Charleston in 1863." *Magazine of American History* 16 (December 1886): 553–60.

Thompson, Robert Means, and Wainwright, Richard, eds. *Confidential Correspondence of Gustavus Vasa Fox: Assistant Secretary of the Navy, 1861–1865*. 2 vols. New York: DeVinne Press, 1918.

Todd, William. *The Seventy-Ninth Highlanders New York Volunteers in the War of the Rebellion, 1861–1864*. Albany: Brandau and Boston, 1886.

Toomb, James H. "The Last Obstructions in Charleston Harbor, 1863." *Confederate Veteran* 23 (1924): 98–99.

———. "Submarines and Torpedo Boats." *Confederate Veteran* 34 (April 1914): 168–69.

Totten, Joseph C. *Report of the Chief Engineer on the Subject of National Defences*. Washington: A. Boyd Hamilton, 1851.

Toutelloutte, Jerome. *A History of Company K of the Seventh Connecticut Volunteer Infantry in the Civil War*. N.p., 1910.

Trumbull, H. Clay. *The Knightly Soldier*. Philadelphia: John D. Wattles, 1892.

Twiggs, H. D. D. "The Defence of Battery Wagner." *Southern Historical Society Papers* 20 (January–December 1892): 166–83.

———. "Perilous Adventure at Battery Wagner." *Confederate Veteran* 12 (March 1904): 104–6.

United States Congress. *Report of the Joint Committee on the Conduct of the War*. Rep. Comm. No. 108, vol. 4, pt. 3, 37th Congress, 3rd Sess., 415–21.

United States of America. *Medical and Surgical History of the War of the Rebellion*. 3 vols. Report Extract of Surgeon J. J. Craven. Washington: Government Printing Office, 1870.

Vizetelly, Frank. "Charleston Under Fire." *Cornhill Magazine* 10 (July 1864): 99–110.

————. "Charleston Under Fire." Edited by Richard Warren. *Confederate Historical Society Journal* 18 (Autumn 1990): 52–63.

————. "When Charleston Was Under Fire." *New Age Magazine* 15 (September 1911): 217–27.

Voris, Alvin C. "Charleston in the Rebellion." In *Sketches of War History, 1861–1865*, 292–341. Cincinnati: Robert Clarke, 1888.

Walkley, Stephen. *History of the Seventh Connecticut Volunteer Infantry.* Southington, 1905.

War of the Rebellion: Official Records of the Union and Confederate Armies in the War of the Rebellion. 128 vols. Washington: Government Printing Office, 1902.

War of the Rebellion: Official Records of the Union and Confederate Navies in the War of the Rebellion. 31 vols. Washington: Government Printing Office, 1901.

Welles, Gideon. *Diary of Gideon Welles.* 3 vols. Boston: Houghton Mifflin Company, 1911.

Wells, Edward L. *A Sketch of the Charleston Light Dragoons.* Charleston: Lucas, Richardson and Company, 1911.

Wheaton, John C. *Reminiscences of the Chatham Artillery During the War 1861–1865.* Savannah: Press of the Morning News, 1887.

Williams, Charles H. "The Last Tour of Duty at the Siege of Charleston." In *Personal Narratives of the Events in the War of the Rebellion.* Providence: N. Bangs Williams and Company, 1882.

Wolsley, Viscount. "An English View of the Civil War." *North American Review* 149 (July–December 1889): 594–606.

Woodford, Stewart L. "The Story of Fort Sumter." In *Personal Recollections of the War of the Rebellion. Military Order of the Loyal Legion of the United States.* Vol. 1. New York: The Commandary, 1891.

Secondary Sources

Adams, William T. "Guns for the Navy." *Ordnance* 45 (January–February 1961): 508–11.

————. "The Ship Shore Duel." *Ordnance* 45 (May–June 1961): 798–800.

Andrew, J. Cutler. *The South Reports the Civil War.* Princeton: Princeton University Press, 1970.

Ballard, Michael B. *Pemberton: A Biography.* Jackson: University Press of Mississippi, 1991.

Berlin, Iva. *The Black Military Experience.* Cambridge: University Press, 1982.

Birkhimer, William E. *Historical Sketch of the Organization, Administration, Material and Tactics of the United States Artillery.* Washington: James J. Chapman, 1884.

Bowen, James L. *Massachusetts in the War.* Springfield: Clark W. Bryan Company, 1889.

Brooks, Ulysses Robert, ed. *Stories of the Confederacy*. Columbia: The State Company, 1912.

Brown, J. Willard. *The Signal Corps, USA*. New York: Arno Press, 1974.

Brown, William Wells. *The Negro in the American Rebellion*. Boston: Lee and Shepard, 1867.

Burchard, Peter. *One Gallant Rush*. New York: St. Martin, 1965.

Burton, E. Milby. *The Siege of Charleston 1861–1865*. Columbia: University of South Carolina Press, 1970.

Carse, Robert. *Department of the South*. Columbia: State Publishing Company, 1961.

Church, Henry F. "The Defenses of Charleston." *Military Engineer* 23 (1931): 11–14.

Civil War Naval Ordnance. Washington, D.C.: Naval History Division, 1969.

Clark, Walter. *Histories of the Several Regiments from North Carolina 1861–65*. 3 vols. Raleigh: E. M. Uzzell, 1901.

Cornish, Dudley Taylor. *The Sable Arm*. New York: W. W. Norton, 1966.

Cullum, George W. *Biographical Register of the Officers and Graduates of West Point*. Vols. 1 and 2. Boston: Houghton, Mifflin and Company, 1891.

Daniels, Jonathan. *Prince of Carpetbaggers*. Philadelphia: J. B. Lippincott Company, 1958.

DeBois, W. E. Burghardt. *John Brown*. New York: International Publishers, 1962.

Epler, Percy H. *The Life of Clara Barton*. New York: MacMillan Company, 1927.

Evans, Clement A., ed. *Confederate Military History*. Vol. 5. Ellison Capers. *South Carolina*. Atlanta: Confederate Publishing Company, 1899.

Fincher, Jack. "I felt Freedom in my Bones." *Smithsonian* 21 (October, 1990): 46–63.

Fowler, G. L. "Ericsson's Monitor and Later Turret Ships." *Engineering Magazine* 6 (October, 1897): 111–19.

Fraser, Walter J. *Charleston! Charleston!: The History of a Southern City*. Columbia: University of South Carolina Press, 1989.

Freeman, Douglas Southall. *R. E. Lee: A Biography*. 4 vols. New York: Charles Scribner's Sons, 1962.

Glatthaar, Joseph T. *Forged in Battle: The Civil War Alliance of Black Soldiers and White Officers*. New York: Free Press, 1990.

Hagy, James W. *To Take Charleston: The Civil War on Folly Island*. Charleston, W.Va.: Pictorial Histories Publishing Company, 1993.

Harrimon, Walter. "General John Bedel." *The Granite Monthly* 3 (September, 1880): 512–15.

Haskins, William Lawrence. *The History of the First Regiment of its Organization in 1821 to January 1st 1876*. Fort Preble, Portland: B. Thurston and Company, 1879.

Higginson, Mary Thacker. *Thomas Wentworth Higginson: The Story of his Life*. Boston: Houghton, Mifflin Company, 1914.

Hippin, James Mason. *Life of Andrew Hull Foote, Rear Admiral United States Navy*. New York: Harper and Brothers, 1874.

Hoole, Stanley W. *Vizetelly Covers the Confederacy*. Tuscaloosa: Confederate Printing Company, 1957.

Irwin, Davis. "Chief Egan's War Record." *American Irish Historical Society Journal*, 7 (1907): 177–82.

Johnson, Robert Erwin. *Rear Admiral John Rodgers*. Annapolis: U.S. Naval Institute Press, 1967.

Jones, Lewis Pinckney. "Ambrosio José Gonzales, A Cuban Patriot in Carolina." *South Carolina Historical Magazine* 56 (April 1955): 67–76.

Jorgensen, Peter C. "The Making of Glory." *Civil War Times Illustrated* 28 (November–December, 1989): 52–59.

Leonard, Mary Hall. *The Days of the Swamp Angel*. New York: Neale Publishing Company, 1914.

Loring, B. U. "The Monitor Weehawken in the Rebellion." *United States Naval Institute Proceedings* 12 (1886): 111–21.

McKay, Martha Nicholson. *When the Tide Turned in the Civil War*. Indianapolis: Hollenbeck, 1929.

McPherson, James. *Marching Toward Freedom*. New York: Alfred A. Knopf, 1967.

Millis, Walter. "The Iron Sea Elephants." *American Neptune* 10 (January 1950): 15–32.

Mitchel, F. A. *Ormsby MacKnight Mitchel: Astronomer and General*. Boston: Houghton, Mifflin and Company, 1887.

Naval History Division. *Rear Admiral John Rodgers*. Annapolis: Naval Government Printing Office, 1961.

Nichols, James L. *Confederate Engineers*. Tuscaloosa: Confederate Publishing Company, 1957.

Pearson, Henry Greenleaf. *The Life of A. Andrew*. 2 vols. Boston: Houghton, Mifflin and Company, 1909.

Pemberton, John C. *Pemberton: Defender of Vicksburg*. Chapel Hill: University of North Carolina Press, 1942.

Perry, Milton F. *Infernal Machines*. Baton Rouge: Louisiana State University Press, 1965.

Phister, Frederick, ed. *New York in the War of the Rebellion* Albany: J. B. Lyon, 1912.

Pickard, Samuel Thomas. *Life and Letters of the John Greenleaf Whittier*. Boston: Houghton, Mifflin, 1894.

Price, Marcus W. "Blockade Running as a Business in South Carolina During the War Between the States, 1861–65." *American Neptune* 9 (January, 1949): 31–62.

———. "Four From Bristow." *American Neptune* 17 (October 1957) 249–61.

———. "Ships that Tested the Blockade on the Carolina Ports." *American Neptune* 8 (April 1948): 196–241.

Quarles, Benjamin. *The Negro in the Civil War*. Boston: Little, Brown, 1953.

Redding, Saunders. "Tonight for Freedom." *American Heritage* (June 1958): 52–55, 90.

Rhett, Claudine. "Frank Harleston—A Hero of Fort Sumter." *Historical Society Papers* 12 (June 1884): 336–42.

Ripley, Warren. *Artillery and Ammunition of the Civil War*. New York: Van Nostrand, Reinhold Company, 1970.

Roberts, William H. "The Neglected Ironclad: A Design and Constructional Analysis of the *U.S.S. New Ironsides*." *Warship International* 26 (June 1989): 109–34.

Rose, Willa Lee. *Rehearsal for Reconstruction: The Port Royal Experiment*. New York: Oxford University Press, 1964.

Ross, Isabel. *Angel of the Battlefield*. New York: Harper and Brothers, 1956.

Russell, Preston. "Glory." *Military Modelling* (June 1990), 342–47.

Smith, Steven D. *Whom We Would Never More See*. Columbia: South Carolina Department of Archives and History, 1993.

Still, William. *Confederate Shipbuilding*. Athens: University of Georgia Press, 1969.

———. *Iron Afloat*. Nasvhille: Vanderbilt University Press, 1971.

Teamah, Robert. *Sketch of the Death of Colonel Robert Gould Shaw*. N.p., n.d.

Tidball, John Caldwell. *Manual of Heavy Artillery Service*. Washington, D.C.: J. J. Chapman, 1880.

Urwin, Gregory J. W. "I Want You to Prove Yourselves Men." *Civil War Times Illustrated* 28 (December 1989): 42–51.

Villard, Oswald, Garrison. "The Submarine and the Torpedo in the Blockade of the Confederacy." *Harper's Magazine* 133 (June–November, 1916): 131–37.

Warner, Ezra. *Generals in Blue: Lives of Union Commanders*. Baton Rouge: Louisiana State University Press, 1964.

———. *Generals in Gray: Lives of the Confederate Commanders*. Baton Rouge: Louisiana State University Press, 1959.

West, Richard S. *Gideon Welles: Lincoln's Naval Department*. Indianapolis: Bobbs-Merrill Company, 1943.

Westwood, Howard C. "Captive Black Union Soldiers in Charleston—What to do?" *Civil War History* 28 (March 1982): 28–44.

———. "Generals David Hunter and Rufus Saxton and Black Soldiers." *South Carolina Historical Magazine* 86 (July 1985): 165–81.

———. "The Cause and Consequence of a Union Black Soldier's Mutiny and Execution." *Civil War History* 31 (September, 1985): 222–35.

Williams, George Washington. *A History of the Negro Troops in the War of the Rebellion 1861–1865*. New York: Bergman Publishers, 1888.

Williams, T. Harry. *P. G. T. Beauregard: Napoleon in Grey*. Baton Rouge: Louisiana State University Press, 1955.

Wise, Stephen R. *Lifeline of the Confederacy: Blockade Running During the Civil War*. Columbia: University of South Carolina Press, 1988.

———. "Magnificent Vessel: The Story of the *New Ironsides*." *United States Navy* 2 (March–August 1977): 34–39.

———. "United States Monitors, 1863." *United States Navy* (September, 1976): 35–40.

Index

Abbott, Joseph C., 221, 234, 238
African-American troops, 44–53, 86–
91, 104, 115, 138, 140, 144, 147,
181, 197, 210, 261; prisoners, 90,
116, 123–127, 216; use in battle,
99–100; result of Battery Wagner
assault, 116–117; pay, 141; health,
185–186; evaluated on Morris
Island, 215–216
Aiken, Hugh K., 235, 243
Aldrich, Alfred Proctor, 126
Alford, Samuel M., 239
Alice, CS, 123–124, 136
Allen, David A., 222
Amelia Island, Fla., 256
Ames, Adelbert, 172, 239
Ames, William, 234, 238
Anderson, Edward C., 123–124, 224
Anderson, George T., 212, 243
Anderson, George W., Jr., 224
Anderson, Richard H., 8
Anderson, Robert, 4, 5
Anderson, Robert H., 272
Andrew, John A., 48, 53
Appleton, John W. M., 101, 103, 104
Army of Northern Virginia, 12, 19
Army of the Potomac, 138
Artillery, 4, 6, 121, 181–182; Blakely
guns, 4, 20, 154, 255; Brooke guns,
20, 182; description, 19–21; Parrott
guns, 43–44, 156–158; use on
earthen forts, 117–118; at Wagner,
132; Whitworth guns, 121, 156–
157; 10-inch Parrott, 157–158;
12.75-inch Blakely Rifles, 177;
ability of Northern gunners, 178–
179; Union breaching batteries,

236–238; in monitors, 258; use of
grape shot, 266
Ashcroft, James E., 222, 235, 238
Atlanta, USS (former CSS), 231, 251
Atwell, Seager S., 237
Augusta, USS, 251
Augusta Dinsmore, USS, 251

Badger, Oscar C., 188, 253
Bailey, James E., 234
Bainbridge, USS, 152, 251
Baker, Scollay D., 209
Balch, George B., 65
Ballenger, Marcus R., 243
Barnwell, Robert, 96
Barton, Clara: at Hilton Head, 64–
65; on Morris Island, 113, 183,
186–187, 279; sums up campaign,
218
Barton, David, 64
Barton, William B., 222
Basinger, William S., 75, 235, 243
Battery Beauregard, 226
Battery Bee, 212, 226
Battery Brown, 194, 236
Battery Cheves, 212
Battery Gary, 212
Battery Glover, 225
Battery Gregg, 61, 82, 84, 92, 95,
129, 134, 148, 156, 162–163, 179,
182, 190–191, 233, 236–238; con-
structed, 12–13; first small boat
attack, 193–194; second small boat
attack, 198; evacuation, 199–204;
renamed Fort Putnam, 210; Garri-
son and commanders, 245–250
Battery Haig, 226
Battery Haskell, 212